Engagement

Each new text comes with access to the exciting learning environment of a robust eBook containing **over 300 tested online links to primary sources, images, field trips, simulations, maps, video, audio, and more.**

Teaching and Learning Styles

Each new text comes with access to **4ltrpress.cengage.com/hist**, where we offer a suite of digital tools—including **interactive quizzing, flash cards, and more**—for the many different learning styles of today's students.

For instructors' different teaching styles, we offer Webtutor on Blackboard and WebCT, as well as PowerLecture™—a suite of PowerPoint® presentations, instructor's manual, and ExamView® computerized testing.

Accessibility

At less than **300 pages**, each volume of *HIST* presents all concepts, definitions, learning objectives, and study tools found in a book twice its size.

Value

HIST offers full content coverage, review cards, and valuable material at **4ltrpress.cengage.com/hist**— all for **$39.95 per split volume and $59.95 for the comprehensive edition.**

Comprehensive
ISBN-10: 0-495-00527-4
ISBN-13: 978-0-495-00527-8

Volume 1 – Through 1877
ISBN-10: 0-495-00528-2
ISBN-13: 978-0-495-00528-5

Volume 2 – Since 1865
ISBN-10: 0-495-00529-0
ISBN-13: 978-0-495-00529-2

WADSWORTH
CENGAGE Learning

HIST, Volume 1
Kevin M. Schultz

Publishers: Clark Baxter and Suzanne Jeans

Senior Sponsoring Editor: Ann West

Senior Development Editor: Sue Gleason

Assistant Editor: Megan Curry

Editorial Assistant: Megan Chrisman

Senior Media Editor: Lisa Ciccolo

Media Editor: Yevgeny Ioffe

Senior Marketing Managers: Diane Wenckebach and Katherine Bates

Marketing Communications Managers: Heather Baxley and Christine Dobberpuhl

Production Manager: Samantha Ross

Senior Content Project Manager: Lauren Wheelock

Senior Art Director: Cate Rickard Barr

Senior Print Buyer: Mary Beth Hennebury

Production Service: Lachina Publishing Services

Text Designer: Dutton & Sherman Design

Senior Permissions Account Manager – Image: Deanna Ettinger

Photo Researcher: Terri Miller

Cover Designer: Bruce Bond

Cover Images: *The Declaration of Independence*, 4 July 1776, 1786–1820, John Trumbull (1756–1843). Oil on canvas, 20⅞ × 31 inches (53 × 78.7 cm), Yale University Art Gallery, New Haven, Connecticut, USA/© SuperStock, Inc./*SuperStock*; Picture Frame, © Alamy; Photography, Jon Chomitz Photography

Compositor: Lachina Publishing Services

For product information and technology assistance, contact us at
Cengage Learning Academic Resource Center, 1-800-423-0563

For permission to use material from this text or product,
submit all requests online at **www.cengage.com/permissions**
Further permissions questions can be emailed to
permissionrequest@cengage.com

Library of Congress Control Number: 2008937532

Student Edition Pkg:
ISBN-13: 978-0-495-00528-5
ISBN-10: 0-495-00528-2

Student Edition:
ISBN-13: 978-0-495-57335-7
ISBN-10: 0-495-57335-3

Wadsworth Cengage Learning
25 Thomson Place
Boston, MA 02210-1202
USA

Cengage Learning products are represented in Canada by Nelson Education, Ltd.

For your course and learning solutions, visit **www.cengage.com**.

Purchase any of our products at your local college store or at our preferred online store **www.ichapters.com**.

About the Cover

The painting that appears on the cover, the iconic *The Declaration of Independence*, was created by John Trumbull between 1817 and 1819, more than forty years after the events depicted. It is a perfect example of the importance of evaluating historical evidence critically and in its original context. Trumbull, one of the most renowned painters in the United States at the time, was best known for his patriotic images. The U.S. Senate, which commissioned the painting, was seeking to adorn its walls in the Capitol with heroic images from the American past, and Trumbull delivered. This huge canvas (12' × 18') depicts the presentation of the Declaration of Independence to the Second Continental Congress on July 3, 1776. Although a presentation of the Declaration certainly occurred, the event was never this formal, nor was it entirely celebratory. Congress edited the draft on July 3 and July 4, before adopting it on the afternoon of July 4. The final version then went to the printers, who produced a completed copy in late July. Only on August 2, 1776, was there a signing ceremony, and even then not all members of Congress signed it. Thus, it is unlikely that all the revolutionary heroes depicted in the painting were actually in Philadelphia at the time, much less in a formal pose in Independence Hall on July 3. Furthermore, fourteen of the lesser-known signers of the Declaration are omitted altogether. And Trumbull wasn't above the use of humor in his paintings: in this one, Thomas Jefferson appears to be stepping on the toes of John Adams, a possible reflection of the political divide that created the first political parties in the United States, which didn't occur until nearly a decade and a half after the presentation of the Declaration. The painting still hangs in the U.S. Capitol, appears on the back of the two-dollar bill, and symbolizes in a single idealized image the wonder of Americans' achieving independence.

Printed in the United States of America
1 2 3 4 5 6 7 12 11 10 09 08

SCHULTZ
HIST
VOLUME 1

Brief Contents

© Icon Ent/Buena Vista/The Kobal Collection/ Cooper, Andrew

© iStockphoto.com/Rich Vintage

© Michael Melford/The Image Bank/Getty Images

© Paul S. Bartholomew/Alamy

Drawn by Earl & engraved by A. Doolittle in 1775   Re-Engraved by A. Doolittle and J.W. Barber in 1832

© American School/The Bridgeman Art Library/Getty Images

© North Wind Picture Archives/Alamy

© iStockphoto.com/Jerry Downs

© Brad Perks Lightscapes/Alamy

Three Societies

on the Verge of Contact

Learning Outcomes

After reading this chapter, you should be able to do the following:

1 Explain current beliefs about how the first peoples settled North America, and discuss the ways in which they became differentiated from one another over time.

2 Describe the African societies that existed at the time the first Africans were brought to the New World as slaves.

3 Describe Europe's experiences during the last centuries before Columbus made his first voyage to the New World in 1492.

> **"We will probably never know when the first people set foot on what we now call the United States."**

People have been living on the landmass we now know as the United States for at least the past 12,000 years—long before civilizations emerged among the Sumerians in Mesopotamia, the ancient Egyptians, the Greeks, and Jesus Christ, whose estimated time of arrival, however incorrect, is the measure by which western European time came to be measured. As a political nation, however, the United States is less than 250 years old, encapsulating roughly just nine or ten generations. Although this book is mostly about that relatively recent political nation and the people who lived in it, this chapter deals with the three groups of people—Indians, West Africans, and Europeans—who came together in North America more than five hundred years ago, setting in motion the process by which America would become an independent nation. This chapter begins in the Ice Age and ends as Christopher Columbus sets foot in North America in 1492, becoming, perhaps, the first European to ever do so.

What do you think?

Calling North American the "New World" is a misnomer.

Strongly Disagree						Strongly Agree
1	2	3	4	5	6	7

LO¹ Native America

The Paleo-Indian Era: The First Settlers (15,000–10,000 years ago)

Arrival

We will probably never know when the first people set foot on what we now call the United States. For a long time, archaeologists believed that the first people came not for fame, fortune, or freedom (as subsequent immigrants would), but simply because they were hungry. According to this theory, about 12,000 years ago, thousands of young adults and their families left their homes in Asia and crossed a narrow passage of iced-over land called Beringia, southwest of today's Alaska. These people were supposedly following herds of wooly mammoths, intending to hunt the animals to feed and clothe their families. Many of these hunters followed the herds south along the western coast of present-day Canada and ended up in what is now the United States. Many of their latter-day ancestors continued southward and, after many generations, made it all the way to the southernmost tip of South America, to a place now called Tierra Del Fuego.

Recent evidence casts doubt on this theory. Carbon dating suggests that the first people on the continent were probably here much earlier than 12,000 years ago. This has prompted a reevaluation of the Beringia theory, with some scholars suggesting that the first settlers came on boats, either following whales across the Pacific from Asia, or coming from Europe, along Greenland, in search of fish, or following the Pacific Coast of today's Alaska, British Columbia, and Washington state (see Map 1.1).

Map 1.1
Settlement of America

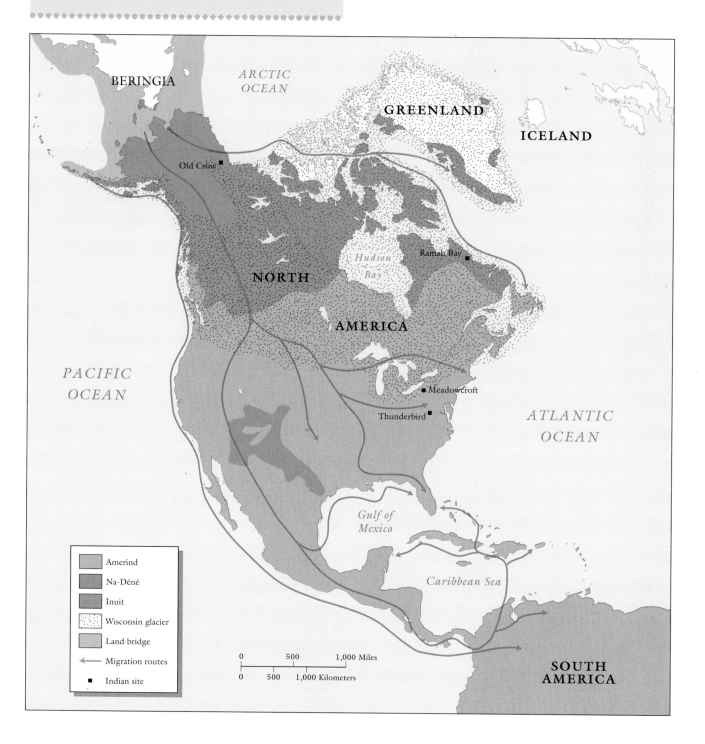

Map 1.1 Settlement of America

In 1996, two men watching hydroplane races in Kennewick, Washington, discovered what turned out to be a 9,000-year-old skeleton. The skeleton, dubbed Kennewick man, baffled scientists, mainly because a physical reconstruction of the skull revealed a man who looked "more like a middle aged European accountant than he did a Paleo-Indian hunter." People with European features were not thought to have been in North America for another 8,500 years, so Kennewick man presented the possibility that North American settlement happened in different waves, from a variety of locations, with older groups dying out, being replaced by yet newer immigrants. Another scientist then suggested that Kennewick man's features resembled those of people living in specific parts of Asia rather than Europe, further complicating the initial origins of humankind in North America. Was he a man with a European face (and genetic origins), an Asian one, or did he resemble one of America's indigenous Indians? Current DNA sampling technology cannot tell us, but a final report written by one of the principal scientists concludes that "methods developed in the near future could be successful in extracting suitable DNA for analysis." Meanwhile, many of today's Indian tribes resisted the supposed European or Asian appearance of Kennewick man because their beliefs maintain that they are the one, true indigenous group in North America. Regardless of the dispute, and regardless of when or from whence they came, their age suggests that calling North America the "New World" might be a misnomer. England, for instance, was not inhabitable until 12,500 BCE, suggesting that the "New World" may actually have a much longer human history than what we now think of as the "Old World." Today we call these initial North American settlers the **Paleo-Indians**.

Meet Kennewick man.

Although the initial origins and timing are in question, what is known for certain is that the greatest flow of people in this early period came between 20,000 and 10,000 BCE, and that sometime between 9500 and 8000 BCE, the ocean level rose due to what we would today call global warming. This covered over the Bering Strait that connected Asia to North America, effectively ending the first major wave of immigration. That path has remained submerged ever since.

Expansion and Development

As these migrants moved from region to region across North America, they adapted their lifestyle according to the climate and the land, as people do. The people of the **Paleo-Indian era** (15,000 to 10,000 years ago) thus lived a wide range of lifestyles, developing many languages and belief systems along the way. Some of the oldest made spears by flaking stones and then chose "kill sites" that large herds traversed. Others hunted herds of animals across great distances. Still others slowly began to cultivate complex systems of sustainable agriculture which allowed them to remain in a single area for years. Still others depended on fishing and the riches of the seas to provide a stable life for their families. Over time, the population of Native North America grew.

Read more about the Paleo-Indians.

Paleo-Indians
The first people to settle North America, roughly 15,000 to 10,000 years ago

Paleo-Indian era
Era beginning about 15,000 years ago and ending about 10,000 years ago, characterized by initial North American settlement

Archaic era
Era beginning about 10,000 years ago and lasting until about 2,500 years ago, characterized by increased agricultural development

The Archaic Era: Forging an Agricultural Society (10,000–2,500 years ago)

Between 5,000 and 8,000 years ago, a monumental transition occurred in how people lived their lives. During the **Archaic era**, agriculture gradually

The development of maize was a remarkable feat of genetic engineering.

sedentary existence
Life in which settlers can remain in one place cultivating agriculture, instead of pursuing herd animals

pre-Columbian era
North American era lasting from 500 BCE–1492 CE, before Columbus landed

became the primary source of sustenance for most of the people of Native North America. This trend was perhaps the most significant development in American prehistory, because settled agriculture permitted the establishment of a **sedentary existence**, without the need to pursue herd animals. Maize, a form of corn, was one key element of this existence. Maize is a highly nutritious cereal, containing more nutrients than wheat, rice, millet, and barley. Its development was a remarkable feat of genetic engineering; Indians in today's southern Mexico some 6,000 years ago cultivated the crop through the careful selection of desirable seeds, ultimately producing corn.

Populations grew larger, not only because food supplies increased, but also because the size of groups was no longer limited by the arduous demands of hunting. Many tribes became semi-

sedentary, settling in camps during the agricultural growing season and then breaking camp to follow the herds at other times of year. Others became increasingly urban in their development, building permanent cities, some of monumental proportions. This was the formative period of the first settled tribes in North America—the immediate ancestors of many of the Indian tribes with which we are most familiar today. The Mesoamerican civilization, founded and developed by the Olmec people, thrived in today's Mexico and served as a precursor to the many maize-based societies that developed throughout North America. Another successful ancient civilization—the people of Norte Chico, in today's Peru—flourished by cultivating cotton, which they used to weave nets and catch the plentiful fish off the Pacific Coast, which they then transported to high-altitude cities in the Andes, some 5,500 years ago. Although nature has reclaimed much of what they created, the developments and accomplishments of these early civilizations are testaments to the capacity of humankind to create and develop monumental societies. One historian has argued that the only way to fully grasp the earth-changing significance of these early civilizations is to take a helicopter ride over undeveloped parts of Mexico and Central and South America, realizing that many of the hills and creeks below are actually the buried remains of temples and canals built by those early civilizations.

The Pre-Columbian Era: Developing Civilizations (500 BCE–1492 CE)

Of all the people living in North America before contact with Europeans, we know the most about the people of the **pre-Columbian era** (500 BCE–1492 CE). The great civilizations of the pre-Columbian world (the phrase means "before Columbus") usually based their economy on agriculture, thus enabling them to endure in a single location long enough to create complex, hierarchical societies and develop long-standing trading networks.

The largest Indian civilization in this period was that of the Incas, who lived on the western coast of South America, from the equator to the southern tip of Chile. The Incas built large cities and fortresses on the steep slopes of the Andes Mountains (and were the beneficiaries of fish deliveries from the people of Norte Chico). Other impressive pre-Columbian societies include the Maya, who, with their step-tiered temples, dominated southern Guatemala and the Yucatan Peninsula (in present-

Many of the hills and creeks below are actually the buried remains of temples and canals built by early civilizations.

>>**Agua Azul Chipas, Mexico**

© Travel Ink/Gallo Images/Getty Images

Aztec calendar

© iStockphoto.com/Soren Pilman

Learn more about the Aztecs through a simulation, "Colonial Expansion."

day Mexico) from the fifth to the eighth centuries, until an internal civil war weakened the civilization so much that it dissipated. The Teotihuacán built a city (named Teotihuacán, about an hour's bus ride from Mexico City) that accommodated perhaps as many as two hundred thousand souls during the fifth century. The Mexica (later labeled "the Aztecs") developed a complex urban society that ruled central Mexico from the ninth to the fifteenth centuries. These were all large, complex societies that, in scientific knowledge, governing capacities, and artistic and architectural development, rivaled any in the world at the time of their particular dominance.

>> **Serpent Mound in Ohio, nearly a quarter of a mile long, is the largest and finest surviving serpentine earthwork.**

© Tom Till/Alamy

The Anasazi

In the present-day United States, two of the largest pre-Columbian cultures were the Anasazi and the Mississippians. In the American Southwest, the Anasazi founded a vast civilization by combining hunting and gathering with sedentary agriculture in order to sustain a large population in the arid desert of present-day New Mexico. As a testament to the grandness of their civilization, between 900 and 1150 CE the Anasazi built fourteen "great houses" in the Chaco Canyon, each one several stories tall and containing more than two hundred rooms. They were perhaps used as large apartment buildings, as the canyon served as the major trading post for turquoise and other material goods. Several of these great houses still stand today, near Albuquerque, New Mexico.

The Mississippians

A second large, pre-Columbian culture to develop on the land now known as the United States was that of the Mississippians, who lived at about the same time as the Anasazi, from 700 to 1500 CE, although their civilization peaked about 1100 CE. The largest Anasazi city was called Cahokia, located eight miles east of present-day St. Louis. Inhabited by more than twenty thousand people (comparable in size to London at that time), Cahokia served as the civilization's crossroads for trade and religion. It was the land's first metropolis. Webs of roads surrounded the city, connecting rural villagers for hundreds of miles in all directions. Many different tribes made up the Mississippian civilization. The Mississippians developed an accurate calendar and built a pyramid that, at the time, was the third largest structure of any kind in the Western Hemisphere. The Mississippians also left many earthen mounds dotting the landscape.

Some of these early civilizations, like the Anasazi, declined about two hundred years before first contact with Europeans and Africans. Others, such as the Aztecs and some of the Mississippians, were still thriving in 1492. Why did these powerful civilizations decline? There is no single answer to the question. Some scholars say that certain civilizations outgrew their capacity to produce food. Others say that battles with enemy tribes forced them to abandon the principal landmarks of their civilization. Still others cite major droughts.

> The Mississippians developed an accurate calendar and built a pyramid that was the third largest structure in the Western Hemisphere.

clan system
Living arrangement in which a tribe was divided into a number of large family groups

matrilineal
Family arrangement in which children typically follow the clan of their mother; married men move into the clan of their wives; most often seen in agricultural societies

polytheistic
Belief system consisting of belief in many deities

animistic
Belief system consisting of belief that supernatural beings, or souls, inhabit all objects and govern their actions

And indeed, not all of these civilizations did decline by the time of first contact with Europeans, and scholars estimate that in 1491 North and South America had perhaps as many as 100 million inhabitants—making it more populous than Europe at the time. These numbers are greatly disputed, however. Regardless, the idea that the Americas were barren "virgin" land before first contact with Europeans is clearly wrong. In 1491, American Indians were thriving and transforming the land to suit their needs.

North America in 1492

By the late 1400s, North America was home to numerous civilizations and tribes, some of which were sizeable, dominating large swaths of land. More than two hundred languages were spoken in North America, among hundreds of different tribes. It was as if each of today's cities spoke its own language and had unique social rituals. Diversity abounded in this land. So did conflict.

Some Social Similarities of Native North Americans

Despite the wide variety of lifestyles developed by the pre-Columbian peoples, there are some broad general similarities among the tribes in North America during the late 1400s. Most of the tribes, for instance, were based on a **clan system**, in which a tribe was divided into a number of large family groups. They were also mostly **matrilineal**, meaning that children typically followed the clan of their mother and that a man, when married, moved into the clan of his wife. Matrilineal societies usually develop when agriculture is the primary food source for a society. In these societies women are in charge of farming (Europeans were universally surprised to see women working in the fields). Thus Indian women maintained the tribe's social institutions while men were hunting, fishing, or off to war. This system was, however, by no means universal in Native North America, but it does signify a level of

sexual equality absent from Europe at the time. Indeed, women were just as likely as men to wield political power in some of these societies. Many Algonkian tribes, for instance, had a female tribal leader.

Learn more about why Chaco Canyon declined.

Land was customarily held in common as well, although there are some instances in which individual rights are said to have existed and others where clan rights existed. Enslavement (usually of captured enemies) was relatively common as well, especially in the tribes of the American Southeast, but Indian enslavement varied in severity, and it is unlikely that enslavement was inherited, meaning that the children of slaves were usually not, by accident of birth, born as chattel.

Most Indian religions were **polytheistic** (believing in many deities) and **animistic** (believing that supernatural beings, or souls, inhabit all objects and govern their actions). Indian religions were usually closely related to the physical world, and local terrain was naturally imbued with spiritual meaning. Placing an emphasis on this world (and not on the next), typical ceremonies featured rain and fertility prayers. Many New England tribes, for example, believed in a ruling deity whom they called Manitou and looked to a dramatic local site (such as Mount Katahdin in Maine) as the source of divine power.

Regional Variations

These broad similarities aside, the tribes of Native America were rich in regional variety (Map 1.2). Most variations depended on how a tribe adapted to its surrounding terrain, and thus it is possible to make generalizations based on region.

The Northeast. Several sizeable societies lived in the northeast corner of the United States, in the area now called New England. These tribes included the Wampanoag, Narragansett, Massachusetts, Mohawk, Oneida, Erie, and Pequot. In general, these groups subsisted on hunting and agriculture, although most of their foodstuffs derived from agriculture. Those that lived along the coast relied on the riches of the ocean. Most of these tribes lived in small villages that were closely surrounded by forests that protected them from attack—something that was always a possibility in the congested northeastern region. Indeed, fear of attack was part of the reason why several of these northeastern tribes

> Women were just as likely as men to wield political power in some of these societies.

Map 1.2
Tribes of North America, 1492

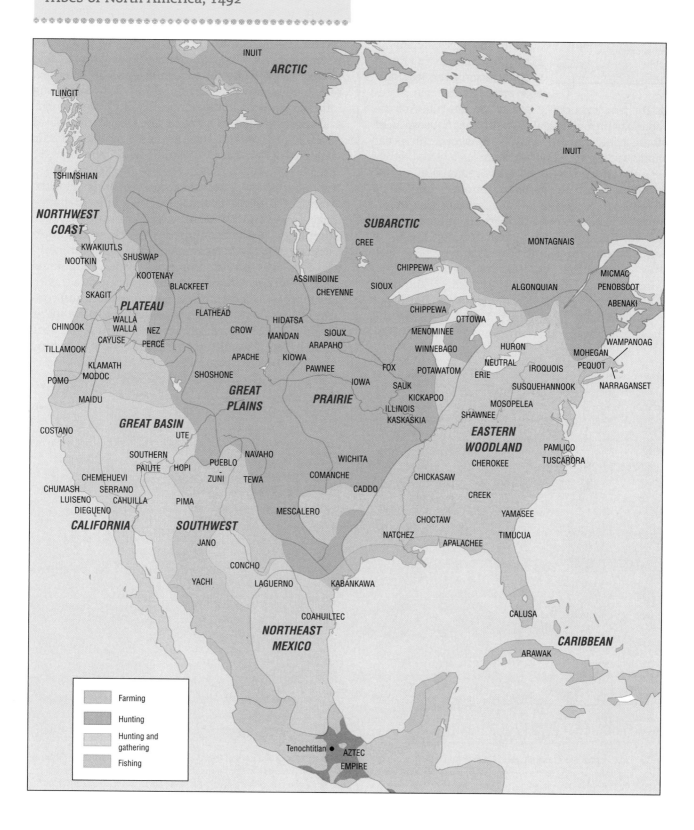

came together to create the **Iroquois Confederacy**, a political and trading entity that maintained relations between several tribes. (Iroquois is actually the European name for the Haudenosaunee Confederation.) The local forests provided the raw materials for wooden houses crafted by the tribes of the Haudenosaunee, who called them "longhouses." Most of these tribes remained small, however, only occasionally trading with one another.

Other tribes developed cross-regional alliances. The tribes within the Haudenosaunee Confederacy developed an elaborate political system that incorporated villages into nations, then nations into a large confederation. The confederation's leaders were charged with keeping peace among the tribes under its auspices in order to assure continuous trade and peaceful relations. The proximity of one's tribal neighbors in the populous Northeast led many tribes to embrace the politics of the Haudenosaunee. Others, however, viewed the tribes of the Haudenosaunee as their bitter enemies.

The Mid-Atlantic. In the Mid-Atlantic region, where New York, New Jersey, Pennsylvania, Delaware, Maryland, and Virginia are today, lived the Lenni Lenape (Delaware), Susquehannock, and Nanticock, among others. The people in these tribes lived on a mixture of agriculture, shellfish, and game. They lived a semi-sedentary life, occasionally leaving their stable villages to follow herds of roaming animals. They, too, remained mostly local, aware of, but rarely venturing into, the lands of another tribe. Disputes over boundaries routinely led to violence. The Indians who lived in the woodlands of the Northeast or Mid-Atlantic were collectively called "Woodlands Indians."

The Southeast. The Southeast—today's Florida, Georgia, North Carolina, South Carolina, Alabama, Mississippi, and Louisiana—was inhabited by the Cherokees (actually named the Tsalagi), Creek, Choctaw, Biloxi, Chicksaw, and Natchez, among others. This was one of the most heavily populated areas of Native America at time of first contact with the Europeans, a fact that would have profound consequences when the Europeans tried to settle there. These tribes subsisted on agriculture, though those living in Florida and the Gulf Coast relied on fishing

© Stock Montage, Inc./Alamy

>> "Their cabins are in the shape of tunnels [*tonnelles*] or arbors, and are covered with the bark of trees. They are from twenty-five to thirty fathoms long, more or less, and six wide, having a passage-way through the middle from ten to twelve feet wide, which extends from one end to the other. On the sides there is a kind of bench, four feet high, where they sleep in summer, in order to avoid the annoyance of the fleas, of which there are great numbers. In winter they sleep on the ground on mats near the fire, so as to be warmer than they would be on the platform."
—French explorer Samuel de Champlain, 1616, referring to an Iroquois longhouse

as well. They developed strong traditions in ceramics and basket weaving; they traded over long distances; and some, such as the Natchez, developed stable, hierarchical political organizations.

The prairies. The prairies, which stretch from today's Dakotas south to Oklahoma, were inhabited by the Omaha, Wichita, Kichai, and Sioux. These tribes usually lived on the edges of the plains, where they lived in semi-sedentary agricultural villages and held major hunting parties every year to hunt bison, which was the chief game animal of the Great Plains. These tribes produced no pottery or basketry, or even much agriculture, as they depended almost entirely on the bison and rivers for their subsistence.

The High Plains. The Indians of the High Plains, which extend from today's Montana all the way south to northwestern Texas, included the Blackfeet, Crow, Cheyenne, Arapaho, and Comanche. Like the Native Americans of the prairies, these tribes depended on bison for a large part of their subsistence (especially after contact with European settlers drove them further west), and their only agricultural crop was usually tobacco (again, after contact), which they used for religious purposes and for pleasure.

The Southwest. In the Southwest, in today's New Mexico and Arizona (and where the Anasazi had lived), lived the Apache and Navajo tribes, along with a large conglomeration of tribes that included the Hopi, Taos, and Zunis to make up what the Europeans called "the **Pueblo people**." These Indians subsisted almost entirely on agriculture, which is a testament to their ingenuity, considering the slight amount of rain that falls in this region. By about 1200 CE, several of these tribes had developed villages made up of several multistory buildings built on strategically defensive sites in canyons and river valleys. By the time Columbus had reached the West Indies, some of these tribes had developed canals, dams, and hillside terracing to control and channel the limited amount of rainwater. Ceramic pots, which were elaborate and sophisticated during this precontact period, were used to transport water as well. This was a society similar in some ways to Europe. According to one European observer in 1599, the Pueblo people "live very much the same as we do," although it is possible he said that simply because the Pueblos were one of the few Indian societies to have men, not women, practice agriculture.

The Northwest. In the Northwest, in today's Oregon and Washington, lived the Chinook, Tillamook, Yuki, and Squamish, to name just a few. These peoples ate fish and shellfish in addition to fruits, nuts, and berries. They made plank houses of cedar, which they sometimes surrounded with dramatic carved totem poles. They were accomplished artists, placing a priority on the arts of carving and painting. These tribes developed the elaborate ornamentation we commonly see on totem poles. Other prized creations were their artistically designed masks. Many of these tribes celebrated annual holidays, maintained social welfare programs, and adhered to a well-developed view of the cosmos.

> **Pueblo people**
> Southwestern conglomeration of tribes including the Apache, Navajo, Hopi, Taos, and Zunis, who lived in today's New Mexico and Arizona

© iStockphoto.com/Alex Pitt

© iStockphoto.com/Adam Korzekwa

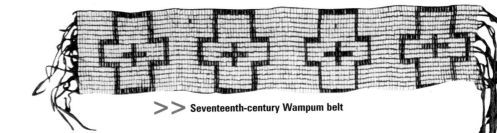

>> Seventeenth-century Wampum belt

© MPI/Getty Images

Intertribal Harmony and Hostility

Most tribal villages coexisted with their neighbors in a fairly stable balance between peace and warfare, at least until territorial disputes, competition for resources, or traditional rivalries set off battle, which happened often. Indians also went to war to bolster their numbers; male captives taken in war were usually integrated into the victorious tribe's village as slaves; females and children were commonly integrated as full members. Some societies, such as the Maya and Aztec, developed an entire culture around warfare. The fact that some Indian groups forged defense alliances, such as the Iroquois Confederacy, demonstrates that protective measures were necessary in a sometimes violent Native America.

But the Haudenosaunee (Iroquois) Confederacy demonstrates something else as well: it shows Indians' interest in and ability to promote peaceful and productive interactions. In many parts of the land, neighboring tribes traded fruitfully with each other. A network of dirt and stone roads traversed the continent. Towns became centers for trade and commerce. Although such trade was small in scale by European standards, the goods exchanged were vital to each village's way of life. These goods included arrowheads, furs, **wampum** (beads made of polished shell), **roanoke** (bracelet-like bands made of wampum), and food. Trade networks could extend over hundreds of miles; for instance, copper goods from the Southwest have been found at Eastern Woodlands sites.

Economics

This trade made up a part of Indian economic life. Tribes traded foodstuffs like corn and meat, sometimes traveling expansive trading routes; they also traded ornamental items such as jewelry and hunting weapons. Their trading grounds provided an early example of what would come to be called the "middle ground" between the native cultures and European traders, after the Europeans had established settlements in the seventeenth and eighteenth centuries.

Despite their willingness to barter in portable goods, a sizeable majority of the people of Native America did not believe that property could be privately owned. Bequeathed to all, land could be used by anyone so long as they cultivated it properly. In practice, however, tribal leaders granted specific parcels of land to a family for a season or two, and tribes frequently fought bloody battles for control of certain plots of land. When large numbers of Europeans arrived in the 1600s, the tribes of Native America would be forced to reconsider their conception of private property.

LO² Africa

Of all the immigrants who came to North America between the sixteenth and eighteenth centuries, roughly 250,000 of them came from Africa, as slaves. This was a not a huge percentage of all immigrants but nevertheless a significant one, dramatically influencing labor, social, and cultural relations in the New World. Understanding Africa's social customs is thus critical to understanding the development of the American nation. A large majority of the transplanted Africans were from West Africa (Map 1.3), and most of the West Africans were from a place called Lower Guinea.

Politics

Africa, the second largest continent on earth (after Asia), is as varied in climate and geography as North America. It follows, then, that there was great range in the way Africans lived their lives. By the time of the first sustained contact with Europeans, in the 1400s and 1500s, some African societies had developed vast civilizations, as trade routes wound through the continent's various regions. Africans had also witnessed the spread of a modern religion, **Islam**, which, in the fourteenth and fifteenth centuries, was probably the most powerful and vibrant religion in the world, expanding rapidly throughout Africa, the Middle East, and Spain. One part of the continent that was transformed by the rise of Islam was West Africa.

Map 1.3
Africa in the Fifteenth Century

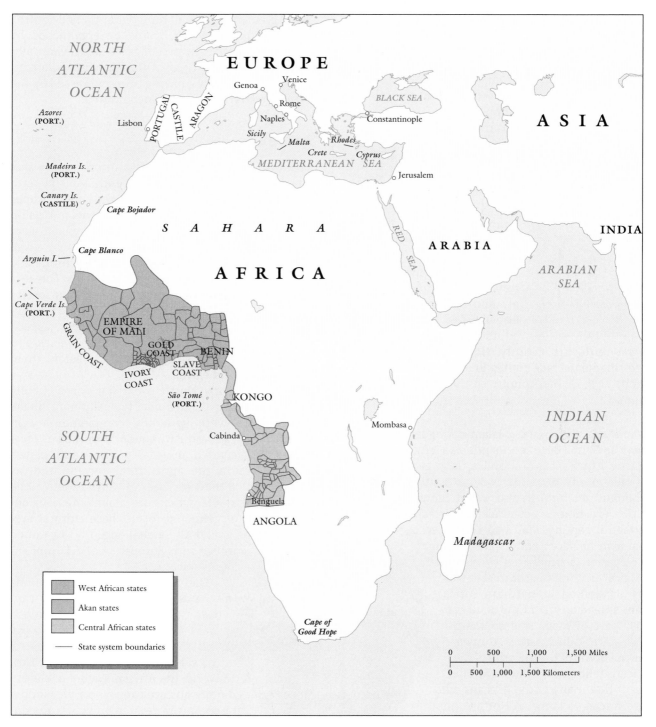

View an interactive version of this map.

NORTH ATLANTIC OCEAN

EUROPE

Genoa
Venice
Rome
Naples
Sicily
Malta
Crete
Rhodes
Cyprus
Constantinople
BLACK SEA

ASIA

Azores
(PORT.)

Lisbon

PORTUGAL
CASTILE
ARAGON

MEDITERRANEAN SEA

Madeira Is.
(PORT.)

Jerusalem

Canary Is.
(CASTILE)

Cape Bojador

S A H A R A

RED SEA

ARABIA

INDIA

Cape Blanco

Arguin I.

A F R I C A

ARABIAN
SEA

Cape Verde Is.
(PORT.)

EMPIRE
OF MALI

GRAIN COAST

GOLD
COAST

BENIN

IVORY
COAST

SLAVE
COAST

São Tomé
(PORT.)

KONGO

Cabinda

SOUTH
ATLANTIC
OCEAN

Mombasa

INDIAN
OCEAN

Benguela

ANGOLA

Madagascar

Cape of
Good Hope

	West African states
	Akan states
	Central African states
—	State system boundaries

| 0 | 500 | 1,000 | 1,500 Miles |
| 0 | 500 | 1,000 | 1,500 Kilometers |

Ghana
West African kingdom that prospered from the eighth to the thirteenth centuries; famous for its gold deposits

Mali
Flourishing Islamic kingdom; it enveloped the kingdom of Ghana by the thirteenth century

Timbuktu
Principal city of the kingdom of Mali; cultural capital of Africa in the thirteenth century

Lower Guinea
Southernmost part of Mali; home to the majority of the Africans who came to America

Songhay Empire
Portion of Mali after that kingdom collapsed around 1500; this empire controlled Timbuktu

Benin
African empire on the Malian coast

Kongo
African empire on the Malian coast

Ghana

The kingdom of **Ghana** ruled West Africa from the eighth to the thirteenth centuries, beginning a tradition of expansive trade throughout Western Africa using horses, camels, and advanced iron weapons to transport goods and ideas. A kingdom as rich in arts and commerce as any in Europe at the time, Ghana was made up of several large cities, where the people produced elaborate works of art and maintained a stable and complex political structure. Ghana was especially famous for its gold. But the kingdom's extensive trade routes caused its eventual demise. In the twelfth century, it lost its trade monopoly, and gold was discovered elsewhere in West Africa. In addition, during the first half of the thirteenth century, North African Muslims used Ghanaian trade routes to invade the kingdom, and by 1235 CE had conquered the ruling parties of Ghana.

Mali. **Mali**, a flourishing Islamic kingdom, rose in power as Ghana declined. Its principal city, **Timbuktu**, became Africa's cultural and artistic capital, drawing students from as far away as southern Europe. Timbuktu's cultural wealth was demonstrated in its rich artistic and economic resources. By the thirteenth century, Mali had enveloped the Ghanaian kingdom and expanded mightily. However, Islam did not permeate all of Mali's territories. In contrast to what was happening in northern Africa, Islam spread slowly in the southernmost part of Mali. This southernmost part, called **Lower Guinea**, was the home of the majority of the Africans who came to America. This meant that many of the Africans who were forced to come to North America via the slave trade maintained their tribal religions rather than Islam. Thus, Islam was not present in North America at this time.

Songhay, Benin, and Kongo. The kingdom of Mali collapsed around 1500—just as sustained contact with Europeans was beginning. Mali was divided, with the largest portion replaced by the **Songhay Empire**, which took control of Timbuktu. Farther along the Malian coast, the empires of **Benin** and **Kongo** maintained control, meaning that they, too, would be approached by European traders in search of goods and, eventually, slaves. By 1500, the ruler of the Kongo people converted to Catholicism, having been impressed by the Portuguese traders he had encountered.

Learn about the fall of the Mali and Songhay kingdoms.

Society

If political control over the region remained in flux in western Africa during the fifteenth and sixteenth centuries, social customs were slightly more stable. Most of the Africans in Lower Guinea lived in kinship groups and, through them, in villages, which were part of larger kingdoms and woven together by a web of roads. The Africans of Lower Guinea were mostly farmers, living in settled agricultural areas. The success of their agriculture allowed some in their society to become artists, teachers, tradesmen, and storytellers—professions that earned their society's respect. Above this group of professionals were nobles and priests, who were mostly older men. Below them were farmers and slaves.

As with many North American tribes, family descent in Lower Guinea was typically matrilineal. Gender roles were generally complementary in Lower Guinea, as women frequently worked as local traders, participated in local politics, and played leading roles in the agricultural society. And, as with the agricultural societies of North America, the presence of stable agriculture meant the development of gendered roles. These cultural systems would all be challenged by sustained contact with Europeans and European-based societies.

The Africans of Lower Guinea also possessed slaves—usually captives from wars or debtors who had sold themselves into slavery to pay off their debt. Unlike the type of slavery that developed in the New World, the African system of slavery did not enslave captives for life, nor did it necessarily deny them access to education. Significantly, the children of slaves

>> **Ghana was especially famous for its gold.**

were not routinely predestined to become slaves themselves; it also was not based on a system of racial classification, as would develop in the United States.

Religion and Thought

Religiously, most of the Africans in Lower Guinea did not embrace Islam; they still believed in their traditional African religions. These religions were as varied as those of Native America, but generally they consisted of belief in a single supreme ruler and several lesser gods. Many of these lesser gods served in worldly capacities—to bring rain and to ensure good harvests, for example. They honored these gods elaborately, through their art and their celebrations. There was no single transcendent spirit mediating between this world and the next (such as Christ), but deceased ancestors served as personal mediators between a person and the gods. This, in turn, nourished a strong tradition of family loyalty.

Africa on the Eve of Contact

On the eve of European contact, then, West Africa was, in general, an agricultural society divided into

Map 1.4
A Typical Manor
Crops on the manor were rotated, with roughly one-third of the fields lying fallow at any given time, to replenish nutrients in the soil.

View an interactive version of this map.

villages organized along matrilineal kinship lines. Some of its people were extremely skilled in the arts, and there was a class of intellectuals who were positioned in houses of learning and supported by kings. Politics advanced in large kingdoms that oversaw and protected their citizens and that allowed for expansive lines of trade. On the whole, West Africans participated in sophisticated societies that had highly developed skills for coping with the diverse geographical settings where they lived.

LO³ Europe

While Africans constituted one large block of immigrants between the sixteenth and eighteenth centuries, the large majority of newcomers to North America came from Europe. These settlers came with a variety of goals and ambitions. Many, but not all, were disappointed in what they found.

Europe up to 1492

Europeans were the initiators of the clash of cultures that would take place in the New World. But until the twelfth century, most of Europe was an economic and intellectual backwater in comparison to China, the countries of Northern Africa, and parts of the Middle East. Intellectual and religious life thrived in Christian Byzantium (encompassing today's Turkey), and the burgeoning Islamic world was spreading episodically through the Middle East, North Africa, and Spain.

A significant factor in Europe's withdrawal from world affairs was feudal lords' domination of large plots of European land called **manors** (see Map 1.4). These men presided over a system of labor that came to be called **feudalism**, in which a lord granted control over a piece of land to an upper-class ally, or vassal. The vassal's grant included authority over all the land's inhabitants. The vassal treated these laborers as servants, guaranteeing them a level of protection in return for a portion

manor
Agricultural estate operated by a lord and worked by peasants in exchange for protection and sustenance

feudalism
System of labor in which a lord granted control over a piece of land, and authority over all the land's inhabitants, to an upper-class ally, or vassal

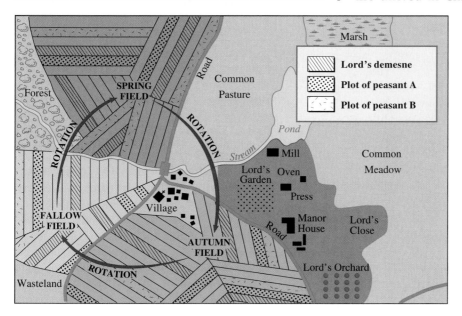

serf
Laborer in the feudal system; protected and controlled by the vassal of the estate

Renaissance
Intellectual and artistic reconnection to the age of Greco-Roman antiquity, starting in the fourteenth century, which lionized the individual

Catholicism
Central religious force in Western Europe; sole institution with moral authority and political power over all of medieval Europe

of the fruits of their labor. In reality, these servants, called **serfs**, forfeited nearly all of their freedoms to the lord and vassal. With the exception of the Catholic Church, the nobleman was the sole authority on the land, serving as governor, judge, and war leader. The lords' overwhelming authority meant that serfs were not free and could not act autonomously. They could not change their profession or even move without approval from their lord.

Medieval Europe was therefore split into myriad feudal territories, which divided it linguistically and economically. It also suffered from political instability due to Muslim expansion and Viking raids. Trade and learning virtually disappeared as a result of the battles among feudal lords and between feudal lords and various invaders. The Catholic Church was the sole overarching institution, and during parts of the medieval period, the Church was at its most powerful. As long as Europe was comprised of hundreds of these feudal fiefdoms and under threat from raiders abroad, there were no entities that could operate as strong nations would: by organizing and controlling various methods of production and trade. The decline of feudalism would propel Europe from its secondary status in world affairs to a dynamic force embarking on far-flung overseas adventures.

 Learn more about feudalism.

The Decline of Feudalism

By the fifteenth century, the feudal system was rapidly declining in Western Europe. In its stead, nations were becoming more powerful. There were four causes for this transition: an economic impetus, a religious one, a biological one, and a political one (see "The reasons why. . ." on the next page). Together, these changes would lead to the rise of nations, which would compete with one another. These nations would look outward and expand from Europe sparking an Age of Discovery, which would lead to sustained contact with the "New World."

Society

Socially, most Europeans in the fourteenth and fifteenth centuries still lived in an agrarian society, on

remnants of the feudal system, although towns and even some great cities had developed since the eleventh century. To ensure a regular food supply, all the members of European villages usually shared their year's crops. As with any society based on agriculture, there were gendered roles in European society. Unlike some African and Indian cultures, women rarely participated in a town's political life or tilled the fields (but they did have lighter duties in the fields, as did children). For the most part, most women's power was limited to their influence on their husbands, children, and servants. In contrast, some women in religious orders (Catholic nuns) operated abbeys and wielded significant power in that realm.

Perhaps the greatest change during the thirteenth through fifteenth centuries was the expansion of European cities, where intellectual life prospered and which demanded surplus agriculture, which could be supplied only when rural farmers expanded their production to bring food to the market. This development further challenged feudal society because it gave serfs the ability to earn money at the market, which allowed them to purchase their freedom from the declining feudal lords.

The Renaissance

By the late fourteenth century, the forces of economic expansion and the development of urban life allowed for a high level of material well-being in the great European cities and the general decline of closed-off feudal living. It was this wealth and expansive mindset that engendered the **Renaissance**, an intellectual and artistic reconnection to the age of Greco-Roman antiquity, when humankind was considered to be more cosmopolitan and not merely a source of labor for feudal fiefdoms. Central to Renaissance artists and thinkers was the idea of humanism, which lionized the individual and therefore directly challenged the declining feudal system.

The Decline of Catholic Europe

If the system of feudalism was declining in the fourteenth and fifteenth centuries, **Catholicism** was still the undisputed religious force in Western Europe. Indeed, the artists of the Renaissance usually used Christian images in order to celebrate the new, more open atmosphere. The Church exerted its greatest power amid the divided feudal society. As the sole institution with moral authority and even political power over all of Europe, the later medieval years witnessed Catholicism's greatest thinker,

Thomas Aquinas (1225–1274), and its most powerful popes, Innocent III (pope from 1198–1216) and Boniface VIII (pope from 1294–1303). Catholicism covered Europe like a cloak, unifying many disparate feudal lands.

Change

By the first quarter of the sixteenth century, two impulses collided to challenge the authority of the Catholic Church. The first occurred in this world: a new attitude toward humankind brought about by the slow urbanization of Europe, the consolidation of monarchical powers, and the rise of popular piety. On

mercantilism
Theory that a nation or state's prosperity was determined by the total volume of its trade

Crusades
Series of campaigns in which Europeans marched to the Middle East in an effort to take control of the Holy Land of Jerusalem, which at the time was controlled by Muslims; battles lasted from 1096 to at least 1291

Black Death
Bubonic plague, which started to spread in 1346 and eventually killed one-third of all Europeans

Hundred Years' War
War waged between France and England in the fourteenth century over who controlled the French throne

{ The reasons why... }

There were four causes for the decline of feudalism:

Expanding trade. The first inklings of the transition away from feudalism can be seen around 1000 CE, when Italian coastal traders began to exploit long-distance trade routes. The riches earned at these trading posts gave several city-states the wealth and power to free themselves from feudal lords. Similarly, merchants began to develop a theory of **mercantilism** (although it would not get that name until Adam Smith coined it, in the late 1700s), which suggested that a nation or state's prosperity was determined by the total volume of its trade. This was based on the idea that the amount of trade in the world was fixed at a certain level; those who traded favorably simply had a larger piece of the pie. This economic theory gained credence as nations increased in power throughout the sixteenth and seventeenth centuries and as European powers competed to develop colonial empires. It would propel these nations overseas and across continents in search of cheaper or more valuable raw materials.

The Crusades. The second reason for the decline of feudalism was religious. The search for riches fused with the power of the Catholic Church to prompt the **Crusades**. The Crusades were a series of campaigns in which Europeans marched to the Middle East in an effort to take control of the Holy Land of Jerusalem, which at the time was controlled by Muslims. These bloody battles were intermittent, lasting from 1096 to at least 1291, and the Europeans never fully succeeded in their mission of permanently capturing the Holy Land. After their bloody

excursions, crusaders brought back luxuries rarely available to medieval Europe, including spices, silks, and gems. Before long, Europeans deemed these goods invaluable (especially the spices). The Italian merchants who supplied these goods grew fabulously wealthy and began to yearn for greater autonomy and freedom from the feudal system.

The Black Death. The **Black Death**, or bubonic plague, which started to spread in 1346, also advanced the decline of the feudal system. It did so in two principal ways. First, it caused the death of one-third of all Europeans, and it did not discriminate by class, meaning that feudal lords died at the same rate as did the poorer members of the continent. Second, the death of so many farmers meant that those who survived became more valuable; this forced feudal lords to grant them more allowances, including greater personal freedom, in order to maintain their loyalty.

The Hundred Years' War. The fourth reason for the decline of feudalism was rooted in politics. **The Hundred Years' War**, waged between France and England in the fourteenth century, was, at its core, a battle over who controlled the French throne, but it is significant for two reasons.

First, it prodded Italian and Iberian merchants to find water routes that connected southern and northern Europe, as they could no longer safely travel by land through France. This spurred several technological advances that would make possible the exploration of North America.

Second, the war allowed the kings to further consolidate their power at the expense of the feudal lords, leading to the rise of several large kingdoms. By the fifteenth century, kings who had long been subjected to the whims of the feudal lords and who did not possess the financial or military power to become absolute rulers began to assert themselves and respond to the mercantilists' demands for organization and protection. The kings did this with considerable popular support; few feudal lords had endeared themselves to their subjects. By the end of the fifteenth century, three strong dynasties had emerged: the Tudors in England, the Valois in France, and the Hapsburgs in Spain. As the power of feudal landlords diminished and that of the kings increased, one idea gained currency: that a person could belong to or identify with a unified nation. This, in some ways, was when the idea of nationalism was born.

Christian humanism
Belief in the importance of the singular individual, as opposed to the institution of the Church; characterized by optimism, curiosity, and emphasis on naturalism

selling of indulgences
Practice of popes using their authority to limit the time a person's soul spent in purgatory, in exchange for cash

Protestant Reformation
Movement that challenged the Catholic Church to return to its unornamented origins; protesters criticized Church rituals, including the Mass, confession rites, and pilgrimages to holy sites

the one hand, merchants did not like priests moralizing about their profits; rulers did not like their authority challenged. On the other hand, the Church's total incapacity to confront and respond to the crises of the fourteenth century, which included famine, plague, and the Hundred Years' War, prompted several movements of popular piety. Together, these challenges led to the development of **Christian humanism**, defined as a renewed belief in the importance of the singular individual, as opposed to the institution of the Church. Optimism, curiosity, and emphasis on naturalism were components of the humanistic worldview. These factors led to renewed interest in the sciences, which began to challenge Christianity as a worldly authority.

The second event concerned humans' relationship with God, and the Church itself helped invite this second challenge. Beginning during the Crusades of the eleventh century, the Church had grown increas-ingly secular in its discipline; it had even begun to sell its favors. For instance, some popes used their authority to limit the amount of time a person's soul spent in purgatory; the cost of this divine favor was usually cash. This practice, which grew throughout the thirteenth and fourteenth centuries, was called the **selling of indulgences**.

The Reformation

These dual challenges sparked the **Protestant Reformation**. At its core, the Reformation was a movement that challenged the Catholic Church to return to its unornamented origins. In addition to questioning the selling of indulgences, the leaders of the Reformation were critical of Church rituals, including the Mass, confession rites that reinforced the hierarchy by putting absolution at the discretion of a priest, and pilgrimages to holy sites. In short, the reformers felt it was faith in God that led to salvation, not the works one did to demonstrate that faith. As protesters (root of the word *Protestant*), the leaders of the Reformation sought a simpler church defined by an individual's relationship to God and the Christ. In Protestantism, the central authority was the Bible; in Catholicism, authority lay with the Bible but also with tradition as espoused by the hierarchy of the Church. The leaders of the Reformation,

>> **Martin Luther took advantage of the invention of the printing press to advocate that scripture be read in local vernacular languages like German and English rather than Latin.**

most importantly Martin Luther (the moral conscience of the movement) and John Calvin (its great organizer), took advantage of the invention of the **printing press** (developed in the 1440s, although not used widely until the 1450s) to advocate that scripture be read in local vernacular languages like German and English rather than Latin. See "The reasons why . . ." for an overview of the significance of the Reformation for the future of Europe.

Europe in 1492

By 1492, Europe was a dramatically different continent from that of just a century earlier. Europeans had fundamentally altered their political, social, economic, and religious structures. Feudalism, headed by hundreds of feudal lords and vassals, had collapsed, and nations, headed by a handful of kings and queens, had become the most powerful political structures on the continent. They covered vast territories and allowed for the easy movement of goods and peoples. Spain was the most powerful nation in Europe at the time, France was the largest, and Portugal had the advantage of superior nautical craftsmanship. Reformers, meanwhile, challenged the righteousness of Roman Catholicism, creating schisms and, eventually, new religious traditions. And in 1492, Spain took control of the city of Granada, ending the northward spread of Islam for at least five hundred years. Merchants had arisen as a powerful force across the continent too, paving the way for capitalism to flourish and for the market to penetrate more deeply into society than it ever had before. The printing press, invented in the 1440s and developed throughout the 1450s, helped democratize knowledge, allowing scientists to share discoveries and news in many vernacular languages.

England was not as powerful as most of the rest of the countries at the time, mainly because it had been divided by internal religious wars for several decades, as Catholics and Protestants brutally vied for control of the country. It would become a powerful force only later, after Queen Elizabeth muted religious conflict, stabilized the economy, and prepared the country to challenge Spain as the most powerful nation in Europe. All that would take place after 1492.

printing press
Invention of the 1440s using metal letter faces to print words on paper

And in the end . . .

At the end of the fifteenth century, three societies, long separated from one another and uniquely developed, stood on the verge of sustained contact. The location of this contact would be the "New World," which included Native North America, as well as Central and South America. Europeans would be the principal catalysts, as their world was in the middle of dramatic changes that led to outward expansion. But the peoples of West Africa and Native America would struggle to shape the outcome of sustained intercultural contact. The battle, both physical and ideological, would begin in earnest in 1492.

What else was happening . . .	
c. 200,000 BCE	The earliest humans appear in Africa.
16,000 BCE	The last Ice Age reaches its coldest point; people in Asia, across Beringia, live in huts made from wooly mammoth bones.
1023	Paper money is printed in China.
1300	Corsets for women are invented.
1300s	The Aztecs make "animal balloons" by creating inflated animals from the intestines of cats and present them to the gods as a sacrifice.
1489	The symbols + (addition) and − (subtraction) come into general use.

{ The reasons why. . . }

The Reformation is important for our purposes for at least two reasons.

Nationalism. It hastened the development of nationalism by fragmenting the unity of Catholic authority over Europe. Freed from that yoke, European nations began to develop unique identities and consolidate wealth, which, in the creed of mercantilism, spurred aggressive attempts to expand in search of greater wealth. This would lead to the Age of Discovery and to sustained contact with both Africa and the New World.

Religious conflicts. The Protestant Reformation triggered several vicious battles over religion, many of which bled over into the New World and provoked people to leave Europe in search of greater religious freedoms.

Contact and Settlement

2

1492–1660

Learning Outcomes

After reading this chapter, you should be able to do the following:

LO **1**   Explain the reasons for Europeans' exploring lands outside Europe, and trace the routes they followed.

LO **2**   Describe the founding of European nations' first colonies in the New World.

LO **3**   Trace the expansion of England's holdings in the southern colonies.

LO **4**   Outline the reasons for and timing of England's founding of colonies in New England.

> ## "At first, the results of contact were generally bad: the tale is mostly one of hunger, disease, and death."

In the collision of cultures that took place in the New World, Europeans were the initiators. Their desire to find wealth and spread Christianity brought Indians, West Africans, and Europeans into sustained contact for the first time. At first, the results of contact were generally bad: the tale is mostly one of hunger, disease, and death. After this difficult start, however, the seeds for a new nation were planted.

What do you think?

The legacy of the initial phase of colonial development was unparalleled freedoms for the settlers, compared to what they could have had in Europe.

Strongly Disagree   *Strongly Agree*
1   2   3   4   5   6   7

LO¹ Exploration and Discovery

Reasons for Exploration

Beginning in the fourteenth century, Europeans took advantage of the new technologies developed during the previous century, especially the nautical advances made during the Hundred Years' War, when large parts of central Europe became battlegrounds that required circumvention.

{ The reasons why . . . }

Europeans sought to explore lands outside Europe for two reasons: to alleviate a trade deficit (and increase wealth) and to spread Christianity.

To alleviate a trade deficit. After the Crusades, many Europeans began to consider spices and other luxuries from the Middle East, India, and parts of Africa true necessities. To reach Europe, the goods had to be shipped from the Far East, through Middle Eastern then Italian traders. This sequence of middlemen drove prices up, leading to a problem: Because the Europeans had few commodities to trade in return, they had to use gold to pay for the goods, and gold supplies subsequently diminished. This trade deficit led to a depression throughout Europe, as a great deal of money was going out and very little was coming in. The depression sparked a scramble to find another way to obtain the desired goods; namely, a cheaper route to the Far East that would avoid Muslim and Italian middlemen.

To spread Christianity. The second factor in European expansion was the mission to spread Christianity, initially Catholicism, around the world. Like many other religions, Christianity has a missionary message within it, and many of the first explorers thought they could simultaneously search for riches and spread the gospel. Competition from the rapidly growing Islamic faith provided further motivation for spreading Christianity, as did the continuing battles between Catholics and Protestants that began during the Reformation. An important consequence of Christianity's messianic message was that Europeans sought not only trade relations with those whom they came into contact, but also dominion over them.

Routes of Exploration

The search for riches and for lands not already in the hands of Christians drew European explorers to several locations around the globe, many of which they encountered quite accidentally. (Indeed, the Americas were perhaps the largest pieces of land ever discovered by mistake.) In 1298, the adventurer Marco Polo wrote that the Orient was the source of many desired goods and that there might be a western route there across the Atlantic Ocean. Others still believed in the existence of an eastern route, through Africa. Both beliefs propelled explorers into the unknown.

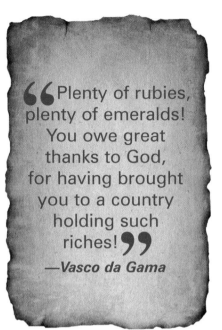

> “ Plenty of rubies, plenty of emeralds! You owe great thanks to God, for having brought you to a country holding such riches! ”
> —*Vasco da Gama*

Eastern Route

Portuguese leaders were among those who still believed that an eastern route could be found (see Map 2.1). Led by Prince Henry the Navigator (1394–1460), Portuguese sailors traveled down the western coast of Africa searching for the dramatic left turn that would lead them to India and the Middle East. After several failures, in 1498, they finally succeeded.

In that year, Vasco da Gama (1469–1524) reached India by rounding the Cape of Good Hope in southern Africa, then heading back north to India. His success made Portugal a wealthy nation throughout the sixteenth and seventeenth centuries.

The Beginnings of European Slavery

Before da Gama's success, however, Portuguese sailors in the 1440s had probed West Africa and made a discovery that would be critical for the development of future relations between cultures. African kings wanted to trade with the Portuguese along the shore, and both sides benefited from the trade in goods. But in the process, the Portuguese also bartered for African slaves. They carried them back to Portugal as living novelties, thus introducing the system of African slavery to Europe during the fifteenth century.

Read a firsthand account of Vasco da Gama's travels.

By the 1490s, the Portuguese had taken control of a previously uninhabited island off the west coast of Africa called São Tomé. São Tomé had the perfect soil for growing sugar, a product much in demand in Europe. Sensing profits, in the 1500s the Portuguese began using African slaves to harvest sugar in São Tomé, thus establishing the first modern economy dependent primarily on slave labor.

The Western Route to the New World

With Portugal's numerous successes, rival Spain acted like a jealous neighbor, and Spanish sailors began advocating the search for a western route to the Orient. After years of delay, the Spanish monarchy finally agreed to fund the costly venture. The first voyage that Spain reluctantly funded, in 1492, was that of Christopher Columbus (1451–1506), a Portuguese-

Fifteenth-century exploring ship

Map 2.1
Routes of Early Exploration

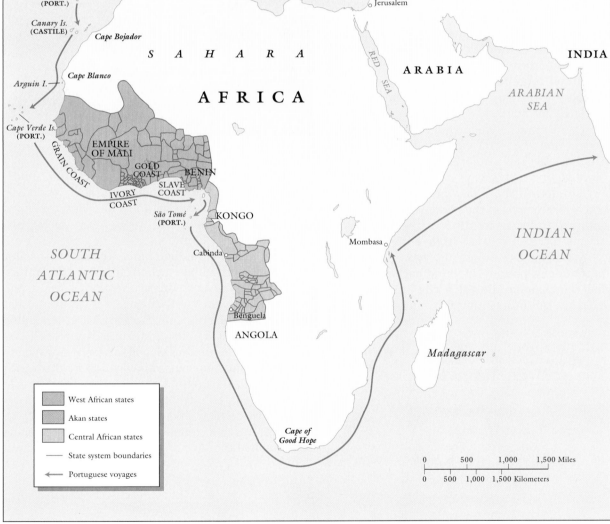

View an interactive version of a similar map.

NORTH ATLANTIC OCEAN

EUROPE

Genoa

Venice

Rome

BLACK SEA

Naples

Constantinople

ASIA

Azores (PORT.)

Lisbon

PORTUGAL

CASTILE

ARAGON

Sicily

Malta

Rhodes

Crete

Cyprus

MEDITERRANEAN SEA

Madeira Is. (PORT.)

Jerusalem

Canary Is. (CASTILE)

Cape Bojador

S A H A R A

RED SEA

A R A B I A

INDIA

Arguin I.

Cape Blanco

A F R I C A

ARABIAN SEA

Cape Verde Is. (PORT.)

GRAIN COAST

EMPIRE OF MALI

GOLD COAST

BENIN

IVORY COAST

SLAVE COAST

São Tomé (PORT.)

KONGO

Mombasa

INDIAN OCEAN

SOUTH ATLANTIC OCEAN

Cabinda

Benguela

ANGOLA

Madagascar

Cape of Good Hope

West African states

Akan states

Central African states

State system boundaries

Portuguese voyages

0	500	1,000	1,500 Miles
0	500	1,000	1,500 Kilometers

trained Italian sailor. The Spanish monarchs, Ferdinand and Isabella, sent him westward with three small ships, the *Niña*, the *Pinta*, and the *Santa Maria*. On October 12, 1492, Columbus and his crew sighted land in the present-day Bahamas. Thinking this was an outlying portion of Asia and India, he called the local inhabitants "Indians." Columbus returned to Spain shortly thereafter, bringing some treasures and, more importantly, tales of the possible riches via the western route. In fact, of course, he had not found Asia or India at all; he was the first European in several centuries to set foot in North America.

 Read Columbus's 1493 letter about his findings.

Predecessors and Followers

Columbus and his crew probably were not the first Europeans to land in North America since the closing of Beringia some ten thousand years earlier. Around the year 1000 C.E., Leif Ericson and a cadre of Scandinavian explorers sailed their brightly colored ships to Greenland and possibly as far south as Cape Cod, in today's Massachusetts. During the following decade or two, Scandinavians made several expeditions to North America, but established neither lasting settlements nor substantive trading posts.

After Columbus, a host of other explorers set out in search of treasures in the Middle and Far East. Many continued to search for the lucrative "passage to the Orient" by sailing west from Europe. John Cabot (c. 1450–1499), like Columbus, was an Italian sailor in search of a patron. He found backing from the English merchants of Bristol, a city in southern England. He set sail in late May 1497 and landed a

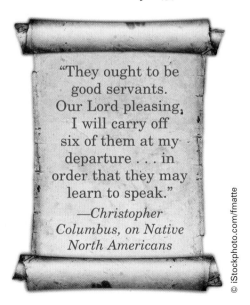

"They ought to be good servants. Our Lord pleasing, I will carry off six of them at my departure . . . in order that they may learn to speak."
—*Christopher Columbus, on Native North Americans*

© iStockphoto.com/fmatte

Christopher Columbus

Image Copyright © The Metropolitan Museum of Art/Art Resource, NY

month later in what is today northeastern Canada. Riding the easterly winds home, Cabot landed in England just two weeks after he departed from Canada. His stories and his rapid return fueled further interest in exploration.

The Americas got their name from the first sailor to realize that he had reached a "new world," rather than the coast of Asia: Amerigo Vespucci (1454–1512). Vespucci explored the Caribbean Sea and the coast of South America from 1497 to 1502. Vasco de Balboa (c. 1475–1519) was the first European to sail the Pacific (1513). Ferdinand Magellan's (1480–1521) crew completed the first circumnavigation of the world from 1519 to 1522 (although Philippine tribespeople killed Magellan shortly before the end of the journey). All these men, and others who explored North America, were prominent players in what historians have dubbed the "Age of Exploration" (see Map 2.2).

LO² Early Settlements and Colonization

Most of these early voyages were intended simply to create trading networks. Few sought to create lasting settlements, and even fewer sought to colonize these exotic lands. However, each European power competitively sought the profits of sustained contact, and this competition for wealth drove them to create encampments that would enable them to defend their claims to those faraway natural resources.

Portuguese

After Columbus's voyage, Spain claimed possession of all of North America. Predictably, the Portuguese would have none of it. They protested Spain's claim. To prevent open conflict between the two Catholic nations, Pope Alexander VI intervened. In 1493, he drew a line on a map that extended from north to south, proclaiming that all land east of the line belonged to Portugal, all land west of it to Spain. The effect of this line, called the **Line of Demarcation**, was to grant all of Brazil to Portugal, while Spain had claim to Central and North America. In 1500, the Portuguese explorer Pedro Cabral accidentally landed in Brazil, beginning what would be Portugal's most profitable colonial venture. As perhaps the first act of modern European colonialism, the pope made his arbitration with no consideration of the peoples already inhabiting the land.

> **Line of Demarcation**
> Line drawn by Pope Alexander IV through a map of the Western Hemisphere. He granted the eastern half to Portugal and the western half to Spain, in what could be considered the first act of modern European colonialism

Spanish

Spain's First Colonies

Despite Portugal's early ambition, it was Spain that established the first colonies in North America. In the process, they began one of the bloodiest

> **Map 2.2**
> **Exploration in the New World, 1492–1542**
>
> View an interactive version of a similar map.

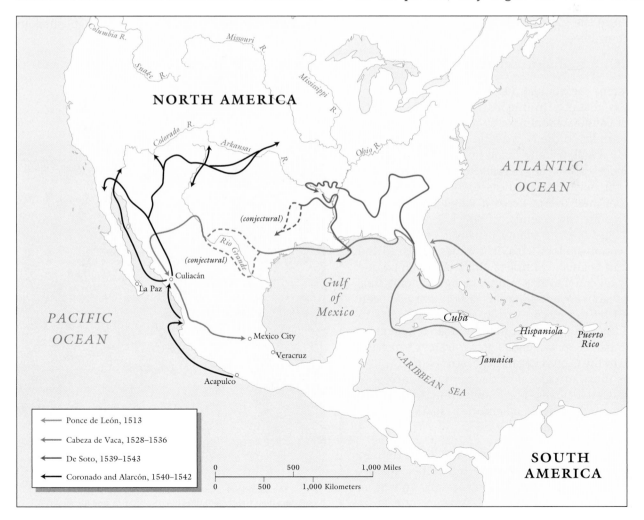

NORTH AMERICA

Columbia R.
Missouri R.
Snake R.
Mississippi R.
Colorado R.
Arkansas R.
Ohio R.
Rio Grande
(conjectural)
(conjectural)

ATLANTIC OCEAN

PACIFIC OCEAN

Culiacán
La Paz
Gulf of Mexico
Cuba
Hispaniola
Puerto Rico
Jamaica
Mexico City
Veracruz
Acapulco
CARIBBEAN SEA

SOUTH AMERICA

Ponce de León, 1513
Cabeza de Vaca, 1528–1536
De Soto, 1539–1543
Coronado and Alarcón, 1540–1542

0   500   1,000 Miles
0   500   1,000 Kilometers

conquistador
One of the Spanish noblemen who sailed to the New World with small armies to vanquish kingdoms there

encomienda
Tribute, usually payable in gold or slaves, demanded of conquered Indian villages by the conquistadors

viceroy
Representative of the Spanish crown who governed conquered Indian villages

chapters in the world's history, as disease and warfare nearly vanquished the native populations of the Caribbean, Mexico, and North and South America. The advent of disease was so bad that perhaps as many as one in five people then living on Earth died in the fifteenth and sixteenth centuries. Furthermore, Spain, searching for gold and other sources of wealth, brutally abused the native populations, often enslaving them and forcing them to work in gold mines to increase Spain's vast wealth. Just two decades after Columbus first crossed the Atlantic, the Spanish had established permanent settlements in Hispaniola, Cuba, Puerto Rico, Jamaica, and Panama. By 1513, the enslaved natives of Hispaniola were producing $1 million worth of gold annually. It would be only a few years before the Spanish expanded their settlements into the interior of North America in search of greater riches.

Spanish Expansion into North America

The system the Spanish used to develop their colonies was distinct. In the early sixteenth century, Spanish **conquistadors**, mostly minor noblemen, led private armies to the New World. These armies were relatively small, usually made up of fewer than one thousand men, but they devastated indigenous populations with weapons and disease wherever they went. Once they had overpowered a kingdom, it became known as an **encomienda**, in which Indian villages were obliged to pay a tribute, usually in gold or slaves, to the conquistadors. This, in essence, enslaved the Indians in Spanish-controlled lands, although no one actually owned another human being. (In doing this, the Spanish were adapting the system that had been enforced by the North African Muslims in order to control the Spanish when they conquered Spain.) As the number of encomiendas grew, **viceroys** reporting directly to the Crown began to govern them.

The most successful of the conquistadors were Hernán Cortés (1485–1547) and Francisco Pizarro (c. 1475–1541), whose adventures sparked widespread interest in the New World.

Cortés and Mexico. Between 1519 and 1521, Hernán Cortés led an expedition of six hundred men against the Triple Alliance (better, if incorrectly, known as the Aztecs) in Mexico and their ruler, Montezuma.

Four weapons allowed Cortés and his men to overrun the huge civilization: horses, which allowed mobility; firearms, which terrorized their victims; the support of other Indian tribes who had suffered under Aztec rule; and, by far the most important weapon, disease. Smallpox was first introduced to the New World by one of Cortés's men and by 1520 had decimated the Aztecs. Under assault from these four weapons, the great civilization of the Aztecs fell into Spanish hands within two years of Cortés's arrival, and, to Cortés's delight, so did the Aztecs' gold and silver reserves. The Spanish built Mexico City on the ruins of the Aztec capital, Tenochtitlán. Hoping to find the same plunder that Cortés had found, Spanish colonists soon arrived in large numbers, and Mexico City became the largest "European" city in America.

Pizarro and Peru. By the 1530s, Pizarro, well aware of Cortés's triumph, explored the western coast of South America from a base he established in

Read firsthand descriptions of Cortés's first contact with the Aztecs.

Experience the battle between Aztecs and Cortés's men through the simulation "Colonial Expansion."

>> The sacrificial practices of the Aztecs were scarcely more brutal than their treatment at the hands of Cortés and his men.

Panama. In 1532, he and his army of just 168 men (mostly untrained soldiers) encountered the tremendous Inca empire of Peru. Initially, like the Aztecs, the Incas welcomed the army, but the relationship quickly soured. Many of the Inca soldiers were off at battle with another tribe because the ravages of smallpox, which had spanned the continent less than a decade after being introduced by Cortés's men and had created political strife for the Incas. In the meantime, Pizarro kidnapped the Inca leader, amassed a huge fortune by ransoming his life, killed him anyway, and seized the Inca capital of Qosqo. With the Inca warriors away, Pizarro faced only mild resistance from what would have been formidable foes. When the Inca soldiers returned, Pizarro and his men were already entrenched in the empire. Pizarro founded the city of Lima as his capital in 1535 and ruled from there until his death in 1541. Again, internal battles within the Indian populations and especially smallpox contributed to the decline of what had been a vibrant civilization.

Florida. In today's United States, the Spanish developed settlements in Florida and the Southwest. The Spanish initially had little interest in Florida, but when French adventurers began to use eastern Florida as a base from which to attack Spanish ships traveling to Mexico and Peru, Spain sent soldiers to drive out the French pirates. In 1565, in order to secure the region, the Spanish conquered the city of St. Augustine from the French. Once established, Florida was a low priority for the Spanish because it did not contain

Read an account of the capture of St. Augustine.

66 Victory! Victory! the French fort is ours! 99

—*from* **The Founding of St. Augustine**

© iStockphoto.com/cornelius30

the riches of Mexico, Peru, or other parts of Central America, but it was important as an outpost guarding against attack.

The American Southwest

The Spanish also explored the American Southwest, heading north from Mexico as far as present-day Colorado. As with St. Augustine in Florida, the Spanish occupied the town of Santa Fe to secure the region against intruders but had little other use for it.

Read more about the founding of Santa Fe.

Results of Spanish Conquest

By the middle of the 1500s, Spanish conquistadors controlled numerous areas surrounding the Gulf of Mexico. There were five principal results of this initial Spanish conquest: financial, biological, racial, religious, and geopolitical.

Financial. Financially, the economic impact of the flow of silver from the mines of these lands was enormous. The influx of minerals made Spain one of the wealthiest nations in the world. Spain could now afford to defend a three-way trade between West Africa, the Americas, and Europe. But the sudden abundance of silver also meant that many people had access to money, causing prices to rise. The result was an inflationary **price revolution,** which badly hurt European laborers and landless agricultural workers, whose wages could not keep up with increasing prices throughout Europe. Increased numbers of impoverished Europeans were driven to emigrate to the Americas in search of a new life.

© Réunion des Musées Nationaux/ Art Resource, NY

Biological. The most important result was the **Columbian Exchange**, in which agricultural products, domesticated animals, and microbial diseases crossed over from one civilization to the other, creating a vast "exchange" that would forever change the world, for good and for ill. As more Spanish came to the New World, they unknowingly carried with them microbes for several diseases to which Indians had not been exposed, smallpox being the most destructive. The direct result of the spreading of these microbes was the death of perhaps as much as 95 percent of the Indian population. The numbers tell the story. Historians estimate that more than 25 million people lived in central Mexico before Cortés arrived; fifteen years after his arrival, more than 8 million had perished. Within a few generations, diseases eliminated two-thirds of the native population. And a century after first contact, the Indian population of Central Mexico was around 700,000. It took less than one hundred years for this population to fall from over 25 million to 700,000. Diseases spread far from the location of their initial inception as well, debatably stretching as far north as New England. This is perhaps one reason why English explorers found so few Indians when they first landed on the Atlantic coast in the 1600s, although diseases affecting New England's tribes may also have come from contact with European fishermen off the coast of Canada. For their part, Indians probably introduced syphilis to Europeans, but syphilis was hardly as deadly as smallpox or measles proved to be. Lest this part of the exchange be used to induce latter-day guilt in Europeans or European-Americans, most historians believe that, due to complex genetic dispositions within the Indian population, there would have been no way to prevent this microbial transmission.

If the exchange of microbes had horrifying ramifications, the mutual transfer of plants and animals led to a more positive biological exchange between the Americas and Europe. Contact allowed the cultures to expand the kinds of food they could grow and animals they could domesticate. Horses and livestock were introduced to the Americas by the Europeans; maize, tobacco, tomatoes, chocolate, and potatoes, all of which had been first cultivated by Indians, came to Europe. The development of sugar plantations in the Caribbean Islands was also a product of the Columbian Exchange, although their dependence on slaves was a corrosive element of the exchange.

Racial. Racially, Spanish exploration began the process of mixing various races of people. For one, the Spanish explorers procreated with Indian women. For another, their diseases had greatly depopulated Native America, a circumstance that expedited the introduction of African slaves as a labor force in the New World. By 1600, the multiracial character of the New World was firmly established.

Religious. In order to convert the Indians, the Spanish often destroyed Indian temples and replaced them with Catholic cathedrals. Catholic friars tried to use the religious symbols of the Indian religions to teach the lessons of Catholicism. But often the Indians transformed Catholic saints into spiritual likenesses of their preexisting gods and goddesses. The most famous example of this religious meshing was the Indian corn goddess and the Virgin Mary. Many Indians were able to accept the Catholic faith on their own terms once it had been hybridized in this way.

Geopolitical. Geopolitically, the Spanish successes meant that other European nations became hungry for conquest. Rivalries grew as nations sought resources they lacked at home. Of the five major results of the Spanish conquest, geopolitical concerns were the most significant in bringing the French and the English into New World exploration.

French

Like the Spanish and the Portuguese, French explorers, too, had been searching for the fabled route to the

>> "How Indians Treat Their Sick," from *Neue Welt und Americanische Historien* by Johann Ludwig Gottfried

© AAA Photostock/Alamy

Orient. They focused on looking for the Northwest Passage that would lead them through today's Canada to the Pacific Ocean. The French never found this nonexistent route, but they did find valuable products, mainly furs, that they could return to France.

The result was the creation of several encampments in present-day Canada that served as French trading posts in the New World. The largest was Quebec, founded in 1608. At these encampments, the French traded for furs with the Indians and spread Catholicism. However, the French were beleaguered by disease, by warfare with the Iroquois (who resented the French's successful trade with the Algonquians), and by the weather of the Northeast. Thus they remained a small but sturdy presence in North America, with holdings that extended great distances but vanished quickly after challenges from the more entrenched English throughout the 1700s. In the mid-1600s, there were only about four hundred French colonists in North America.

English

The English were slow to enter into New World exploration because the Tudors were still consolidating their Crown in the early 1500s, when Portugal, Spain, and France were busy traveling abroad. Furthermore, the Tudors at this time were closely allied with Spain (both were still Catholic) and did not want to challenge Spain's dominance in the New World. Also during the early 1500s, the English textile industry was booming, so wealthy individuals invested in textile businesses rather than in high-risk overseas ventures.

By the middle of the 1500s, this English disinclination toward exploration began to change. There were religious, social, economic, and geopolitical motives for this transition (see "The reasons why. . ." below).

Planting Colonies, Not Marauding Wealth

Despite hopes to the contrary, England (and all other European nations other than Spain) did not find

{ The reasons why . . . }

There were four key reasons why the English became more interested in exploration in the mid-1500s:

Religious. After several contentious decades during which Catholics and Protestants fought bitterly over whose faith was the rightful inheritor of the Bible, Protestant Queen Elizabeth I came to the throne. Queen Elizabeth's support of the Reformation suddenly turned England into Europe's leading opponent of the increasingly powerful Catholic Spain. Their rivalry increased after Spain supported two unsuccessful Roman Catholic plots to assassinate Elizabeth for her support of the Reformation (whether Pope Sixtus V was aware of these attempts remains an open question). Making things worse, in 1588, Spain tried unsuccessfully to invade England. This intense rivalry meant that the English were unwilling to allow Catholic Spain to convert all the non-Christians of the New World without competition from the surging English Protestants.

Social. Meanwhile, the enclosure of farms and the inflationary price revolution created a glut of impoverished Englishmen seeking to escape poverty by leaving England. But the poor were not the only English affected by limited economic possibilities. The English gentry was growing, and after the Church of England separated from the Catholic Church, traditional opportunities for the younger sons of nobles to serve in the Catholic Church were closed. With little unsettled land remaining in England, many members of the English upper class were willing to seek their fortune in the colonies.

Economic. The third motive for English expansion was that the textile markets of Antwerp, Belgium failed in the late 1500s, a development that left English producers without this market for their cloth. As a result, many wealthy individuals stopped investing in textiles and looked for new opportunities, such as New World exploration. In addition, the English economy was burdened by importing large quantities of raw materials, which created a dangerous trade imbalance. The New World had the potential to supply the English with these raw materials at cheaper prices.

Geopolitical. Fourth, Queen Elizabeth's durability as a monarch, reigning for over fifty years, stabilized the Tudor throne, meaning that England could now participate wholeheartedly in New World ventures. The bitter relations between Spain and England had erupted into war after Elizabeth knighted the British pirate Francis Drake for his exploits raiding Spanish treasure ships from 1578 to 1580. The Anglo-Spanish war, most noted for the defeat of the Spanish Armada, led to an English victory. For our purposes, the Anglo-Spanish war is significant for two reasons. First, it established England as ruler of the sea, prompting it to begin exploring the New World, and second, it signaled the decline of Spain as a world power. Now other nations could more successfully capitalize on the promises of the New World.

plantation
Large farm staffed by an entire family in an agricultural economy

lost colony of Roanoke
Second settlement by English colonists at Roanoke; deserted sometime before 1590

joint stock company
Company that sold stock to numerous investors in order to raise large sums of money

great wealth through quick plundering of existing civilizations in the Americas. England's wealth from the New World came instead through prolonged colonization, the development of substantial economies, and the exploitation of agricultural resources. As illustrated by Sir Walter Raleigh's explorations, it would take time and experience for the English to learn to focus on such endeavors. The desire for quick riches has persisted as a human flaw through the ages.

Sir Walter Raleigh and Roanoke. Sir Walter Raleigh was the first Englishman to found a New World colony. Raleigh received a royal patent to claim New World lands in the name of the queen, who was eager to check Spain's colonial expansion. In 1585, he established his first colony, using the Spanish conquistadors as his model. Like the Spanish adventurers who had conquered the Aztecs and Incas, Raleigh and his men sought gold and silver, and planned to exploit native labor to mine these treasures.

But there was a hitch in Raleigh's plan. Hoping to avoid conflict with the Spanish, Raleigh decided to focus his search to the north of Spain's territories in Mexico and South America. He and his men established their base at Roanoke, on the outer banks of modern-day North Carolina, a region lacking mineral wealth. Frustrated in their search for New World gold and silver, Raleigh's men abandoned the colony within a year.

After the first Roanoke settlement failed, Raleigh decided to continue his efforts on a different basis. He returned to the same region because he still wanted to avoid the Spanish, but this time he declared that he would not seek easy treasure. Learning from his initial failure and drawing on the experience of English settlements in Ireland earlier in the century, Raleigh decided that his second colony would consist of **plantations.** Instead of sending conquerors, he sent whole families to the New World; he hoped to re-create English society and its agricultural economy. Poor English farmers would perform the labor on the plantations, while transplanted gentry would perform their traditional functions of land ownership and governance.

But Raleigh's second Roanoke colony ultimately

Do a CSI Roanoke where *you're* the crime scene investigator.

failed as well. Voyages to resupply the colonists were delayed, and by the time a ship finally reached Roanoke in 1590, the outpost was deserted, perhaps after an attack by a local Indian tribe that was outraged after the colonists killed a tribal leader and displayed his head on a stake. The fate of the roughly one hundred settlers has never been conclusively determined, and the second Roanoke settlement came to be known as the **lost colony of Roanoke.**

Lessons of Roanoke. Although Roanoke was a catalogue of failures, it did teach the English two lessons. First, Raleigh had discovered that the formula for successful English colonization would not be quick strikes for gold but rather a plantation model that would create self-sustaining settlements. Second, Raleigh's efforts demonstrated that more than one person needed to fund such ventures—the demands were too great to be borne by a single purse. This realization resulted in the expansion of **joint stock companies**, or companies that sold stock to numerous people in order to raise large sums of money. At first, the English used joint stock companies to finance trade and, in the second half of the sixteenth century, English investors started a number of joint stock companies for ventures in the Old World. In 1553, the Muscovy Company traded for furs and naval stores in Russia; in 1581, the Levant Company was founded for trade with the Turkish Empire; in 1585, the Barbary Company focused its attention on North Africa; in 1588, the Guinea Company traded in West Africa; and in 1600, the East India Company formed to trade in Asia. Many of these companies

© Service Historique de la Marine, Vincennes, France, Lauros/Giraudon/The Bridgeman Art Library

>> **What became of the colonists left at the stockade on Roanoke Island? No one knows.**

were highly successful, and they encouraged many English investors to consider establishing colonies overseas by the early 1600s.

LO³ England Founds the Southern Colonies, 1607–1660

These two lessons observed, if not always adhered to, the English began to expand their holdings in the New World. Between 1600 and 1660, more than 150,000 English people left for the New World. Most went to the West Indies, and perhaps slightly less than a third crossed the Atlantic in order to settle the eastern coast of North America.

Virginia

Jamestown

Despite 115 years of contact, the year 1607 is often regarded as the first year of American history. It was in that year that the English established their first lasting colony in the land that would become the United States: **Jamestown**, in present-day Virginia.

Begun by the Virginia Company of London (a joint stock company), Jamestown began with 104 colonists, some of whom favored the plantation model of settlement, others of whom favored the conquistador model. Failure bedeviled them, however, mainly because of a harsh drought and because this group of settlers included too many English gentlemen who had little desire either to work the soil or to build fortifications. Most notably, John Smith attempted to unite this first group of settlers, but his rise to power insulted many of the gentleman explorers, who had him shipped back to England. The first years for these settlers were difficult, as disease, lack of food, poor management, and hostile relations with Indian tribes took a toll. Historians now call the winter of 1609–1610 the **starving time**, when food supplies were so scarce that at least one colonist resorted to cannibalism. Only the continued arrival of new colonists kept the settlement functioning. From 1607 to 1609, more than 900 settlers arrived in Jamestown. Only 60 survived the first few years.

Read John Smith's *Generall Historie of Virginia*.

Take a tour of Jamestown.

> From 1607 to 1609, more than 900 settlers arrived in Jamestown. Only 60 survived the first few years.

Jamestown Finally Succeeds

Jamestown eventually succeeded, and its success depended on two things: Indian relations and tobacco.

The Powhatan Confederacy. First, the English settlers, badly in need of food, relied on a group of six Algonquian villages known as the **Powhatan Confederacy** (named after its leader). Powhatan and his tribe saw the English settlers as allies who would accept food in return for knives and guns, which would help Powhatan secure his confederacy against other tribes. The relationship between Powhatan's tribe and the Virginians was often difficult and sometimes violent, especially when crops were limited. But the tribes of the Powhatan Confederacy did assist the settlers throughout their struggling early years.

Tobacco. Second, in the early 1610s, the English settlers hit a jackpot: They successfully cultivated tobacco. The Spanish had introduced the crop to Europe in the late 1500s after first encountering it in the Caribbean. Tobacco had been a tremendous success in the markets of Europe, making it, along with sugar, one of the most profitable **cash crops** of the New World. By 1612, the Virginia settler John Rolfe (best known for making peace with the local tribes by marrying Pocahontas, the daughter of a local chieftain) had successfully cultivated an imported strain of tobacco in Jamestown. The colonists shipped the first crop to England in 1617, and by 1620 they had delivered 40,000 pounds of the cured plant back to England. Within a few years, shipments had climbed to 1.5 million pounds. Virginia was about to boom.

Jamestown Grows

The success of tobacco made Jamestown a more appealing place to be. But cultivating tobacco requires labor. To meet this need, early tobacco growers attempted to follow the Spanish model and force Indians to work in their fields. Such efforts were hampered by several problems: Indians objected to the concept of growing surplus crops for cash;

Jamestown
English settlement of 1607 in present-day Virginia

starving time
Winter of 1609–1610 in Jamestown, when food supplies were so scarce that at least one colonist resorted to cannibalism

Powhatan Confederacy
Group of six Algonquian villages in present-day Virginia, named after its leader

cash crop
Agricultural product grown primarily for sale. Examples include sugar and tobacco harvests.

indentured servitude
System of labor whereby Virginia farmers paid the Atlantic passage for English and Irish workers in exchange for four to seven years of their work on farms or plantations

head right
50 acres of land granted by the Virginia Company to any individual who paid his or her own passage across the Atlantic. This put more property in private hands.

"seasoning"
Period of several years during which indentured servants were exposed to the New World's microbes. Many did not survive

royal colony
English settlement whose governor was chosen by the King

House of Burgesses
Assembly of landholders chosen by other landholders, with which the royal governors were forced to work

Read Rolfe's first-hand account of conditions in Jamestown at the end of its first decade.

Read more about the economic aspects of colonial tobacco culture.

Read a contract of indenture.

>> **Tobacco was a currency, also used to pay fines and taxes. For example, persons encouraging slave meetings were to be fined 1,000 pounds of tobacco; owners letting slaves keep horses were fined 500 pounds tobacco; if a person wanted to become married, he had to go to the rector of his parish and pay the man so many pounds of tobacco.**

language barriers made it difficult for English planters to explain their demands; and, chiefly, the colonists lacked the military force required to enslave Indians. In 1619, Dutch traders imported a small number of Africans to Jamestown, who performed much of the backbreaking work of establishing a town. However, due to cost considerations, the institutionalized importation of Africans was slow to progress throughout the seventeen century.

The result was the expansion of a system of labor called **indentured servitude,** in which English and Irish poor sold their labor for four to seven years to a farmer who would fund their voyage across the Atlantic. To encourage their importation, the Virginia Company offered a **head right** of 50 acres to any individual who paid their own passage, which put more property in private hands. Throughout the 1600s, almost 80 percent of the immigrants to Virginia were indentured servants, most of whom were young lower-class males. These servants had to endure several years of **"seasoning,"** a period of time during which they were exposed to the New World's microbes. Many did not survive.

Consequences

Jamestown continued to grow in size and in population. This expansion had three major consequences: increased hostility with Indians, change in leadership of the colony, and the introduction of African slavery.

Increased hostility with Indians. Local Indian tribes were leery of the growth of Jamestown, which was rapidly encroaching on lands to which they had previously had access. After Powhatan died in 1618, his successor, Opechancanough, began planning an attack to expel the colonists. A fierce assault in 1622 resulted in the death of 357 English colonists, or one quarter of the Jamestown settlement. Angered, the settlers felt the attack gave them justification to destroy every Indian they encountered. Hostilities brewed.

Change to royal control. A second result of Jamestown's growth was a change in who controlled the colony. Opechancanough's attack of 1622 wiped out vital infrastructure and subsequently bankrupted the Virginia Company of London, which had had a grant for the land from the Crown. This, combined with internal conflicts within the company, led England's King James I to seize the colony and place it under royal control. Virginia thus became a **royal colony**, with a governor chosen by the King. But the colonists fought for their liberties and forced the governor to work with an assembly that would be chosen by the landholders (a democratic method carried over from the Virginia Company). This assembly was called the **House of Burgesses**. Although the King maintained control, the colony enjoyed self-government and had its own political body within which it could air grievances. America's struggle for political liberty had begun.

Introduction of African slavery. The third major result of Jamestown's growth was the introduction of African slavery into the colonies that would become the United States. Throughout the 1600s, indentured servitude remained the preferred source of labor, but slaves were a small, significant part of the labor force as early as 1619. However, slavery did

>> At the age of twenty-one, Pocahontas visited London, where she was presented to King James I and the court. In March 1617, she and her husband, John Rolfe, departed for home, but it soon became clear that Pocahontas would not survive the voyage. She died of pneumonia or tuberculosis and was taken ashore and buried far from her home.

not become legally defined or a dominant source of labor until late in the seventeenth century.

Maryland

Founding

Following Virginia's success, in 1632, the king of England granted the region that we now call Maryland to George Calvert, a lord whose royal name was Lord Baltimore. Lord Baltimore created the first of the **proprietary colonies**, or colonies overseen by a proprietor who was allowed to control and distribute the land as he wished. The King granted Lord Baltimore the land in part to end a religious problem, because Lord Baltimore was a prominent English Catholic looking for a haven for members of his faith. The first settlers landed in Maryland in 1634, with large numbers of Catholics but even a slightly larger number of Protestants. Learning from the mistakes of Roanoke and Jamestown, the colonists under Lord Baltimore developed an economy based on the plantation model, raising corn and livestock for food and tobacco for profit.

Politics and the Toleration Act

Although Lord Baltimore and his sons at first attempted autocratic rule over Maryland, they quickly opted to create a legislature in the model of the House of Burgesses, which allowed the colonists a good amount of self-rule. Self-rule had its problems, though: As more Protestants came over from England, Lord Baltimore realized that he must protect his fellow Catholics. The result was one of the major landmarks in the history of liberty: the **Toleration Act of 1649**, which granted freedom of worship to anyone who accepted the divinity of Jesus Christ. The act did not end religious disputes between the colonists, as Protestants continued to battle Catholic rule in the colony. But it did prevent legal action from being taken on account of one's faith. Christians, whether Catholic or Protestant, could not be imprisoned for their faith.

Life on the Chesapeake

Although Maryland and Virginia prospered, mainly due to tobacco, life on the Chesapeake was generally miserable. Virginia and Maryland remained a collection of tiny villages made up of numerous small farms worked by indentured servants. Three quarters of those who came over were young males, and most died during their seasoning period. Families were unstable: Marriages were fragile, childbirth a risky undertaking, and growing up with both parents a rarity. In this atmosphere, the population was slow to establish churches and schools. Most homes were crudely built, with few partitions, and the quality of life could adequately be described as bleakly rustic.

proprietary colony
Colony overseen by a proprietor who was allowed to control and distribute the land as he wished

Toleration Act of 1649
Act granting freedom of worship to anyone who accepted the divinity of Jesus Christ. This meant that neither Catholics nor Protestants could be imprisoned for their faith.

Read the Toleration Act.

LO⁴ Founding the New England Colonies, 1620–1660

Why More Colonies?

Despite the harsh reality of life in the colonies, the promise of wealth and freedom fueled England's desire for more colonies.

Puritans
Group of believers who wished to reform or purify the Church of England by removing its hierarchy, its emphasis on work as payment to God, its allowance of prayers for communal salvation, and its promotion of missions

Separatists
Group of believers who wished to separate completely from the Church of England because they believed it was irrevocably corrupted

Mayflower
Ship containing Separatists who sailed from Holland and landed in Plymouth, in present-day Massachusetts, in 1620

Financial Impulses

Financially, the English had seen the wealth that successful cultivation of a cash crop like tobacco could generate, and this furthered investors' interest in colonial development.

Religious Impulses

In 1559, Queen Elizabeth reestablished the Church of England as a body distinct from the Catholic Church. Nevertheless, several groups in England felt she had not gone far enough in freeing Christianity from the yoke of the Catholics. One of these groups was the **Puritans**, who wished to reform, or purify, the Church of England by removing its hierarchy, its emphasis on work as payment to God, its allowance of prayers for communal salvation, and its promotion of missions. Another dissenting group was the **Separatists**, who wished to separate completely from the Church of England because they believed it was irrevocably corrupted. Both these groups were buttressed by England's social problems, which created a large number of poor people who feared the power of an overarching institution such as the Church of England.

Massachusetts
The Accidental Landing

In order to escape the Church of England and worship according to their understanding of the Christian faith, a group of Separatists departed from England. First, they went to Holland, then after receiving a land grant from the Virginia Company of London, they sailed on the ship *Mayflower* in 1620, destined for Virginia. The winter winds caught them, and they were blown off course, landing in present-day Massachusetts, in a town they called Plymouth. Weakened by the crossing and fearful of storms, they decided to establish their pure Christian community there. The Plymouth colony was born.

These Separatists had no title to land this far north, however, and they knew this would be a problem if other settlers arrived with a proper patent. To remedy this problem, and to establish ground rules for governing once they landed, they signed an agreement that bound each member to obey majority rule

... life on the Chesapeake was generally miserable.

Replica of the Mayflower

In 1623, the settlers divided their land among the people, which rewarded those who were willing to work hard. The ingenuity and drive of these early settlers, in addition to some help from London benefactors, helped them pay off their debts to the Virginia Company by 1627, a remarkably quick repayment that encouraged others to migrate to Massachusetts. They also had stable governmental self-rule, as one of the new settlers, William Bradford, ruled with a strong, level hand and consulted numerous colonists before making decisions.

Learn more about Plymouth.

Mayflower Compact
An agreement that bound each member of the Separatist group in Plymouth to obey majority rule and to promise to defend one another from potential eviction. This agreement set a precedent for democratic rule in Massachusetts.

and to promise to defend one another from potential eviction. This was the **Mayflower Compact**, an agreement that set a precedent, in rhetoric if not always in reality, for democratic rule in Massachusetts. It was also grounded in the notion of Christian unity, lending a messianic fervor to the mission: In their minds, they were there because God wanted them to be there. One year later, in 1621, they secured a patent to the land from the Crown.

Participate in a simulation of the founding of a new colony.

Settling

After a difficult first winter in 1620, during which half of them died or returned to England, the Separatists established farms and developed a fur trade in today's Maine. The local Wampanoag Indians viewed their presence—and all European presence—as a short time to enjoy trading with the Europeans, after which the Indians would expel the Europeans. By 1621, however, the Wampanoags had been ravaged by disease and needed help fending off their rivals in the interior. The Wampanoag leader thus made a decisive deal: They would allow the European visitors to stay if they would agree to ally with the Wampanoags. Once the agreement was settled, a harvest festival enjoyed by the two peoples in 1621 became the symbol for the event we today know as Thanksgiving. The settlers were bound to be permanent residents.

Expansion

Encouraged by the developments at Plymouth, English Puritans (not Separatists) sought to formalize Massachusetts as a royal colony. This was done in 1629 under the name of the Massachusetts Bay Company. Its charter was special, however, in that it did not stipulate that decisions about the colony had to be made in England, thus implying that those who lived under the charter would enjoy self-rule. This encouraged a larger group of Puritans, who were under increasing assault in England for their religious beliefs, to migrate.

Led by John Winthrop, 1,000 Puritans set out for their religious haven of Massachusetts; between 1630 and 1640, 25,000 more followed. Their success, supported by the cultivation of cereals and livestock, made the Puritans believe that "God hath sifted a nation"—that God had wished the Puritans to settle the Americas as the world's Promised Land. As John Winthrop told them before they arrived, "We shall be as a city upon a hill [and] the eyes of all people are upon us." Their so-called "errand into the wilderness," as it was described in a 1670 sermon, was an attempt to form an exemplary religious community, one that would inspire reform in Old England.

Politics

Politically, the Puritans were not democrats but theocrats, believing in a state that forced all of its inhabitants to hold a specific religious orthodoxy within an established church. This unity of belief, combined with the fact that most of the immigrants came as families, allowed the development of tightly knit communities based on a less rigid hierarchy of labor exploitation than that found in the Chesapeake.

By 1634, the people of Massachusetts began to reject the absolutism of the Puritan theocracy (it had not lasted long), although the colonists did not reject the religious nature of the colony. They also demanded a legislature, which had been approved in the royal charter. The legislature was composed of two separate houses: one an elite board of directors, the other a larger house made up of popularly elected deputies. This was a less-than-representative form of representative government, though: Only selected church members were allowed to vote for the deputies who represented them.

Society

As Massachusetts prospered through the cultivation of grains and cereals, small towns appeared throughout present-day Massachusetts, Maine, New Hampshire, Connecticut, and Rhode Island (see Map 2.3). Small villages composed of several families were the central institution of Massachusetts. They dotted the New England coast and the central New England rivers. Large farmlands surrounded the villages, and the villagers would trudge each morning from their homes to work the outlying lands, then return to the central village at nightfall.

The town's land was parceled out to families depending on each family's size and needs. Successful families were expected to give back to their community by helping out the poor or the unlucky. Importantly, the tightly knit nature of these sparse communities and the priority placed on families meant that diseases were much less likely to ravage their population than those of the Virginia and Maryland colonies. Infant mortality in Massachusetts fell below that of Europe, resulting in a remarkable population boom during which the population doubled every twenty-seven years.

Even the most successful of the colonists often remained less powerful than the town's minister, however, as biblical orthodoxy was demanded of all settlers. Single men and women were required to live with a family so as not to appear promiscuous. In response to a need for religious education, the Puritans founded Harvard College in 1636. New England also was fertile ground for famous writers and poets during this period.

Rhode Island

Beginnings

In Massachusetts, the persistent demands of religious orthodoxy rankled some settlers, and one of the biggest troublemakers was Roger Williams, the minister of Salem, Massachusetts, who hoped for a "purer" form of religion than even the Puritan founders had institutionalized. Most importantly, he suggested that there should be a clear division between the practice of religion and the politics of state. He believed that politics necessarily impeded the soul's progress toward perfection. Williams's teachings obviously contradicted the Puritan notion of a commonwealth based on devotion to God, and Williams was expelled from Massachusetts. He left Massachusetts with a small band of followers, walking to what is today Rhode Island and founding the town of Providence.

A second group of dissenters was also destined for Rhode Island. The leader of this second group was a charismatic woman named Anne Hutchinson. Hutchinson, a married woman who worked as a midwife, defied the orthodoxy of Massachusetts by stressing that only God determined who merited grace, not ministers or powerful men. More importantly, she disputed the notion of a single orthodox scripture, suggesting instead that humankind's relationship with God was a continual process of divine revelation, rather than based solely on a fixed

Anne Hutchinson's trial

Map 2.3
New England in the 1640s

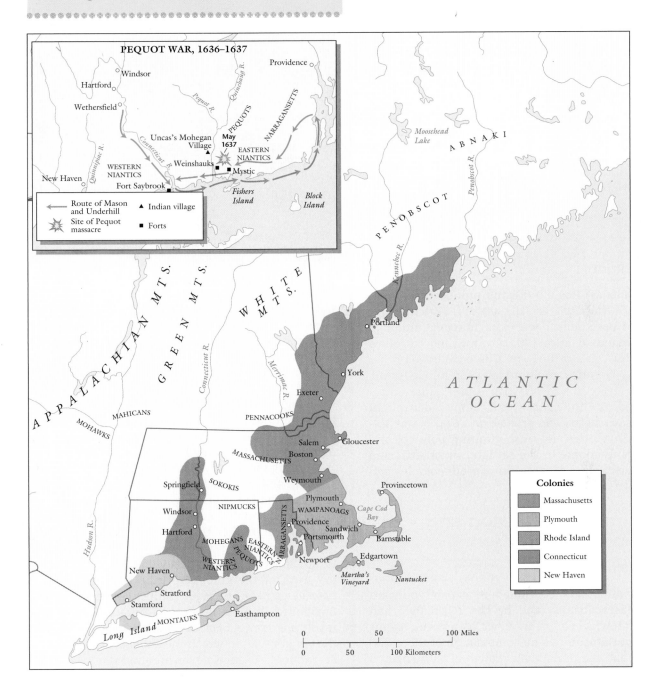

PEQUOT WAR, 1636–1637

Windsor

Hartford

Wethersfield

Providence

Pequot R.

Quinebaug R.

PEQUOTS

NARRAGANSETTS

Uncas's Mohegan Village

May 1637

EASTERN NIANTICS

Quinnipiac R.

WESTERN NIANTICS

Weinshauks

Mystic

New Haven

Fort Saybrook

Fishers Island

Block Island

Connecticut R.

→ Route of Mason and Underhill
✦ Site of Pequot massacre
▲ Indian village
■ Forts

Moosehead Lake

A B N A K I

Penobscot R.

P E N O B S C O T

Kennebec R.

APPALACHIAN MTS.

GREEN MTS.

W H I T E M T S.

Connecticut R.

Merrimac R.

Portland

York

A T L A N T I C
O C E A N

Exeter

PENNACOOKS

MAHICANS

MOHAWKS

MASSACHUSETTS

Salem

Gloucester

Boston

Weymouth

Hudson R.

Springfield

SOKOKIS

NIPMUCKS

Windsor

Hartford

MOHEGANS

WESTERN NIANTICS

EASTERN NIANTICS

PEQUOTS

NARRAGANSETTS

WAMPANOAGS

Plymouth

Providence

Sandwich

Portsmouth

Newport

Provincetown

Cape Cod Bay

Barnstable

Edgartown

Martha's Vineyard

Nantucket

New Haven

Stratford

Stamford

Easthampton

Long Island MONTAUKS

Colonies

■ Massachusetts
■ Plymouth
■ Rhode Island
■ Connecticut
■ New Haven

0   50   100 Miles

0   50   100 Kilometers

Antinomianism
Theological philosophy stressing that only God, not ministers, determined who merited grace. Instead of a single orthodox scripture, this belief suggests that humankind's relationship with God was a continual process of divine revelation. Anne Hutchinson led a group of Antinomian dissenters and was banished from Massachusetts for these beliefs.

Pequot War
Bloody battles of the 1630s between New England colonists and the Pequot tribe of Indians

scripture from thousands of years ago. This theological turn came to be called **Antinomianism**. Hutchinson was also an able leader and a persuasive preacher who won over many followers, and Boston's clergy saw her and her Antinomianism as a threat to their community and their leadership atop it. To silence her, they put her on trial, found her guilty of sedition and contempt, and banished her. She and her followers left Massachusetts and founded Portsmouth, Rhode Island, just southeast of Providence.

Settlement

In Providence, Roger Williams promised religious and civil freedom to all settlers. Hutchinson's town of Portsmouth was less tolerant, although it continued to attract those unwilling to follow Massachusetts's orthodoxy. This encouraged other religious "heretics" to found towns in Rhode Island, such as Newport and Warwick. A preliminary charter founding Rhode Island as a colony independent of Massachusetts was granted in 1644. It was followed by another in 1663, granting political and religious freedoms to the settlers, which attracted a wide range of dissenters from other colonies and Europe.

Continued Expansion and Indian Confrontation

Expansion

Puritan dissenters continued to expand outward from Massachusetts, and by the 1630s they had founded towns in what are now Connecticut, Maine, and New Hampshire. The combination of these dissenters and the remarkable growth of New England meant that the ideal of puritanically pious communities was untenable. What grew instead was a dynamic agricultural society fueled by a seemingly insatiable land hunger. Almost as soon as it had started to proliferate, the Puritans' hope of a "pure" society was beginning to fade.

>> New Englanders effectively exterminated the Pequot tribe in the bloodbaths of the 1630s.

© American Antiquarian Society, Worcester, Massachusetts, USA/ The Bridgeman Art Library

Indian Battles and the Pequot War

As had happened in Virginia, New England's growth led to confrontation with the land's inhabitants, the tribes of Indians. Although the Puritans had several Indian allies, John Winthrop had prepared New Englanders quite early for the possibility of conflict, agreeing to train all male colonists to use firearms, forbidding Indians' entering Puritan towns, and forbidding Puritans' selling firearms to Indians.

During the first years of settlement, conflict was sporadic and light, no doubt in part because European diseases had killed off as much as three quarters of the Indian population before the colonists arrived at Plymouth. In fact, the Puritans viewed this dying as the work of God, who, they felt, divinely wished to transform New England's wilderness into a shining work of the Lord. One tribe remained strong, however, and by the 1630s conflict between the New Englanders and the Pequots became inevitable. The result was a series of bloody battles collectively called the **Pequot War**, in which the supposedly pious New Englanders effectively exterminated the tribe, gruesomely killing men, women, children, and the elderly. With the Pequots now removed from power, the colonists were assured control over all the southern tribes of New England. The blood shed during the Pequot War foreshadowed the dark nature of Indian–colonist relations that was just over the horizon.

Learn more about what life was like in 1628 New England.

And in the end ...

Historians still debate the legacy that modern America inherited from this initial phase of colonial development, but some parallels are clearly visible. For instance, the freedom to worship as one pleased had its origins in both Maryland and Rhode Island during a time when that level of tolerance was unknown elsewhere in the world. There was a considerable expansion of political freedoms and self-rule that one would never have encountered in England. And economically, it was plausible and possible that one could work one's way out of one's class and become a landholding farmer. This sense of economic mobility also transcended any similar experience one might encounter in Europe.

On the other hand, each of these democratic impulses had considerable limitations. In religion, by 1660, every colony besides Maryland and Rhode Island had restrictions on what faith one could hold; the two exceptions existed because minority sects had begun them in order to find freedom from harshly restrictive colonial magistrates or the dangers of popular opinion. In politics, the right to participate in political life was limited to landholding farmers or orthodox religious adherents (depending on whether one lived in the South or the North). Economically, although there was some mobility, one had to endure tremendous hardships in order to realize it. Most who came seeking great wealth were promptly disappointed. Nevertheless, with the Chesapeake in the South and New England in the North, these were America's colonial beginnings. They would only grow, as we will see in the next chapter.

What else was happening . . .

1492	The Spanish peso is first put into circulation.
1498	The first toothbrush is made from hog bristles.
1501	The first flush toilet is invented.
1540	The first horses arrive in North America, when Spanish explorer Francisco Vasquez de Coronado, traveling through Kansas, lets about 260 of them escape.

CHAPTER 3

Expansion

and Its

Costs,

1660–1700

Learning Outcomes

After reading this chapter, you should be able to do the following:

LO¹ Describe the changes in European development of North America during the period from 1660 to 1700, and analyze the four distinct areas that began to emerge.

LO² Discuss the English colonists' experiences up to 1700 with Native American tribes.

LO³ Discuss the English colonists' experiences up to 1700 with African slaves.

LO⁴ Discuss the European wars that had an impact on North America.

"No matter where one lived, daily life in the early colonies was grueling."

During the hundred years between 1660 and 1763, the English colonies in North America not only scratched out a living in a harsh environment, but grew and expanded into a sizeable power central to the British empire. In 1660, England had only a few colonies in the land that would become the United States. They were in New England, with its numerous small towns, and in the Chesapeake, in its large tobacco-producing farms sprawling along the region's riverbanks. In total, there were about seventy thousand people of non-Indian origin living in these regions. There was not much commerce between these European settlements, and no matter where one lived, daily life in the early colonies was grueling.

One hundred years later, the landscape had changed considerably. By 1763, there were thirteen English colonies in four distinct regions: New England, the Middle Colonies, the Chesapeake, and the Southern Colonies. Each of these regions enjoyed a vibrant economy based on the commerce, agriculture, and industry that flourished there. Intellectually and culturally, English colonies on American soil had begun to develop a style all their own. The colonial non-native population reached 1 million by 1750, with colonists pushing toward lands in the west that would accommodate their growing numbers.

This chapter explores this development from 1660 to 1700, paying particular attention to the expansion of British America (Map 3.1 on page 43), the decline of the Indian populations along the Atlantic coast, and the subtle transition from indentured servitude to race-based slavery. It also examines how the growing North American colonies became crucial players in the "Wars for Empire" between the European powers. Chapter 4 will focus on the solidification of the four distinct colonial regions, the development of the American slavery system, and the attempts by the British Crown to reassert control over colonial America, efforts that would ultimately trigger the Revolutionary War. But first, to the initial expansion of English holdings in North America from 1660 to 1700.

What do you think?

When the first Africans arrived in the North American colonies, they were not treated badly.

Strongly Disagree						*Strongly Agree*
1	2	3	4	5	6	7

commonwealth
A kingless republican government

Restoration
Period of English history when the Stuarts were restored to the throne (1660–1685)

Navigation Acts
Regulations that dictated where colonial producers could ship their goods, stipulated that colonists must transport their goods in English ships, and listed a group of products that colonists were permitted to sell only to England

enumerated articles
Goods (tobacco, sugar, cotton, indigo) listed in the Navigation Acts that colonists were permitted to sell only to England

proprietary colonies
Colonies owned and ruled by an individual or a private corporation, rather than by the Crown

LO¹ Expansion of English Holdings in North America, 1660–1700

English Motives for Further Expansion

The English Civil War. The initial impetus for English colonial expansion came from the homeland. In 1649, revolutionaries led by Oliver Cromwell executed the English king, Charles I, igniting a civil war that lasted a decade and a half. The revolutionaries intended to create a kingless republican government called a **commonwealth**, founded on concepts like taxation only with representation, limited government, and antimonarchical beliefs—all of which would become central ideas of the American Revolution more than a century later. Cromwell's commonwealth dissolved into chaos in 1658 when he died, leaving the revolution without a leader. Conservative military men took control of the country, and, in 1660, a group of generals invited Charles II to fill his late father's position as king of England. After twelve years of civil war, the Stuarts (the family that had controlled the throne since 1603) regained power. This period of English history is called the **Restoration** (1660–1685), and it was significant for colonial North America because King Charles II used the colonies to tighten control of his initially unstable leadership and to pay off debts incurred during his fight to recover the throne.

Tightening royal control. To reinforce control over the colonies (which, in general, had been sympathetic to Cromwell and which had engaged in more trade with the Dutch because of the decline in English trading), Charles II first enacted strict trade regulations. Passed by Parliament in

1651, the first of these regulations, known collectively as the **Navigation Acts**, dictated where colonial producers could ship their goods, stipulated that colonists must transport their goods in English ships, and listed a group of **enumerated articles** (tobacco, sugar, cotton, indigo) that colonists were permitted to sell only to England. The goal of these measures was to prevent the transfer of resources from England to its rivals, France and the Dutch Republic. It was also intended to curb the growth of colonial North America, which the Crown saw as a potential threat to English producers.

Paying off debts. The Navigation Acts meant that the colonies could be lucrative for those who controlled them, because the acts ensured an English monopoly on the first sale of all colonial goods. Thus, to pay off his debts, Charles II offered land in the New World to his supporters, where they could establish colonies called **proprietary colonies**, which were colonies owned and ruled by an individual or a private corporation, rather than by the Crown. If the proprietors ruled them successfully, they could become extremely wealthy.

The Creation of Colonies During and After the Restoration

Proprietary colonies were the chief means of colonial expansion between 1660 and 1700, and it was through them that the large gap of land unsettled by Europeans between Massachusetts and Virginia, as well as the lands between Virginia and Florida, were colonized. During the Restoration, friends of Charles II created five proprietary colonies: Carolina (present-day North and South Carolina), New York, Pennsylvania, and East Jersey and West Jersey (later joined to become New Jersey). The proprietary colony of Georgia was founded after the Restoration. The proprietors of these colonies were free to establish governments as they wished, so long as their laws did not contradict those of England. As such, each of the proprietary colonies developed quite differently from one another. The expansion of colonial America had begun.

Carolina

Three years after returning to his father's throne, Charles II granted the vast territory of Carolina to a group of eight noblemen who had supported him during the com-

Tobacco ships in the James River, Virginia Colony, 1600s.

Map 3.1
English Settlement between 1660 and 1700

View an interactive version of a similar map.

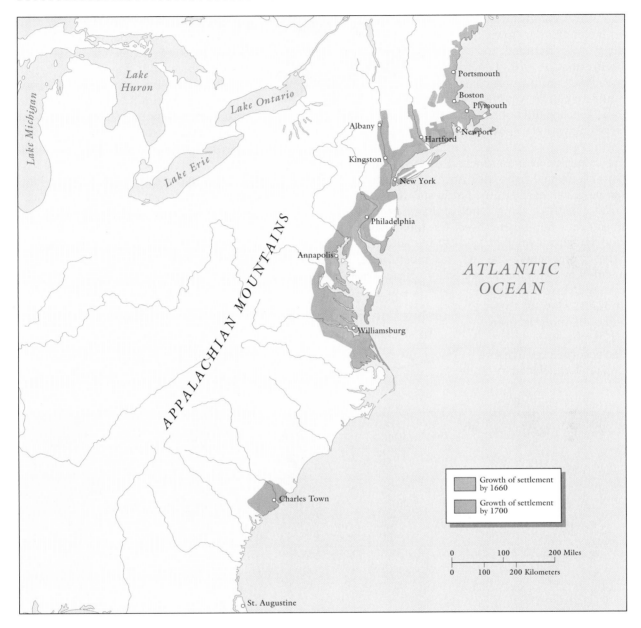

Lake Huron

Lake Michigan

Lake Ontario

Lake Erie

Albany

Portsmouth

Boston
Plymouth

Hartford
Newport

Kingston

New York

Philadelphia

Annapolis

APPALACHIAN MOUNTAINS

ATLANTIC
OCEAN

Williamsburg

Charles Town

Growth of settlement
by 1660

Growth of settlement
by 1700

0   100   200 Miles

0   100   200 Kilometers

St. Augustine

monwealth. According to the grant, the Carolinas extended from Virginia south to the northern tip of today's Florida, and west all the way to the Pacific Ocean. The eight proprietors set up elaborate rules (in a constitution drafted by the philosopher John Locke) and encouraged the establishment of large plantations. Two-fifths of each county was to be set aside for the proprietors, thus ensuring the continued wealth of the founders.

The failure of proprietorship. Things did not turn out as Carolina's proprietors had hoped. Basically, they misunderstood that the American context of abundant land would not accommodate the hierarchical society of England with its noble titles and haughty proprietors. Many of the earliest settlers of Carolina came from the Caribbean rather than England, because a temporary dip in sugar prices made the Caribbean islands less appealing. These settlers were accustomed to self-rule, not the hierarchical society the proprietors intended to emulate. They also brought slaves with them, meaning that, from its earliest history, Carolina was powered by small-scale entrepreneurs and slave laborers. It later had the distinction of being America's first colony dependent on slave labor. Charles Town (later Charleston) was founded in 1670 after the decimation of Indian tribes in the area, but Carolina was considered highly undesirable; its weather was hot and humid, and tobacco did not thrive in the colony's soil. Everything was going badly.

Rice. The colony's fortunes reversed in 1693, when Carolinians discovered from their African slaves that rice could be grown easily in the fertile soil. Rice culture spread rapidly, making Carolina lucrative and suddenly creating an urgent need for more labor. This labor crunch meant that by 1720 the southern part of the colony, where the soil was most fertile, was populated by twice as many slaves as European freemen or indentured servants. Most of these slaves had been imported from Barbados, in the West Indies, which had become a key marketplace for the worldwide slave trade.

> Carolina had the distinction of being America's first colony dependent on slave labor.

The large number of slaves in Carolina made Charlestown the center of North America's early slave trade, which would begin to prosper in the 1680s and 1690s.

Life. Few Europeans lived in the southern part of Carolina because life there was so miserable. Diseases spread rapidly, and population growth remained low. Despite the proprietors' hopes for a harmonious existence with the Indians, before rice made Carolina lucrative its principal export was captured Indian slaves who were sold in New England and the West Indies. This meant continued warfare with Indian tribes—yet another reason to avoid the southern part of Carolina. Within the first three decades of the colony's founding, the two largest tribes on the Carolina coast were largely extinct.

In the northern part of the colony there were fewer diseases and lower humidity, which led to the development of a different kind of society. Tobacco farmers from Virginia developed small farms and advocated self-rule there. Although slavery existed, it never became the main labor supply. By 1698, the differences between the south and the north had become so marked that the proprietors chose to divide the col-

Few Europeans lived in the southern part of Carolina because life there was so miserable.

>> Map of New Netherland, by N. J. Visscher, 1650–1651, based on a manuscript map compiled by Adriaen van der Donck in 1648.

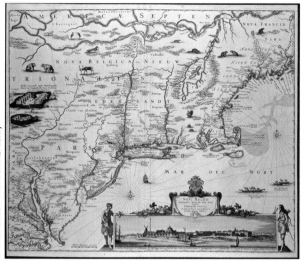

onies in two; they became South Carolina and North Carolina in 1712.

New York

New York was also a proprietary colony, but polyglot and diverse from the beginning. It developed much differently than Carolina did.

The New York Dutch. New York began as a Dutch colony, founded long before the Restoration, in 1624, when the Dutch claimed New Jersey and New York. The Dutch based their claims on the voy-

Take a virtual tour of New Netherland.

age of Henry Hudson in 1609 and Peter Minuit's purchase of the island of Manhattan for a small amount of trinkets and jewelry. They called their territory New Netherland. This was a bold move because the English were developing colonies south of New York in Virginia and north of it in New England.

During the early 1600s, the Dutch had moderate success trading furs with the Iroquois. But their biggest success lay in the port town of New Amsterdam (later New York City). There, a multicultural group of traders gathered to trade and barter near the Atlantic. By 1660, the population of New Amsterdam reached ten thousand.

The English take over. Competition over commerce led to bitter relations between the English and Dutch, and three small "Anglo-Dutch" wars broke out between the two nations, fought mostly in the English Channel, between 1652 and 1675. In 1664, England's Charles II wrested New Amsterdam

from the Dutch and granted it to his brother, the Duke of York. Renaming the colony New York, the duke ruled it severely and autocratically for two decades. But his attempts to restrict the rights of New Yorkers were resisted by the diverse mix of settlers and traders, who fought to keep New York free for commerce and expression.

Pennsylvania

Outdoing even New York's polyglot character, William Penn established the most diverse of the proprietary colonies. Penn was named after his father, a royal courtier, to whom the king had become indebted because of gambling losses. When the elder Penn died, the younger William Penn inherited claim to the debt. And when Charles II began imprisoning religious minorities in the 1670s, Penn, a newly converted Quaker, traded the debt for a North American colony.

Quakers. The **Quakers** are Protestants who believe that God's will was directly transmitted to people through "the inner light" of divine knowledge that a

>> William Penn meeting with Native Americans on the site of the city of Philadelphia

person possesses within his or her being. This belief was in opposition to the Protestant mainstream, which made the Bible the center of the religious experience. The Quakers also rejected the concepts of Original Sin and predestination, further alienating them from the Protestant core.

In the 1600s, there were social differences between Quakers and Protestants as well. Quaker meetings employed no professional ministers (whom they derisively called "hireling ministers"), relying instead on laypeople (non-ordained faith-community members). Quakers, sometimes called the Society of Friends, rejected class distinctions as well, which prevented them from deferring to social superiors. Furthermore, the Quakers argued that any believer was as capable as any other of transmitting the truth about God's will, including women, a policy that threatened traditional Christian distinctions between the sexes. In an era of religious intolerance and political instability, the Quakers were distrusted and even outlawed.

Fleeing England. In 1674, Penn, along with ten other Quakers, purchased the proprietary rights to West Jersey. Penn drafted an egalitarian constitution for the colony, which protected the right of trial by jury, prohibited capital punishment, allowed almost all free males the right to vote, and sought to ensure good relations with the Indians. His constitution required settlers to purchase any land taken from Indian inhabitants and extended the right of trial by jury to Indians (with the stipulation that juries in the trial of an Indian would be half Indian, half English).

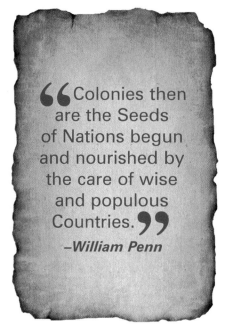

> 66 Colonies then are the Seeds of Nations begun and nourished by the care of wise and populous Countries. 99
> –William Penn

Although many considered such policies radical, Penn enjoyed good relations with both Charles II and the Duke of York. In 1681, Charles granted him Pennsylvania ("Penn's wood")—which he had named after Penn's father. The sale of "Penn's wood" accomplished two things for the king: it relieved him of his gambling debt to Penn's father, and it relieved him of the Quakers. In 1682, the Duke of York sold Penn three additional counties from his own vast New World landholdings. In time, these counties would become Delaware.

Creating Pennsylvania. Recruiting settlers was the key to creating Penn's idyllic vision. Penn's promotion of the colony rested on two factors: religious freedom and a liberal land policy that allowed easy access to land. Penn dispatched agents throughout Europe to advertise the colony, and the response was overwhelming. In 1682, the population was about one thousand; two years later, it had grown to four thousand; by the end of the 1680s it had risen to twelve thousand. Although not yet as large as the Massachusetts Bay colony, Pennsylvania's population continued to grow. Penn was also successful in promoting peaceful relations with the Indians; Indian refugees migrated to Pennsylvania from other lands where they had faced violence from colonists.

Read Penn's "Some Account of the Province of Pennsilvania."

Penn did permit slavery. He owned slaves personally and allowed other colonists to do the same. Like most northern slaves, slaves in Pennsylvania were Africans used primarily as domestic workers. Although some Quakers spoke out publicly against slavery as early as 1688, slavery lasted in Pennsylvania until the 1780s.

New Jersey

The Duke of York granted the southern portion of his colony to two friends, one of whom sold his portion to a group of Quakers. This led to the creation of East Jersey, which bordered New York, and West Jersey, which bordered Pennsylvania. Although they retained certain differences, by 1702 both areas had developed substantially, earning a single royal charter. To attract settlers, the proprietors of New Jersey promised both generous land grants and a limited freedom of religion. For these reasons, Puritan New Englanders and Dutch New Yorkers migrated there, prompting significant growth by 1726. The two colonies were united and renamed New Jersey.

Georgia

Georgia was founded after the Restoration as a proprietary colony. The chief motives for its settlement were to create a buffer between Spanish Florida and the Carolinas, and a haven for English debtors and persecuted English Protestants, a place where they could live comfortably. James Oglethorpe, the utopian lead proprietor, led the first settlers to Savannah in 1733. It was his vision, as an opponent

> **❝** I received information that a plot for a general uprising of the Christian Indians was being formed and was spreading rapidly. This was wholly contrary to the existing peace and tranquillity in this miserable kingdom, not only among the Spaniards and natives, but even on the part of the heathen enemy, for it had been a long time since they had done us any considerable damage. **❞**
>
> *—Don Antonio de Otermin, governor of New Mexico during the Pueblo Revolt*

of Britain's policy of imprisoning those who could not pay their debts, that fashioned Georgia as a colony where the "worthy poor" could start anew.

The colony grew slowly because the charter stipulated that no one could own enough land to develop a large-scale plantation. Furthermore, slavery was initially prohibited because of Oglethorpe's vision for the colony and because the Spanish in Florida had promised freedom to any slave who would serve in their military, which would have meant a collection of slaves eager and able to desert Georgia for Florida. It was only in the 1750s that the Crown, to whom the proprietors had returned the charter, succumbed to local demands from English planters and allowed slavery.

 Read the story of the semi-utopian James Oglethorpe and Savannah.

Where Were the Spanish?

As the English planted deeper roots in colonial North America, the Spanish were pulling their roots out. Their main limitation was an unwillingness to develop colonial settlements, preferring instead to bring home quick profits after a brief period of having conquered and controlled resource-rich lands. They established some settlements, like those founded by Catholic friars eager to convert Indians, although these permanent settlements frequently conflicted with local Indian tribes and persuaded Spain that permanent settlement was not worth the investment.

New Mexico

In New Mexico, for example, the Pueblo people rejected the forced piety of the Spanish Catholic friars, and in a dramatic 1680 rebellion, a shaman named Popé led the **Pueblo Revolt**—an uprising of several villages spanning several hundred miles across the New Mexican landscape. The villagers burned Spanish farms, destroyed churches, and killed half the friars. Reeling from the revolt, the Spanish left the Southwest for more than a decade. They returned in the 1690s with a more tolerant outlook, and the Pueblo people welcomed them only because they felt they needed European weaponry to fight their tribal enemies.

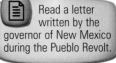 Read a letter written by the governor of New Mexico during the Pueblo Revolt.

Florida

The Spanish faced similar resentments in Florida. But here the resentments were compounded by the proximity of colonial competitors, the English and the French. When England and France went to war in the War of Spanish Succession in 1701, British Carolinians attacked Spanish Florida (the British feared that Spain and France were becoming too closely allied). The result was the devastation of all Spanish strongholds in Florida, except St. Augustine. And, because English colonists outnumbered Spanish settlers, the Spanish were slow to resettle Florida. By 1700, the Spanish presence in the future United States was limited to a few Catholic missions and a few increasingly smaller settlements.

 Read more about the origins of Florida.

Conclusion

Between 1660 and 1700, Britain had crafted the beginnings of a large colonial empire in North America. It had seeded permanent colonies and established itself as the European nation claiming the biggest stake to the land, ahead of the Dutch, French, and Spanish, whose primary colonial interests lay elsewhere. These English colonies were not wholly stable yet, nor were they particularly unified. Furthermore, each colony was made up of a mix of people, including Europeans from different countries, Indians from many tribes, and, increasingly, slaves.

LO² Indians

As Britain's colonial holdings expanded into the American interior, they encroached on lands that were already inhabited. The initial encounters between Europeans and the tribes of Native America had mixed outcomes. In their search for gold and other riches in the 1500s, the Spanish annihilated many tribes with violence and disease. The French, without a large settled presence in the New World, had mostly positive trade arrangements with the tribes near Quebec. The English had at first cautiously engaged the Indian tribes for trade and protection, but as their settlements expanded, suspicion and enmity between the two groups increased. In Jamestown, for instance, relations between the Powhatan confederacy and the first settlers were generally nonviolent until the expansion of Jamestown provoked Powhatan's successor, Opechancanough, to attack. In New England, the Pequot War symbolized the violent direction that relations were taking.

These first encounters had elements of both trust and suspicion, but the situation worsened over time. By the beginning of the 1700s, it had become clear that the two peoples would not share the New World. Most English colonists believed that any Indian who stood in their path to settlement could be exterminated. Indians responded in kind to this threat. Competition for land was the key motive. Violence, disease, and the market economy were the principal means of effecting change.

What Went Wrong?

There were five general reasons why the situation deteriorated so drastically after 1660:

The Middle Ground

Although the decimation of Native America is the most significant story of Euro-Indian relations, positive interactions occurred during the colonial era as well, usually over trade. In this "middle ground," where trading took place, the two groups operated as equals. Indians and Europeans shared rituals, such as tea and rum drinking, gift giving, and pipe smoking. This middle ground was noticeable in situations when colonists encountered large groups of Indians, meaning the groups meeting were close to equal in number, and it allowed contact that benefited both Indians and colonists.

Read more about the "middle ground" at Chicago.

Colonial Land Lust, Colonial Democracy

But the central story of Indian relations with the colonists is one of violence. In the first half of the 1600s, most outbreaks of violence between English colonists and Indians were short-lived. The deadlier conflicts occurred between Indian tribes seeking to win the European trade. The bloodiest of these intertribal battles were the **Beaver Wars** (1640–1680s), in which the Iroquois, seeking beaver pelts to trade with the French, forced the Hurons and their supporters out of the Northeast altogether, leaving the Iroquois Confederacy as the single most significant collection of tribes between northern Canada, southern Virginia, and the Mississippi River. They decimated their competition and forced the survivors to flee across the Mississippi River.

By the 1670s, enough English settlers had moved to the colonies that colonists and Indians could engage in prolonged wars. These wars established a pattern of violence that would last for the dura-

{ The reasons why . . . }

- Land lust of the English colonists grew as the initial colonies succeeded, prompting perpetual incursions on Indian lands.

- Religious differences between the two groups prevented each group from having a common understanding of the other.

- Cultural differences about land use, gender roles, and language created further misunderstandings and resentments.

- Both sides were willing to use violence to resolve conflict.

- Perhaps most important, the European powers were viciously protective of their lucrative New World holdings. Throughout the 1700s the Europeans fought several wars to defend them, and the battleground of this "great war for empire" (as historians have called these wars) was often the New World, forcing colonists and Indians to take sides. In the short term, Indians could profit from the situation by selling their support to one European power or the other. But as England pursued increasing world dominion, the tribes of Native America could no longer play one side off the other, and England (and eventually the United States) could subject the Indians to their will, at times violently.

>> In an area historians have called "the middle ground," Indians and Europeans shared rituals, such as tea and rum drinking, gift giving, and pipe smoking.

tion of contact between the two groups. Although highlighted by several large-scale battles, conflict between Indians and North American colonists was continual, making every outing a potentially perilous adventure. Two events of the 1670s, however, greatly influenced colonist–Indian relations: Metacom's War and Bacon's Rebellion.

Metacom's War (King Philip's War), 1675–1676

The first large-scale conflict was **Metacom's War** (sometimes called "**King Philip's War**"), which broke out in Plymouth, Massachusetts in 1675. "King Philip" was the name the English gave to Metacom, the son of the Wampanoag chief, Massasoit. Massasoit had befriended the Plymouth settlers in the 1620s (his generosity thus giving Americans the model for today's Thanksgiving), but by the 1670s, the English settlement in Massachusetts had grown to 50,000. The New Englanders had expanded onto Indian territories

and forcibly subjected the Wampanoags and other tribes to English law. The settler's cattle trampled native cornfields, demonstrating the differences in concepts of land use between the two peoples and the arrogance of some New Englanders, who felt God had granted them the land to cultivate. The younger generation of Indians had had enough.

The result was war. Many tribes joined Metacom in battling the settlers, although several tribes that had converted to Christianity sided with the English. Over a period of fourteen months in 1675 and 1676, Metacom and his followers attacked fifty-two of the ninety Puritan towns, destroying thirteen of them completely. They attacked towns in four colonies: Plymouth, Massachusetts Bay, Rhode Island, and Connecticut. Before the tide of battle had turned, Metacom's forces pushed the area of English colonization almost back to the coast. The story of Mary Rowlandson, a young New England settler, dates from King Philip's War. Metacom's forces kidnapped her and held her hostage for three months before ransoming her back to her family; she wrote a wildly popular account of her tribulations, giving many colonists a first-hand look at Indian life.

Read Mary Rowlandson's account of her capture.

The tide of war turned against the Indians in 1676. The English retaliated against them for Metacom's assaults, and the colonists' most significant victory

Metacom's War
First large-scale conflict between colonists and Native Americans, waged in Plymouth, Massachusetts Bay, Rhode Island, and Connecticut (1675–1676)

King Philip's War
British colonists' name for Metacom's War, because they referred to Wampanoag leader Metacom as King Philip

INDIAN WARFARE OF THE COLONIAL EPOCH.

Map 3.2
New England During Metacom's War, 1675–1676

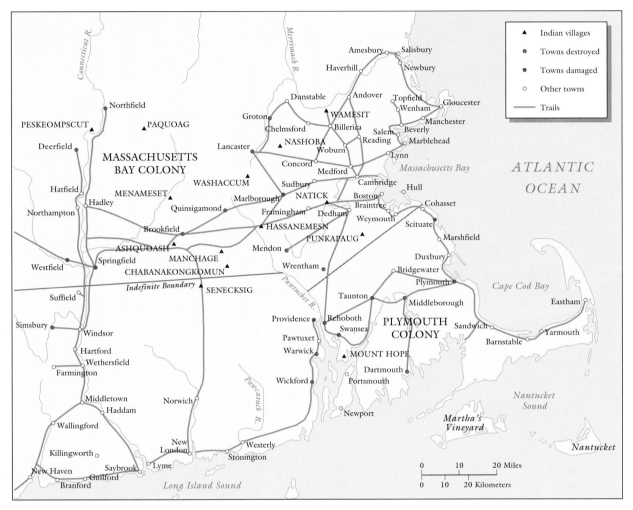

View an interactive version of this map.

came after a New England boy escaped captivity, returned home, and then led the colonists to the exact location of the tribes. The fighting ended in 1676 when Metacom fell in battle at the hands of an Indian who was acting as a scout for the colonists. The colonists placed Metacom's head on a stake and let it stand in Plymouth town square for 25 years.

New England's Indians paid a heavy price for their resistance. Algonquian communities were decimated from Narragansett Bay to the Connecticut River Valley. Many died from disease and starvation, in addition to the thousands who were killed in battle. Both sides suffered: Metacom's War killed one in ten of New England's colonists. Metacom's War showed an early, if uneven, willingness of Indian tribes to unite to fight colonists.

Bacon's Rebellion, 1676–1677

The impact of Metacom's War was felt beyond New England. Metacom's message of pan-Indian resistance to English settlement spread (aided by the fact that all Indians faced the same frustrations as Metacom had), and in 1676 warriors from the Potomack and Susquahannock tribes of the Chesapeake began to raid English outposts in

Virginia. The English governor of the colony, Sir William Berkeley, showed a reluctance to retaliate, favoring instead a policy of keeping a strict boundary between Indian and colonial land (and of keeping his bountiful trade relations with several tribes going). His disinclination to fight, and his unwillingness to compromise (or even listen to) the demands of the laboring people, or "middling sorts" who aspired to own land, sparked a revolt among the colonists, called **Bacon's Rebellion**.

Nathaniel Bacon was a young, well educated, and charismatic member of the Virginia colony council. He was also related to Berkeley through marriage. Bacon advocated immediate retaliation against the Potomack and Susquahannock tribes. After Berkeley denied his bid for a commission to attack the Indians (Berkeley recognized that arming hundreds of young colonial men—mostly former indentured servants—would pose a threat to the colony), Bacon raised his own militia to fight the Native Americans.

Bacon's Laws

Bacon's militia quickly vanquished the Indians in the area. Fearful of where Bacon might go next, the governor dispatched three hundred militiamen to stop him. Bacon was captured and released, and then continued to seek a commission to attack the tribes. Berkeley resisted. A series of standoffs ensued, with Bacon variously being imprisoned or on the run. In the process, Berkeley became acutely aware of Bacon's wild popularity among the settlers and, to quell the potential uprising, passed a series of laws that democratized the politics of Virginia. Commonly called **Bacon's Laws**, the new rules granted the franchise to all freemen, inaugurated elections of the members of the legislature (rather than offering legislators lifetime appointments), and granted greater representation in taxation. In sum, Bacon's Laws reduced the influence of the ruling elite in Virginia, setting a precedent for free white man's democracy. This was a meaningful step in the expansion of colonial liberty.

It was also an attempt to win back some of the popularity Bacon had attracted. After the passage of Bacon's Laws, Berkeley persisted in his attempts to quell any rebellion, but it seemed that would be impossible without granting the militia a commission to kill local Indians and cultivate their lands—something he would not allow. The continued standoff prompted Bacon and his army to attack Jamestown in the summer of 1676, forcing Berkeley to flee. Bacon invited his troops to plunder the plantations around Jamestown, especially those of Berkeley's supporters, and throughout the summer, Bacon's ragtag army fought with Indians and Englishmen alike.

During the late summer of 1676, Berkeley organized a counterattack against Bacon's anti-Indian, anti-upper-class forces. Berkeley's men, with superior arms, chased Bacon around eastern Virginia, capturing several of his supporters but not the rebel himself. When 1,100 English troops arrived to help Berkeley, Bacon went on the run, contracted an infectious fever, and died. Other rebels tried to maintain control of the colony, but Bacon's death brought the rebellion to a rapid close. Berkeley remained in power. He later tried to repeal several of Bacon's Laws, but these efforts were overruled by more moderate members of the Burgesses.

Results

Bacon's Rebellion succeeded in pushing the Potomack and Susquahannock tribes farther west, opening up more land for Euro-American settlement. But Bacon's Rebellion is significant to American history beyond that.

- Bacon's Rebellion reflected the land lust of the growing colonial population.
- It demonstrated that the settlers were willing to use violent means in order to gain that land, usually against Indians, but sometimes against the English gentry.
- It made wealthy colonists less willing to import indentured servants, who, as the rebellion proved, would do nearly anything to get land once they were freed from their condition of servitude. This was one factor that led to a rise in the importation of African slaves. It also initiated an upper-class proclamation of the similarity of all men perceived to be white; by importing more slaves and creating a racially divided population, the upper classes of Virginia sought to limit class conflict by prioritizing racial differences. This was a turning point in the history of North American race relations, which buttressed a trend toward the expansion of the American slave system and the decline of indentured servitude.

Read Governor Berkeley on Bacon's Rebellion.

> **Bacon's Rebellion**
> Revolt among colonists, led by Nathaniel Bacon, triggered by Virginia governor Sir William Berkeley's unwillingness to listen to the demands of the laboring people who wanted to attack several nearby Indian tribes (1676–1677)
>
> **Bacon's Laws**
> Series of laws that democratized the politics of Virginia, granted the franchise to all freemen, inaugurated elections of the members of the legislature, and granted greater representation in taxation

LO³ The Expansion of American Slavery

Motivations

Europe's slave trade with Africa began in the 1400s and increased in the 1500s and 1600s as a means of relieving a labor shortage in the areas surrounding the Mediterranean. Labor needs arose in the New World during the late 1500s and 1600s after Europeans realized that sugar could be grown easily in the West Indies and South America. (Europeans had discovered sugar in their travels during the Crusades, and it became so popular and expensive in Europe that it was among the first items Columbus transported from the New World, in his second voyage of 1493.) Cultivating sugar is labor intensive, and once Europeans had exhausted and exterminated native populations in the West Indies and South America, their search for labor led them to African slaves. This was made easier by the fact that the established trade routes between Europe and Africa had made Africans eager for European goods, especially guns. Thus, in a mutually beneficial trade system, beginning in the early 1600s West African kingdoms competed with one another to supply slaves to the Europeans in return for European goods.

But what began so easily was not so easily stopped. As the Atlantic slave trade grew, West African kingdoms grew leery of supplying Europeans with more slaves because they were fearful of the overwhelming demand. Some Europeans resorted to kidnapping slaves from West African villages.

Why the Transition from Indentured Servitude to Slavery?

In the early 1600s, the North American colonies relied mainly on European (and some African) indentured servants for labor. At least 70 percent of those in the Chesapeake came as indentured servants from England. By the 1680s, however, African slaves had begun to replace indentured servants as the colonists' preferred labor source, and by the early 1700s, there were few indentured servants in the colonial labor pool.

Despite the variety of benefits of indentured servitude (the ability of landowner and laborer to communicate easily, similarities in culture and religion between the two), there were several problems with it in North America. Many servants ran away once they landed in the New World because, as Europeans, once they escaped, they blended in easily there. Most of those who did remain confronted the wet climate of the Chesapeake, which was so unhealthy that many servants died shortly after arriving in America. Those who survived were habitually sick and unable to work. Indentured servants also earned their freedom once their term of indenture (usually seven years) expired. At that point, some of them acquired land and began competing with their former masters, a situation that most masters did not welcome, as proved by Bacon's Rebellion. Finally, as England's economy improved, fewer people signed up to become indentured servants in the first place. By the 1680s, the practice of indentured servitude diminished rapidly. Slavery replaced it. In need of labor, North American colonists tapped into the slave trade system that had developed during the 1600s.

Africans Transition from Servants to Slaves

In 1619, when the first Africans arrived in Virginia, they were treated like indentured servants, which meant not generously, but not inhumanely either. They lived alongside European colonists in their landowner's house, and some earned their freedom after their term of service. But as the number of Africans in the Chesapeake increased during the 1680s, European and Euro-American colonists crafted a wide-ranging slave society, developing laws that would make slavery an enduring, race-dependent institution.

By the late 1630s, colonists had already begun to differentiate between indentured servants and slaves, but the first major law specifically regarding slavery emerged in Virginia in 1662. It stipulated that the condition of the mother determined the condition of the child; if a mother was a slave from Africa—or had African heritage—her child was to be a slave as well. This allowed male slaveholders to exploit African American females and, at the same time, produce new slaves. In 1664, Maryland enacted an "anti-amalgamation" law, which outlawed interracial sex and marriage, rendering any relationship between a male colonist and a female slave illegal, and any relationship between an African American male slave and a female colonist intolerable. Virginia followed suit, declaring in 1691 that any colonist who married a "Negro, mulatto, or Indian" would be banished from the colony. In 1682, Virginia passed a law that used specific racial differences to differentiate between servants and slaves, thus ensuring African Americans and Euro-

Americans were treated differently by the law. Thus, even before the rapid expansion of slavery in the 1680s and 1690s, colonial laws differentiated people by strict racial classifications. These differences grew markedly after slaves were brought to the American colonies in greater numbers throughout the 1700s.

Slave Codes

Slowly race became the central factor determining who was perceived as a freeman worthy of "natural rights" and who was not. In 1705, Virginia codified the racial orientation of the system with a series of **slave codes**, meant to govern the new system of labor. The slave codes meant that, in most areas, especially in the Southern Colonies and the Chesapeake, it became impossible for an African American to live as a free person. The codes declared that all "Negro, mulatto, and Indian" servants brought into the region were slaves, or "real estate." This guaranteed slaveholders *permanent* ownership of the black bondspeople they purchased. It also allowed masters to punish their property and, because no one would deliberately destroy their own property, Virginia lawmakers said there was no need to enact laws prohibiting slaveholders from killing their slaves. The codes stated that slaves needed written permission to leave their plantation, would receive severe physical punishments for any wrongdoing, and no longer had any legal standing. Virginia's slave codes served as a model for other states to emulate, which they readily did. English colonists were constructing a legalistic slave society.

LO⁴ Wars for Empire

Propelled by the desires of landless young men and attracted by the potential profits of a slave-based

{ Some slave codes ... }

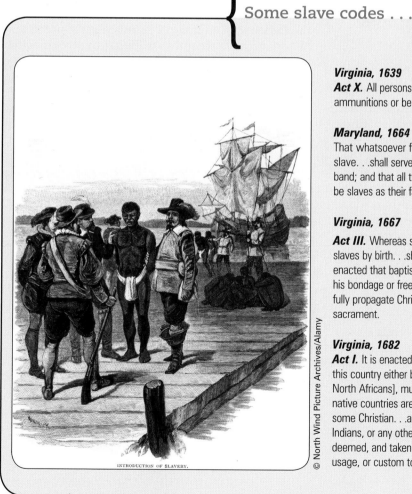

INTRODUCTION OF SLAVERY.

© North Wind Picture Archives/Alamy

Virginia, 1639
Act X. All persons except Negroes are to be provided with arms and ammunitions or be fined at the pleasure of the governor and council.

Maryland, 1664
That whatsoever free-born [English] woman shall intermarry with any slave. . .shall serve the master of such slave during the life of her husband; and that all the issue of such free-born women, so married shall be slaves as their fathers were.

Virginia, 1667
Act III. Whereas some doubts have arisen whether children that are slaves by birth. . .should by virtue of their baptism be made free, it is enacted that baptism does not alter the condition to the person as to his bondage or freedom; masters freed from this doubt may more carefully propagate Christianity by permitting slaves to be admitted to that sacrament.

Virginia, 1682
Act I. It is enacted that all servants. . .which [sic] shall be imported into this country either by sea or by land, whether Negroes, Moors [Muslim North Africans], mulattoes, or Indians who and whose parentage and native countries are not Christian at the time of their first purchase by some Christian. . .and all Indians, which shall be sold by our neighboring Indians, or any other trafficing with us for slaves, are hereby adjudged, deemed, and taken to be slaves to all intents and purposes any law, usage, or custom to the contrary notwithstanding.

economy, the English colonists pushed west into North America. There, they ran into an obstacle other than Indians: the French. Beginning in the late 1600s, the French recognized the rich potential of North America and fortified their posts from the Great Lakes to New Orleans, traveling down the Mississippi River and usually developing friendly relations with Indian tribes along the way. Their only significant settlements, however, were at Quebec and New Orleans. Nevertheless, the increased French presence brought them into conflict with the English. When France and England had disputes in Europe, their battles had New World ramifications. Beginning in the late 1600s, European wars had North American fronts as well as European ones.

King William's War and Queen Anne's War, 1689–1713

The first of these carryover battles lasted from 1689 to 1697, and its most significant theaters were in Europe and the Caribbean. But it also reached the North American mainland, where it was called **King William's War**. King William's War began when New York's governor, Thomas Dongan, goaded the Iroquois into attacking tribes that were friendly with France. The French fought back by attacking the Iroquois and, eventually, English colonists in northern New England and New York. England in turn attacked various French outposts, with minimal success. The New World front had stalemated without significant gains for either side. Nevertheless, King William's War was influential for three reasons: (1) it prompted the French to fortify their New World position, creating a stronghold of settlers for the first time; (2) it demonstrated the ways Europeans manipulated Indians (and vice versa) in efforts to conquer the land; and (3) in its wake, the Iroquois

established better relations with the French and agreed to remain neutral in future conflicts.

The second English-French war started four years later, when the French king angled to put his grandson on the newly vacant Spanish throne. The other European powers rejected this power play and attacked France. This was the War of the Spanish Succession, called **Queen Anne's War** in the New World. Twelve years of battle between the Spanish in Florida, the French in the North American interior, the English along the coast, and the various Indian tribes friendly to one group or another, finally ended with an English victory.

Queen Anne's War was significant for two reasons: (1) success gave the English a base on the Hudson Bay, further promoting their expansion westward, into the interior of America; and (2) it ushered in a period of relative peace in Europe, which allowed France and England to fortify their positions in the New World, so that when later battles came, both sides were better entrenched. Over time, the increasing economic and social strength of English colonies threatened the French, who feared that the alliances they had built with the Indians would falter. It should also be noted that historians have recently attributed the Salem witch trials to fears triggered by the Indian Wars. Because these witch trials were prosecuted during Queen Anne's War, they suggest how the European Wars for Empire were felt in even the smallest of New World hamlets. (The witch trials will be discussed in greater detail in Chapter 4.)

What else was happening . . .

17th century	The average woman in America gives birth to thirteen children.
1655	The Dutch of New Amsterdam use lotteries to raise money for the poor.
1666	The Great Fire destroys three-fourths of London, killing only sixteen and helping halt spread of the bubonic plague.
1670	Paris café starts serving ice cream.
1686	Christian Gabriel Fahrenheit invents the thermometer.

And in the end . . .

By 1700, then, the North American colonies had developed into established, but not yet prospering, outliers in Britain's colonial web. They were stably situated along the Atlantic seaboard, and it seemed inevitable that they would continue to settle farther into the interior of the continent. It was clear that Europeans (and especially the English) would not blend into the lands of Native America or mix with its inhabitants, but would seek dominion over the areas they controlled—areas that they expanded widely from 1660 to 1763. Also by 1700, the colonists had established slavery as the primary system of labor in the New World. From these roots, a system of racialized slavery would expand on American soil. These trends would only continue from 1700 to 1763, as the colonies developed economically and socially, coming to be understood as four distinct regions. As these regions became stronger and more established, when later "Wars for Empire" broke out the North American colonists could ponder independence. But in 1700 those thoughts were still years away.

4

Expansion *and* Control,

1700–1763

Learning Outcomes

After reading this chapter, you should be able to do the following:

LO¹ Describe the development of the English colonies during the 1700s, including a discussion of each group of colonies: New England, the Middle Colonies, the Chesapeake, and the Southern Colonies.

LO² Discuss the impact of the Enlightenment and the Great Awakening on colonial society in America.

LO³ Chronicle the development of slavery in the American colonies, and analyze the reasons for changes in attitudes and in the legal system that helped the distinctively American slave system to flourish.

LO⁴ By 1763, American colonists had become used to making their own decisions and taking care of their own needs. Describe the events in England that contributed to this situation, and explain their effects on the colonists.

> **66** *One historian has called this developing society 'an empire of goods' because of the large number of goods newly available for purchase.* **99**

As colonial society grew, by 1700 four distinct regions had developed: New England (Massachusetts, Rhode Island, New Hampshire, Connecticut), the Middle Colonies (New York, New Jersey, Pennsylvania, Delaware), the Chesapeake (Virginia and Maryland), and the Southern Colonies (North Carolina, South Carolina, Georgia) (see Map 4.1). Each region had a unique economy based on its geographical location and its founding ideology, and each region's society developed in response to those two factors.

This chapter explores the development of these four unique regions, the expansion of an intellectual and cultural life distinct from that of Britain, and the ways in which African slavery became ingrained in the life of colonial North America. This chapter concludes with Britain's attempts to regain control of its increasingly feisty and independent-minded colony, an effort that would eventually foster a revolution.

What do you think?

The strangeness of the Salem witchcraft episode reveals the anxiety of the time, sparked mostly by wars with Indians, but also by the rapid social and economic changes the colonists were experiencing.

Strongly Disagree   Strongly Agree
1   2   3   4   5   6   7

LO¹ Expansion of Colonial Economy and Society, 1700–1763

New England

Economy

Like most other colonists, most New Englanders were farmers. New England's hilly land and a short growing season encouraged **diversified farming**, a system in which a single home could farm many different crops that would sustain the household throughout the year. Farmers lived in towns and walked each day to their fields to tend their crops. Livestock was allowed to graze on community-owned land, such as the town common. New Englanders were consistently alert to new economic opportunities. They grew surplus agricultural goods to trade for tools and other finished goods such as furniture. At first their surplus was limited to grains and cereals, but by the early 1700s New Englanders were trading meat, dairy, and orchard products as well. In the mid-1600s and throughout the early 1700s, New Englanders also maintained an active trade in furs, fish, and timber.

In this highly agrarian society, New Englanders often produced their own furniture and agricultural implements, and spun their family's flax and wool to make clothing. Over

diversified farming
System in which a single home could farm various crops to sustain the household throughout the year

© Paul S. Bartholomew/Alamy

Map 4.1
Settlement by 1760

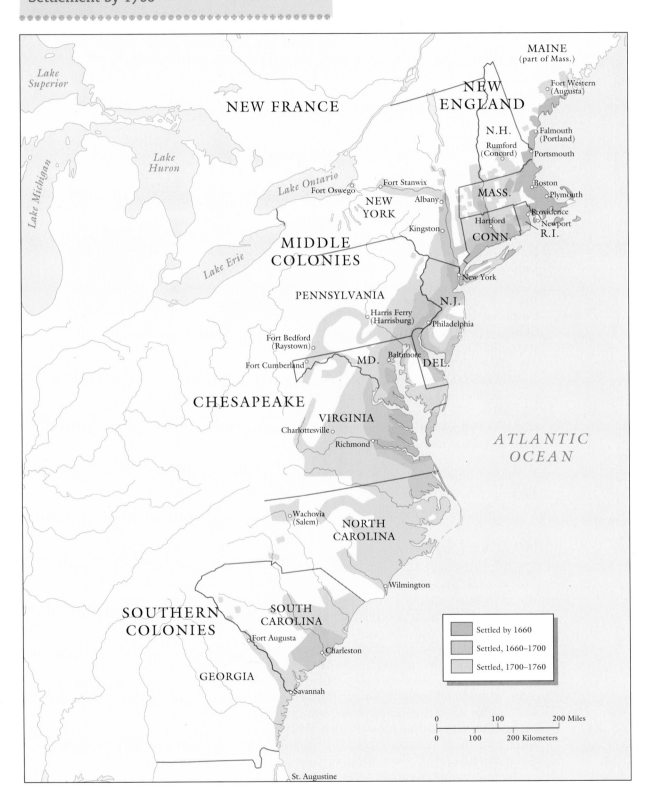

MAINE
(part of Mass.)

NEW FRANCE

NEW ENGLAND

N.H.

Fort Western
(Augusta)

Falmouth
(Portland)

Rumford
(Concord)

Portsmouth

Lake Superior

Lake Huron

Lake Michigan

Lake Ontario

Fort Oswego

Fort Stanwix

Albany

MASS.

Boston

Plymouth

NEW YORK

Hartford

Providence

Lake Erie

Kingston

CONN.

Newport

R.I.

MIDDLE COLONIES

New York

PENNSYLVANIA

N.J.

Harris Ferry
(Harrisburg)

Philadelphia

Fort Bedford
(Raystown)

Fort Cumberland

MD.

Baltimore

DEL.

CHESAPEAKE

VIRGINIA

Charlottesville

Richmond

ATLANTIC OCEAN

Wachovia
(Salem)

NORTH CAROLINA

Wilmington

SOUTHERN COLONIES

SOUTH CAROLINA

Fort Augusta

Charleston

GEORGIA

Savannah

	Settled by 1660
	Settled, 1660–1700
	Settled, 1700–1760

0   100   200 Miles

0   100   200 Kilometers

St. Augustine

>> **By the mid-1700s, one-third of all ships used by England were built in New England.**

time, some small industries developed around New England's two principal products: fish and lumber. New Englanders used local timber to establish a shipbuilding industry, and by the mid-1700s, one-third of all ships used by England were built in New England, a truly remarkable statistic.

Developing industries require money, salesmen, and trade routes, and the merchants who met these needs became prominent players in the development of New England from 1700 to 1763. The merchants brought in capital and managerial expertise, and when land opened up in the west, the commercial leaders of New England were some of the first speculators, originating the practice of western land speculation around 1670.

These commercial adventurers also participated in a pattern of trade that came to be called the **Triangular Trade**, although it was much more complicated than a simple triangle. The New England colonies traded fish and grains to England and to southern Europe, in return for wine, spices, and gold. They also sold their goods to the West Indies in return for sugar and molasses. The New Englanders then distilled the molasses to make rum and traded it, along with other manufactured goods, to Africa in return for slaves and gold. The gold from this trade allowed New Englanders to purchase manufactured goods, tools, and linens from England. New Englanders in turn sold their manufactured ships to England. By 1763, this was a thriving arena of commerce that gave the colonies a good deal of economic independence,

which later supported their insistent demands for increased political independence.

Society

In 1660, New England had a population of more than 30,000 people of European descent. These people lived a mostly provincial life, in small, family-centered towns. By 1700, the population had tripled to 90,000. By 1760, it had reached 450,000. Still, most of these people lived in small towns.

The dramatic increase in population reflected the stability and importance of families, and an environment hospitable to life and commerce. Some immigrants came, and slaves were forced to come, but most of the growth was due to a high birthrate in the colonies. This burgeoning population was the impetus for rapid westward expansion. A family with six sons could not divide its land six ways and bequeath a plot of land large enough for each son to ensure his prosperity or success. Some of the children had to strike out on their own.

One English import that crossed the Atlantic successfully was a social system demarcated by class. Theoretically at the top of the system was a small group of aristocrats—governors, judges, and wealthy businessmen with English backgrounds—who endeavored to live a properly refined life above the rest of the population. A bigger group in New England society was what the colonists called the "natural aristocracy"—merchants and wealthy landholders

halfway covenants
Processes by which baptized individuals who had never had a personal conversion to Christ were counted as partial members of a Protestant church and were allowed to have their children baptized

jeremiad
A long speech or literary work emphasizing society's fall from purity and grace to its current depraved state

who made their fortunes in the New World and were not deemed special because of their titles. These men dominated economic affairs and owned an increasingly larger and larger percentage of the area's wealth. A group of commercial middlemen, farmers, and artisans constituted the class in the middle and made up the majority of the population. Slaves, employed by the wealthiest members of the natural aristocracy, dwelled at the bottom of the social structure.

Life

With the growth that occurred between 1660 and 1763, the now-idealized image of an agricultural and religiously orthodox New England receded into the past. In its place emerged an increasingly commercialized society characterized by economic mobility and social differentiation. New England remained overwhelmingly agricultural, but the small towns became increasingly connected to one another.

This was a significant transition from a century earlier. In the 1660s, colonial New England was a provincial land freckled with unconnected towns. There were few roads in the 1660s, and they connected only the largest towns. By the 1700s, this had begun to change. Commerce had grown exponentially. Colonists tracked the markets in England and knew which ships were carrying which goods. One historian has called this developing society "an empire of goods" because of the large number of goods newly available for purchase.

As the population multiplied, colonists pushed westward and developed one town after another, creating a large half-circle of small towns around any large Atlantic port city. The cities' hinterlands filled with people, as family plots that were too small for the number of sons vying for independence meant a constant migration westward in search of land. These hinterland towns lay on the margins of the bustling economic and social world of New England's cities.

This robust growth meant that the religious and social orthodoxy enforced by the Puritans could not last. Prosperity weakened the younger generations' commitment to the strict religious practices of their forefathers. Ministers slowly lost stature, no longer defining New England life as they had when the Puritans first arrived. Although the number of church congregants remained stable, by the mid-1660s, some church leaders attempted to stimulate membership growth. They instituted "**halfway covenants**," whereby baptized individuals who had never had a personal conversion to Christ were counted as partial members of the church and were allowed to have their children baptized as well. These "halfway" members were usually brought to the front of a church, where members could watch to see if they were about to experience a conversion. By 1700, Puritan ministers had also begun to rely on the **jeremiad**—a long speech emphasizing society's fall from purity and grace to its current, depraved state—as a way to stir up congregations.

Salem Witchcraft Trials

The demise of the Puritans' religious utopia is illustrated by a case concerning a group of preteen and teenaged girls in Salem, Massachusetts. In 1692, two girls were playing with an older female slave who taught the girls African voodoo tales. The girls later became seized with fits, and soon other girls in Salem were behaving strangely as well. Searching for an explanation, the town's leaders accused the female slave and two other women of practicing witchcraft. Soon, the village elders accused several others of being witches, too. Once started, accusations flew wildly. Before long it became apparent that divisions between social classes, gender, commercial professions, and religiosity determined who was accused and who was not, as the poor were accused more readily than the wealthy, as were those who had fallen away from

> 66 Abigail was much disquieted by the apparition of Martha Kory, by which apparition she was sometimes haled to & fro. & somtimes pinched, & somtimes tempted to put her hand to the Devils book, & that she hath several times seen her at the Devils sacrament. 99
> —*Testimony of Abigail Williams at the Salem witchcraft trials*

©Andrew Fox/Alamy

Experience the Salem witchcraft hysteria. Would you have survived?

Read a collection of primary source documents from the trial.

View a Google Earth™ exploration of Salem.

the church. Recent research demonstrates that unmarried women of property were prominent targets as well. Before the accusations slowed, twenty people had been executed. The strangeness of the Salem witchcraft episode reveals the anxiety of the time, sparked mostly by wars with Indians, but also by the rapid social and economic changes the colonists were experiencing.

Conclusion

New England life moved more and more toward commerce and trading. The wealthiest became wealthier during the 1700s, and the rich attempted to re-create the privileged life of urban England. They built large homes and filled them with English furnishings. They replicated elitist social structures, picturing themselves as the new aristocracy. And they occupied public office. To flaunt their wealth, some possessed slaves. By 1760 New England no longer looked like the Puritan ideal. Instead, it looked

a lot like England, though with greater economic and social mobility, and a higher rate of literacy.

Families of middling wealth owned farms or small businesses that produced handmade goods. A laboring class consisted mostly of young men waiting to inherit land from their fathers or preparing to enter a craft. In time, most of this laboring class would own property and enjoy some level of wealth. The number of poor grew as well, although they

© Robert Harding Picture Library Ltd/Alamy

>> By 1760 New England no longer looked like the Puritan ideal. Instead it looked a lot like England, though with greater economic and social mobility, and a higher rate of literacy.

would remain few in number compared to those living in European cities.

Despite the decline of the church's importance, the slow growth of the cities, and the rise of New England, commerce helped New Englanders maintain their commitment to family life. If all else was changing, these values remained constant. The sexual division of labor continued (as imported from England): women remained in charge of "indoor affairs" (raising children, preparing food, cleaning house, doing laundry) and men took charge of "outdoor affairs" (cultivating fields, chopping wood, and conducting the daily business transactions, such as buying horses and selling crops). In sum, New England consisted mostly of stable, agriculturally based families, an expanding economy that led to the growth of some cities, and a rapid westward migration to accommodate the growth of the population.

The Middle Colonies (New York, New Jersey, Pennsylvania, Delaware)

Economy

Life was slightly different in the Middle Colonies. With a warmer climate, farms in the Middle Colonies were larger, and farmers lived on their farms rather than in the village. Many of the farms achieved relative self-sustenance, and some were so bountiful that they exported goods. Fruit, livestock, and wheat were the principal exported crops of the region, wheat being the biggest export. Indeed, by the early 1700s, New York and Pennsylvania were sometimes known to English traders as the "bread colonies." Agricultural production grew 2 to 3 percent every year from 1700 to 1770, and the best farmers in the Middle Colonies could afford to bring nearly 40 percent of their produce to market, meaning that this area rapidly grew wealthier than New England, as money from England poured in.

As in New England, families in the Middle Colonies produced their own furniture and agricultural implements and spun their family's flax and wool to make clothing. Clay from the riverbeds allowed them to build houses of brick, usually two stories high. Unlike the many small towns of New England, commerce focused on the two hubs of the Middle Colonies: New York and Philadelphia. The chief industries of the Middle Colonies developed around corn and wheat. Mills built alongside rivers ground corn or wheat into flour. Nearly all of these goods were traded overseas, passing through New York or Philadelphia to get there.

The success of the mills allowed the Middle Colonies to participate in the Triangular Trade by supplying wheat, grain, and excess fish to England and southern Europe, where they were traded for wine and gold. They traded other surplus items, such as meat and horses, to the West Indies in return for sugar and molasses. As in New England, they turned the molasses into rum, which they shipped with other goods to Africa in return for slaves and gold. Some Middle Colonies families were slaveholders, and by the 1760s slavery was generally well established there, although most families owned only small numbers of slaves.

Society

In 1660, just 5,000 non-Indian people lived in the Middle Colonies. In 1710, that number had grown to 70,000. By 1760 it was 425,000. The high rate of childbirth fueled this growth as well as (unlike New England) continued immigration from Scotland, Ireland, Germany, and England.

In the Middle Colonies, there were several members of the natural aristocracy who owned enormous tracts of land. These people grew wealthier and wealthier throughout the 1700s as they sold some of their extensive lands. Below them socially were urban merchants and small family farmers, who comprised the majority of the population. Below these groups were tenant farmers who rented the farms they worked. And in the cities there was a growing number of poor. There were also around 35,000

© iStockphoto.com/Vlado Janžekovi

© North Wind Picture Archives/Alamy

slaves in the Middle Colonies in 1770, most of whom worked in the agricultural areas of New York, usually cultivating wheat. Slavery was also visible in the cities, usually because the wealthiest colonists liked to have a servant in tow, to show off their wealth. Furthermore, by 1750, New York City was a major hub of the American slave trade.

Life

Life in the Middle Colonies can be examined by looking at the big cities (Philadelphia and New York) on the one hand, and everywhere else on the other. Family farms owned and worked by one family produced huge amounts of grain. In New York, however, large landowners owned baronial estates and had tenants work their lands. As in New England, the population boom propelled youngsters off family plots and farther west. Some tried to purchase farms; some were reduced to tenant farming. In most areas, the sexual division of labor continued, with women controlling indoor activities and men controlling outdoor activities. Families remained generally stable and, in the absence of large villages, the number of people living on a farm grew.

The cities were booming as well. In 1765, almost one out of every five Pennsylvanians lived in a sizeable town. A professional class of lawyers, craftsmen, and millers emerged. The populace founded urban institutions such as centers of public education, newspapers, theaters, fire departments, and libraries. More so than the other colonies, the Middle Colonies' thriving population was diverse. In New York City and Philadelphia, many languages were spoken, and people often grouped together by language. In general, the laboring people of the Middle Colonies exerted an impressive amount of control over civic life, as a ruling elite was slow to emerge. This civic input combined with devotion to family and to individual happiness and formed the cornerstone of Middle Colonies society.

The Chesapeake

Economy

The Chesapeake was the third of the four major regions in colonial North America. The Chesapeake had more fertile soil than either New England or the Middle Colonies, which influenced the development of a distinctly different society. Tobacco was the chief product, and, rather than developing a diversified economy, farmers in the Chesapeake remained tied to this single lucrative crop. For instance, in the late 1600s, tobacco generated 90 percent of the enormous wealth in Virginia and Maryland. Flour and grains came in a distant second as exports, growing in importance only in the mid-1700s. From 1660 to 1763, tobacco

Tobacco was king of the Chesapeake.

© iStockphoto.com/Jan Tyler

>> In most areas, the sexual division of labor continued, with women controlling indoor activities and men controlling outdoor activities.

was king of the Chesapeake. Its production influenced everything else in the colony.

There were hardly any developed industries in the Chesapeake, largely due to the scarcity of towns. There were few towns because of the region's dependence on tobacco, which meant that people lived on huge stretches of land where tobacco could be farmed. Virginia did mine some iron ore. After 1730, when grain became profitable, mills sprang up along the rivers. Indeed, just before the American Revolution, the Chesapeake's mills had developed into one of the strongest sectors of the economy. But this was a late development. The Chesapeake relied on its staple crop for its wealth, and the anemic growth of other industries would suffer because of it.

Cities, too, failed to develop. By the middle 1700s, the Chesapeake had only one sizeable city in Baltimore, which was developed as a port town for the area's grain. Other than that, most of the Chesapeake's cities (such as Norfolk) were little more than small towns.

Instead of living in cities or towns, the people of the Chesapeake settled on farms. Key to a farm's success was access to a riverbank where product could be transported to market. Thus, a developmental map of the Chesapeake would show a number of large farms moving farther and farther up the major rivers. In 1660, there were around 35,000 non-Indians living in the Chesapeake. By 1760 that number reached 500,000. Just under two-fifths of this total (about 190,000) were slaves, most of whom worked on tobacco plantations that lined the major waterways.

Society

In this economically minded society, social relations were based on knowing one's place in the social hierarchy and deferring to one's superiors. At the top of the structure were the few families with access to public land who profited from selling tobacco and grain. They increased their wealth throughout the 1700s, constructing a visible structure of leadership and power. They modeled their lives after those of the landed English gentry, not wealthy Londoners. They set themselves up as an elite with social responsibilities, which allowed them to gain total control over political and religious institutions. By the mid-1700s, commentators were noting the extravagance and indulgences of this elite. They sat high above the less affluent free colonists, who were usually small landholders and who were, in turn, socially above the slaves.

Life

The majority of the people in the Chesapeake lived on widely scattered farms and plantations. Because settlements were scattered, individual households grew larger and larger in size. It was common to live with one's siblings for most of one's life. Throughout the 1700s, kinship networks among neighbors prospered.

As roads slowly developed, settlements began to spring up farther from the rivers. Horses provided the main mode of transpor-

>> Governor's palace at Williamsburg, Virginia, the seat of royal power in the colony, exemplified the standard to which wealthy Virginia families aspired.

tation. By the 1750s, the Chesapeake supported a rural commercial network along these roads, where merchants, innkeepers, and traders could hawk their wares. Life was slowly moving away from being entirely agricultural, although in contrast to New England and the Middle Colonies, urban life in the Chesapeake was nonexistent.

Until 1700, there were many more men than women in the Chesapeake. This meant that many people married late and that women possessed ample power. The region suffered from high death rates, economic inequality among free people, and weak social institutions, such as churches (where a sense of community could develop). This began to change around 1700. A temporary lull in tobacco prices slowed the rush of new arrivals, allowing Chesapeake society to settle down as its sex ratio evened out. In addition, after 1675 slavery replaced indentured servitude as the preferred type of labor. By 1720, slaves made up 25 percent of the population, a percentage that stabilized at about 40 percent by 1760, when almost 50 percent of families owned slaves, usually in small numbers. The declining number of indentured servants meant the eventual decline of a class of free white people, who would have constituted the region's middle rung of society. Because of the growth of slavery, this middle rung remained narrow in the Chesapeake; there was little middle class to speak of.

For women, this meant a changed domestic life, and a less influential one. With the model of the landed English gentry before them, Chesapeake society viewed men as benign patriarchs presiding over their flock of dependents. This meant that women's roles in the region declined in importance from 1660 to 1760.

As opposed to the variety of religions in the Middle Colonies and, increasingly, New England, throughout the 1700s the Anglican Church became entrenched in the life of the Chesapeake. Anglicans did not demand strict adherence, unlike Puritans, meaning that the Chesapeake institutions remained generally secular. This situation was aided by the fact that there were few ministers in the growing region, and the gentry did not care to pay for more to come (see Map 4.2).

Throughout the 1700s, then, the Chesapeake developed a strongly aristocratic social structure and a largely rural, English model of living. This stood in contrast to New England, which featured small towns, family relations, and social mobility. It also stood in contrast to the Middle Colonies, which relied on New York and Philadelphia as central urban hubs to support the many middle-rung farmers. Life in the Chesapeake was more deferential regarding status, more rural, and, at the top, more luxurious and comfortable.

The Southern Colonies

Economy

Impressive as it was, the wealth of the Chesapeake could not compete with that of the Southern Colonies. The Southern Colonies were like the Chesapeake in that they relied overwhelmingly on a few staple crops. However, they were unlike the Chesapeake in that life was generally so miserable there that few colonists resided there permanently. Only two towns of any size were established, and no social models of leadership developed. The wealthy landowners enjoyed the profits, but they chose to live elsewhere.

The staple crops of the Southern Colonies were tobacco, rice, and indigo, and they dominated the region's economic life. Cotton would become significant only after 1793, when Eli Whitney invented the cotton gin, which allowed the cultivation of the crop on lower-quality land, thus expanding the amount of cotton that could be grown. By the early 1700s, however, large plantations started springing up to grow those staple crops. Slave labor was the key to their development, allowing a few successful farmers to develop large plantations of over a thousand acres.

There was little industrial development in the Southern Colonies. Local artisans and their apprentices developed small establishments for manufacturing guns and other ironware. For the most part, however, the people of the Southern Colonies relied on trade with England for their industrial goods. This led to the creation of well-developed routes of commerce along waterways. It also allowed the Southern Colonies to participate in the Triangular Trade, shipping their tobacco, rice, and indigo to England in return for manufactured goods.

Society

Because of the miserable living conditions, including the heat, humidity, and insects, the Southern

> By the mid-1700s, commentators were noting the extravagance and indulgences of the Chesapeake elite. They sat high above the less affluent free colonists.

Map 4.2
Forms of Government and Religions in the
Colonies, 1720

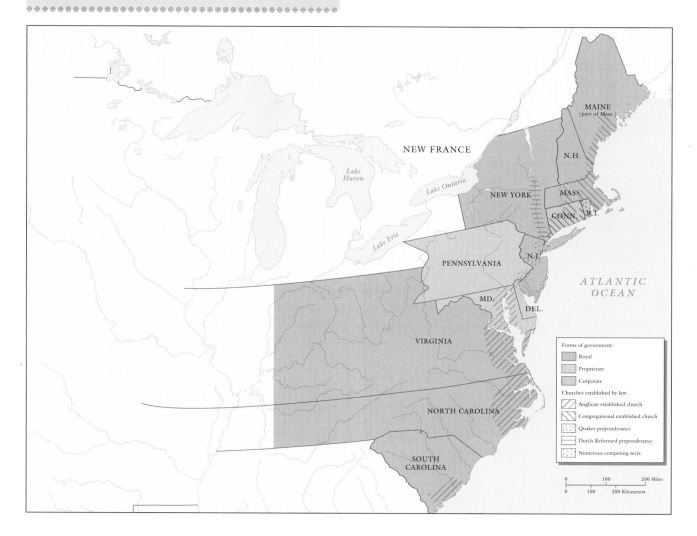

Colonies were slow to grow in population. In 1660, there were very few non-Indian settlers. In 1710, there were 26,000, and in 1760 there were just 215,000, about 95,000 of whom were slaves. The social structure reflected this differentiation. Plantation bosses were heads of large fiefdoms. There was a tiny middle class of lawyers, merchants, and skilled workers who usually lived in the region's few small towns or worked in the lumber mills of North Carolina. The bulk of the working class was made up of slaves imported from Africa.

Life

There was a difference in lifestyle between the upper and lower Southern Colonies. In the lower colonies (today's South Carolina and Georgia), life expectancy continued to be perilously short. Few people lived to be sixty, and many died before they were twenty. This meant that, for the most part, those who could live elsewhere did.

Nevertheless, the lucky and the entrepreneurial amassed great wealth in the Southern Colonies. The commercial gentry who enjoyed this wealth lived a stylish life, usually in the manner of the English elite, enjoying West Indian accent pieces for their home's furnishings. They customarily owned two homes: one on their plantation (where they spent little time), and one in either Charleston or Savannah. To make use of the gentry's wealth and leisure time, these two cities developed such institutions as libraries, theaters, social clubs, and concert houses.

>> Town homes in Charleston, South Carolina

© iStockphoto.com/Rod Pasibe

In the Southern Colonies, communities were not always based around families, mostly because there was no certainty that parents would survive long. Law enforcement was slack, depth of religious commitment was shallow, and interest in public education was limited. The wealthy frequently sent their children to England to be educated.

In dramatic contrast to this pleasant life they were leading, white Southerners developed draconian slave codes to govern the lives of their slaves. Punishment for slave insurrections was severe, travel for slaves was limited, and accumulation of wealth denied. Yet, there were few slave revolts, probably because most slaves did not yet work in gangs. The single major uprising, the Stono Rebellion of 1739 in South Carolina, was put down brutally and spurred the reinforcement of strict slave codes (see page 73). However, because of the high rates of white absenteeism from their plantations, there was little owner oversight, meaning that slaves actually led a slightly freer life than the laws dictated.

LO² Expansion of Colonial Intellectual and Cultural Life

> **Enlightenment**
> A movement to prioritize the human capacity for reason as the highest form of human attainment

The expanding economic and social life of the 1700s gave some people the time and inclination to engage in intellectual and cultural pursuits. It also allowed Americans to participate in a monumental transition affecting much of the Western world, a movement away from medieval thought toward that of the Enlightenment. This was important for American history because Enlightenment ideals played a substantial role in the American Revolution and in the development of the American political system that was to come.

The American Enlightenment

The European Enlightenment

The American **Enlightenment** stemmed from the European Enlightenment, which was a movement to prioritize the human capacity for reason as the highest form of human attainment. In the early 1600s, most people of the Western world believed (1) in the unquestioned primacy of rulers (spiritual and secular); (2) in humans' incapacity for social change; and (3) that our time here on earth is a temporary interlude on our journey toward either eternal salvation or damnation. In the 1500s, European scientists, most notably Copernicus, began to question these beliefs, and by the 1600s educated people were postulating whether natural laws (not divine ones) governed society and the universe, and whether these natural laws were accessible to humans through the use of reason. The most prominent of these thinkers were John Locke and Jean-Jacques Rousseau. Locke argued that one's environment was more significant than divine decree in the development of one's character, and Rousseau contended that individuals had "natural rights" to life, liberty, and property, which even a king or a pope could not deny. The key Enlightenment economist was Adam Smith, who postulated a natural balance in the economy determined by laws of supply and demand. Each of the central ideas put forward by these thinkers implied that progress was possible as people achieved more and more of their natural rights and that people had a stake in their own life and were entitled to reject authority if certain rights were denied.

The American Enlightenment and Religion

These ideas inspired both harmony and conflict with religious leaders, and many of the most consequential American intellectual outpourings from the colonial period are either rejections of or support for the Enlightenment. Cotton Mather, for instance, produced important sermons as he refined a Puritan theology that articulated the centrality of God to an individual's well-being. William Bradford, John Winthrop, and Edward Johnson wrote histories of New England, giving special testament to the sacrifices made to religion by the colonial founders, but also hedging a bit toward the Enlightenment by praising the individual fortitude of those founders. And religion animated the poems of Anne Bradstreet, Edward Taylor, and Michael Wigglesworth. The American Enlightenment did not produce many atheists or agnostics, but it did begin a process whereby religious thinkers tried to find a balance between science and religion.

Education

The necessity of training ministers, especially in New England, led to the creation of an educational system, and the Enlightenment ideals of individual progress and human reason prodded the slow democratization of the system over the course of the seventeenth and eighteenth centuries. Reflecting this balance between religious and secular ideals, America's first

college, Harvard, was founded in 1636, not as an official church school, but under the prevailing Puritan philosophy and with a mission to create a literate ministry. In 1642, Massachusetts passed a law requiring parents to teach their children to read. In 1647, it passed a law requiring towns to maintain a primary school. Although they did so more slowly than New England, the Middle Colonies also launched endeavors in public education.

Over time, the presence of schools grew, especially in New England. Secondary schools opened there in the 1700s. They would not be established southward in significant numbers until after the revolution. Nine colleges were founded during the colonial period, four of them in New England. All, like Harvard, were in some way church schools.

Read Cotton Mather on the need for education.

The Secular Press

Religious leaders were losing some of their primacy in colonial America, especially in New England. Enlightenment ideals took hold with many laypeople, as did the secular practices of politics and commerce. This was reflected in the expansion of nonreligious newspapers throughout the 1700s, especially in New England. The first newspaper was published in Boston by Benjamin Harris in 1690, and the first regularly published paper was the *Boston News-Letter*, begun in 1704. By the middle of the 1700s, every major town had its own newspaper (although they published more about events in Europe than about

Harvard College, founded in 1636

John Peter Zenger's trial

those in the colonies). In 1741, Andrew Bradford published the first magazine, the *American Magazine*. The title alone reflects the unity that the colonists were beginning to feel.

The freedom encouraged by Enlightenment ideals also led to expansion of liberties, as in the case of John Peter Zenger, a New York newspaperman who was arrested after publishing an attack on the gov-

ernor. Zenger was acquitted of the crime (because his attack was factually correct), setting a crucial precedent for freedom of the press; truth became a legitimate defense against a charge of libel, no matter how elevated in rank the alleged libel victim was. Illustrating the deep antiauthoritarianism that ran through the case, the jury, in coming to its decision, defied the wishes of the judge.

Take an interactive look at the trial of John Peter Zenger.

The Great Awakening

The Great Awakening

During this expansion of Enlightenment ideals, American churches experienced a revival. A combination of Enlightenment ideals and a general unhappiness with social and economic developments bred dissatisfaction with the direction American life was taking. Many colonists felt that the established religions had overly accommodated the Enlightenment, allowing rationalization too much free rein in the spiritual world; many colonists had also begun to feel alienated from the mainstream establishment and the traditions that ensconced them in power.

In response, ministers and laypeople alike originated a Protestant revival that emphasized the notion that individuals could find heaven if they worked hard enough (not just if they were predestined to go) and that allowed—even invited—emotional expressions of religion. Ignoring tradition, this new group of preachers stressed

Read Jonathan Edwards on the Great Awakening.

"The congregation was extraordinarily melted by every sermon; almost the whole assembly being in tears for a great part of sermon time."

– *Jonathan Edwards on Great Awakening preacher George Whitefield's sermons*

that all were equal in Christ. The result was the growth and development of several new Protestant denominations, which invariably emphasized the laity's role in matters both spiritual and temporal, as well as a more emotional type of religion. Called the **Great Awakening**, it was America's first large-scale religious revival.

Old Lights versus New Lights

Jonathan Edwards was the intellectual leader of the Great Awakening, although itinerant evangelical preachers such as George Whitefield played a considerable role in fomenting the revival. These itinerants advocated an emotional style of religion and sometimes attacked the local ministers, who they felt were both too beholden to tradition and too accommodating of Enlightenment ideals. By the time it had run its course (by about 1745), the Great Awakening had opened a tremendous rift among Protestants. On one side were the **Old Lights**, who condemned emotionalism and favored a more rationalistic theology favored by elements of the Enlightenment; on the other were the **New Lights**, who supported evangelism, the new methods of prayer, and equality before Christ. The revival slowed during the 1750s. The Great Awakening is significant for at least five reasons. (See "The reasons why. . ." below.)

LO³ African Slavery

An intricate and harsh slave system developed alongside the American Enlightenment and the Great Awakening. It was especially brutal in the Southern Colonies, although slavery existed everywhere in colonial North America. Numerically speaking, the colonies that would become the United States were a tiny part of a much larger **Atlantic slave trade**, a huge system of trade and migration that brought millions of slaves to the New World and Europe and that served as a pillar in the economy of one of the earliest forms of globalization. Europeans and colonials forced perhaps as many as 12 million Africans to cross the Atlantic. Many died during the arduous passage, masking the true number of forced migrants. About 75 percent of slaves came from West Africa. The other 25 percent came from Southwest Africa. A majority of the Africans went to colonies controlled by Spain or Portugal: about 2 million to Brazil and 3 million to the West Indies, usually to work on sugar plantations. Roughly 350,000 Africans, less than 5 percent of the total, came to the future United States. Of this 350,000, Europeans forced 10,000 Africans to come during the 1600s and the remainder during the 1700s. Although some would become free after earning enough money to purchase their freedom, more than 95 percent of colonial Africans remained slaves for life.

Enslavement

Capture

The process by which the captured slaves came to North, South, and Central America was rationalized by the profits to be made. Acquired either through barter between a European slave trader and an African kingdom or through kidnapping, the enslaved Africans were bound at the neck in a leather brace. The slave trader connected a gang of slaves together by chains attached to these neck braces. Then the chained gang was marched to the coast, a journey sometimes as long as 550 miles, which could take up to two months. Once on the

{ **The reasons why . . .** }

The Great Awakening was significant because:

- It increased the number of churches in colonial America, as ministers formed new sects to meet the demands of the population.

- It strengthened evangelical sects, such as the Baptists, who became prominent in the Chesapeake and sought to overturn the aristocratic social structure.

- It inspired the founding of several colleges (for example, Princeton, Brown, Rutgers, and Dartmouth).

- It demonstrated the persistence of religion *in conjunction with* Enlightenment ideals in America.

- It severed colonial ties to established structures of authority (religious authority, in this case), serving in some ways as a precursor to revolution.

African coast, the traders herded their captives into stucco pens to be inspected and sorted by desirability. Some traders branded the slaves with hot irons to mark their property. Then the slaves waited in captivity for cargo ships to arrive.

The Middle Passage

When the ships arrived, slave traders forced the slaves from their pens and onto canoes, and paddled them out to the larger ships. At this point, some slaves jumped overboard, keeping themselves under water long enough to drown.

Once aboard the transport ship, slaves faced the "**middle passage**," their horrible journey across the Atlantic. Traders packed the ships until they were overfilled. They cuffed the slaves and kept them belowdecks, away from fresh air. The captives were denied access to latrines, and the stench in the holds became unbearable. Many captives vomited in response, making the stench even worse. The Europeans fed the slaves paltry food. They threw sick slaves overboard to try to prevent the spread of diseases. They force-fed with a mouth wrench those who sought to commit suicide by starvation. Because the slaves came from varied tribes, it was likely they did not speak one another's language, cutting them off completely from

Read a doctor's account of the Middle Passage.

the life they once knew. The middle passage took between four and eight weeks, and more than one in four captives died along the way. In the seventeenth and eighteenth centuries, any trans-Atlantic journey was perilous and potentially fatal, but especially so for the captured Africans.

middle passage
Perilous journey across the Atlantic endured by captives from Africa

To a New Life

Once in the New World, slave traders auctioned off their cargo in public squares, chiefly in New York and Charleston, but in several other cities as well. Potential buyers inspected the captured men and women's teeth, underarms, and genitals. Strong young men were the most valuable, but women of child-bearing age were also prized because they could have children who, by law in the 1700s, were also the slaveholder's property. Then the buyer transported the slaves to what lay ahead: a life of ceaseless labor. In total, the journey from African village to New World plantation routinely took as long as six months.

This process began in the 1600s and continued into the 1800s, although the 1780s were the years of the Atlantic slave trade's peak. Before the American Revolution, there were only a few scattered movements to protest the slave trade and the practice of slavery (primarily by the Quakers, the Mennonites,

TO BE SOLD on board the Ship *Bance-Island*, on tuesday the 6th of *May* next, at *Ashley-Ferry*, a choice cargo of about 250 fine healthy NEGROES, just arrived from the Windward & Rice Coast.—The utmost care has already been taken, and shall be continued, to keep them free from the least danger of being infected with the SMALL-POX, no boat having been on board, and all other communication with people from *Charles-Town* prevented.

Austin, Laurens, & Appleby.

N. B. Full one Half of the above Negroes have had the SMALL-POX in their own Country.

and a few other religious groups). Much of European society simply accepted the horrors of slavery as a necessary cost of colonial expansion.

The Spread of Slavery

Expanding the Trade

Tobacco, rice, and indigo—the three staple crops of the Southern and Chesapeake colonies—all demanded significant labor, and by the late 1600s, the favored form of labor in the American colonies was rapidly becoming African slaves. Between 1680 and 1700, the average number of slaves transported on English ships rose from five thousand slaves a year to more than twenty thousand.

Slavery in the North

Although slavery was most common in the Southern Colonies and the Chesapeake, it was legal in *all* English colonies in America. In the North, slaves worked as field hands on farms and as domestic servants, dockworkers, and craftspeople in cities. But because of their labor-intensive cash crops, the market for slaves was much more lucrative in the South and the Chesapeake. Nevertheless, many northerners were involved in the trade. Northern traders, especially from Massachusetts, New York, and Rhode Island, engaged in and profited from the slave trade before the United States outlawed the importation of slaves in 1808.

Life under Slavery

Variety

The daily life of a slave in colonial America depended on where he or she lived. In New England, where only about 3 percent of the population was African during the colonial era, slaves worked as field hands on small farms, as house servants for wealthy colonists, or as skilled artisans. Slaves could be isolated from one another (and most were), or they could live in a port town like Newport, Rhode Island, where slaves made up 18 percent of the population.

In the Middle Colonies, some slaves worked as field hands on small farms, while smaller numbers worked in cities in nearly every labor-intensive occupation. Neither of these regions relied on gang labor.

In the Southern Colonies and the Chesapeake, most slaves were field hands who grew sugar cane, rice, tobacco, or cotton. Some were house servants who cooked, cleaned, and helped care for children. A very few were skilled artisans. As arduous as the southern labor system was, however, plantation life allowed for development of a slave culture. This was possible because of the large number of slaves who could gather together after working hours.

Slave Life

The plantations where slave life developed most fully were entirely in the South, especially in the lower South, where slaves outnumbered other colonists. Many slaves here spoke Gullah, a hybrid language of several African tongues. They preserved several African religious traditions, such as a couple's jumping over a broomstick to seal a marriage. Over time, these traditions merged with Christianity in the same way that Catholic images merged with the traditional beliefs of Native America.

For slaves, family life was unpredictable, fragile, and subject to the arbitrary whims of their owners. Children typically stayed with their family until they were eight, at which time they were sometimes sold. Masters occasionally raped or coerced female slaves into sexual relations, further demonstrating their limitless power over their property. Nevertheless, families did struggle through, and wherever possible, strong family structures emerged. The hazards and difficulties inherent in the process of sustaining a family life under these conditions led slave men and women to take on roles different from those of their masters. Slave women, for instance, worked both in the field and in the home. Slave men, meanwhile, took on occasional domestic duties.

Rebellion and Resistance

Despite the horrific nature of slave life, slave rebellions were infrequent, principally because slave owners had taken such drastic measures to maintain control over their slaves. The few slave rebellions that did arise met with violent resistance and led to even tighter controls. One planned insurrection in New York City in 1740 ended with the burning of thirteen slaves and the hanging of eighteen others (along with four white allies).

The most notable slave revolt of the 1700s—the **Stono Rebellion**—occurred in Stono, South Carolina, in 1739, when, on a quiet Sunday morning, a group of mostly newly arrived slaves marched into a firearms shop, killed the colonists manning the shop, stole several firearms, and marched south, probably in an effort to get to Florida, where the Spanish government promised England's slaves freedom. After traveling only a few miles, the number of slaves had grown to more than one hundred.

 Learn more about the Stono Rebellion.

They marched from house to house, murdering slave owners and their families as they went. After ten miles, the band was met by an armed militia, which killed at least thirty of the rebelling slaves and captured almost all of the rest. Nearly all who were captured were killed.

In response to the rebellion, South Carolina passed the **Negro Act**, which consolidated all of the separate slave codes into one code that forbade slaves from growing their own food, assembling in groups, or learning to read. This sharp response to the Stono Rebellion continued a pattern of harsh legal retributions for slave insurrections.

Slavery and Racism

In the end, slavery promoted the rise of extreme, sustained racism against African Americans in North America. Since their arrival in the Chesapeake in 1619, dark-skinned people had been considered of lower status by Europeans. But because until the 1680s there were so few African slaves in the American colonies, they were generally not treated harshly. During this early period, a few slaves broke the bonds of enslavement and became landowners and politically active freedmen. Yet as the cost of indentured servants went up and that of slaves went down, slaves were employed as the central labor force of the South and the Chesapeake. And as the number of slaves rose, so did restrictions on Africans and African Americans. Rabid manifestations of racism emerged out of owners' growing fears. The result was the creation of a caste-like system of segregation in which African Americans were considered inherently inferior to Europeans and Euro-Americans, and sometimes less than human. At the same time, religious writers, philosophers, scientists, and lay writers (among them, Thomas Jefferson) concocted theories about the "inferior" nature of African Americans, thus creating an intellectual framework to support the economic reality. Slavery lasted until the Civil War, and elements of this racial caste system have persisted well into the twentieth century.

Explore a wide variety of images and documents related to slavery.

Religious writers, philosophers, scientists, and lay writers (among them, Thomas Jefferson) concocted theories about the "inferior" nature of African Americans.

Stono Rebellion
Slave rebellion in South Carolina in 1739; this was the largest slave uprising of the century

Negro Act
South Carolina state law which consolidated all of the separate slave codes into a single code that forbade slaves from growing their own food, assembling in groups, or learning to read

salutary neglect
Hands-off style of relations between the Crown and the colonies; a loose system of oversight where the Crown ignored governance of its colonies and enforcement of its trade laws so long as the colonies provided England with cash and crops

Glorious Revolution of 1688
Overthrow of King James II by Protestant factions; his exit left the crown to William and Mary

King George's War
Continued New World battles between England and France (1744–1748)

LO⁴ Attempted Expansion of English Control

Slavery was, of course, a huge part of the economic expansion of the early 1700s—an expansion that led to increased interest in the colonies from the British Crown. Most importantly, the exceptional production of raw materials had propelled the colonies into a second stage of economic development, whereby manufacturing and industry began to prosper. This stimulated economic competition between the North American colonies and England, which the Crown could not tolerate.

Salutary Neglect

The Glorious Revolution

Any attempt by the Crown to reassert control of the colonies would aggravate the colonists because they had become accustomed to a hands-off style of relations between the Crown and the colonies, a relationship labeled **salutary neglect**. The principle developed in the late 1680s, when, upon King Charles II's death in 1685, his brother, James II, became king and promptly attempted to make England Catholic once again. This created such a severe rift within England that it fell into near civil war. Unlike the Cromwellian revolution of the 1650s, however, this second revolution was bloodless, and in the so-called **Glorious Revolution of 1688**, Protestant factions forced James II to flee England. His exit left the Crown to his Protestant daughter and son-in-law, William of Orange and Mary II, more commonly referred to as William and Mary.

For the colonists, the result of the Glorious Revolution was looser governance by the Crown and the removal of many of the proprietors who had founded the colonies. William and Mary continued to have a definite economic interest in the colonies, establishing a Board of Trade to oversee affairs and collect data. They also established a privy council to administer colonial laws. But, in general, royal administration over the colonies grew much looser with the decline of the proprietors.

Salutary Neglect

The colonists loved, advocated, and fought for the loose system of oversight that came to be called salutary neglect. The concept is simple: the Crown would essentially ignore governance of its colonies and enforcement of its trade laws so long as the colonies continued to provide England with sufficient cash and produce. Politically, this system gave colonial assemblies a high level of legitimacy, which was accomplished at the expense of the royal governors. Of course, the risk of salutary neglect was that, if England ever decided to enforce the laws on its books, a serious conflict was inevitable. This is exactly what would happen in the French and Indian War, yet another of the "Wars for Empire" that occurred from 1754 to 1763.

The French and Indian War, 1754–1763

The truce from Queen Anne's War lasted nearly thirty years, but the battles between the European powers were not over. In **King George's War** (1744–1748) England and France continued their New World spat, but the war ended with resolutions concerning only Europe; the exact New World ramifications remained unclear.

Meanwhile, English colonists pushed deeper into the Ohio Valley, further infuriating the French, who were already established traders there. Eventually the French attempted to build a series of military strong-

>> **The risk of salutary neglect was that, if England ever decided to enforce the laws on its books, a serious conflict was inevitable.**

© iStockphoto.com/James Thompson

holds that would intimidate the English, the largest of which was Fort Duquesne in today's southwest Pennsylvania. Virginian colonists who were speculating on lands in the west retaliated by building Fort Necessity nearby. When the Virginians sent an inexperienced young militia colonel named George Washington to deter the French from building more forts, a skirmish between the French and the English ignited yet another war. This war would be the most consequential one yet.

George Washington was swiftly forced to surrender, and it looked as though the French were going to control trade relations in the American interior for the foreseeable future. But English merchants in London lobbied to use this backwoods dispute to forge a war that would eject the French from North America once and for all. Without the French, London merchants would have a monopoly on much of the New World trade, which promised to be incredibly lucrative. They succeeded in their lobbying, and a hesitant Crown used this minor provocation to start a major war. It was in this contrived way that a skirmish on the Pennsylvania frontier exploded into a world war that involved France, England, Austria, Russia, Prussia, Spain, and numerous Indian tribes. In Europe, the war was called the **Seven Years' War**; in North America, it was the **French and Indian War**.

The Albany Congress

The coming war put the English colonists on high alert. A major war was about to erupt on their soil. To discuss the matter, seven of the colonies sent representatives to Albany, New York, in the summer of 1754. The meeting, called the **Albany Congress**, represented the first time the mainland English colonies met for a unified purpose.

The Albany Plan

Part of their purpose was to convince the Iroquois to join the English side in the battle, but the Iroquois chose to remain neutral in order to preserve their trade routes. Another part of the colonists' strategy was to develop what would have been the first-ever colonial union under the **Albany Plan**, drafted by the printer, scientist, and, later, politician Benjamin Franklin. The plan would have placed all of England's colonies in America under a single president-general, appointed by the Crown, whose responsibility would be to manage all activity on the frontier and handle negotiations with Indians. It also would have created a single legislature, made up of representatives from

each of the colonies, whose number would depend on how much in taxes each colony paid. The union failed to materialize, however, mainly because the colonists felt allegiance only to their particular colony and (to a lesser extent) to the Crown. They did not yet identify with their fellow colonists. England was unhappy with the prospect of colonial unity, but slowly, the colonists were beginning to perceive the need for it. The French and Indian War did much to solidify the feeling that the English colonies along the Atlantic Coast would share one fate and should, perhaps, unite.

The Battles

As the colonists had foreseen, war came, and under the leadership of General James Braddock, the English fared badly. Braddock's attempts to raise money to help supply his troops from the colonists provoked colonial ire. His patronizing attempts to work with Indian tribes also failed. Worse, he bumbled his way from one military defeat to another. Within three years, two-thirds of his troops were dead, including Braddock himself.

In 1758, the English began to take the conflict more seriously. They sent a large army under the leadership of Jeffrey Amherst to take over military operations. What followed was warfare marked by extreme brutality on all sides. After a year, the English were prevailing, and a year later, in 1760, hostilities largely ended. In 1763 the three warring nations (Spain, England, and France) signed the **Treaty of Paris** (Map 4.3), which laid out the so-called Proclamation Line giving England the western interior of North America, Canada, and Florida. Spain received Louisiana from France, and the Mississippi River became the boundary between England's holdings and Spain's. France had been evicted from North America.

The French and Indian War was significant to the colonies for five reasons:

- France was forced to give up its land claims in Canada. This was disastrous for Indians in the north, because they had been surviving by playing

Seven Years' War
European label for the world war (1754–1763) between France, England, Austria, Russia, Prussia, Spain, and numerous Indian tribes

French and Indian War
Colonial label for the Seven Years' War

Albany Congress
Meeting of representatives from seven colonies in Albany, New York in 1754, the first time the mainland English colonies met for a unified purpose

Albany Plan
Concept for the first-ever colonial union, drafted by Benjamin Franklin

Treaty of Paris
1763 agreement between Spain, England, and France that made the Mississippi River the boundary between England's holdings and Spain's, and evicted France from North America

one European power off another. Freed from competing with the French, the English could dictate the terms of trade and land possession.

- The colonists gained experience dealing with the English army. They disliked its hierarchical style, especially after having experienced extensive self-rule in the colonies. For their part, the English saw the colonists as ragtag and undisciplined. This led to increased contempt between the two peoples.

- The French and Indian War allowed the English colonies to see themselves as a united body distinct from England. The Albany Congress proved to be the first demonstration of an increasingly unified colonial identity.

- The war was costly for England, and its attempts to recoup its losses through taxes on the colonies led directly to the Revolution.

- The French and Indian War led to increased feelings of pan-Indianism against white settlers.

Pan-Indianism

With all the lands east of the Mississippi River now belonging to England, Indian tribes had to adapt. No longer could one tribe negotiate with one group of colonists and play the European nations off against one another to win concessions. Now Indian–colonial relations were centralized in London. The Indians recognized this transition and began to realize an increased unity between tribes in opposition to the English. Simply put, in the aftermath of the French and Indian War, many of the tribes of Native America shifted from favoring a tribal identity to assuming a racial one, or **pan-Indianism**. This was especially true in the Northwest, between the Great Lakes and the Appalachian Mountains, where contact with the colonists was most sustained.

Neolin

In the late 1750s and 1760s, **Neolin**, a Delaware prophet, began preaching a return to old Indian ways, as they were before Europeans had come to America. Central to this revitalization movement was the notion of purging all European habits, such as reliance on material goods, use of alcohol, and belief in Christianity. Neolin traveled to several tribes preaching his message of pan-Indianism and anti-Europeanism.

Pontiac's Rebellion

By 1763, several Indians had followed Neolin's advice and come together to present a unified front against the colonists. Under the leadership of

>> **Pontiac and his Native American allies visit British officer Major Gladwyn.**

Pontiac, chief of the Ottowa, they were ready to protest English intrusion into their lands and attempt to drive the colonists back across the Appalachians. The resulting battles in **Pontiac's Rebellion** were brutal, with the English attempting to introduce smallpox into Indian communities (through infected blankets) and Indians deliberately poisoning English troops' drinking water (by putting rotten meat in springs upriver from English camps). The English troops were better equipped for warfare, however, and the tribes of Native America, without the French available to help, could not withstand the English armies. They were beaten back, pushed farther west.

> **pan-Indianism**
> Movement in which many of the tribes of Native America shifted from favoring a tribal identity to assuming a racial one
>
> **Neolin**
> Prophet from the Delaware tribe, who began preaching a return to old Indian ways
>
> **Pontiac's Rebellion**
> Brutal battles between Ottowa Indians and English troops in 1763

And in the end . . .

Little did England suspect that, although it had won the Wars for Empire, it had done so at great cost: it had sparked the process of colonial unification. The fight for political freedom was about to begin. During the years between 1700 and 1763, the North American colonies had developed into a stable, manufacturing economy that could potentially rival many European nations. It had large numbers of free white farmers and slave laborers performing much of the backbreaking labor. It also had a growing class of merchants and wealthy landowners who provided leadership and governance. As the French and Indian War was fought on American soil, many colonists began to feel themselves a people apart from their Mother Country. The initial and uncertain itching for political independence had begun. Many colonists could not, or would not, fathom the idea—they had too much to lose. But many outspoken colonists felt that if England persisted in proclaiming the end of salutary neglect, and intended to intrude upon colonial affairs more pointedly, there would be trouble.

What else was happening . . .	
1709	Bartolomeo Cristofori invents the piano.
1712	The last execution of a witch takes place in England.
1751	Benjamin Franklin sends up a kite during a thunderstorm and discovers that lightning is a form of electricity.
1752	The first eraser is put on the end of a pencil.

Toward
Revolution
1763–1776

5

Learning Outcomes

After reading this chapter, you should be able to do the following:

LO 1 What were Britain's main reasons for attempting to change its management of the American colonies during the mid-1700s?

LO 2 Explain how the colonists responded to the new acts, and trace the evolutionary process that brought the colonies closer to true rebellion.

LO 3 Trace the path to revolution in America from the Townshend Acts of 1767 to the meeting of the First Continental Congress.

LO 4 Explain how the American Revolution began, and describe the first battles of the conflict.

> ❝*The British came to see the colonists as not only resisting the demands of their mother country, but also as getting free armed protection from the world's most powerful army.*❞

Getting the colonies organized for the French and Indian War revealed a number of problems for Britain, the most serious of which was the lax enforcement of royal policies in the colonies, the principle that was labeled salutary neglect. The tradition of salutary neglect meant that the colonies were slower to mobilize when the British demanded adherence to their dictates. It also meant that the colonists paid few taxes. After the expensive French and Indian War, the British came to see the colonists as not only resisting the demands of their mother country, but also as getting free armed protection from the world's most powerful army. The colonists, the British also pointed out, also benefited from having had that army remove the colonists' most powerful competition (the French) from the land. Should they not pay for these benefits?

As the French and Indian War came to a close, Britain decided to remedy these problems through a series of reforms that tightened control over the colonies and limited the areas where colonists could settle. The colonists resisted these encroachments, however, for

What do you think?

Boycotts were meaningful because simple participation in a colonywide boycott radicalized the population, making them choose loyalties.

Strongly Disagree						*Strongly Agree*
1	2	3	4	5	6	7

>> The English saw the colonists as a bunch of headstrong upstarts.

they had become accustomed to the self-rule implied in salutary neglect. In addition, since the Enlightenment, Englishmen had sought to protect their "natural rights" from encroachment by their rulers. It did not matter if the ruler was a king or a parliament: if either institution violated one's rights to life, liberty, and property, all Englishmen felt they could reasonably rebel. From the colonists' perspective, they hoped that England's King George would protect them from what they saw as the enmity of a jealous Parliament. The English, on the other hand, saw the colonists as a bunch of headstrong upstarts, demanding rights without assuming the responsibilities inherent to them. As this rhetoric escalated, conflict escalated as well.

Explore an interactive module showing life on the eve of the American Revolution.

LO¹ British Attempts to Rein in the Colonies

The British plan to reform colonial relations had three main goals: (1) to tighten control by eliminating absenteeism and corruption of royal officials in the colonies and by limiting widespread smuggling, by which colonists were avoiding taxes, tariffs, and regulations; (2) to limit the areas where colonists could settle; and (3) to raise greater revenue from the colonies.

Tightening Control

England began its attempts to rein in the colonies in 1760, shortly before the end of the war with France. In that year, the **Privy Council**, which advised the Crown on various matters, issued the "Orders in Council," which required absentee officials to occupy their posts instead of collecting the salary and then paying a substitute to occupy the post. The Privy Council also rewarded officers and crews of naval vessels for seizing smuggling ships. There ought to be no more absentee colonial leadership, and smugglers were to be punished for avoiding taxes.

Limiting Settlement

The next major reform was the Proclamation of 1763, which did three things: (1) placed a moratorium on government sale of western lands; (2) put trade with Indians under royal control; and (3) forbade settlement west of the Proclamation Line (see Map 4.3), which followed the crest of the Appalachians. Its thrust was to control British settlement and push the colonists into the newly acquired colonies of Canada and Florida. Royal officials also believed that the policy would protect British manufacturing, because if colonists moved too far from the Atlantic coast, they would develop their own manufacturing industries rather than import British goods.

Many colonists who were merely frustrated by the Orders in Council were infuriated by the Proclamation. After all, in their minds, the French and Indian War had been fought so that the colonists *could* move farther west. Many colonists had celebrated the British victory, believing that the removal of the French from the region would make westward colonial expansion a possibility. King George's proclamation directly contradicted this belief. Ultimately, the Proclamation of 1763 was impossible to enforce. Settlers moved across the line anyway, and the royal government lacked the resources to stop them.

Raising Revenue

The final piece of reform was George Grenville's plan for paying off Britain's debt. The British had tried to prevent the colonists' evasion of royal taxes earlier in the 1700s, most notably with the 1751 Writs of Assistance, which gave British officials the right to inspect not only places of work, but also private homes. The colonists valiantly fought this infringement on their liberties, although they did not persuade the Crown to reverse the decision. Grenville, who became England's prime minister in 1763, contributed to these woes. He convinced Parliament to pass several specific acts in the 1760s that significantly increased the Crown's interference in the economy of its colonies.

The first of these acts was the **Sugar Act of 1764**, which was technically a *cut* in taxes on molasses and

© iStockphoto.com/Vaide Dambrauskaite

>>Colonists bristled at the idea of British soldiers living in their houses.

© Kelly-Mooney Photography/Corbis

sugar brought into the colonies from non-British colonies in the West Indies. But it was troublesome to the colonists because, even though it reduced the assessment on sugar, it increased enforcement of tax collection. The act signaled the end of the era of salutary neglect. Furthermore, the act taxed items besides sugar, including indigo, pimento (allspice), some wines, and coffee. Britain was now evidently looking to the colonies as a source of direct revenue.

The **Quartering Act of 1765** was the next intrusive act. It required the colonies to feed and house British troops stationed in their territory. Colonists bristled at the idea of British soldiers living in their houses, and the colonial assemblies often refused to provide the money required to feed and house these soldiers.

Most disruptive of all, however, was the **Stamp Act**. Passed by Parliament in 1765, the Stamp Act mandated the use of stamped paper for all official papers, including diplomas, marriage licenses, wills, newspapers, and playing cards. The stamp, embedded in the paper (not a topical stamp), indicated that a tax had been paid on the document. Grenville insisted that revenues from the tax go directly to soldiers protecting the North American colonies. He also mandated that those who avoided using taxed paper would be tried in a Crown-operated vice admiralty court, rather than by a trial of one's peers. Not only had the Crown declared its intention to raise revenues from the colonists, it also indicated that it was ready to enforce its actions.

Quartering Act of 1765
This act required the colonies to feed and house British troops stationed in their territory

Stamp Act
Passed in 1765, this act mandated the use of stamped (embedded) paper for all official papers, including diplomas, marriage licenses, wills, newspapers, and playing cards

LO² Beginnings of American Resistance

Colonial Response to British Reforms

The Sugar Act was widely unpopular. New Englanders in particular saw that the new regulations threatened their profitable (though now illegal) rum trade.

The Stamp Act provoked a much stronger backlash than the Sugar Act had. This was so for three reasons:

The reasons why. . .

- The Stamp Act applied to the kinds of goods used by merchants and lawyers, which stirred up an educated and powerful opposition.

- Although Parliament passed the Stamp Act in March, the act did not go into effect until November 1, 1765. This gave colonists time to organize.

- The Stamp Act was a direct tax on the colonists (instead of a regulation of trade), and the proceeds were meant to pay the salaries of colonial officials, something that the colonists themselves had done in the past. Taxing the colonies so that the Crown could pay these salaries undermined colonial control over royal officials and seemed to indicate that Parliament was limiting colonists' liberties. Royal control appeared to be growing more onerous.

circular letter
Communication among a number of interested parties which was sent from colony to colony in order to keep the disparate colonies together, or united; a primary form of communication for the colonies during the revolutionary period

Stamp Act Congress
Gathering of colonial leaders from nine states in New York City in October 1765 to discuss resistance to the Stamp Act; one of the early instances of collaboration between colonies and of identifying Parliament as the opposition rather than the king

The Stamp Act Congress

To try to force Parliament to repeal the Stamp Act, opponents in Massachusetts initiated a **circular letter** inviting all of the colonies to send representatives to a congress to discuss resistance to the Stamp Act. This was a radical move; convening an intercolonial congress without British authorization was an illegal act. Despite this, the **Stamp Act Congress** convened in New York City in October 1765, with representatives from nine colonies in attendance.

Although it began as an act of defiance, the Stamp Act Congress was largely conciliatory to the Crown. It acknowledged that the colonies were "subordinate" to Parliament in matters of administration, but it maintained that the colonists' rights as Englishmen were infringed upon when Parliament levied taxes without providing the colonists with representation in Parliament. Resolutely noninflammatory, the Stamp Act Congress avoided words like *slavery* and *tyranny*, which were common in editorials of the day. Nevertheless, it did declare that taxes had never been imposed on the colonists by anyone other than colonial legislatures. It also differentiated between the Crown, to which the Stamp Act Congress pledged allegiance, and Parliament, to which it acknowledged a grudging "subordination." In the end, the congress showed the colonists' increasing tendency to collaborate as a single unit; it also began a pattern of finding fault with Parliament rather than with the king.

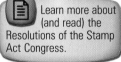
Learn more about (and read) the Resolutions of the Stamp Act Congress.

Boycotts

In addition to these legalistic declarations, there were other, more potent forms of protest. In Boston, New York, Philadelphia, Charleston, and smaller ports, merchants signed agreements not to import British goods until the Stamp Act was repealed. In New England, women's groups called "Daughters of Liberty" organized local boycotts against cloth and tea imported from Britain. These women also held

Tax stamp

"spinning bees" that encouraged American women to show loyalty to the resistance by producing homespun cloth. Locally produced clothing was a sign that one was a "patriot."

The boycott proved effective, especially in New York, where boycotters shut down the port. British exports to the colonies declined, and the opposition party in Parliament began to advocate repealing the Stamp Act. The boycotts were also meaningful because simple participation in a colonywide boycott radicalized the population, making them choose loyalties. This was becoming larger than a protest of elite lawyers. The very clothes that people wore became a form of protest.

> **The very clothes that people wore became a form of protest.**

Rioting

Although the Stamp Act Congress and boycotts proved fruitful, rioting proved to be the most effective means of pro-

test. To coordinate the riots, several colonists formed groups called the **Sons of Liberty**. Typically led by men of wealth and high social standing (such as Samuel Adams), the Sons of Liberty served as leaders in organizing protests and intimidating stamp officials. Mobs in Massachusetts, New York, Rhode Island, and South Carolina burned the homes of stamp officials and hanged effigies of tax collectors, occasionally even tarring and feathering them. As a result of this intimidation, all known stamp officials resigned before the Stamp Act went into effect on November 1, 1765. When the Crown offered the positions to others, they refused the jobs. Furthermore, when the stamps and stamped paper arrived in America, colonists sent them back to England, destroyed them, or locked them away.

Ideological Opposition

In addition to these physical forms of protest, several colonial assemblies sent Parliament written protests, called "resolves." The wording of the resolves was usually influenced by political pamphlets that circulated at the time. Both the pamphlets and the resolves are significant because they articulated the ideas of liberty that positioned the colonists against Britain all the way to the Revolution.

The central drafters of the pamphlets called themselves **Radical Whigs** (which referred to the opposition party in England, the Whigs). Radical Whigs such as James Otis of Massachusetts argued that, because the colonists were not represented in Parliament, Parliament had no authority to tax them. These men coined the phrase "no taxation without representation." The Radical Whigs claimed that the principle that taxation required representation had precedent in British law (in the Magna Carta) and was one of the basic English liberties.

In Virginia, Patrick Henry followed this same line of reasoning. He argued that the Stamp Act was unconstitutional because only the Virginia legislature had the authority to tax Virginians. He introduced a series of *Resolutions Against the Stamp Act* to the Virginia Legislature and asserted that anyone who supported the Stamp Act was an enemy to Virginia.

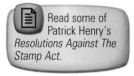
Read some of Patrick Henry's *Resolutions Against The Stamp Act*.

Several of his *Resolutions* were passed by the Burgesses and forwarded to Parliament, indicating the level of radicalization provoked by the Stamp Act.

John Adams of Massachusetts framed another argument against Parliament's right to tax the colonists. In his *Instructions of the Town of Braintree to their Representative*, Adams argued that allowing Parliament to tax the colonists without their consent threatened the sanctity of private property and personal liberty. If Parliament could seize colonists' property, Adams argued, then colonists were dependents of Parliament and not free men. Furthermore, Adams railed against Parliament for creating the specific courts (called vice admiralty courts) that denied the colonists the right to a trial by a jury of one's peers. More than anything else, Adams argued, the colonists wanted liberty; they did not want to become slaves to the whim of a Parliament over which the colonists had no control.

Benjamin Franklin and Daniel Dulany (a celebrated Maryland attorney) promoted another argument against the Stamp Act. They insisted that colonists accept Parliament's right to regulate trade through the use of duties designed to protect the British empire—a form of taxation they called **external taxes**. What the colonists objected to, according to these writers, was the Stamp Act's imposition of an **internal tax** that directly affected the internal affairs of the colonies. Dulany and Franklin feared that internal legislation threatened private property. Both the Crown and many colonists questioned the validity of this distinction between the two forms of taxation, but theirs was a milder argument than that of Adams, who rejected all taxes. This was a more nuanced, conciliatory line of reasoning, but it also demonstrated strong opposition to the Stamp Act.

Read Adams's *Instructions of the Town of Braintree to their Representative*.

View a short film about Benjamin Franklin's life.

Opposition to the Opposition

Not all colonists agreed with these dissenters. In fact, a large portion of colonists did not care one way or another about the Stamp Act, while some, such as James Otis, opposed the Stamp Act *and* resistance to it, favoring instead to advocate for a Parliamentary repeal. Still others, such as Lieutenant-Governor Thomas Hutchinson of Massachusetts, defended the Stamp Act as a fair policy. Hutchinson personally disliked the Stamp Act but believed that, because Parliament

Sons of Liberty
Groups of colonial leaders who organized protests and intimidated stamp officials; their actions caused the resignation of all known stamp officials

Radical Whigs
Political activists and pamphleteers who coined the phrase "no taxation without representation"

external taxes
Duties designed to protect the British empire, part of Parliament's right to regulate trade, as argued by Benjamin Franklin and Daniel Dulany

internal tax
Duties that directly affected the internal affairs of the colonies; according to Benjamin Franklin and Daniel Dulany, this internal legislation threatened private property

virtual representation
Theory endorsed by Parliament that said the House of Commons represented the interests of all the king's subjects, wherever they might reside; this was the pretext for rejecting the colonists' demand for actual representation

deputy representation
The practice of the people's interests being advocated by a deputy; also known as actual representation

Declaratory Act
Passed by Parliament in 1766, this act affirmed its authority to legislate for the colonies "in all cases whatsoever"; largely symbolic, this Act became one of the nonnegotiable claims that Parliament was unwilling to relinquish throughout the struggle.

was the supreme legislative body in the Empire, everything it did was constitutional. Hutchinson said that no matter how inconvenient the Stamp Act was, duty and law required obedience. Hutchinson became a focal point of the rioters, who viewed him as a stooge of the Crown. They sent Hutchinson fleeing, and a mob eventually pulled the roof off his house and trashed all of his possessions. In 1765, resentments were heating up.

In Britain, few people accepted any of the colonists' arguments. They shouldered a heavy tax burden already, so most of them felt that the colonists were asking for a better deal than British subjects living in the mother country received. The British regarded the colonists' ideological arguments as mere rationalizations for avoiding paying taxes.

Members of Parliament also rejected the opposition to the Stamp Act. They argued the dubious point that the House of Commons represented the interests of all the king's subjects, wherever they might reside. This theory of **virtual representation**, they said, was vital to Parliamentary legitimacy because many regions within England were not directly represented in Parliament. In addition, in some areas that *were* represented in the House of Commons, the people had no say in who represented them. Instead, the local nobility or the king selected their representative. King George himself owned the right to appoint over fifty members to the House of Commons—more than 10 percent of the entire body. Under this questionable theory, Parliament rejected the colonists' demand for actual or **deputy representation**.

Repeal of the Stamp Act

A trade recession that gripped the British economy in late 1765 ended the bitter dispute. With a downturn in the economy, the king withdrew his tacit

John Adams

"No freeman should be subject to any tax to which he has not given his own consent."
– *John Adams, 1765*

support of the Stamp Act for fear that the opposition to it would damage revenues too much. His withdrawal of support doomed the Stamp Act, and Parliament eventually repealed it. In repealing the act, however, Parliament made it clear that it was yielding not to the colonists' demands, but to the king's. To make this clear, on the same day it repealed the Stamp Act, Parliament passed the **Declaratory Act**, which affirmed its authority to legislate for the colonies "in all cases whatsoever." Although it was largely symbolic, the Declaratory Act became one of the nonnegotiable claims that Parliament was unwilling to relinquish throughout the struggle. Its leaders would rather go to war than have Parliament lose any of its authority.

News of the Declaratory Act perplexed American leaders, leaving them to wonder whether Parliament had accepted the distinction between internal and external taxation. If the distinction was not accepted, the Declaratory Act asserted Parliament's raw power over the colonies because it gave no concessions on the issue of representation. Most colonists, however, overlooked such abstruse concerns and simply celebrated the Stamp Act's repeal. When Parliament passed few new taxes in 1766, many colonists believed that the crisis was over. They were wrong.

LO³ Taxation Without Representation, 1767–1773
The Townshend Acts of 1767

In 1766, Charles Townshend, who believed it was fair for England to tax the colonies in order "to provide their own safety and preservation," was installed as Britain's chancellor of the Exchequer. The first act he sponsored did not impose a new tax on the colonies, but it did alert colonists that their struggle with Parliament was not over. In the **Restraining Act**, Townshend suspended the New York Assembly for failing to comply with the Quartering Act. This bred suspicions that Townshend would deal harshly with the colonies. It also pushed the debate beyond mere revenue issues, such as taxation without representation, and into the realm of infringement on the colonists' self-government and self-rule.

The British regarded the colonists' ideological arguments as mere rationalizations for avoiding paying taxes.

The Townshend Acts

Townshend confirmed the colonists' worst fears in the summer of 1767, when he steered new taxes through Parliament. Townshend considered the colonists' distinction between internal and external taxes invalid, but he saw how he could use it to his advantage. He intended to raise revenue with new, *external* duties on the goods that the colonists imported from Britain. The resulting **Townshend Acts** laid duties on glass, lead for paint, tea, paper, and a handful of other items. The Townshend Acts also demanded the collection of duties and bolstered the importance of colonial governors who were friendly to the Crown. Once again, this threatened the previous status quo of salutary neglect.

Opposition

Opposition to the Townshend Acts followed the pattern of the Stamp Act opposition slowly—largely because of internal splits among mer-chants. But many colonists evetually began to boycott British goods again. Women stopped wearing silks and satins or serving tea and wine, making fashionable what they saw as a modest, patriotic life. By 1769 the boycotts were effective in every colony, having been spread by colonial newspapers, which shared information and important essays.

One essay, published in all but four colonial newspapers, offered a distinctive ideological protest to the Townshend Acts. Posing as a simple country gentleman resisting a corrupt government, the prominent lawyer John Dickinson wrote a series of essays called *Letters from a Farmer in Pennsylvania*—in both Britain and America. Dickinson explained that the colonies had tolerated earlier duties because they accepted the idea that Parliament should regulate trade. The purpose of the Townshend duties, however, was not regulation, but revenue. Dickinson considered this unconstitutional.

Read Dickinson's twelve short letters.

The Boston Massacre

Opposition to the Townshend Acts triggered rioting as well. Radicals in the Massachusetts legislature

Restraining Act
In this act, chancellor of the Exchequer Charles Townshend suspended the New York Assembly for failing to comply with the Quartering Act

Townshend Acts
These acts of 1767 instituted duties on glass, lead for paint, tea, paper, and a handful of other items

© iStockphoto.com/lillisphotography

>> "Whoever seriously considers the matter, must perceive that a dreadful stroke is aimed at the liberty of these colonies." – John Dickinson, 1767

Boston Massacre
Incendiary riot on March 5, 1770 when British soldiers fired into a crowd and killed five people

Gaspée incident
Conflict that occurred when colonists from Providence boarded and burned the English naval vessel *Gaspée*

committees of correspondence
Organized groups of letter writers

drafted a circular letter rejecting the Townshend Acts that was sent to all the colonies. Written primarily by Samuel Adams, the letter urged all merchants to enforce the boycott. In one case, colonist John Hancock's sloop *Liberty* arrived in port in Boston with a cargo of wine. Colonists held the customs official hostage as the wine was unloaded without payment of the required duties. Similar protests followed in other towns. In response, the British sent troops to restore order, and by 1770 British troops were quartered in New York, Boston, and other major towns. The conflict was growing increasingly tense.

On March 5, 1770, a crowd of Boston rebels began throwing snowballs, oyster shells, and other debris at a British sentry in front of the Customs House, prompting the British captain to order more guards outside. When a stick hit one of the soldiers, he fell, and someone shouted, "Fire!" prompting a British guard to shoot into the crowd. Hearing the report, other soldiers shot into the crowd, and in the end,

>> A color print of the Boston Massacre by Paul Revere, used as propaganda to spur on the cause of colonial rebellion.

five colonists lay dead and six were wounded. The colonists called this the **Boston Massacre**. Nine British soldiers were tried for the act, and two were convicted of manslaughter (they were all defended by the future president John Adams). The "Massacre" served as important propaganda for the colonial agitators, despite the fact that the English had followed the rule of law and that most of the soldiers were found innocent in a colonial court of law.

Read an eyewitness account of the Boston Massacre.

Repeal

The same day as the Boston Massacre, Parliament repealed most provisions of the Townshend Acts. But, as a symbol of its continued control, Parliament left the tax on tea in place; the colonists accepted the tea tax and dropped their boycott, claiming victory in the conflict.

But this sort of compromise meant that Parliament and the rebelling colonists had not reached a clear agreement, leaving the situation ripe for future conflicts. For the next several years, no major issue emerged to galvanize colonial opposition, lulling many in Britain and in the colonies into the belief that the crisis was over. This was a relief to the Crown, as well as to the many colonists who were content with the colonies' relationship to the royal government. Furthermore, royal officials in America did their best to foster this pacified view, asserting that subordination of the colonies had finally been achieved. This, however, was merely the surface view.

Local Conflicts, 1770–1773

The *Gaspée* Incident

If unified colonial opposition declined between 1770 and 1773, local conflicts continued, demonstrating that colonists remained assertive and that royal control was tenuous. The most noteworthy example was the **Gaspée incident**. In Rhode Island, colonists from Providence boarded and burned an English naval vessel, the *Gaspée*, which had run aground while in pursuit of a colonial ship accused of smuggling. This was quite a radical move. Britain assembled a royal commission of British officials in America to identify the perpetrators and remand them to England for trial. The local commission, however, shortly became the target of colonial protest. **Committees of correspondence**, or organized groups of letter writers, coordinated opposition to the extradition of the suspects, and, as a result, the perpetrators of the *Gaspée* incident were never identified or tried.

© Eon Images

Committees of Correspondence

Massachusetts's colonists also continued their resistance to royal policies. In 1772, several Bostonians set up a committee of correspondence to inform other Massachusetts towns and other colonies of their grievances, "as Men, as Christians, and as Subjects." This organization aimed to stir up dissent and unite the colonists in their opposition. Several other colonists from towns outside of Boston joined these committees, creating a method for the relatively quick transmission of information between the colonies. As letters circulated from one committee to the next, they passed along information, helping to unify opposition to the Crown.

Choosing Sides

Although local colonial opposition to Crown policies was significant between 1770 and 1773, it was not as widespread as the protests that emerged in response to the Stamp Act or the Townshend Acts. And, although some colonial leaders tried to transform local concerns into colonywide grievances, most issues never achieved more than local prominence, mainly because most colonists were reluctant to engage in a full-on confrontation with the Crown.

> Women were the key players in reducing tea consumption, while men were the staunchest advocates of using violent means.

Within cities like Boston, New York, and Philadelphia, wealthy people remained mostly supportive of the Crown, while artisans and merchants, who had been financially stung by several economic acts passed by the Crown, were the most avid patriots. Many people did not favor conflict and could not imagine rebellion. New England's slaves, meanwhile, attempted to use the language of political freedom to their benefit, and in 1773 and 1774 they petitioned the colonial government for their freedom. When the legislature passed a bill on their behalf, the royal governor vetoed it. Regardless, the slaves made it clear that whoever promised to free them would earn their support.

In the Southern Colonies and the Chesapeake, many of the most powerful families remained supportive of the Crown, whose policies had enriched them in the first place. Meanwhile, those living in rural areas were more supportive of the rebels, mainly because they felt slighted by the meager amount of self-rule that the colonial elite granted them. These internal cleavages would persist through the Revolutionary War, although between 1770 and 1773, they were less visible because no single issue materialized to stoke the fires of dissent. In 1773, however, an issue emerged that would prod more and more colonists toward open opposition to royal control.

The Tea Act, 1773

In 1773, Parliament passed the **Tea Act**. The act was designed not to anger the colonists, but to give the East India Company a monopoly on the sale of tea to North America (the company was badly in debt and had influence in Parliament).

The Act

The Tea Act had three provisions: (1) it lowered the colonists' duty on tea; (2) it granted the East India Company the monopoly; and (3) it appointed royal agents who were to pay the duty in England and then sell the tea to the colonists. This last provision meant that colonial merchants could no longer sell tea. Prior to the Tea Act, most colonists had bought smuggled Dutch tea because it was cheaper than the English variety. The Tea Act was designed to bring British tea to the colonies at a lower price, thus undercutting the illegal Dutch trade. Because tea was the most common beverage consumed by the colonists, Parliament and the East India Company hoped that the colonies would be pleased with the measure and buy more tea.

Colonial Response

This was not the case, for two reasons. Naturally, powerful colonial tea merchants were upset at losing the business. In addition, the timing of the act meant that many colonists interpreted it as yet another move to establish Parliament's authority. Radical Whigs pointed out that until 1773 the duty on tea had been paid in Britain. But now, under the Tea Act, the duty would be collected from British agents who had collected the revenue from the Americans. Instead of a tax laid in England and collected in England, it was a tax laid in England and collected in America.

The colonists responded as they had before, only more violently. They published protests and pressured anyone concerned with the enforcement of the law to send tea back to Britain. They forged a campaign of intimidation by threatening anyone who tried to enforce the Act. In short, the colonists

Boston Tea Party
Protest staged December 16, 1773, when an organized squad of roughly sixty colonists dressed as Mohawk Indians boarded Hutchinson's ship and dumped 342 chests of tea into Boston Harbor

planned to nullify the Tea Act by refusing to comply with it. Women were the key players in reducing tea consumption, while men were the staunchest advocates of using violent means.

The Boston Tea Party

Most of the tea-bearing ships that encountered resistance simply returned to England. But in Boston, the tea issue was especially sensitive because Governor Thomas Hutchinson's son was one of the major consignees, and Hutchinson was determined to support his son's enterprise. In addition, Hutchinson viewed the Tea Act as a chance to demonstrate his fidelity to the Crown in the face of the most rebellious colony in North America. Thus, when Bostonians pressed to have the tea returned to England, Hutchinson said that was fine, so long as they paid the tax on the tea first.

The rebelling colonists refused, and in this impasse, the ship simply sat in Boston Harbor. The deadlock could not last: by law, the tax had to be paid within 20 days, which, in this case, meant it had to be paid by December 17, 1773. Governor Hutchinson vowed to have the tea unloaded and the tax paid on the day of the deadline. To prevent this, on the night of December 16, an organized squad of roughly sixty colonists dressed as Mohawk Indians boarded the ship and dumped the entire cargo—342 chests of tea—into Boston Harbor. Historians are unsure why they chose that particular disguise to commit their act of protest.

For Boston radicals and other alert colonists, the **Boston Tea Party** was momentous. Bostonians were proud that they had made a powerful strike against the Crown, and they noted that discipline among their ranks was maintained. Beyond the tea, the squad did not commit vandalism or destroy any other property.

But they also recognized that they had pushed the conflict to a new level. After the destruction of British property, they could only speculate on how the British government would react to this new provocation. Refraining from buying tea was essentially a passive protest; destroying an entire ship's worth was an active protest.

Read a participant's eyewitness account of the Tea Party.

The Coercive Acts, 1774

Parliament's response came quickly. A few members of Parliament argued that the Tea Party's ringleaders should be arrested. The majority disagreed, recalling the failure of the government to bring to trial the perpetrators of the *Gaspée* incident. To avoid the

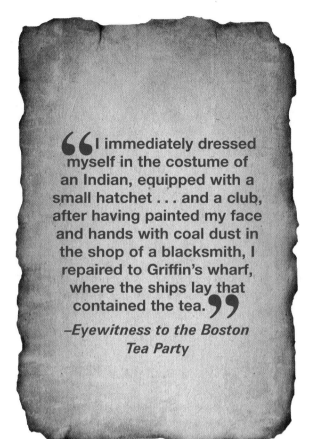

> **"I immediately dressed myself in the costume of an Indian, equipped with a small hatchet . . . and a club, after having painted my face and hands with coal dust in the shop of a blacksmith, I repaired to Griffin's wharf, where the ships lay that contained the tea."**
>
> —*Eyewitness to the Boston Tea Party*

difficulties of prosecuting the individual Bostonians, Parliament opted to pass punitive legislation—the so-called Coercive Acts—in 1774.

The Coercive Acts

The laws that came to be called the **Coercive Acts** actually comprised four separate acts, most of which attempted to punish Massachusetts for the Tea Party. Parliament thought it could attack Massachusetts and thus divide the colonists in order to reconquer them. The four Acts were: (1) the Boston Port Act, which closed Boston's harbor until the town paid for the destroyed tea; (2) the Massachusetts Government Act, which terminated most self-government in the colony; (3) the Administration of Justice Act, which dictated that any British official charged with a capital offense in the colonies could be tried in Great Britain (this issue had arisen after the trials that resulted from the Boston Massacre); and (4) the Quartering Act, which applied to all the colonies and allowed the British Army to house troops wherever necessary, including private buildings.

Read the Coercive Acts.

The Quebec Act

A fifth act followed the same year. In 1774, Parliament passed the Quebec Act, which straightened out several legal issues in Canada. But the act also did two other things: (1) it guaranteed French Canadians the right to practice Roman Catholicism, which appalled the colonists, especially in New England, where almost everyone was a Protestant unaccustomed to accommodating other religions; and (2) the act declared that much of England's holdings across the Proclamation Line of 1763 (everything west of the Appalachian Mountains) would be governed from Quebec. The colonists were infuriated that the Crown was governing this land from the north rather than the east. After all, many colonists felt they had fought for possession of this land during the French and Indian War. The colonists' widespread anti-Catholicism and their land lust led them to link the Quebec Act and the Coercive Acts, referring to them together as **Intolerable Acts**.

Colonial Response

The various acts were intended to break the colonists' spirit, to dissolve colonial unity, and to isolate Massachusetts. But the actual consequences were different. At the most basic level, Bostonians refused to pay the penalties required by the Port Act. A small number of pro-British merchants offered to pay the fines on the city's behalf, but a group of rebellious colonists threatened them, too. The rejection of the offer was a strong measure of the colonists' convictions because the port closure inflicted considerable suffering on the people who depended on trade to maintain their economic well-being.

Through committees of correspondence, colonists everywhere heard of Massachusetts's plight. Virginia, South Carolina, and Connecticut sent food. Unity among the colonies grew and, rather than isolating Massachusetts, the Acts unified the colonies.

The First Continental Congress

This colonial unity is best seen in the meeting of the First Continental Congress. In May 1774, Rhode Island, Pennsylvania, New York, and Virginia called for an intercolony congress to address the growing crisis (doing so without consent from the Crown,

Coercive Acts
Four separate acts, passed in 1774; meant to punish Massachusetts for the Tea Party. The four Acts were: the Boston Port Act, the Massachusetts Government Act, the Administration of Justice Act, and the Quartering Act

Intolerable Acts
Colonists' collective label for the Quebec Act and the Coercive Acts

which was still illegal). In September, delegates from twelve colonies met in the **First Continental Congress** at Philadelphia to consider the American response to the Coercive Acts. Only Georgia was absent, principally because Creek Indians were actively fighting Georgians over western expansion, and the colonists there felt they needed British defensive support.

The delegates considered several plans of action. Ultimately, the congress created the **Continental Association**, which supervised a boycott of British trade. The association was prefaced with a "Declaration of Rights," which asserted the natural-rights foundation of the colonists' resistance, affirming the trio of natural rights put forward by John Locke—"life, liberty, and property." This was not yet independence, though. The delegates to the first Continental Congress tried to maintain a balance between supporting colonists' rights and affirming the role of the Crown. In 1774 they were pursuing autonomy, not independence. They agreed to meet again the next year.

LO⁴ The Shot Heard 'Round the World

Militia Preparations

Meanwhile, back in Boston, local militias were preparing for battle. Parliament, these men felt, had pushed far enough; they would no longer tolerate more infringements on their liberties. Furthermore, who knew what the Crown would do next to plague their economic existence? Massachusetts colonists stockpiled guns in several locations outside Boston, while militia groups drilled defiantly in town squares. They developed a "Provincial Congress," which assumed the role of a colonial government outside the Crown. Other Massachusetts counties organized conventions to unify the resistance. In some areas, colonists opposed the Administration of Justice Act by closing courts rather than permitting the governor's appointed judges to sit.

Other colonies followed Massachusetts's lead, organizing their own provincial congresses, committees, and conventions. Patriots near urban centers formed committees of correspondence in order to circulate news, information, and instructions throughout the colonies. Not all colonists were so enthusiastic for war though, especially outside the cities that were affected most by Britain's policies. But there was a growing sense that the conflict between Britain and its North American colonies might result in a full-scale rebellion.

Britain's Response to the Preparations

The colonists' military preparedness became evident to the British in September 1774, when Massachusetts patriots responded to false rumors that the royal governor had ordered the British Army to seize colonial gunpowder and that British troops had fired on the people of Boston. Roughly three thousand colonists responded to the "Powder Alarm" by converging on Boston, a city of approximately 15,000 inhabitants. Many more patriots were on the road to Boston when news came that the rumors were untrue. The governor, Thomas Gage, realized that his army was outnumbered and that the colonists were prepared to actually fight. In response, he ordered the construction of fortifications across the small strip of land that connected Boston to the mainland and asked Parliament for 20,000 more British troops.

Lexington and Concord

By the spring of 1775, tensions were at a fever pitch. Feeling threatened, the British secretary of state pressured Gage to curb the colonists' military planning. So, in April 1775, Gage sent troops to the town of Concord, about twenty miles northwest of Boston, to capture the colonial military supplies hidden there and to arrest the patriot leaders John Hancock and Samuel Adams.

The British soldiers were thus armed and resolute when they left Boston on April 18, 1775 (see Map 5.1). Despite the soldiers' efforts to move quietly, Boston patriots detected the troop movement and sent Paul Revere, William Dawes, and Dr. Samuel Prescott on horseback to alert the colonists in the countryside between Boston and Concord (only Prescott made it all the way to Concord; the others were captured on the way). On the morning of April 19, a militia assembled in Lexington to halt the British before they reached Concord. The British, still the most powerful army in the world at the time, did not back down. The American militia captain ordered his men (called **"Minutemen"** because they were ready on a minute's notice) to retreat after the much stronger British forces ordered them to disperse. As some of the rebelling colonists retreated, someone fired a shot (both sides later claimed that the other fired first), and the British soldiers began firing on the militia. The colonists suffered eighteen casualties (eight killed and ten wounded), while the British suffered only one.

After the British rout of the Minutemen, the British marched to Concord, but by the time they arrived, Hancock and Adams had fled, and it is uncertain whether the cautious British would have exacerbated the already explosive situation by carrying out the capture of these two prominent colonists. Instead, when they took their position at one end of the North Bridge in Concord, they were met by another armed militia, which positioned itself at the opposite end of the bridge. The militia fired on the British troops and forced them to alter their route back to Boston. This was the first time Americans had fired against the British Army (colloquially referred to as the Redcoats) in a formal confrontation. It was also the first time the Redcoats had been forced to retreat in the face of an American enemy.

The Minutemen made the Redcoats' return to Boston a nightmare. Militiamen gathered from surrounding towns to pursue the British the entire way, firing from behind stone walls and trees. The British suffered heavy casualties and, once in Boston, found themselves besieged by thousands more militiamen. Over the course of the day, the Americans suffered 95 casualties, while the British suffered 273, including 73 dead. This was a marked escalation of the colonial conflict; for the first time, Americans had killed British soldiers in battle.

Watch a film about Lexington, Concord, and the "shot heard 'round the world."

Colonial Response to Lexington and Concord

Following the battles of Lexington and Concord, the colonists had to determine what their best response might be. Had an all-out war begun? What about the many colonists who did not support the rebellion?

On May 10, 1775, the **Second Continental Congress** gathered in Philadelphia to answer this

Map 5.1
Lexington, Concord, and Boston, 1775

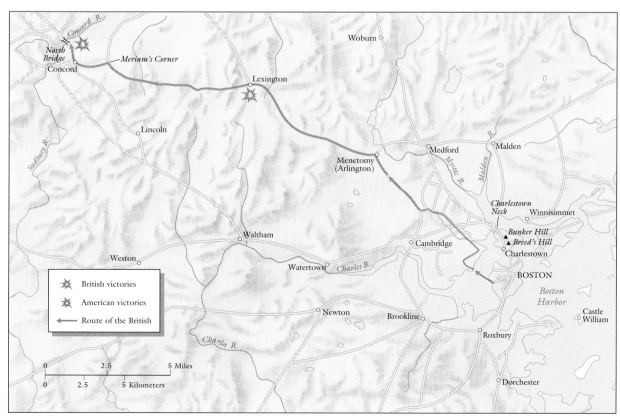

Legend:
- ✸ British victories
- ✸ American victories
- ← Route of the British

question. The congress enacted several policies, including acknowledging the militia companies surrounding Boston as the core of a new "Continental Army" and appointing as its general a Virginian, George Washington. (The selection of a Virginian was meant to balance the predominance of Massachusetts militiamen in the army, thus showing colonial unity.) The Second Continental Congress passed resolutions supporting war, which included a sharp rejection of all authority under the king in America. It also adopted the "Declaration of the Causes and Necessity of Taking up Arms." These were bold, brave actions, although no one was sure whether this was a battle over grievances against Parliament or one with a goal of independence.

Regardless, without formally declaring the colonies' independence, the Continental Congress was beginning to behave more like the government of an independent nation than that of a territory within an empire. The congress remained cautious about the word *independence*, though, and in July 1775 it approved the "**Olive Branch Petition**," written by John Dickinson, which declared that the colonists were still loyal to King George III and implored the king to seek a peaceful resolution to the conflict. The king ignored the petition, viewing the colonists as insubordinate subjects of the Crown.

The Battle of Bunker Hill

Within weeks, the hesitancy shown at the Second Continental Congress vanished. Local battles inspired this eagerness, especially the biggest battle, which occurred in Boston. After Lexington and Concord, thousands of men from throughout the colonies joined the Minutemen around Boston to besiege the British military. On June 17, 1775, the British Army sent troops across the Charles River to capture the colonists' cannons located on Breed's Hill, which overlooked Boston and was connected to nearby Bunker Hill by a saddle of land. The colonists had fortified Breed's Hill because they could fire their cannons at British ships in Boston Harbor from there. The ensuing battle was fought primarily on Breed's Hill but came to be known as the **Battle of Bunker Hill**. It was the first all-out battle of the Revolutionary War. Although British troops forced the patriots to abandon their hilltop position, the colonists inflicted heavy casualties on the British. In one particularly brutal episode, the British lost one thousand men in an hour. The British killed around four hundred Minutemen.

> For the first time, Americans had killed British soldiers in battle.

THE FIGHT AT CONCORD BRIDGE, APRIL 19, 1775.

© North Wind Picture Archives/Alamy

What else was happening . . .

1700s	American innkeepers think nothing of requesting that a guest share his bed with a stranger when accommodations become scarce.
1760s	Because the British Macaroni Club's members are known for having affected manners and long, curled hair, "macaroni" becomes a slang term for "dandy." The song "Yankee Doodle" is invented by the British to insult American colonists. The section where Doodle puts a feather in his cap and calls it macaroni is a slap at the ragged bands of American troops.
1769	Shoelaces are invented in England.
1772	Joseph Priestley invents soda water.
1773	Seamstress Betsy Ross and her husband, John, begin renting the Philadelphia house where she will sew the first American flag.

And in the end . . .

When news of the Battle of Bunker Hill spread through the colonies and reached Britain, it had two key effects: (1) it prompted thousands of additional colonists to join the opposition to Britain, as small conflicts spread across the land; and (2) it convinced Britain that many colonists, not just a handful of troublemakers, were part of the rebellion.

Because of this realization, Parliament issued the **American Prohibitory Act**, which declared the colonies to be "in open rebellion," forbade commerce with the colonies by blockading their ports, and made colonial ships and their cargo subject to seizure as if they were the property "of open enemies." Now that Parliament had declared the colonies to be in rebellion, this meant that any leaders who were caught could be tried for treason and executed. This raised the stakes dramatically. A rebellion was turning into a revolution.

American Prohibitory Act
This Act declared the colonies to be "in open rebellion," forbade commerce with the colonies by blockading their ports, and made colonial ships and their cargo subject to seizure as if they were the property "of open enemies"

6

The Revolution

Learning Outcomes

After reading this chapter, you should be able to do the following:

LO **1** Describe the long-term causes and more immediate events that led the colonists into a true revolution against Britain.

LO **2** Discuss the various phases of the American Revolution, and analyze the circumstances that eventually helped the colonists win a conflict that Britain, by rights, should never have lost.

LO **3** Assess the significance of the American Revolution to the following groups: colonists, slaves, native populations, and women.

> **"** *Ostensibly, the battle was between freedom and tyranny (if you were a patriot), or about the responsibilities of being an Englishman (if you were a Loyalist).* **"**

After the "long train of abuses" leading up to the Declaration of Independence, from 1776 to 1783 American patriots fought a difficult war with Britain. Ostensibly, the battle was between freedom and tyranny (if you were a patriot), or about the responsibilities of being an Englishman (if you were a Loyalist). In reality, choosing sides was much more personal, depending, for instance, on whether your landlord was a Loyalist or a patriot, whether you thought political freedom would improve your business, or whether you felt the earnings you made from a slave-based economy were threatened. All colonists, of course, were forced to choose sides, although many remained ambivalent about each position. Loyalists were scorned, but revolutionaries would be punished brutally if their side lost the war. Choosing sides was no small matter, and the consequences could be deadly.

But the war and the political independence that followed made up only one of several revolutions that took place during these years. The revolutionary war brought with it fundamental questions about freedom and liberty, and about what kind of society Americans wanted. How far would the American Revolution go in promoting equality? Would economic and educational differences be eradicated by a leveling state? Would slavery be abolished? How different would the new society look compared with the old?

LO¹ From Rebellion to Revolution

Underlying Causes

There were both long-term, underlying causes for the revolution and short-term, precipitating events. Between 1660 and 1763, the colonies had formed a unique society distinct from that of England. Perhaps most importantly, they had developed a dynamic economy in manufacturing and developing goods, as well as supplying raw materials to trading partners in both the Old and New Worlds. In other words, the colonies were not just a primary economic supplier (supplying raw materials to a mother country), but a well-rounded economic system unto themselves. Of course, many wealthy southerners owed their fortunes to slave-based cash crops that were then traded with England, so these colonists shied away from confrontation with the Crown. Nevertheless, large sectors of the North American economy were becoming increasingly independent of England.

© iStockphoto.com/Sean Locke

Along similar lines, property ownership was more common in the colonies compared to England. This meant that, with the notable exception of slaves, the people working the land owned it, which gave them something to fight for should their position be threatened. The colonies also had developed without the titled aristocracy or widespread poverty found in England, two further factors in making the colonies an entity unique from England. And, in fact, each colony had developed a self-elected government, something they were not willing to give up easily.

Precipitating Events

These long-term causes could not have detonated into a war without several precipitating sparks. Three were substantial: (1) increased local conflicts; (2) the uncompromising attitude of Britain; and (3) a shift in opinion among the colonists—toward revolution.

The Widening War

At the local level, the war's scope was widening even before any official declaration of war. In 1775, for instance, Ethan Allen and his "Green Mountain Boys" attacked and captured Britain's Fort Ticonderoga and Crown Point in backwoods New York. The Continental Army invaded Canada and captured Montreal but failed to capture Quebec. In Charleston, patriots beat back an attack by a British fleet. Virginians forced the royal governor, Lord Dunmore, to retreat from the mainland to a British warship in the harbor at Norfolk. These local conflicts, organized without assistance of any unified colonial body, indicated a widening war between England and the colonies.

Lord Dunmore's actions are significant, however, for another reason. After retreating to an offshore ship as he awaited British military support, Dunmore issued a proclamation offering freedom to any slave who agreed to fight for the British. His program, "Liberty to Slaves,"

>> The King's uncompromising attitude presented the colonists with few options other than revolution.

angered the colonists, who would later cite Dunmore's actions in the Declaration of Independence. To many colonists, liberty was meant only for Europeans and Euro-Americans, and it stung that the governor was offering it to slaves. Within weeks of Dunmore's call, between five hundred and six hundred slaves responded, and before the war was over, several thousand more fought for Britain and for their freedom. Only during the final months of the war were colonists forced to press slaves into service, delaying doing so mostly because they feared arming them as enemies.

Learn more about Lord Dunmore and read his proclamation.

Uncompromising Britain

As the war widened, King George III grew increasingly angry at the colonies for their continued insubordination. He rejected the "Olive Branch Petition" of the Second Continental Congress. He denounced the colonists as rebels in August 1775. He hired mercenaries from Germany, called "Hessians," to fight the colonists. And in December 1775 he closed all American ports. This last action was particularly significant because it made independence absolutely necessary in order to open trade with other countries. The King's uncompromising attitude presented the colonists with few options other than revolution.

The Shift in American Opinion

Finally, popular opinion had gradually shifted toward independence. In the end, somewhere between one-fifth and one-third of the colonists remained loyal to Britain throughout the war. Most prominent in this group were wealthy landholders and slave owners who had the most to lose in a revolution. Furthermore, a large percentage of colonists remained indifferent to both the British and the revolutionaries. Nevertheless, the decline of salutary neglect and the spread of local violence led many colonists to side with the revolutionaries. Thus, in addition to this being a revolutionary war, it was also very much a civil war.

Choosing Sides

The Loyalists

Why remain loyal? Colonists were reluctant to withdraw from the British Empire for at least six reasons:

- Many still felt a strong attachment to Britain, and many still had family and friends there.
- Many also had strong commercial ties with Britain (the slave-based economy of the southern colonies was particularly dependent on such trade). To rebel was to risk their present and future wealth.
- Some feared that France or Spain might take over if Britain was driven out of the colonies, and they preferred British rule to that of some other European nation.
- Some of the smaller religious groups felt that Britain had protected them from more powerful denominations that could potentially flourish if the new American state adopted a national religion.
- Economically, it was often a matter of settling small scores. If, for instance, your landlord was a revolutionary, you were likely to be a Loyalist; if your landlord was a Loyalist, you were likely to be a patriot.
- Some colonists doubted the colonies' ability to throw off British rule. After all, Britain was the most powerful nation in the world, with the mightiest army.

© Powered by Light/Alan Spencer/Alamy

Although all the colonies had some pro-Crown families, geographically most Loyalists lived in the southern colonies and New York.

The Revolutionaries

Why revolt? Each rebelling colonist had a different motive for supporting a break with England, and these reasons were just as complicated as those for remaining loyal.

Personal and commercial considerations were vitally important. But perhaps most influential was the ideology of republicanism. **Republicanism** was the idea that government should be based on the consent of the governed and that the people had a duty to ensure that their government did not infringe on individual rights. The American Revolution was the first serious modern attempt to craft a government based on these principles.

Republicanism set down deep roots in England before it flowered on American soil. The British Radical Whigs of the 1600s, for example, harked back to the classical Roman ideal of a "republican society," in which governmental power was curtailed by the actions of the people, who were presumed to be virtuous and willing to sacrifice for the public good. Drawing on these Roman ideals, the Radical Whigs outlined a theory according to which a government was legitimate only when it was based on an agreement between the members of a society and government. In this formulation, the members of society would agree to sacrifice a degree of liberty and the government would maintain security and order, but otherwise avoid infringing on a person's access to life, liberty or property. Any ruler who transgressed natural laws was a tyrant, and under tyranny the rebellion of a people was justifiable. (Republicanism was different from liberalism, which viewed any government as an unwanted infringement on individual liberty.)

Republican ideas spread throughout the colonies in the 1700s, mainly by the work of two English authors—John Trenchard and Thomas Gordon—who wrote a short book called **Cato's Letters**. In America, Cato's Letters and other Radical Whig writings were quoted every time Britain attempted to raise taxes after the French and Indian War.

But the best known expression of republican ideas in revolutionary America was corset maker

Republicanism
The theory that government should be based on the consent of the governed and that the governed had a duty to ensure that their government did not infringe on individual rights

Cato's Letters
Book that spread Republican ideas throughout the colonies; written by English authors John Trenchard and Thomas Gordon

Common Sense
Influential political pamphlet written by Thomas Paine, published in January 1776, containing a simple wording of republican ideals

Thomas Paine's political pamphlet *Common Sense*, published in January 1776. Its simple wording of republican ideals nudged the colonists further toward independence. Paine asserted that the king never had the welfare of his subjects in mind and that he was entirely concerned with his own exercise of power. Paine also argued that independence was the only answer to this problem, using language so powerful that it made any other course of action seem absurd. He set forth a vision of America as a dynamic, independent nation, growing in population and prosperity, with a kindly government doing a substantial amount of economic and political leveling to ensure equality. Pointing to the tremendous growth of the American colonies in the eighteenth century, Paine argued that America was more than just capable of maintaining independence from Britain; America was so strong, he claimed, that independence was inevitable.

Paine's pamphlet was enormously influential in changing the minds of those who had opposed independence. Emerging just as local conflicts

© iStockphoto.com/Mark Grenier

>> *Common Sense* was reprinted several times; in total, 150,000 copies were distributed throughout the colonies—a number equivalent to 15 million copies being distributed in the United States today.

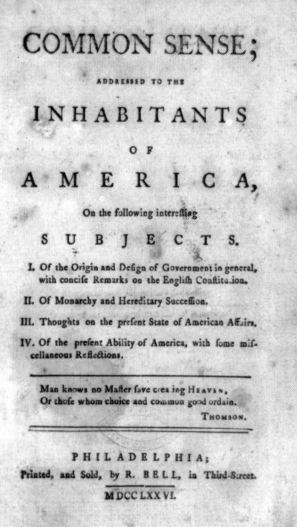

COMMON SENSE;

ADDRESSED TO THE

INHABITANTS

OF

AMERICA,

On the following interesting

SUBJECTS.

I. Of the Origin and Design of Government in general, with concise Remarks on the English Constitution.

II. Of Monarchy and Hereditary Succession.

III. Thoughts on the present State of American Affairs.

IV. Of the present Ability of America, with some miscellaneous Reflections.

Man knows no Master save creating HEAVEN,
Or those whom choice and common good ordain.
THOMSON.

PHILADELPHIA;

Printed, and Sold, by R. BELL, in Third-Street.

MDCCLXXVI.

© Eon Images

spread, *Common Sense* was reprinted several times; in total, 150,000 copies were distributed throughout the colonies—a number equivalent to 15 million copies being distributed in the United States today.

Explore an interactive module on choosing sides in the American Revolution.

Read *Common Sense*.

The Declaration of Independence

The increase of local conflicts, Britain's inflexibility, and the spreading of republican ideals made a break

with Britain inevitable by 1776. But independence was expedited further by events on the ground. In March 1776, the Continental Army forced the British to evacuate Boston, ending the eleven-month siege of the city that had begun after Lexington and Concord and the Battle of Bunker Hill. Rather than sail for home, however, the British army headed for New York, where more Loyalists resided than in any other colony. Rather than establish their base where the colonists were united in opposition (Boston), the British hoped to divide the colonies by setting their base of operations in an area less committed to independence.

The Drafting

With this crisis at hand, Richard Henry Lee, a Virginia delegate to the Continental Congress, proposed, on June 7, 1776, that the colonies officially declare their independence. With regional balance in mind, the congress created a committee to draft a declaration. The committee consisted of John Adams of Massachusetts, Roger Sherman of Connecticut, Robert R. Livingston of New York, Benjamin Franklin of Pennsylvania, and Thomas Jefferson of Virginia, who was selected as the principal draftsman. After the committee made minor revisions to Jefferson's first draft, the committee presented the Declaration of Independence to the congress on June 28, 1776.

> View a film about the drafting of the Declaration of Independence.

> Read the Declaration.

The Declaration

The document consisted of two parts: (1) a preamble justifying the revolution on the basis of natural rights, as espoused in the language of republicanism and (2) a list of grievances accusing George III of tyranny and therefore justifying revolt.

The Signing

Once the congress had read the Declaration, they debated it and made several major changes (the most important one was deleting Jefferson's tortured assertions that England had been responsible for implanting the evil institution of slavery in the New World and then, through Lord Dunmore, provoking slave rebellions). Then the Continental Congress unanimously approved the Declaration of Independence on July 2, 1776, by a vote of 12 to 0. (The delegation from New York abstained from voting because it had not received instructions from its colony legislature, but the delegates themselves stated that they were in favor of independence.) Two days later, on July 4, John Hancock, as president of the congress, may have signed the edited document; other delegates added their signatures to a clean copy of the Declaration in early August. But with the congress's July 2, 1776 declaration, the Revolution now had a goal—political independence for the American colonies. What had begun as a struggle to secure the rights and liberties that the colonists felt they deserved as British subjects had become a war to secure American nationhood.

LO² The War for Independence
The Opposing Sides
The Continental Army

The colonists had declared their independence, but now they would have to fight for it. But how could they? They had long been protected by the British, and, other than a few small colonial militias, they had no standing army.

>> **The army of the patriots was often ill equipped, undermanned, and hungry.**

Efforts to build one began in earnest even before the Declaration of Independence. It was an uphill battle. The army of the patriots, called the Continental Army, was often ill equipped, undermanned, and hungry. From the beginning, recruitment was a problem. Many colonists wanted freedom, but not many wanted to give their lives for it. The Continental Congress had to offer large bounties of land to induce men to enlist, and eventually it reduced the term of service to just three months. Congress set enlistment quotas for all the new states, but the states rarely met them. At any given time, there were usually ten thousand poorly trained troops in the Continental Army. They were usually hungry and unpaid, but the Continental Congress could not help because it did not have much money itself. As fighting progressed, the army had to live off the kindness of surrounding farmers (hoping they were patriots and not Loyalists).

The Continental Army acted under the orders of George Washington, a patrician Virginia tobacco farmer whose wealth came from his wife's family. He believed in the republican ideology to the very marrow of his bones. And he had a brilliant grasp of the war's military strategy. He recognized that, because of the ideological nature of the revolution and the nature of his ragtag army, his chances would be better if he did not try to win every battle. Indeed, if he refused to engage the British at all and made them wear themselves out in pursuing him, he could win simply by surviving.

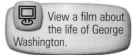

View a film about the life of George Washington.

The Revolutionary Government and Finances

Washington received his orders from the Continental Congress, the only centralized authority in the colonies, although it had no legal standing or charter document. The Continental Congress could only request assistance from the various states, which had no obligation to grant those requests. Although the revolutionaries planned a national government in 1777, its founding charter (the Articles of Confederation) was not completed until 1781. Throughout the revolutionary war, then, the revolutionaries had no official central authority.

This hindered them organizationally, and worse, it meant that the revolutionaries could not easily raise money. They had neither the power to levy

> The main way they raised money was simply to print it and hope people would accept the bills.

George Washington

© George Washington in the uniform of a Colonel of the Virginia Militia during the French & Indian War (1755–63) (colour litho), Peale, Charles Willson (1741–1827) (after)/Private Collection, Peter Newark American Pictures/The Bridgeman Art Library

© iStockphoto.com/Lee Pettet

taxes nor the infrastructure of a treasury. The main way they raised money was simply to print it and hope people would accept the bills. The Continental Congress issued these **bills of credit** throughout the war. The states issued their own money as well, almost all of which was generally more stable than the Continental dollars. Toward the end of the war, the phrase "not worth a Continental" became common, suggesting the centralized currency's lack of buying power and the widespread lack of faith in it. Only after 1781, when Robert Morris became superintendent of finance, did monetary conditions improve, mainly because he could borrow from friendly European nations.

Read more about how the revolutionaries paid for the war.

The British Army

The British, on the other hand, had the most powerful army in the world, supremacy of the seas, and an organized hierarchy of authority that extended all the way to the king. But it also had the more difficult military task of trying to destroy Washington's army, which was adept at running up hills and into forests in order to avoid being captured. The Crown sent seasoned British troops who were well armed and accustomed to large battles on vast battlefields. It also had hired German mercenaries, the Hessians, to fight the revolutionaries. Many times, the British outnumbered the revolutionaries and were better trained and better armed, but they confronted three insurmountable problems: (1) Britain could never supply its troops adequately, especially as Washington prolonged the war by constantly retreating inland, away from places where British ships could easily resupply British troops; (2) Washington avoided directly engaging the British troops, so the regimented British army was subjected to unaccustomed guerrilla warfare as it chased him around the countryside; and (3) other European nations (notably France) eventually supported the revolutionaries. These other nations were only too glad to see mighty Britain humbled by upstart New World backwoodsmen.

The First Phase of the War, 1775–1779

The first half of the war took place in the North (see Map 6.1 on page 103). The

bills of credit
Currency printed by the Continental Congress

second half was fought in the South. Generally speaking, the Americans' strategy was to run and survive. They attacked only when they were convinced of victory.

Early British Successes

After evacuating Massachusetts in March 1776, the British army repositioned on Long Island and pressed to drive patriot forces from New York City. Their goal was to isolate New England (which it saw as the center of resistance) by taking control of New York City and the Great Lakes, then subduing the South, leaving Massachusetts stranded in its revolutionary fervor.

In July 1776, 34,000 British troops delivered a crushing defeat to the patriots on Long Island. They forced the revolutionary army of 18,000 to give up New York City. The patriots withdrew all the way to New Jersey, then to Pennsylvania. Fleeing was militarily embarrassing and bad for morale, but it was tactically sound: so long as the Continental Army remained intact, the colonies were still fighting for independence.

Crossing the Delaware

This first loss was a terrible blow to morale. Recruitment suffered, and Washington realized he needed a victory. Furthermore, most of Washington's soldiers were enlisted only through the end of 1776, so Washington feared that without a victory before the end of the year, the majority of his soldiers would not

© Eon Images

>> **The American victory at Trenton, after Washington's crossing the Delaware, had little strategic significance, but it boosted morale and energized the revolution.**

Battle of Saratoga Battle in New York state in 1777 between the Continental Army and General Burgoyne's British army troops; Burgoyne surrendered

reenlist. Washington decided on a bold, brilliant action. On Christmas night 1776, the army crossed the ice-filled Delaware River and captured Trenton, New Jersey, which at the time was held by 1,500 Hessian mercenaries working for the British army. The American victory at Trenton had little strategic significance, but it boosted morale and energized the revolution.

Reversal of Fortune

Because the loss at Trenton was of minor strategic importance, the British let it go, and, in 1777, British leaders planned a two-pronged invasion that they hoped would finish off the war. British General John Burgoyne was to lead his army south from Canada. At the same time, General William Howe was to capture Philadelphia, the seat of the colonial government, then sail up the Hudson River to join Burgoyne, completely isolating New England and testing the revolutionaries' unity.

At first, the plan was successful. Burgoyne's army captured outposts in New York (Fort Ticonderoga) and began moving south. Meanwhile, Howe drove the patriots from Philadelphia on September 26, 1777 (forcing the Continental Congress to flee the capital), and headed north. Then the British faced obstacles. General Burgoyne's troops were slowed by assorted Loyalists seeking protection from the revolutionary fervor of the northern states, which allowed guerrilla fighters and an organized camp of the Continental Army to catch up and harass the British troops. By the time Burgoyne neared the Hudson River, the Americans had forced him to halt, and, while he waited for reinforcements, 6,000 Continental soldiers surrounded him. Recognizing their advantage, the Americans attacked. At the end of the fighting, Burgoyne surrendered all 5,700 men who remained of his army. This was the **Battle of Saratoga**. The American victory there proved two things: that the patriots could defeat sizeable regiments of the larger British army and that, if the British were to win this war, it was going to be a long, expensive affair.

Read a secret "spy" letter from Howe to Burgoyne.

The French Alliance

The Battle of Saratoga was also significant in that it convinced several European powers to fight against the British, including Spain and the Dutch. Obtaining the support of France, however, was key. The French

From the perspective of the winter at Valley Forge, the revolutionary war would not last long.

F.C. YOHN

allied themselves with the Americans for two reasons: they wanted to help weaken the British Empire, and they wanted access to New World trading posts, which they had lost in the French and Indian War. Up until this point, the French had been reluctant to advocate a losing cause, however, and the Saratoga victory helped alleviate these concerns.

In addition to France's backing, the Americans also received aid from an influential Frenchman. The Marquis de Lafayette, a nineteen-year-old nobleman committed to the Republican cause in France, volunteered for the American fight. Lafayette became an instrumental leader in the American army and played a key role in several pivotal American victories. The youngest of all the generals in the war, Lafayette successfully lobbied the French to more fully support the patriots' cause.

The Winter of 1777–1778

Aside from the victory at Saratoga and the French commitment to enter the conflict, the Americans were slowly losing the war. General Howe's forces were continually besting George Washington's troops, enabling the British to capture Philadelphia and other locations. And Washington, keeping with his chief tactic, kept on running. As a result,

Map 6.1
Revolutionary War in the North

 View an interactive version of this map.

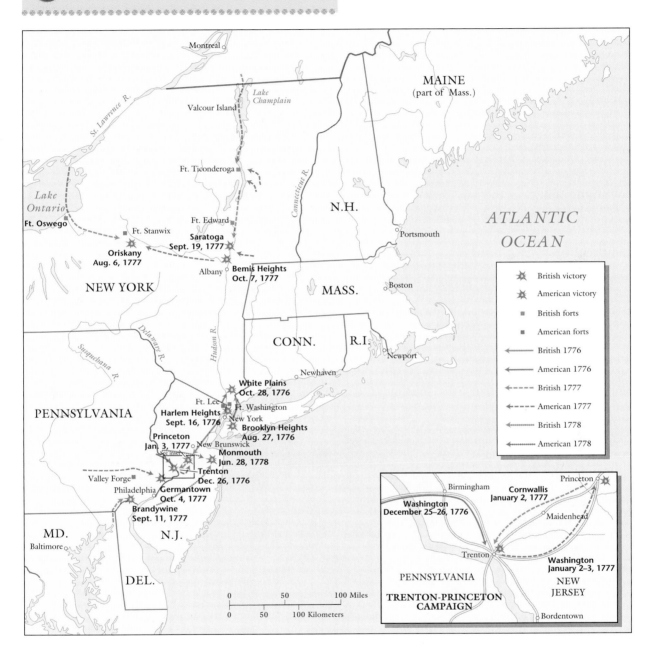

while Howe's army wintered in the comforts of Philadelphia, Washington and his army stayed twenty miles away in the wilderness of Valley Forge, Pennsylvania. It was a harsh winter, and Washington's men were close to starvation. They were poorly equipped and, although the country had enjoyed one of its best harvests ever, the congress had allowed the military supply system to deteriorate into chaos. The men's clothes were threadbare and the troops were losing heart. From the perspective of the winter at Valley Forge, the revolutionary war would not last long.

The Second Phase of the War, 1778–1781

A Peace Offering

But the victory at Saratoga reemerged to stimulate the revolutionary fervor once again. When the snow finally melted, the colonists realized the British had changed tactics. The patriots' victory at Saratoga meant that Britain had to commit more troops to America, and to do this it needed to raise money, most plausibly by raising taxes in England. This was unpopular in England, and the people's resistance to increased taxes forced Parliament to make a peace offering to the revolutionaries. Parliament's offering would have maintained the colonial status of America but abandoned British attempts to tax them—returning things to the way they had been in 1763. To the patriots, this offer was unacceptable; they now wanted freedom.

Giving up on New England

So instead of attempting the costly venture of replacing Burgoyne's troops in an effort to capture New England, the British planned to contain New England by holding New York, while harassing the coastline and the South (see Map 6.2). They also aimed to demoralize the patriots and break the will of the fighters. For example, the British recognized that the American treasury had little to offer its generals, so the British tried to "buy" major American leaders, hoping that the defection of prominent patriots would spread disaffection. The purchase of General Benedict Arnold in 1779 (for more than £10,000) was their chief victory on this front. But aside from Arnold, Britain's bribery policy proved unsuccessful.

Britain's Southern Plan

Meanwhile, the British prepared to invade the southern colonies. British leaders understood that the South possessed more abundant natural resources than the North, so they sought to preserve their claim to at least that region. They also believed that Loyalists were abundant in the South, so they hoped to exacerbate divisions along Loyalist–patriot lines. They had several reasons to believe this, the main one being that, in the South, the revolutionary war really was a civil war. This civil war was being fought between frontiersmen, who generally favored independence, and landholders, who usually sided with the British in order to protect their assets. These two factions had battled among themselves during the early years of the war in countless backwoods battles. The British miscalculated in their estimation of Loyalist support in the South, however. For one thing, Loyalists lacked the fervor and militancy of the patriots. For another, Loyalists were not as prevalent as British leaders had hoped. The British plan was doomed from the beginning.

In 1779, the British landed a large army at Charleston. Commanded by General Sir Charles Cornwallis, the army speedily captured Savannah, Georgia, and Charleston, South Carolina. Through 1780, Cornwallis continued to capture southern towns, and he planned to march north to subdue the rest of the colonies, particularly Virginia, which he viewed as crucial to holding the South.

Washington and Greene's Strategy for Victory

In 1780, the Continental Army in the South, now led by Nathanael Greene, attempted to counter Cornwallis's successes by fleeing inland, sucking the British army farther into the continent, away from the coast and easily accessible British support. This approach served two purposes: it stretched British supply lines, and it countered British attempts to rally Loyalist opposition. By drawing the British away from their supplies, Greene hoped to force them to "live off the land," a military euphemism for stealing food from the populace. Greene and Washington expected that any support for the British would evaporate as hungry British soldiers began to raid farms.

Their plan succeeded. For several months, Cornwallis pursued the Continental Army across the Carolinas. British supplies gradually ran low and, just as Washington and Greene had predicted, the troops began stealing from once-sympathetic farmers. On top of this, when the two armies actually fought, the

> **❝**I saw several of the men roast their old shoes and eat them, and I was afterwards informed by one of the officers' waiters, that some of the officers killed and ate a favorite little dog that belonged to one of them.**❞**
> —*Joseph Plumb Martin, Continental soldier, on northern campaigns of the winter of 1780*

Map 6.2
Revolutionary War in the South

View an interactive version of this map.

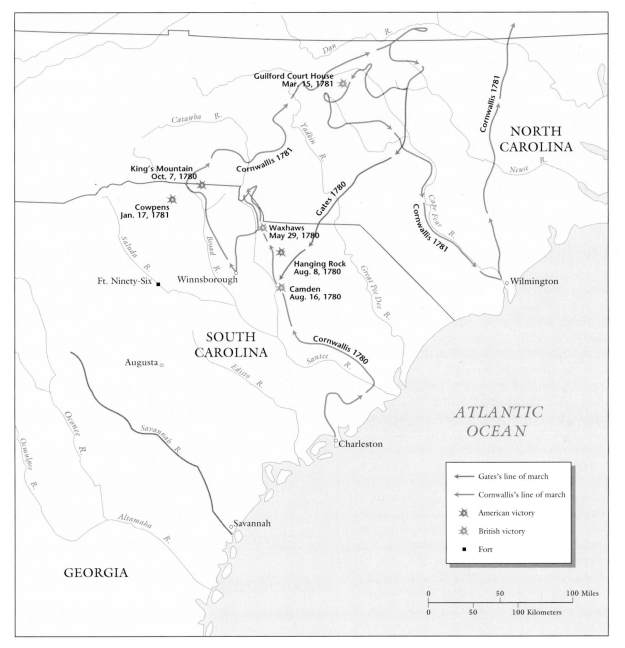

Map legend:
- Gates's line of march
- Cornwallis's line of march
- American victory
- British victory
- Fort

Continental soldiers inflicted major casualties on the British. Although the British won most of the engagements, meaning that they took control of the territory being fought over, the Continental strategies made British victories costly.

Read a Continental soldier's account of his experiences in 1780.

In early 1781, Cornwallis was forced to cease his pursuit and take his army north, into Virginia, to await reinforcements. Faced with mounting casualties, he planned to reunite with his naval fleet at Chesapeake Bay.

Yorktown and Victory

The problem with Cornwallis's plan was positioning: while Cornwallis waited for the British fleet (which the French had forced to retreat to New York), his army was stranded at the tip of the Yorktown peninsula in Virginia. Washington seized the opportunity to attack. He moved a combined force of American and French troops across the lower peninsula; the American victory was complete when the French naval fleet arrived just before the British fleet could rescue Cornwallis's 27,000-man army.

After a night of bombardment, on October 19, 1781, Cornwallis turned his sword over to Washington. More accurately, an emissary for Cornwallis handed it to American General Benjamin Lincoln, whom Washington appointed to accept the surrender when he learned that the British commander had refused to offer his sword personally. When news of Cornwallis's surrender reached England, King George III grudgingly accepted defeat.

Newburgh Conspiracy

It took more than a year after the last major battle before a peace treaty was crafted, however, and while negotiations were ongoing, the armies remained mobilized. Unpaid and undersupplied, several American military leaders proposed a coup, seeking to take control from the relatively impotent Continental Congress in order to implement a tax to pay for unpaid expenses, including their own salaries. The Continental Army was at the time positioned in Newburgh, New York, about 60 miles north of New York City, which was still occupied by the British, and thus the plan became called the Newburgh Conspiracy. With the British in close striking range, any hint of turmoil within the Continental Army might have provoked Britain to resume hostilities. But Washington rapidly quashed the proposed conspiracy, principally by demonstrating the costs of the war on him personally. The generals were not the only ones who had suffered during the war, he said, reminding them that independence was more consequential than worldly gain. Washington's words derailed the revolt, but the unrest demonstrated the significance of the peace treaty that was to come.

Peace Negotiations, 1782–1783

Conflicts Among the Allies

With battle over, the American team of negotiators—Benjamin Franklin, John Jay, and John Adams—found themselves in a difficult situation. They traveled to Paris for the talks in 1782, with instructions to consult with the French. However, the Americans knew that both France and its ally, Spain, had territorial goals of their own in the New World, goals that the Americans did not want to encourage. As a result, Franklin, Jay, and Adams determined that it was in their best interest to negotiate with the British separately and deal with the French later.

The Treaty of Paris

The treaty that Franklin, Jay, and Adams fashioned in 1782 included so many provisions favorable to the Americans that it has frequently been called the greatest triumph in the history of American diplomacy. To guarantee that France did not have the best trading rights to the New World, Britain offered generous terms to the Americans in terms of land and trading rights. America and Britain signed a treaty in November 1782. In doing so, Franklin, Adams, and Jay violated one of the provisions of the Franco-American Alliance of 1778: namely, that neither France nor America would negotiate a separate peace with the British. Nevertheless, the French were eager to end the war, and on January 2, 1783, preliminary treaties were signed between Britain and France and Britain and Spain, and on February 4 hostilities formally ceased. All parties signed the Treaty of Paris in September 1783.

There were five major parts to the Treaty of Paris of 1783: (1) American independence; (2) American expansion west to the Mississippi River and north to the Great Lakes (a much greater area than Americans had thus far settled); (3) freedom of all parties to travel the Mississippi River; (4) that Spain would retain control of Florida; and (5) that "no lawful impediment" be placed on British merchants seeking to recoup debts from America.

View a map of America after the Treaty of Paris.

LO³ Significance of the War

The six long years of the Revolutionary War were filled with suffering. A doctor in the Continental Army suggested that American losses totaled 70,000, but the number of war-related deaths was more likely 25,000, with perhaps another 25,000 injured. Disease and infection killed off many more. Indeed, the war took place in the midst of a widespread smallpox epidemic, which may have killed as many as 130,000 colonists. (Washington wisely had his troops inoculated, perhaps his smartest move in the entire campaign.)

Furthermore, the war had divided the colonists between Loyalists, rebels, and those who were indifferent to either side. It had also greatly disrupted daily life, as soldiers were recruited to join the army and leave their families for extended periods of time, women were asked to shoulder a heavier burden in their household and in civic life, and slaves contemplated their future in a new American republic, one that showed little sign of granting them freedom. Beyond this disruption of daily life, the American war for independence had six major results.

The Impact on Politics

Politically, the American Revolution was the first world conflict whose winners embraced the promise of the Enlightenment. In promising the "natural rights" of life, liberty, and property, the American Revolution served as an ideological model for later revolutions in France and in Central and South America, among others.

But the revolution was not just a bellwether of liberty, it was also a bellwether of republican democracy. The American revolutionaries hoped that their struggles would curb the system of Old World aristocracy. They no longer wanted to be ruled by a few powerful people with long-entrenched methods of perpetuating their wealth and status. Many also did not want an established church that denied the freedom of belief. No one was sure what would arise in the place of Old World aristocracy, but they knew that, after the revolution, the old system was dead. Eventually, this awareness would lead to the formal separation of church and state and limited (but growing) access to the ballot. (During the revolutionary era, access to the ballot was still dependent on owning property, which usually excluded women and African Americans, but the revolution geared up the machinery for a more expansive democracy in the future.)

The Impact on American Nationalism

Before the American Revolution, the colonists living in what became the United States did not think of themselves as having a national culture fundamentally unique from England's. In terms of nationality, most colonists considered themselves as their great-grandfathers were, English. But the French and Indian War and the American Revolution unified the colonists under a new, ideological definition of what it meant to be an American. A nation is composed of people who recognize that they share certain qualities that set them apart from other nations, whether those qualities are ideological, political, linguistic, religious, cultural, racial, or historical. For Americans, in the revolutionary era and after, a strong belief in democracy and the experience of fighting for their political independence was the impetus for the mounting tide of patriotism that followed the Revolutionary War.

Explore an interactive module about building a new nation through symbols.

The Impact on Slavery

The Revolutionary War also illustrated the contradiction between slavery and liberty, and triggered the abolition of slavery in the North. During the war, slaves participated in the fight on both sides, although the British welcomed them more willingly than the revolutionaries. Cornwallis himself employed 5,000 slaves, promising to free them after

© American School/The Bridgeman Art Library/Getty Images

>> **The experience of fighting for their political independence was the impetus for the mounting tide of patriotism and patriotic imagery that followed the Revolutionary War.**

manumit
To willingly free one's slaves

the war. Many slaves simply fled their masters during the confusion of battle. In all, there were about 50,000 fewer slaves after the war than before it. Some former slaves went to New England, some went to Canada, and many stayed in the South to live free.

After the war, the progress of formal abolition was slow and gradual, but it was progress nonetheless. Some advances were even made in the South, where the vast majority of slaves lived (see Map 6.3). Virginia and Maryland made it easier for owners to **manumit** (or willingly free) their slaves, and many revolutionaries chose to do so. By 1800, one in ten African Americans in the Chesapeake region was free. This meant there were large communities where escaped slaves could hide in the growing cities of the Chesapeake. Nevertheless, slavery had not been abolished in the South, and leaders like Thomas Jefferson, who were well aware of the contradiction between the practice of slavery and the rhetoric of independence, never freed their slaves.

The most dramatic changes occurred in the North when abolition was set in motion legally. Vermont outlawed slavery in its first constitution in 1777. In Massachusetts and New Hampshire, slaves sued for their freedom—and won. In the Middle States, where the slave population was larger, progress was slower, but both Pennsylvania and New York favored gradual emancipation, which, in Pennsylvania's case, meant that all slaves born in 1780 or later were free when they turned twenty-one. Throughout the North, five states allowed African Americans to vote and in total, by 1810, three-quarters of the 30,000 African Americans living in the North were free. By 1840, there were only 1,000 slaves in the North, and the freed slaves and their children had developed large social institutions, including various sects of historically black churches and numerous fraternal organizations, such as the African American Masons.

Perhaps most importantly, however, by 1790, all states except Georgia and South Carolina had outlawed the importation of slaves from abroad. As Americans began to consider the political meanings of liberty and freedom, they were confronted by the obvious contradiction of having freed themselves of the Crown while others lived in slavery. After the revolution, only compromise would keep the issue of slavery at bay, as the North and South took different tactics in handling the contentious issue.

Read one Quaker's attempt to point out inconsistencies between American freedom and slavery.

The Impact on Native America

The war also greatly affected the fate of Native Americans; the Indians were generally worse off after the war than before it. By the time of the revolution, there were few tribes still living on the Atlantic coast. Disease and violence had decimated the tribes of that region. The most powerful tribes in contact with the colonists lived between the Appalachian Mountains and the Mississippi River, where the Iroquois dominated in the North and the Choctaw, Seminole, Creek, and Cherokee dominated in the South. Both the English and the Americans sought their help during

Map 6.3
Distribution of Slave Population, 1790

View an interactive version of this map.

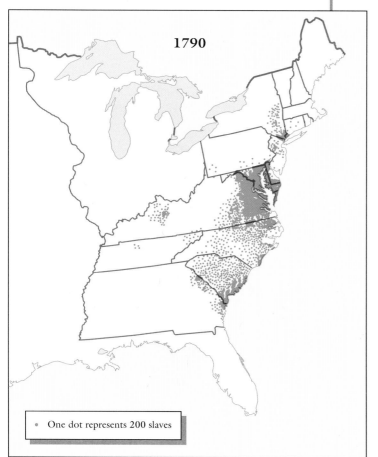

1790

• One dot represents 200 slaves

the war. Some, such as the Cherokee, sided with the British. For their efforts, American frontiersmen fiercely attacked Cherokee towns, driving them back almost to the Mississippi. The battles throughout Native America were unspeakably harsh, as the war often served as a pretext to remove Indian tribes and empty Indian land for land-hungry colonists. Anyone could become a casualty on the frontier.

The Iroquois faced the direst outcome. During the war, the Iroquois vowed to remain neutral, but their neutrality did not last. Two Iroquois tribes, the Oneida and the Tuscaroras, joined the Americans at the urging of their Presbyterian minister, Samuel Kirkland. The remaining four tribes of the Iroquois Confederacy sided with the British, participating in frequent attacks on several American cities. By 1779, the Americans fought back forcefully, killing Iroquois men, women, and children, and torching their fields as they left. By the end of the war, nearly one-third of the Iroquois nation was dead. Their supremacy in the land between the Appalachians and the Great Lakes did not survive the war.

In addition to these violent encounters, with the war over, the tribes of Native America had to contend with an expanding nation of settlers who respected no practical western boundary and answered to no governmental authority preventing them from moving farther west. This portended a grim outlook for American Indians.

The Impact on Women

Women played key roles during the revolution. They enforced boycotts, sewed clothing made of nonimported fibers, raised impressive funds for the Continental Army, and sometimes even engaged in battle. This was a significant shift from the colonial era, when women only rarely protested their total exclusion from politics. New Jersey's constitution of 1776 opened the franchise to "all free inhabitants" who were worth at least fifty pounds, thus allowing many New Jersey women to vote for the first time.

But immediately after the war, women generally lost out politically as the new nation decided how far it would extend the rewards of citizenship. In many states, women were not eligible to own property. And, in every other state besides New Jersey, there is no evidence that women were ever offered the vote. In 1807, even New Jersey rescinded its offer of the franchise. Men confined women's role to that of "Republican motherhood," which historians now describe as a double-edged identity—one that put women in charge of raising young male republicans through a demanding path of education, religious adherence, and political engagement, but also confined women's role to familial relations outside the realm of direct intervention in the public sphere.

The Impact on Religious Minorities

Many historians have pointed to the Great Awakening of the 1730s and 1740s as laying part of the foundation for the revolutionary events of the 1760s and 1770s. With its emphasis on personal religious experience rather than the authority of the ministers, and as one of the first events to create a shared experience for people from New England to the southern colonies, the Great Awakening has been viewed as an early form of revolutionary activity. Colonists were also afraid that, around 1763, Parliament was planning to establish a bishop of the Anglican Church for America. They feared that any such appointment would extend England's official church to the colonies.

© Eon Images

>> Molly Pitcher: Fact or Fiction? It is true that women played a significant role in the revolution. One in particular, however—nicknamed Molly Pitcher—has achieved legendary status for taking her husband's place in battle when he was incapacitated. It is not clear whether the New Jersey woman known as Molly Pitcher was based on Mary Ludwig Hayes, who was praised for her courage at the Battle of Monmouth, or Margaret Corbin, who similarly fought at the Battle of Fort Washington.

Two American actions after the war reflected their concerns about an established church: (1) most of the new state constitutions included some guarantee of religious toleration, although a few of the states that already had an official church (like Massachusetts) moved more slowly toward disestablishment; and (2) the democratic ideals of the revolution called into question public financial support of churches that were not attended by everyone.

The best-known representation of these ideas came in 1776, when Thomas Jefferson drafted a bill for the Virginia legislature that called for the disestablishment of the Episcopal Church. Jefferson's **Virginia Statute of Religious Freedom** was one of the accomplishments that Jefferson himself was most proud of. It immediately influenced several state constitutions, and several states made their ratification of the United States Constitution in 1787 contingent upon an amendment promising that the federal government would not infringe on religious liberties.

At the same time, the revolution led to the creation of several divisions of American churches, such as the Methodist Episcopal Church of America and the Presbyterian Church of the United States. Two "freedom churches" also opened, both of which stressed the brotherhood of man and the freedom of conscience: the Universalist Church (1779) and the Unitarian Church (1785). Thus, not only did the revolution inspire laws mandating the separation of church and state, but it also encouraged the creation of two major anti-dogmatic sects.

See numerous primary sources connecting the revolution with religion, including a revolutionary flag.

Read the Virginia Statute of Religious Freedom.

And in the end ...

The war generated a bewildering mix of emotions and warnings. It set the patriots free from English control, but it also drew boundaries that the future nation would have to observe when it created its new government and society. It set in motion the ideals of the Enlightenment, but it also provoked the question of how far republican democracy would extend—not just politically, but socially and economically as well. Many revolutionary leaders feared that too much freedom might lead to chaos: if everyone were free, who would ensure order? On the other hand, too little freedom might trigger a second revolution.

With the war over, the leaders of the new nation confronted yet another daunting task: forming a new nation that embodied the revolutionary spirit without letting that spirit extend to anarchy.

What else was happening . . .	
July 4, 1777	The United States celebrates its first birthday. Ships lined up on the Delaware River discharge thirteen cannon shots in honor of the thirteen states.
1778	New Orleans businessman Oliver Pollock creates the $ symbol.
1787	The first U.S. penny, designed by Benjamin Franklin, is minted.
1790	The cornerstone of the mansion known as the White House is laid.

{ Read It Your Way! }

"I liked how you could access the eBook online; you could do your reading anywhere."
– *Ashlee Whitfield, Student, Grand View College*

"I liked the questions that were asked (reflection questions, multiple choice) at the end of each of the supplementary documents that were attached to the eBook chapters. They helped me reflect on what I read."
– *Ashley Mariscal, Student, University of Texas at Brownsville*

"I liked the different options that you had: two different books, the eBook and the regular one. There were eBook links you could click on to find further information about that subject in the chapter plus good review questions at the end."
– *Rachel Montieth, Student, Grand View College*

We know that no two students read in quite the same way. Some of you do a lot of your reading online.

To help you take your reading **outside the covers** of *HIST*, each new text comes with access to the exciting learning environment of a robust eBook containing **over 300 tested online links to:**

- **Primary source documents**
- **Audio**
- **Historical simulations**
- **Video**
- **Maps**
- **Interactive modules**
- **Images**
- **Websites**
- **Virtual field trips**

Confederation *and* Constitution
1783–1789

Learning Outcomes

After reading this chapter, you should be able to do the following:

LO 1 Describe the first state constitutions written and adopted after the United States declared its independence.

LO 2 Analyze the federal government as it existed under the Articles of Confederation.

LO 3 Describe the most significant issues that the United States had to deal with under the Articles of Confederation, and explain how the Articles failed to live up to the needs of the new country.

LO 4 Explain the need for the Constitutional Convention that met in Philadelphia in 1787, and describe the process of writing the Constitution.

LO 5 Describe and explain the major provisions of the Constitution created by the Philadelphia convention, especially concerning the separation of powers and the rights given to individual states.

LO 6 Explain the procedure established for ratification of the Constitution, describe the actions of its supporters and its opponents, and explain how and when ratification was eventually achieved.

"Could Americans design a government able to provide liberty and strong enough to protect that liberty?"

By 1783, the nation was officially independent, but it had three immediate problems: (1) it had amassed a huge war debt from fighting for independence; (2) it suddenly had vast lands to control in the West; and (3) it had to re-create a system of trade after England's protections

had been withdrawn. These problems were intensified because the ideology that had propelled the revolution—republicanism—strenuously warned against a strong central authority, and most Americans were repelled by the idea of a home-grown authoritarian yoke. They wanted their day-to-day freedoms. They wanted the liberties promised in the Declaration of Independence. Which begs the obvious question: What were those freedoms and, just as important, what price were people willing to pay for them? Could Americans design a government able to provide liberty and strong enough to protect that liberty?

This was the primary concern from the moment the colonists declared their independence in 1776. Their first attempt to find an appropriate balance (through a government established under the Articles of Confederation) proved unsuccessful. The Articles made the federal government too weak to address the nation's pressing needs. By 1787, Americans had scrapped the Articles and designed an entirely new structure of government. This new government, as defined in the United States Constitution, placed more power in a central authority than most Americans had anticipated or wanted. But a Bill of Rights protected the liberties they sought to preserve. Although not perfect, what they created in the Constitution has served the nation for more than two hundred years.

This chapter explores the development of the American government between 1783 and 1789. It begins by examining the state constitutions that served as testing grounds for the federal constitution, then it examines the strengths and weaknesses of the Articles of Confederation before addressing the current U.S. Constitution and its Bill of Rights.

LO¹ State Constitutions, 1776–1780

Between 1776 and 1780, while the fighting continued, all of the thirteen states except Connecticut and Rhode Island drafted their own constitution. Most changed their constitution several times, meaning that there was a good deal of experimentation going on. The ideas laid out by John Locke, Jean-Jacques Rousseau, John Trenchard, Thomas Gordon, the English Parliament, and the colonial legislatures were put to the test at the state

© iStockphoto.com/Rich Vintage

>> New Jersey's constitution of 1776 opened the franchise to "all free inhabitants" who were worth at least fifty pounds, thus allowing many New Jersey women to vote for the first time. Note that there is also an African American man waiting to vote.

© The London Art Archive/Alamy

Learn more about the Pennsylvania State Constitution of 1776.

level during these years. These state constitutions worked out ideas that would influence the federal system.

Content

Most of the state constitutions had several common elements, three of which are particularly important: Bills of Rights, limits on participation, and separation of powers.

Bills of Rights

Each state constitution included a **bill of rights** that protected the "natural rights" that many Americans felt were threatened by England's prerevolutionary laws. Most of the bills of rights guaranteed the freedom of the press, the right of popular consent before being taxed, and protections against general search warrants. Most states guaranteed the freedom of religion, although some limited political participation to Christians only.

Limits on Participation

Almost universally, the state constitutions broadened the base of people who could participate in government by relaxing property-holding qualifications. Pennsylvania, for instance, gave the vote to anyone who paid taxes. And New Jersey opened the vote to "all free inhabitants" worth at least fifty pounds. Nevertheless, each state maintained limits on who could vote and who could hold public office. These limits usually concerned owning property or adhering to a particular religion. Women and teenagers were almost universally excluded from voting, except, sometimes, when they owned property.

Separation of Powers

As they tinkered with various forms of government, each state recognized that creating several different branches of government and giving each of them different responsibilities prevented one person or one body from becoming overly tyrannical or exerting an excess of authority. This was called the **separation of powers**. In the 1780s, John Adams of Massachusetts developed the theory behind separation of powers, one he called "mixed government." Most of the states operated according to separation of powers, in that they had a weak elected governor, a powerful legislature that changed membership frequently, and courts whose judges were named for life to ensure they were beholden to no one.

Results

The various state constitutions were valuable forums for working out different types of government. Many worked well in the local context of their state; many were adapted frequently. However, none of the state constitutions addressed the issue of how the states would participate in and contribute to a national body. The balance between states' rights and federal rights had yet to be found.

LO² The Articles of Confederation, 1777–1787

Origins

Americans managed to fight more than half the revolutionary war without any legitimate federal government. The Continental Congress had assumed a number of rights and responsibilities associated with a federal government, such as creating the Continental Army, printing money, managing trade, and dealing with debt. But it had done these things without having been granted authority by the people or some other sovereign power. Feeling the need to legitimate their actions and define the colonies' collective sovereignty, the revolutionaries realized they had to form a governing body. So between 1776 and 1777 the Continental Congress drafted the **Articles of Confederation**. The following year, it presented the document to the states for ratification, and, by July 1778, eight states had ratified the document. But full unanimity of the thirteen states, which was required before it could go into effect, would not be reached until 1781.

Articles of Confederation Document that defined the colonies' collective sovereignty; drafted by the Continental Congress between 1776 and 1777, then ratified by the thirteen states by 1781

Mechanics

The experimentation that had taken place in the states did not affect the Articles of Confederation, which were drafted too early to be substantially influenced by the state constitutions. Thus the Articles did not innovate; they basically codified the way things were in the late 1770s. John Dickinson, the prominent lawyer who had drafted the ideological tract *Letter from a Farmer in Pennsylvania,* was the principal author of the Articles. Although he initially voted against independence (he felt the colonies were ill prepared), the Continental Congress invited him to draft the new system of government. Fundamentally conservative, the Articles provided for each state's independence, granting very little power to the overarching federal government. The central government was simply an administrative agency that provided a meeting place for debate and enacted some very minimal, hard-to-enforce rules.

Division of Powers

Powers Reserved for the Federal Government

The Articles placed all power in a single legislature, which was the system followed under the Continental Congress. This meant no separation of powers. There was no president, monarch, or prime minister to serve as the executive power. Instead, there was a "Committee of the States," in which one representative from each state was seated. This was the most centralized authority, and its powers were minimal. The Continental Congress, on the other hand, had five powers under the Articles: (1) to declare war and make peace; (2) to make international treaties; (3) to control Indian affairs in the West; (4) to establish a currency; and (5) to create and maintain a postal service.

Powers Reserved for the States

The states, meanwhile, maintained the all-important right to levy taxes and regulate commerce

© North Wind Picture Archives/Alamy

>> Carpenters' Hall in Philadelphia was chosen as the site for the Continental Congress.

Unfortunately, these were perhaps the two most pressing needs of a nation conducting a war, precisely because they are the actions that keep money rolling in. If the states would not provide enough funds to fight a war, what could the federal government do? Under the Articles of Confederation, it could do nothing.

Achievements of the Articles

We can already begin to guess at the flaws and limits of the Articles, but they also represented significant achievements. From a philosophical perspective, two stand out: (1) the Articles established the United States as a government of laws that placed limits on the government's authority, and (2) the Articles created a national citizenship, which gave equal rights to qualifying members. There would be no titles or codification of classes in America.

Weaknesses

The weaknesses of the Articles outweigh their achievements. Three stand out: (1) the inability to raise funds; (2) the need for unanimity to make changes; and (3) the lack of authority over internal trade.

Inability to Raise Funds

The war had sunk the new nation badly in debt, and the Articles declared that Congress could not levy taxes. Furthermore, with a massive debt, it was hard to find creditors. This combination spelled immediate trouble for the new nation.

The Need for Unanimity to Make Changes

In 1781, nationalists in Congress chartered a national bank to help consolidate the national debt and facilitate credit. In order for the bank to operate, however, Congress needed capital to create a system of reserves. To get that capital, Congress passed a bill that put a 5 percent tax on all imported goods. However, the Articles of Confederation required that all bills receive unanimous approval before becoming law. Tiny Rhode Island, reliant on foreign trade for its economy, would not assent to the tax. Without Rhode Island, the bill died, as did these early plans for a national bank. In matters legislative, the need for unanimity was a clear problem.

Lack of Authority over Internal Trade

Finally, commerce between the states suffered because there was no centralized authority to manage it. Because each state had its own currency, its own levels of inflation, and its own taxes, it was difficult to transport goods across state lines or engineer large programs that would encompass an entire region. The Articles provided no national policy on commerce, and throughout the first half of the decade, delegates from southern states resisted efforts to devise one. They feared that such a policy would allow northern merchants to monopolize the trade of southern agricultural products, bypassing southern merchants and traders.

 Learn more about (and read) the Articles of Confederation.

LO³ Day-to-Day Operations of the Confederation

In addition to these constitutional problems, the government under the Confederation faced three other significant challenges—managing the Western expansion, foreign relations, and debt—which further underscored the Articles' strengths and weaknesses.

The Western Problem

The most pressing challenge concerned land in the West. During and after the Revolution, Americans continued their seemingly perpetual push westward, and in the 1780s large numbers of Americans moved to western Pennsylvania, Kentucky, and the Nashville region. They were slowly populating the area between the Appalachian Mountains and the Mississippi River. But as these pioneers moved west, they began to enrich the states that had charters in the West. (Recall that many of the original colonial charters specified northern and southern boundaries, but usually made the western boundary the Pacific Ocean.) These stipulations bred jealousy among states that had no claims on western land. Maryland, in fact, refused to ratify the Articles of Confederation until the largest western landholder, Virginia, ceded its western holdings to the federal government (Map 7.1).

Land Cessions

In 1784, Congress finally persuaded Virginia to cede much of its land to the federal government. But Virginia and other large landholders did so only on the condition that they be allowed to keep small "reserves" of land for later use, a condition the Continental Congress had to grant. By 1802, eighteen years later, all states had ceded their western

Map 7.1
Western Land Claims after the Revolution

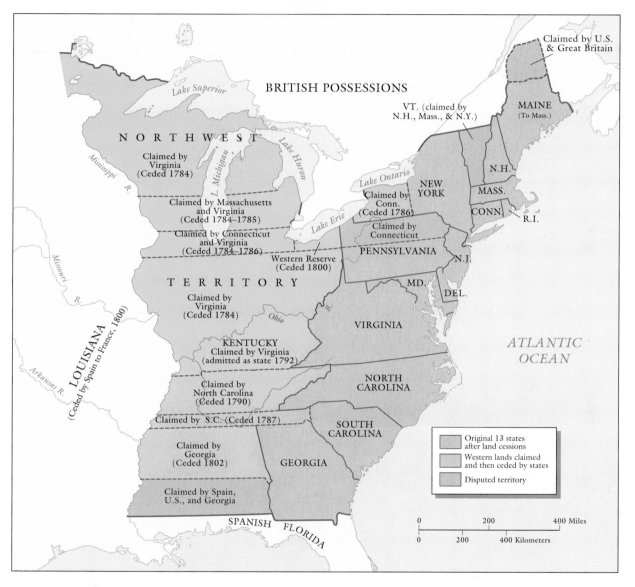

lands to the federal government. The inability of the federal government under the Articles to make this happen sooner showed that it could not bully the states into doing what it wanted, even if what it wanted was what was best for the young nation.

Organizing Territories

With continued westward migration and calls for the federal government to oversee that expansion, Congress devised several plans to organize the western territories. Congress passed the Land Ordinance of 1785, which surveyed the immense western territory, divided it into townships six miles square, and set prices for its sale to individuals. This plan favored wealthy speculators because small farmers could not afford an entire "township," thus requiring speculators to act as intermediaries, which drove prices up.

Furthermore, two years later Congress passed the great achievement of the government under the

Articles of Confederation, the **Northwest Ordinance of 1787**, which established territorial governments in the Great Lakes region and set a pattern for future western development. The Ordinance crafted boundaries for territories and developed laws by which a territory could be included in the nation. When the male population of a territory reached 5,000, it could elect a legislature and send a delegate to Congress. When the population reached 60,000, the territory could enter the Union as a state, on equal status with all other states, including the original thirteen. The Northwest Ordinance also contained something absent from the Articles: a Bill of Rights. In addition, the Ordinance prohibited slavery in the territories, a point that would become increasingly contentious as westward expansion continued throughout the first half of the 1800s.

Read the Northwest Ordinance.

Overall, the Confederation enabled easier access to western lands. But because it could not fund a standing army, the government had little capacity to protect the settlers who moved there.

The Problem of Foreign Relations

The second important issue confronted by the government under the Articles of Confederation had to do with foreign relations. Most significantly, with a weak federal government, Americans found it difficult to secure their borders. Three groups took advantage of this weakness: the English, the Spanish, and pirates.

The English

Although the United States had won its independence, Britain retained a few forts along the U.S.-Canadian border. They did this to protect their lucrative fur trade and to ensure that the United States would pay off its loans to British creditors. The United States badly wanted these forts removed, but did not have the muscle to push them out. Again, the United States had no standing army and could not afford to maintain one.

The Spanish

From a foreign relations perspective, there were three main problems with Spain: (1) the Treaty of Paris was

>> "Plan of an American new cleared farm," 1793

Library of Congress, Prints & Photographs Division, LC-US262-2766

unclear about who controlled a piece of land called the Yazoo Strip, which was the boundary between Spanish Florida and American Georgia; (2) the Spanish controlled the mouth of the Mississippi River and were able to close off this central access point to the American interior, should they ever wish to; and (3) the Americans wanted access to Spanish traders in the West Indies, but Spain was reluctant to allow this access because they did not want the United States to become dominant in the Western Hemisphere.

In 1784, Spain made a proposition to the United States: Spain would grant Americans access to the Spanish West Indies (which would benefit American traders), but it would cut off access to the Mississippi River (so that Spain could limit the amount of goods that came down the Mississippi into the open market). Needing nine votes in Congress to pass the measure, the treaty floundered, winning only seven. It was revealing that all seven votes came from northern states, infuriating the South, which would be hurt economically if the Mississippi River were closed off to American traders. The Spanish eventually reopened the Mississippi but charged high duties to American merchants.

Pirates

In the 1780s, American forces were also impotent in the face of Mediterranean pirates, who preyed on American trade ships in the Atlantic and the Caribbean. Without the capital to maintain a strong army or navy, the government under the Articles could do little to stop the marauding of American ships and pillaging of American goods.

The Debt

Despite these two serious issues (the West and foreign relations), the overarching problem facing the new nation was debt. This had three visible political ramifications: (1) those who held the debt wanted to be repaid; (2) the rank-and-file of the army grew angry when the government could not pay all the back pay it owed the soldiers; and (3) farmers grew angry because inflation had priced them out of the life to which they were accustomed.

Promissory Notes and Bonds

To finance the Revolutionary War, the American government had sold bonds, which had to be repaid, plus interest, at a certain time in the future. Furthermore, the government had issued several promissory notes, mostly to farmers and usually after the army had seized farmers' property in order

to wage battle. Both types of these debt-holders wanted to be paid back.

> **specie**
> Gold or silver, which has intrinsic value, used as payment instead of paper money, which has extrinsic value

An Angry Army

In 1783, with the war over, the Continental Congress called for the demobilization of the Continental Army. But it shortly became evident that the government could not pay the soldiers their back pay. Officers petitioned on behalf of the soldiers' grievances, sometimes threatening violence if the payments were not made. In one standoff, troops protested in front of Philadelphia's Independence Hall, forcing the Continental Congress to abandon Philadelphia (it moved to Princeton, New Jersey, until the threat quieted down). Only George Washington's words could soothe the troops. But this signaled troubles to come; after all, the Continental Congress was still unable to raise revenue.

Angry Farmers

Meanwhile, inflation continued to rise, meaning that prices increased dramatically. Farmers were hit the hardest. They had enjoyed rising prices for their goods during the war and had increased their spending, sometimes to the point of indebtedness. After the war, with no army to feed, markets shrank. At the same time, Britain prohibited American ships from trading in the West Indies. This limited the size of the market even further. As a result, agricultural goods flooded American markets, lowering prices and dropping farm wages by as much as 20 percent. When creditors demanded payment from the farmers in gold or silver (a form of payment called **specie**), most farmers were unable to pay their debts. Although most of the farmers' debts were small, foreclosure threatened many. Some were about to lose their farms or were imprisoned after being convicted in debtors' court.

Shays's Rebellion

The financial burden seemed unbearable to those who had just fought for independence. In Massachusetts, a tax increase compounded these problems. In 1786, rural towns in Massachusetts petitioned its state assembly for a moratorium on taxes and on lawsuits against debtors. When the assembly rejected their petitions, angry crowds gathered at several county courthouses to stop the courts by force. Daniel Shays, a former Continental Army officer, emerged as the leader of the protesters.

Fed up with the Massachusetts government's failure to address the problem of inflation and with its apparent favoritism toward coastal merchants who did not require the large and costly infrastructure that farmers did, on January 26, 1787, Shays led 1,200 men to seize control of the federal arsenal in Springfield, Massachusetts. This potential coup was formally called **Shays's Rebellion**. The Massachusetts government had prepared for such a move (after protesters had stormed the debtors' courts), and a force of 4,400 soldiers from New England was ready to defend the arsenal. Tellingly, these troops were funded and led into battle by East Coast merchants, not country farmers. The troops opened fire on Shays's army. Six died. This seemed to be the beginning of a civil war between the commercial class and the farming class, the wealthy and the poor. But, unprepared for formal combat, Shays's followers quickly abandoned their siege, and during the next few weeks Shays's Rebellion waned. Despite the rebellion's dissolution, unrest continued to haunt leaders in Massachusetts and other states. Shays's Rebellion was a warning that the federal government would have to address the problem of debt in order to prevent a lower-class uprising. Under the Articles it was impossible for it to do so.

>> **Shays's Rebellion was a warning that the federal government would have to address the problem of debt in order to prevent a lower-class uprising.**

The Failure of the Articles of Confederation

Despite these underlying problems with the Articles of Confederation, a financial collapse was the last straw. In 1783, England banned all American ships from the West Indies and put limitations on specific competitive items. Few other countries granted protective treaties with the United States, knowing that America was too weak to honor them. Meanwhile, the individual American states began to levy their own tariffs in order to raise money. This meant that the states with the lowest tariffs received the most trade, which led to hostile competition between the various states within the Union. The federal government's attempts to pay off its debt by simply asking the states for help was not working and was in fact promoting further discord. With a single veto, both New York and Rhode Island rejected proposed revenue-raising tariffs. Change had to come.

Calls for Change

At the urging of Virginia and Maryland, in 1786 (months before Shays's Rebellion), congressional representatives made plans to meet in Annapolis, Maryland, to discuss the problem of commerce. Only five states sent delegates, but several prominent figures were there, including James Madison, Alexander Hamilton, and George Washington. The convention's main success was in reaching a consensus to call a general meeting of delegates for the purpose of amending the Articles of Confederation. They agreed to meet again in May 1787, in Philadelphia.

LO⁴ The Constitutional Convention

Although it started out as an effort to amend the Articles of Confederation, the meeting in Philadelphia rapidly became a Constitutional Convention, aimed at creating an entirely new government. There were substantial differences of opinion, however, and the Constitutional Convention debated these issues throughout the summer of 1787.

Membership

One matter on which there was complete agreement was that George Washington should be the president of the convention. Washington's reputation and integrity protected the convention from accusations that it had usurped the authority of the Congress.

>> Most delegates were young (average age: forty-two), wealthy, and wanted to strengthen the national government in order to protect trade and promote economic and social stability.

In addition to Washington, fifty-four other delegates attended. The states had elected members to go to the meeting who were, for the most part, members of the social and educational elite. Most were young (average age: forty-two), wealthy, and wanted to strengthen the national government in order to protect trade and promote economic and social stability. They were leery of democracy, however, because Shays's Rebellion had demonstrated that democracy could be messy. Most of the delegates were also lawyers (more than half were college graduates), which meant they would respect and honor the rule of law.

Preliminary Plans

There were several key divisions at the convention (northern states versus southern, merchants versus farmers), but none was as important as that between the large states and the small ones. Two plans, prepared before the convention even began, highlighted the differences between the two.

The Virginia (Large States) Plan

James Madison of Virginia was clearly the star of the convention. A thirty-six-year-old Princeton graduate, Madison was well read in political science. He came to the convention with an agenda, summarized as the Virginia Plan. The **Virginia Plan** sought to scrap the Articles of Confederation, create a Congress with two houses, establish a federal judiciary, a president who was elected by Congress, and a centralized system of government in which Congress had veto power over the actions of the states. Membership in Congress would be determined by population, which would clearly favor the large states.

The New Jersey (Small States) Plan

For obvious reasons, smaller states objected to the Virginia Plan. Under the Articles of Confederation, all states had received an equal voice in Congress, regardless of size. To counter the Virginia Plan, New Jersey delegate William Paterson proposed an alternative—the **New Jersey Plan**—which called for revising the Articles of Confederation rather than replacing them altogether. Paterson's plan strengthened the federal government in many ways, but it proposed giving each state equal representation in a bicameral legislature, defined as a legislature with two houses with differing rules regarding responsibilities and duration of a member's term.

Drafting the Constitution

A Compromise

The convention was deadlocked over apportionment of representatives until Roger Sherman of Connecticut

>> James Madison of Virginia was clearly the star of the convention.

Virginia Plan
This proposal, known as the large states plan, sought to scrap the Articles of Confederation and create a Congress with two houses, with representation in Congress being determined by population, favoring the large states

New Jersey Plan
This proposal suggested revising the Articles of Confederation rather than replacing them altogether

Great Compromise
Plan to grant each state equal representation in the upper house (to be called the Senate) and representation that was proportional to population (1 representative for every 30,000 people) in the lower house (the House of Representatives)

three-fifths clause
Section of the Constitution that allowed southerners to include three-fifths of their slave population for both representation and the apportionment of federal taxes

came up with a compromise. He suggested granting each state equal representation in the upper house (to be called the Senate) and representation that was proportional to population (1 representative for every 30,000 people) in the lower house (the House of Representatives). This plan was ultimately approved (after Benjamin Franklin reproposed it and conceded to the larger states the power to have all funding bills originate in the lower house). Sherman's plan is called the **Great Compromise** because it broke a stalemate that could have been fatal to the development of a new federal constitution.

Slave State versus Free State

But the large states–versus–small states debate was only one of the many divisions that would bedevil the convention, and indeed, the Great Compromise had raised another problem. How do you count the population of each state? Should only voters count? Only taxpayers? Should women count toward the total? Although the conventioneers had ready answers for many of these questions, the issue became volatile when it touched on slavery.

In the early 1780s, in the aftermath of the revolutionary war (when the Atlantic slave trade was at its height), southerners were on the defensive over the issue. The spread of abolitionist ideas in the North threatened their labor supply. In addition, southerners feared that freed slaves would seek vengeance against their former masters. The southern delegates wanted a constitutional guarantee that slavery would be legal in the new nation, and they needed political power in order to ensure that slavery would continue. Thus, in a stroke of historical irony, this demand meant that southerners wanted slaves to be included in their population, which would grant the South more representatives in the House. Northerners objected, arguing that, because slaves would not have an active political voice, their numbers should not be included.

Yet another compromise allowed southerners to include three-fifths of their slave population for both representation and the apportionment of federal taxes. This **"three-fifths clause"** demonstrated that, despite the new nation's stated commitment to freedom and equality, African Americans still were treated as far less than equal by white Americans—and that this inequality would be enshrined in the American Constitution.

Delegates also had to forge a compromise regarding the slave trade. Some southerners threatened to secede from the Union if the slave trade was abolished, but many delegates (both northern and southern) considered the trade inhumane. George Mason, a Virginia slaveholder himself, even predicted that slavery would cause "the judgment of heaven" to fall upon the nation. But the majority of delegates felt that the survival of the nation was at stake and agreed to yet another compromise. Ultimately, antislavery delegates agreed to permit the slave trade for twenty more years, until 1808. In exchange, proslavery delegates granted Congress the authority to regulate commerce with a simple majority (rather than the two-thirds vote desired by most southerners).

East versus West

The final compromise of the convention was made between eastern and western states. Easterners were afraid that western expansion would allow the government to be controlled by agricultural interests rather than commercial ones. To compromise, the convention granted Congress (and not the president) the power to admit new states to the nation, which meant that the eastern states that were already a part of the nation would have the power to regulate the number of new (western) states that could enter.

> George Mason, a Virginia slaveholder himself, predicted that slavery would cause "the judgment of heaven" to fall upon the nation.

Learn more about the Constitutional Convention and read Madison's original notes.

LO⁵ The Constitution

Once these compromises were agreed upon (after the convention had gone on for four months), the convention established the structure of the new government in a constitution. The U.S. Constitution developed mostly out of the Virginia Plan, although considerable concessions were made to small states, southern states, and eastern states. The convention created a government of three branches—executive, legislative, and judicial—granting unique powers to each branch.

The Powers Given to Congress

The convention allocated several specific powers to Congress. Its intention was to make Congress the most powerful branch, allowing it to do five things: (1) collect taxes and raise revenue; (2) regulate commerce, both foreign and domestic (except on the issue of slavery, where compromise meant that it could not touch the issue until 1808); (3) declare war; (4) maintain an army; and (5) make any changes necessary to pursue these powers. By controlling the government's purse strings and by demanding that all laws originate in Congress, the Constitutional Convention wanted to ensure that no singular authority would possess too much power.

The Executive Branch

The convention also created an executive branch, consisting of a president and his cabinet.

How Elected

Because of their experience with King George III, most Americans initially favored keeping power in the hands of elected legislators. Yet, after the failure of the Articles of Confederation, those at the Constitutional Convention realized that this system did not work. As an alternative, the Virginia Plan proposed to have Congress elect the president. Another plan would have the president serve a life term. A third plan would have three presidents serving simultaneously. Finally, Gouverneur Morris, an influential delegate from Pennsylvania, insisted that the executive should not depend on Congress for his office. Instead, Morris proposed to have him elected directly by the people to two terms of substantial length.

Although this plan certainly had its merits, the Framers of the Constitution remained fearful of true democracy. So they created in the Constitution an **Electoral College**, which was composed of

Electoral College
Group composed of delegates from each state equal in number to its total apportionment in Congress (number of senators plus number of representatives); these delegates cast votes for president

delegates from each state equal in number to its total apportionment in Congress (number of senators plus number of representatives). The college was to ensure that only qualified candidates, not populist hooligans, got elected. Each delegate in the Electoral College was to vote for two people. The person who received the most votes would be president; the one with the second most votes would be vice president. Anticipating that several people would run for president (and not anticipating the two-party system), the House of Representatives would decide the president if no one received a majority of the votes.

Powers

The Constitution also gave the president the power to do five things: (1) make treaties, but only if two-thirds of the Senate approved them; (2) oversee the army and navy as commander-in-chief; (3) name diplomats with the consent of the Senate; and, most important, (4) execute the laws passed in Congress and (5) veto acts of Congress that he did not feel were constitutional (or, as it was understood after Andrew Jackson, in the country's best interests). The president was to be powerful, but also somewhat deferential to Congress.

The Judicial Branch

The Constitution also provided for a federal system of courts, headed by a Supreme Court and several regional courts. The president was to name the judges to the courts to serve lifetime appointments. The judges had jurisdiction over constitutional questions, cases in which the United States itself was a party, and cases between two or more states or between the citizens of two or more states. The Framers also included a supreme law of the land clause (or Supremacy Clause), which made the Constitution supreme over state laws in all legal cases.

Federal and State Powers

Conscious of the necessary balance between state and federal powers, the Framers of the Constitution forbade states from making their own money, levying customs, or infringing on the obligation of contracts (all things that the states had done during the era of the Articles of Confederation). Other than that, states maintained significant power. By design, if a power was not specifically given to the federal government, the states controlled it.

Relationship of the Government and the Governed

There were other transitions as well. Under the Articles, the central government was not permitted to reach the individual—that was the sovereign right of the states. But under the new Constitution, the federal government could rule individuals directly. Perhaps the most significant change in this regard was granting the federal government the power of taxation. The revolutionary commitment to representation was not abandoned, however, as the legislative branch of government, which represented the people most directly, held the exclusive right to tax.

Read the U.S Constitution.

LO⁶ The Ratification Debate

In September 1787, the Framers of the Constitution presented their work to the states for ratification. The Constitution needed the states' approval in order to become the law of the land. Otherwise, the Articles of Confederation would still rule. The conventioneers urged each state to hold a special convention to discuss ratifying the new document and it voted that approval by nine states was enough for the Constitution to take effect—deliberately avoiding the need for unanimity.

A Slow Start

A few states ratified the Constitution almost immediately: smaller states, such as Delaware, Connecticut, and New Jersey, supported the Constitution because it promised to strengthen their position in conflicts with their larger, more populous neighbors. The Great Compromise had secured their votes. Georgia ratified quickly as well, because it felt threatened by Indian conflicts and the Spanish presence in Florida. The people of Georgia needed protection. But the only large state to ratify the Constitution before the end of winter 1788 was Pennsylvania. In the other states with a large population—particularly New York, Massachusetts, and Virginia—concerns about the loss of sovereignty generated opposition. They wanted to ensure their rights.

The Federalists

Factions speedily formed. In an effort to undercut opposition, supporters of the Constitution took the name **Federalists** and began openly campaigning for the Constitution's ratification. The Federalists emphasized that the new government would not end state autonomy. They also contemplated a Bill of Rights that would prevent the new centralized government from infringing on what were thought of as natural rights.

To influence the debate in the key state of New York, in 1787 the Federalists John Jay and Alexander Hamilton wrote a series of essays that came to be called the **Federalist Papers**. The essays appeared in pamphlets and were condensed in newspapers. Soon James Madison of Virginia added his own essays to the series. The Federalist Papers were to become the most important tool in the ratification debate, as well as America's most significant contribution to political theory. The Federalist Papers defended the Constitution article by article and addressed many of the complaints of opponents, such as the concerns about the size of the new nation. It was a tool of ideological warfare in the name of the new Constitution.

The Federalists' choice of a name was meaningful too. Supporters of the Constitution emphasized that the new government was designed around the principle of **federalism**, which is the philosophy of government in which states and nation share the responsibility of government, with no one group or agency possessing sufficient power to dominate the other. This was an attempt to assuage notions that the new government would slide into tyranny.

Read the Federalist Papers.

The Anti-Federalists

The name "Federalists" impelled opponents to take the name "Anti-Federalists." The **Anti-Federalists**, who included many prominent patriots, including Patrick Henry, John Hancock, and Samuel Adams, preferred a weaker confederation of states and a more direct democracy. In fact, Anti-Federalists did not really oppose federalism, but they did object to the concentration of power in a centralized government regardless of how it divided power. They believed that centralized governments threatened the sovereignty of the states and the liberties of individuals. At the very least, the Anti-Federalists wanted an explicit Bill of Rights to safeguard those liberties. Because of their steadfast defense of individual rights, historians often view the Anti-Federalists as idealistic patriots concerned about how much liberty they would have to sacrifice in order to earn federal security.

The Debate

The Federalists attempted to address the concerns of their opponents by arguing that the rights of the states and of individuals were adequately protected by state bills of rights. However, the Anti-Federalists maintained that, if the Constitution were the supreme law of the land, its provisions would have preeminence over any state legislation. Thus, Anti-Federalists—especially those from the powerful states of Massachusetts, New York, and Virginia—insisted on the addition of a federal Bill of Rights before they would consent to ratification. The Federalists, on the other hand, resisted any amendments because they knew that the addition of new sections to the Constitution meant that the entire process of ratification would have to start over.

Compromise ultimately broke the deadlock. In Massachusetts, the Anti-Federalist leader, John Hancock, changed his position after Federalists promised him that the insertion of a Bill of Rights in the Constitution would be the first order of business for the new government. Such conditional ratification provided New York and Virginia with an acceptable formula for their own voting; they shortly consented to the new Constitution.

The compromise came just in time. In June 1788, New Hampshire voted to ratify the Constitution, becoming the critical ninth state, putting the Constitution into functional operation. But it

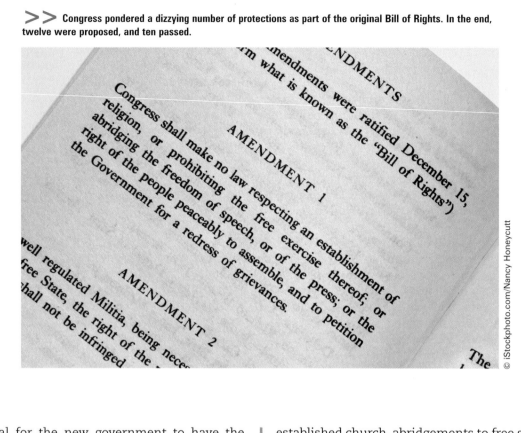

>> Congress pondered a dizzying number of protections as part of the original Bill of Rights. In the end, twelve were proposed, and ten passed.

was crucial for the new government to have the support of the larger states of Massachusetts, New York, and Virginia if it was going to succeed. With these larger states now supporting the document, by the end of the year, twelve states had accepted the Constitution (Rhode Island finally ratified the Constitution in 1790). The new United States government was launched.

The Bill of Rights

Massachusetts, Virginia, and New York had all agreed to ratify the Constitution only if Congress hastened to the task of drafting a Bill of Rights that would protect individual freedoms from the threat of potentially tyrannous federal government. It began the task of crafting these rights even before the Constitution was fully ratified. Congress pondered a dizzying number of protections, many of which were borrowed from the various state constitutions. In the end, twelve were proposed, and ten passed.

The first two amendments, which specified the number of constituents of each representative and compensation for congressmen, did not pass. The remaining ten became the Bill of Rights.

We can see in each amendment a specific grievance that emerged during the "long train of abuses" that led to the Revolution, including: the fear of an established church, abridgements to free speech and peaceful gatherings, attempts to disarm the people, the quartering of soldiers in private homes, the forcible removal of private property, unreasonable searches by the federal government, the denial of a trial by one's peers, and the suspension of protections under the law. The Bill of Rights was to defend against the kind of tyranny that the revolutionaries had encountered in the run-up to the Revolutionary War. The final amendment making up the Bill of Rights pronounced that any power not delegated to the federal government by the Constitution was reserved for the states, thus ensuring a balance of power between the new government and the state governments.

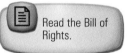

Read the Bill of Rights.

And in the end ...

The Constitution has survived, relatively unchanged, as the basis of the United States' republican government for more than two hundred years. The first ten amendments—the Bill of Rights promised by the Federalists—were added in 1791. Since then, only seventeen more amendments have become law. Some of the fundamental debates, including the question of the balance of power between the states and the federal government, continue today. Interpretations of the framers' intentions have changed over time, but the American frame of government created in 1787 has demonstrated impressive flexibility and longevity.

More than just a political document, the Constitution also sparked essential debates that would continue to preoccupy the American nation. What would be the role of African Americans? Was America a nation only for white people? And what about women as citizens? Was there any justification for their exclusion from voting? How long would that justification be sustainable? And what would be the nature of the relationship between the Americans and the Indians, both of whom had good reasons to think of the land as theirs? Who would decide? The Constitution took a stand on many of these issues, coming out in ways that make it look anything but democratic.

Through amendment and custom, the American nation would slowly achieve greater democracy. The initial steps were taken in the first years of the new nation, a period that historians today call the Federalist era.

CHAPTER 8

Securing *the New* Nation
1789–1800

Learning Outcomes

After reading this chapter, you should be able to do the following:

LO¹ Describe the creation of the federal government under the new Constitution.

LO² Describe how disagreements over how the United States should be governed led to political divisions, and discuss some of the individuals who took strong stands on each side.

LO³ Outline the country's development of a two-party political system.

LO⁴ Discuss the issues of John Adams's presidency, and explain how he and the country dealt with them.

LO⁵ Explain the convoluted political process that made Thomas Jefferson president in 1800, including the constitutional change designed to mend the problem.

"A blueprint is not a building."

Although the war had been won and the Constitution ratified, the debate about the size, shape, and duties of the federal government continued. A blueprint, after all, is not a building. Some, like New York's Alexander Hamilton, were worried that common people could not handle

democracy and would be confused by the challenges of running a modern nation. Others, like Thomas Jefferson, were concerned that a powerful centralized federal government would likely take away coveted liberties.

The stakes were high, as the unformed nation struggled to establish itself on the periphery of the European economic system. Daily life went on, of course: people went to school, got married, had families, bought slaves, moved west, and built new homes. But they did so during a time of heightened worries about the political stability of their new nation. Was American independence going to be temporary? Could the country's leaders pull the nation together? Politics of the 1790s were fraught with questions, anxiety, and passion. And the social life of the new nation would not change dramatically until the 1810s and the Market Revolution (which appears in Chapter 10).

In the end, the political center held, but not in a way that anyone had predicted. Nearly all the founders disliked political partisanship, yet they helped usher in the two-party system that we know today. They also preached the virtues of liberty and equality but went to great extremes to safeguard both the practice of slavery and the continued seizure of Native American lands. Thomas Jefferson advocated a rural, agrarian republic, yet the stability enjoyed and the land acquired during his presidency helped foster an economic revolution—one that we will encounter in the following chapters. But, first, to the decade following the ratification of the Constitution, when the central role of the federal government was to secure the new nation. This chapter examines the development of the new government, the rise of the two-party political system, and the first peaceful turnover of power in the "bloodless revolution" of 1800.

LO¹ Creating a New Government

From 1789 to 1800 the federal government was remarkably small. In 1800, the Department of State had only three employees, plus representatives in London, Paris, Madrid, Lisbon, and The Hague. The entire Treasury had a total of about seventy-five employees. The War Department consisted of the secretary of war, two clerks, and a messenger. The Post Office numbered seventy-five offices. The legislative branch had only twenty-six senators and sixty-four representatives. For a nation suspicious of centralized power, a small federal government was appropriate.

As the new government began operations in 1789, it became clear that, although the Constitution outlined a framework of

> **From 1789 to 1800 the federal government was remarkably small.**

© North Wind Picture Archives/Alamy

Naturalization Act of 1790
Legislation which declared that, among immigrants to the U.S., only "free white persons" could become citizens of the United States

patronage
System of granting rewards for assisting with political victories

government, the exact roles of its three branches were not clearly defined. Establishing precedents would be the mission of the first group of federal politicians.

The First Citizens

According to Article 4, Section 2 of the Constitution, the states dictated who was and was not a citizen. They more or less confined citizenship to white, property-holding males, although there were a few exceptions to this generalization. Immigrants could become citizens as well, and in the **Naturalization Act of 1790**, Congress declared that, among immigrants, only "free white persons" could become citizens of the United States. This obviously limited black people, Native Americans, and Asians. (These restrictions continued for almost a century, until 1870, when African Americans were allowed to become citizens.) White women also had few property rights and, once married, anything a woman owned became the property of her husband. It was not until 1920 that women were granted full citizenship.

Read the Naturalization Act of 1790.

The First Congress

The first federal election under the new Constitution was held late in 1788. Most of the men elected were sympathetic to the arguments laid out in the Federalist Papers. At its first meeting in the capital city of New York, the first Congress had four major tasks: (1) setting up a system of federal courts; (2) securing the Bill of Rights that had been promised during the ratification period; (3) establishing the executive department; and

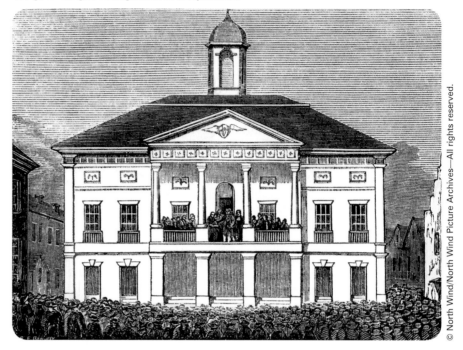

>> Federal Hall in New York City, the first capitol building of the United States, on the day of George Washington's inauguration as first president.

(4) raising revenue. By addressing these pressing issues in a relatively tidy manner, the first Congress demonstrated its strength compared to the Continental Congress under the Articles of Confederation. The new government seemed to be working.

Courts

The Judiciary Act of 1789 created three circuit courts and thirteen district courts to accompany the Supreme Court established by the Constitution.

Rights

James Madison proposed to Congress seventeen amendments to the Constitution, twelve of which Congress approved and ten of which the states later ratified. These ten amendments are known as the Bill of Rights.

Executive Department

Congress created five executive posts: (1) the secretary of state, (2) the secretary of war, (3) the secretary of the treasury, (4) the attorney general, and (5) the postmaster general. These positions were to be filled by the president, meaning that the president would control **patronage**,

> It was not until 1920 that women were granted full citizenship.

defined as the granting of rewards for assisting with political victories (although in these early years, these jobs were not viewed as lucrative because the federal government was so small). Under President George Washington, these positions (except that of postmaster general) would serve as his cabinet of advisors.

Revenues

James Madison, who had played an essential role at the Constitutional Convention, was elected to the House of Representatives from Virginia. His work was equally indispensable during the first term of Congress. In 1789, he persuaded Congress to pass the **Hamilton Tariff of 1789**, which imposed a 5 to 10 percent tariff on certain imports. This act's success freed the federal government from constant worry about economic shortfalls.

Take a virtual tour of the activities of the First Federal Congress.

The First President

The least surprising outcome of the nation's first election was installing George Washington as president. His stature as an honest war leader made him the obvious choice to lead the new government. He never ran for

> Washington had to be talked into coming back and serving his country once again.

the office, and indeed, had retired from public life altogether before he was elected. Washington had to be talked into coming back and serving his country once again.

As he formulated his approach to the office, Washington was aware that he had no contemporary role models; the American republic was truly an experiment. "I walk on untrodden ground," he said. "There is scarcely any part of my conduct which may not hereafter be drawn in precedent." Washington established several important precedents while in office. Three of the most significant concerned the presidential manner, the cabinet, and relations with Congress.

The Presidential Manner

Washington displayed a dignified and formal manner as president. In the debate about how people should address him, Washington remained quiet. Federalists proposed calling him "His Excellency" or "His Highness," but Anti-Federalists rebuffed the proposal, favoring a less lofty title. Without any insistence from Washington himself, he came to be called simply "Mr. President." This endowed him with importance, but not regal entitlement. Washington also dressed formally (never in military attire, always in American-made suits), conducted affairs in a formal manner, and decided not to use his veto power unless he deemed a law unconstitutional. He wanted people to take the office of president seriously, but without encouraging the office to usurp the will of the people as expressed by Congress.

The Cabinet

Washington's second important precedent concerned his cabinet. Congress voted to create several departments within the executive branch, but the Constitution did not explicitly outline the

>> **Washington in retirement at Mount Vernon after the war.**

responsibilities of these departments (which were collectively known as the president's "**cabinet**"). With the cabinet's role open to interpretation, Washington assembled this group with an eye toward gathering differing viewpoints. He hoped that including a range of opinions within the government would keep leaders working together in the nation's interests rather than fighting among themselves for power.

Washington appointed Thomas Jefferson the first secretary of state. In addition to heading American diplomatic relations, Jefferson's office was also in charge of the census, patents and copyrights, public lands, and the mint. Washington's treasury secretary was Alexander Hamilton, a close friend who had served as his aide-de-camp during the revolution. Henry Knox was secretary of war, as he had been under the Continental Congress during the 1780s. Knox commanded an army of five thousand men, most of whom were deployed for defense against Native Americans in the western territories. Samuel Osgood was the postmaster general, in charge of mail delivery. Edmund Randolph was the attorney general, who met with the cabinet as Washington's personal advisor.

Reflecting the balance of perspectives that Washington sought, Hamilton and Knox favored a strong centralized government, whereas Jefferson and Randolph favored greater power at the state level. Jefferson and Randolph were from Virginia, Hamilton from New York, Knox and Osgood from New England. When Washington began consulting them on official matters (or, more commonly, asking Randolph to solicit their opinions), the cabinet system was born.

Relations with Congress

The Constitution required that the executive branch draft treaties with the "advice and consent" of the Senate, but the first time Washington endeavored to make a treaty, the resulting bickering with Congress led to an inconclusive treaty. From then on, Washington decided to negotiate treaties first, then submit them to Congress for approval.

Read Washington's First Inaugural Address.

Explore Washington's life in a series of interactive modules.

> **"I walk on untrodden ground. There is scarcely any part of my conduct which may not hereafter be drawn in precedent."**
> –*George Washington*

© iStockphoto.com/Matthew Hertel

This established a precedent. Washington also took seriously his role of informing Congress of the state of the union once a year, thus demonstrating that he was ever attentive to the will of the people.

LO² Political Divisions

During its first decade, this small government had serious problems to confront, and the confrontations sparked factionalism. Whose side you chose in the debate depended on your vision for the nation. Some, like Washington, Hamilton, and Adams (who, as a political group, would come to be called the Federalists), wanted a strong federal government that would assist merchants and industry in order to create a buoyant, market-based nation. Others, like Jefferson and Madison (who would come to be called the Democratic-Republicans), preferred a weaker federal government that would allow the preservation of "natural rights" and of slavery. Two issues illustrated these competing visions—problems over government finance and foreign policy.

The Problem of Finance

During the revolutionary war, the Continental Congress had taken out loans to fund the war. Foreign investors held $12 million worth of notes; domestic bondholders were owed $48 million. To establish good credit and to maintain authority over the states, the federal government had to pay off the loans.

Hamilton's Financial Plan

As treasury secretary and an author of the Federalist Papers, Alexander Hamilton promoted economic policies aligned with his vision for a strong, centralized government. He proposed an economic plan that favored the interests of the commercial and mercantile elite. His plan had four key components: (1) consolidating the loans that Congress took out during the revolutionary war into one national debt, which would commit the wealthy people who were owed money to the success of the federal government; (2) consolidating the individual states' loans into the national debt, making the states beholden to the federal government and thus strengthening its authority; (3) raising revenue through the sale of bonds, the sale of public lands, the establishment of tariffs, and the imposition of an excise tax on whiskey; and (4) creating the First Bank of the United States, which would hold the government's revenue and issue bank notes (paper money) that would be legal tender throughout the country.

The bank was the linchpin of the plan. It would benefit the business classes, who could capitalize on the stability provided by a bank. It would organize the loans and the debt as well. But it would also expand the power of Congress and, therefore, of the federal government. A national bank was not mentioned in the Constitution, but the Constitution did grant Congress the power to do anything "necessary and proper" to carry out its delegated powers. If Congress could successfully charter a bank (which it did in 1791), it would assume a vast amount of **implied powers** through a loose interpretation of the words in the Constitution—a position called **loose constructionism**. This would in turn make the federal government more powerful.

Opposition to Hamilton's Plan

Thomas Jefferson and James Madison led the faction that immediately opposed Hamilton's policies. Because Jefferson was a towering figure in the new government, this faction came to be called

© iStockphoto.com/Stefan Klein

© iStockphoto.com/Robert Dodge

The bank was the linchpin of the plan.

Democratic-Republicans
Faction that coalesced in opposition to Alexander Hamilton's economic policies and Jay's Treaty; led by Virginians like Thomas Jefferson and James Madison; also known as the Jeffersonians

strict constructionism
Literal interpretation of the Constitution, arguing that the original meaning of those at the Constitutional Convention should not be adapted to fit more recent times

the Jeffersonians, although they preferred to be called the **Democratic-Republicans**. The Democratic-Republicans had three problems with Hamilton's plan (see "The reasons why. . .").

Jefferson, Madison, and their supporters envisioned an agrarian nation made up of independent farmers, not laborers and industrialists who were dependent on others. Their plan for an agrarian nation, of course, also allowed for, indeed depended on, the perpetuation of slavery. (Hamilton, meanwhile, ardently opposed slavery, believing that it denied individual liberty and favored the wealthy, established aristocracy of the South over the merchants of the North.)

Congressional Impasse and Washington, D.C.

The deadlock over Hamilton's plan for the national government to assume the still-outstanding state debts was ultimately broken by a compromise on an entirely separate issue: the location of the national government. Between 1789 and 1793, the federal government of the United States was in New York City. In 1793, the government moved south to Philadelphia, but southern leaders wanted the government to be located even farther south, in Virginia. They also wanted it to be located *outside* a big city, because many of Jefferson's supporters considered big cities sinkholes of corruption.

Washington, D.C., in 1800

Over dinner and wine one night, Jefferson and Hamilton struck a deal: Hamilton instructed supporters of his economic plan to favor relocating the seat of government along the Potomac River, and Jefferson allowed Hamilton's plan to pass through Congress. With this compromise, the economic legislation passed, the First Bank of the United States was created (it lasted until 1811), and the stage was set for the national government to move to Washington, D.C.

The Whiskey Rebellion

Opposition to Hamilton's economic policies was not limited to Democratic-Republicans in the government. In western Pennsylvania, Hamilton's decision to tax whiskey proved divisive. Before railroads or canals were built, western farmers depended on slow, halting, horse-based transport and had difficulty

{ The reasons why . . . }

The Democratic-Republicans had three problems with Hamilton's plan:

- The Democratic-Republicans thought that honoring all debts was unfair because many of the Americans who had purchased bonds to fund the revolutionary war—often widows and soldiers—had been forced to sell their bonds for less than their face value during the hard economic times of the 1780s. Commercial speculators bought the bonds from them at low prices, and Hamilton's plan would reward these speculators unfairly.

- They also believed that nationalizing the state debts was unfair because some states (especially southern states like Jefferson's Virginia) had already made headway in paying off their debts by selling western lands. If the debts of all states were pooled together,

then the residents of the states that had already reduced their debts would have to pay a disproportionate share of the national debt.

- Creating a bank was contentious because many Americans—particularly southerners—argued that the creation of a national bank would serve the interests of only financiers and merchants. They believed it would offer little aid to farmers and plantation owners. The Democratic-Republicans considered these groups the most virtuous citizens of an agrarian republic. Arguing that the creation of a bank was not within the purview of the federal government, the opponents of Hamilton's plan favored a more literal interpretation of the Constitution—a position called **strict constructionism**.

© iStockphoto.com/Jacom Stephens

transporting their crops without spoilage. They found it easier to distill their grain to whiskey and ship it in that form. A tax on whiskey was a serious threat to their livelihood. To make matters worse, Hamilton's plan taxed small producers of whiskey more than it did large producers, in part because the tax was an effort to demonstrate to small farmers and western-ers the government's authority to tax them. This gave rise to accusations of East Coast elitism.

In 1794, many westerners attacked the tax men who tried to collect the whiskey tax. When Washington and Hamilton attempted to bring some of the rebels to justice, they chose whiskey produc-ers in western Pennsylvania as their test case. The rural Pennsylvanians fought back, eventually riot-ing and overrunning the city of Pittsburgh, where they were to be tried for tax evasion. This was the **Whiskey Rebellion**. Alarmed by the direct refusal to adhere to the dictates of the federal government, George Washington issued a proclamation declaring the farmers in rebellion and sent a newly organized army of nearly thirteen thousand to quell the revolt. Washington himself at times led the troops. But by the time the army reached western Pennsylvania, the reb-els had gone home. Washington ultimately pardoned the two men who were captured in the dispute.

Results

From this time forward, the western prov-inces were firmly Anti-Federalist, favoring the small-government approach of the Democratic-Republicans. But Washington's message was clear:

the national government would not allow extralegal protests to effect change. In a nation of laws, change would come only through peaceful means.

The Problem of Foreign Policy

Through the 1790s, there were still no formal politi-cal parties, but clear divisions were apparent. Both politicians and everyday Americans had to deter-mine what kind of nation they wanted. In the Whiskey Rebellion, the Pennsylvania farmers sought to defend their idea that the federal government should not reach too deeply into the pockets of everyday Americans. They lost that particular battle, but the sympathy they aroused from the future Democratic-Republicans showed that their com-plaints did not go unheard.

As a new nation, the United States also had to travel the often-treacherous terrain of foreign policy. And here too, almost every decision made by the federal government was liable to be framed in divisive language. Would the nation support other Enlightenment-based revolutions, like the one tak-ing place in France? Would it challenge England when it infringed on American liberties in the seas? The answers to these questions only increased political divisions.

The Pinckney Treaty

In one rare instance, The **Pinckney Treaty of 1796** (also called the Treaty of San Lorenzo) was an accomplish-ment everyone could celebrate. The tax on whiskey

impressment
Practice of capturing and forcing sailors from other nations into naval service

Jay's Treaty
Treaty in which the British agreed to evacuate military posts along the frontier in the Northwest Territory and make reparations for the cargo seized in 1793 and 1794 while the United States lifted duties on British imports for ten years

remained after the Whiskey Rebellion, but opposition to the policy cooled when the treaty with Spain gave Pennsylvania farmers an easier way to get their crops to market. The Pinckney Treaty opened the Mississippi River to American shipping and allowed Americans the "right of deposit" at New Orleans, which meant that American merchants could warehouse goods in the city. The Pinckney Treaty was popular, a notable foreign policy achievement in a decade of political controversy. Other foreign policy decisions divided American leaders in the 1790s. In particular, government officials clashed over the French Revolution and the conduct of trade with certain foreign nations.

The French Revolution and the Citizen Genêt Affair

In 1789, growing discontent with the king spurred the French people to overthrow their monarchy, inciting the French Revolution. Most Americans were initially pleased with the news, thinking that they themselves had been on the front line of an inevitable transition to republican governments around the world. But by the early 1790s, the news from France grew worse: the country had erupted into violence, and one leader after another had been deposed, creating chaos and a reign of terror. The French could not agree on what liberty was, who was deserving of it, or how it could be governed fairly.

Public opinion in America was divided over the French Revolution. The disorder in France alarmed many Federalists, and criticism increased when the revolutionaries executed the former king, Louis XVI, and his wife, Marie Antoinette, in 1793. At the same time, many Federalists (especially in New England) viewed England as the United States' natural trading partner. When Britain declared war on France in 1792 (other European nations saw France's chaos as an opportunity to make territorial gains, prompting Europe-wide battles), many New Englanders were concerned that too much support for France's revolution would sour trade relations with England. Meanwhile, the Democratic-Republicans continued to sympathize with the revolution, supporting its attempt to create a republican government.

In the United States, the conflict came to a head when an ambassador from the revolutionary French Republic, Edmond Genêt, arrived in the United States on April 8, 1793. Genêt's mission was to raise support for the new French government, particularly because the revolution had brought France into conflict with England and Spain, key trading partners of the United States. Genêt received a mixed reception. Many Americans remembered the French contribution to the American Revolution and welcomed him. Others pointed out that America's alliance had actually been with the now-deposed French king, not the new French Republic. To avoid entanglement, Washington issued a neutrality proclamation three weeks after Genêt's arrival, on April 22, 1793.

Genêt ignored the proclamation and very publicly tried to recruit American soldiers and advocate American attacks on British ships. This was a direct challenge to Washington's stance on neutrality, so the president issued a proclamation in August 1793 that France recall Genêt. (Genêt was allowed to stay in America, however, after a new French government demanded his arrest and Washington became aware that Genêt would likely be executed if he returned to France. Washington opposed Genêt's methods, not Genêt himself, and thus allowed him to stay.)

Besides creating a diplomatic nuisance, the Genêt affair was significant because it delineated further distinctions between Washington's Federalists and Jefferson's Democratic-Republicans. Jefferson opposed President Washington's neutrality and realized that Washington had started looking more to Hamilton for advice on foreign affairs than to him. Recognizing his loss of influence, Jefferson resigned as secretary of state in July 1793, a sign of the growing divisions within American political leadership.

U.S. Neutrality and Jay's Treaty

The rebuke of Genêt did not end Washington's problems maintaining neutrality. Indeed, neither France nor Britain respected American neutrality, with the British sometimes performing the terrible act of **impressing** (capturing and forcing into service) American sailors into its navy. Other British policies, unrelated to the war with France, also aggravated Americans. For example, the treaty that ended the American Revolution decreed that the British evacuate their forts on the American frontier, but a decade after the agreement was reached, Britain still occupied the forts. In addition, Britain closed its ports in the West Indies to American ships.

To address these issues, in 1794, Washington sent New York's John Jay to Britain. Jay had served as the first Chief Justice of the Supreme Court and helped negotiate the treaty that ended the American Revolution.

In 1795, Jay returned with **Jay's Treaty**. In it the British agreed to evacuate military posts along the frontier in the Northwest Territory and make reparations for the cargo seized in 1793 and 1794. But Jay made several concessions: for instance, the United States lifted duties on British imports for ten years. Furthermore, the treaty avoided addressing other important issues, such as the impressing of American sailors.

Jay's Treaty brought the conflict over foreign relations (whether to support France or England) to a boiling point. Jefferson's partisans were brutal in their attacks on the Federalists, claiming that Jay's Treaty was a betrayal of the 1778 alliance with France and a humiliating capitulation to the British. At public rallies, protesters burned Jay in effigy. The vehemence of the opposition caused Washington to hesitate in signing the treaty, although he did sign it eventually. Nevertheless, Jay's Treaty indicated growing divisions within American politics, divisions that would contribute to the rise of a two-party political system.

Indian Relations

Indian Resistance in the Northwest

If problems of finance and foreign policy were hardening the opposition of the two political factions, they could at least agree on the policies toward Indians. Once again, it was the Americans' westward expansion that provoked the conflict. In 1790, a huge coalition of Indian tribes (including the Chippewa, Ottawa, Shawnee, Delaware, Pottawatomi, and others) attacked American settlers north of the Ohio River, in what is today Ohio. Buttressed by British promises of support, the Native Americans were successful in defeating several American battalions until 1794, when the American Army finally secured a victory in the Battle of Fallen Timbers. President Washington intended to clear the Ohio River Valley for settlement and had finally done so at that battle. The result was the **Treaty of Greenville** (1795), which forced the Indian tribes of the Old Northwest westward, across the Mississippi (Map 8.1). This signaled peace in and white settlement of the Ohio River Valley for two decades.

The South

At about the same time, the Creeks near Georgia were battling to prevent further American encroachment on their lands. The Spanish were the real beneficiaries of the Creek war, because the Creeks served as a buffer between Spain's Florida territory and the American settlers in Georgia. Anxious to avoid continued attacks by the Creeks, George Washington called the Creek leader, Alexander McGillivray, to New York to pursue a treaty. The parties agreed to terms that legitimated the Creek presence and ended hostilities until 1792, when McGillivray accepted better terms from the Spanish. Small wars continued in the South and Southwest until 1794, at which time Tennesseans, hoping to establish Tennessee as a state, successfully pushed the Creeks farther west and south.

A New Policy

The continuing violence led the United States to revise its Indian policy. In 1790, Congress passed the first of the **Indian Trade and Intercourse Acts**, which made it illegal for Americans to trade with Native American tribes without formal consent from the federal government. The acts also made it illegal to sell land to or buy land from Native Americans without similar federal consent. This last part began the process of defining "Indian territory," the lands where Indians could live and work.

LO³ The Rise of Two-Party Politics

Despite the factions' willingness to come together to fight Indians, by 1795, after the uproars caused by the Citizen Genêt affair and Jay's Treaty, the two major divisions of opinion had crystallized into political parties: the Democratic-Republicans and the Federalists. Each party considered itself the inheritor of America's revolutionary ideology and viewed its opposition as illegitimate.

The Democratic-Republicans

The Democratic-Republican Party (often called the Republican Party or the Jeffersonian-Republicans) coalesced in opposition to Hamilton's economic policies and Jay's Treaty. James Madison and a few other Virginians were the architects of the new organization. They transformed a loose collection of "Democratic-Republican societies" into a disciplined party whose members voted with consistency. In 1792, Thomas Jefferson assumed the party's leadership.

Treaty of Greenville Agreement which forced the Indian tribes of the Old Northwest westward across the Mississippi in 1795

Indian Trade and Intercourse Acts Laws which made it illegal for Americans to trade with Native American tribes without formal consent from the federal government and also made it illegal to sell land to or buy land from Native Americans without similar federal consent

Map 8.1
The West, 1790–1796
The Battle of Fallen Timbers and the Treaty of Greenville pushed white settlement across Ohio and into Indiana.

In general, the Democratic-Republicans favored limited government. They opposed the national bank and other measures that enhanced the power of the federal government, and they sided with France over Great Britain because of the feeling of shared republican brotherhood with France. It should be noted, however, that their sense of self-rule also included the right to own slaves if one so desired. Jefferson found supporters among southern landholders and among free workers and laborers everywhere.

The Federalists

The **Federalist Party** grew out of the faction of American leaders that endorsed Hamilton's economic policies and Jay's Treaty. They supported Washington's presidency and helped John Adams succeed him in 1796. In general, the Federalists supported the stability provided by a centralized government and were suspicious of the whims of the populace. The Federalists supported a strong governmental role in economic affairs and the stability of trade with Britain. They were mostly wealthy merchants, large property owners, or conservative farmers. New England and the Middle Colonies were Federalist strongholds.

The Slavery Issue

Aside from finance and federalism, another issue caused a rift between the two parties: slavery. To be sure, most Federalists were not abolitionists, but many of them were less committed to the continuation of slavery than the Democratic-Republicans. This division was illuminated in each party's reaction to the Haitian Revolution.

The Haitian Revolution

In 1791, slaves in Santo Domingo, Haiti, revolted, killing planters and burning sugar plantations. Led by Toussaint L'Ouverture, the slaves declared independence from their French overlords. In America, the Federalists supported the revolution (in this instance, *they* were the ones mindful of their own republican roots). George Washington kept up trade relations with Haiti and sought to recognize the independent nation made up mostly of former slaves.

Democratic-Republicans were aghast at Washington's actions. The Haitian Revolution had forced a flood of white landholders to decamp to America's southern states, who told of the violence they had witnessed and warned against the potential creation of a black republic near the coast of America. When Thomas Jefferson became president in 1800, he reversed the nation's position on the Haitian Revolution and supported French attempts to crush the slave rebellion. (The French lost this effort in 1803, and Haiti became the first black republic and Latin America's first independent state.)

There were three results of the Haitian Revolution in the South. First, southern lawmakers tightened black codes, citing fear of slave insurrec-

tions in America. Second, the revolution also hardened planters' conviction that the South was meant to maintain slavery. This reliance on slavery had deepened after the invention of the cotton gin in 1793, which made labor-intensive cotton profitable in much of the South. Finally, the revolution underscored France's increased reluctance to maintain their possessions in the New World, a sentiment that led to the Louisiana Purchase of 1803 (see Chapter 9).

Gabriel's Conspiracy

Yet another result of the Haitian Revolution was the spread of revolutionary fervor among American slaves, which sparked **Gabriel's Conspiracy** in 1800. After the American Revolution, New York and Philadelphia became havens for free black people, and nearly all of the northern states had developed plans to free their slaves. The opposite was happening in the South, where slavery was becoming more and more entrenched.

In 1800, several churchgoing African Americans learned of the events in Haiti and planned a similar attack on Richmond, Virginia. They intended to burn the town and capture the governor, James Monroe. After heavy rain postponed the attack, several conspirators leaked the plan. State leaders hanged twenty-six rebels, including the leader, a slave named Gabriel. A second attack in 1802 (led by a slave named Sancho) was also preemptively stopped. These two attempts by slaves to overthrow the system resulted in the continued tightening of the laws governing slaves. Most significantly, all postrevolutionary talk of emancipation in the South ended due to white fears of black insurrection. The harsh measures were meant to stifle slaves' hopes of escaping the system, and they worked.

> **❝**I am ready to join them at any moment. I could slay the white people like sheep.**❞**
> —*Slave recruit to Gabriel's Conspiracy*

See documents related to Gabriel's Conspiracy.

LO⁴ Adams's Presidency and Dealing with Dissent

George Washington easily won reelection as president in 1792, but as the election of 1796 approached,

Washington decided not to run for a third term. Exhausted by his years as president and by the continual attacks of the Democratic-Republican press, Washington encouraged Americans to come together under a nonpartisan system. His hopes were not realized. The Democratic-Republicans and the Federalists both began organizing local meetings of their supporters. In his heartfelt Farewell Address, Washington rued these divisions, but both parties were sufficiently well organized to field candidates in the election of 1796. The two-party political system was born.

Read Washington's Farewell Address of 1796.

Adams's Election

When Washington's vice president, Federalist John Adams, announced his candidacy for president, the Democratic-Republicans nominated Thomas Jefferson to oppose him. After a particularly partisan campaign, rife with intense bickering and dissention, Adams received seventy-one electoral votes and became president. According to the Constitution, the candidate with the second highest number of electoral votes was to be vice president, and, by previous arrangement among Federalist electoral voters, Adams's running mate, Thomas Pinckney of South Carolina, was meant to receive the same number of votes as Adams less one, with one supporter withholding his vote. This would have given Pinckney seventy votes and the vice presidency. Confusion and trickery muddled the plan, though, and, communications were slow. No one was sure who was supposed to hold back his vote for Pinckney, and so, several did. The result was

that, instead of Pinckney, it was Jefferson who took second place, with sixty-eight electoral votes. Thus, Adams's opponent, Thomas Jefferson, became his vice president. From 1797 to 1800, there would be no harmony in the federal government.

The XYZ Affair

Upon entering office in 1797, Adams immediately faced a foreign policy crisis called the **XYZ Affair**, which further divided the two factions. The French had interpreted Jay's Treaty as an indication that the United States was siding with Great Britain in the trade wars, and they retaliated by raiding American merchant ships. France was angry at what it saw as a rebuke to the clan of republican brotherhood. Adams sent three envoys to France to defuse the situation, and the French foreign minister sent three agents to meet them (designated X, Y, and Z in official French documents). It became evident that X, Y, and Z's real purpose was to extort money from the Americans as a prerequisite for negotiations. When news of "the XYZ Affair" reached the United States, Americans were outraged at France's galling lack of respect.

Result—The Quasi-War

Meanwhile, the French continued to raid American ships. The Adams administration responded to these raids by repudiat-

> Adams's opponent, Thomas Jefferson, became his vice president. From 1797 to 1800, there would be no harmony in the federal government.

>> "Cinque-têtes, or the Paris Monster," an outrageous contemporary political cartoon on the XYZ Affair, shows staunch Americans resisting threats and demands for money from revolutionary France, depicted as happily devouring frogs, guillotining aristocrats, and supporting the Haitian revolution (notice Toussaint L'Ouverture seated at the far right).

ing America's 1778 alliance with France, and a so-called "quasi-war" erupted between the two nations. From 1798 to 1800, the naval fleets of both countries openly plundered each other's ships. As Franco-American relations deteriorated, Adams feared the outbreak of a full-scale war between the two nations. This was significant because it put Adams on the defensive regarding dissent within the American government. In his mind, America was on the verge of an international war.

Lyon retaliated by spitting in Griswold's face, and the two men began wrestling on the floor of the House of Representatives.

Alien and Sedition Acts

Adams's concerns about dissent became problematic because partisanship had continued to escalate during his term. For example, in 1798, a fight broke out on the floor of the House of Representatives

when Matthew Lyon, a pugnacious Democratic-Republican congressman from Vermont, declared that aristocratic Federalist representatives were perpetually duping the people. Roger Griswold, a Federalist representative from Connecticut, asked Lyon if he meant to defend the people with a wooden sword. (Griswold was referring to the fact that, during the American Revolution, Lyon had been court-martialed for cowardice and forced to wear a wooden sword as punishment.) Lyon retaliated by spitting in Griswold's face, and the two men began wrestling on the floor of the House of Representatives.

The Alien and Sedition Acts

Attempting to bring such bitter conflicts under control, Adams pushed a series of measures through

Congress known collectively as the **Alien and Sedition Acts**. They turned out to be his undoing.

The Alien and Sedition Acts consisted of three separate acts, the third of which would have the biggest impact on Adams's future: (1) the Alien Enemies Act authorized the deportation of the citizens of enemy nations; (2) the Alien Friends Act allowed the government to detain and deport noncitizens for almost any cause. Because many of the most active Democratic-Republicans were recent British immigrants, the Alien Friends Act was regarded as a deliberate assault on the party; and (3) the Sedition Act set fines and prison sentences for anyone found guilty of writing, speaking, or publishing "false, scandalous and malicious" statements against the government.

The two Alien Acts had little impact, but the Sedition Act was explosive. Several Democratic-Republican newspaper editors were jailed for violating the new law. Federalists used the law to jail Matthew Lyon, the Democratic-Republican representative who had wrestled on the House floor. But not only did the act make political martyrs out of the jailed Republican-Democrats, it provoked their party colleagues to fight back.

Calling the Alien and Sedition Acts a violation of the First Amendment's guarantees, Thomas Jefferson and James Madison collaborated anonymously to pen a set of resolutions denouncing the acts. In 1798, the legislatures of Virginia and Kentucky adopted resolutions—called the **Virginia and Kentucky Resolutions**—proclaiming the Sedition Act to be an infringement on rights protected by their state constitutions. The resolutions declared that each state had the right to nullify federal laws within their borders.

This bold challenge to federal authority was called the **doctrine of nullification**. No other state endorsed the resolutions, but they provided the intellectual framework for sectional divisions that were to come. They also set the stage for the bitter election of 1800.

LO⁵ The "Bloodless Revolution" of 1800

The Campaign

The candidates in the election of 1800 were the same as those in 1796, Jefferson and Adams. Four years of controversy, however, had intensified the bitter rivalry between the two men. Citing the Alien-Sedition Acts, Democratic-Republicans accused Adams of harboring monarchical ideas and called him a slave to British interests. Federalists castigated Thomas Jefferson as an atheist (he had composed his own personal copy of the Bible by cutting out everything but the words spoken by Christ) who would follow the lead of the French revolutionaries and instigate a reign of terror in the United States. The campaigning was vitriolic, to say the least.

The Mistake

John Adams gave his opposition unexpected help by reopening negotiations with France. In terms of international relations, the negotiations were a success; they resulted in a peace treaty that brought the quasi-war to an end. In terms of Adams's candidacy, because most of his fellow Federalists were pro-British, his efforts to smooth things over with France divided his own party. The Federalist Party had already suffered in the controversy over the Alien and Sedition Acts. Now they were divided over whether the United States should negotiate with France.

The Election

As the election of 1800 approached, the Federalists were too divided to give Jefferson any real competition. Hamilton, in fact, jockeyed to get the Federalists to dump Adams as their candidate. In contrast, the Democratic-Republican Party was well organized, and the final tally in the Electoral College gave Jefferson and his running mate, Aaron Burr of New York, a clear margin of victory.

Results

The assumption of power by the Democratic-Republicans did not go off without a hitch, however. Ironically, the Democratic-Republicans were, in a way, too organized. Jefferson and Burr received seventy-three votes apiece in Electoral College voting. This was a problem because the Constitution did

Map 8.2
The Election of 1800

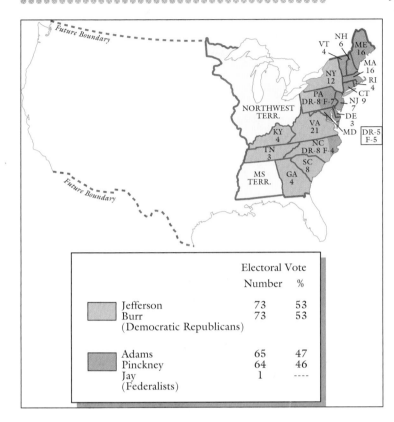

		Electoral Vote	
		Number	%
	Jefferson	73	53
	Burr	73	53
	(Democratic Republicans)		
	Adams	65	47
	Pinckney	64	46
	Jay	1	----
	(Federalists)		

lame duck
Politician who is not returning to office and is serving
out the rest of his or her
term with little influence; a
soon-to-be-out-of-office politician or Congress

decision. Some Federalists decided to support Burr and deny Jefferson the presidency, and, although Burr did not openly support this movement, he also did not denounce it. Hamilton, however, distrusted Burr more than he disliked Jefferson. Using his influence among the Federalists, Hamilton helped his old rival Thomas Jefferson to victory on the thirty-sixth ballot. To ensure that the shenanigans of the 1800 election would never be repeated, in 1804 the United States adopted the Twelfth Amendment to the Constitution, allowing electors to vote for president and vice president separately.

And in the end . . .

Although party politics had increased tremendously between 1796 and 1800, the election of 1800 was valuable in demonstrating that an opposition party could defeat the party in power without causing a total breakdown of government or a civil war. This was a tremendous accomplishment. When Adams and the Federalists handed over the reins of power peacefully, optimism ran high that the nation had passed a critical test. After 1800, opposition became a cornerstone of the American system of government, as did the two-party system. The so-called bloodless revolution of 1800 paved the way for active, peaceful political dissent in American life.

not provide for a two-person ticket (with one designated as president and the other as vice president). Rather, it stated that the candidate with the most electoral votes became president and the candidate with the second most assumed the vice presidency. In the event of a tie, the decision was placed in the hands of the House of Representatives.

In the election of 1800 (Map 8.2), Democratic-Republican candidates had also won control of both houses of Congress, but the new Congress did not sit until after the presidential election was settled. Therefore, it was the **lame-duck** (or, soon-to-be-out-of-office) Federalist Congress that would make the

What else was happening . . .

1791	Early bicycles are made in Scotland.
1798	The first soft drink is invented.
1800	Worcestershire sauce is invented.

Jeffersonian

Democracy

1800–1814

Learning Outcomes

After reading this chapter, you should be able to do the following:

LO **1**   Define Jeffersonian Democracy, and explain how Jefferson's presidency both defined and contradicted that political philosophy.

LO **2**   Discuss the reasons for and the results of the War of 1812.

> ## "Democratic-Republicans brought politics to the people in a new, more personal way. "

Jefferson's election marked a reversal in American politics. Jefferson's apprehension of an overly strong centralized government led him to advocate a vision of a farmers' republic, led by an agrarian upper class. To realize this vision, he attempted to roll back several of the Federalist policies,

although he did not go as far as many of his supporters hoped. At the same time, Jefferson dramatically expanded the boundaries of the nation to allow for continued westward expansion. All this occurred during a similarly dramatic expansion of America's social and economic life, which is the subject of Chapter 10. This chapter examines Jefferson's presidency, the meaning of "Jeffersonian Democracy," and the rule of the Jeffersonians through the War of 1812.

LO¹ Jefferson's Presidency

Jeffersonian Democracy

In addition to being the beneficiaries of the country's first bloodless revolution, the Democratic-Republicans were instrumental in transforming the political culture of America. The Federalists never relished the notion of making appeals to the public, preferring instead for the people to call on their leaders to act on their behalf. In contrast, Jefferson's Democratic-Republicans eagerly cultivated popular opinion. They founded highly partisan newspapers that spread throughout the country. They campaigned at the grass roots, staging political barbecues and clambakes. They also led virulent attacks on their Federalist opponents. The Federalists never mastered this aggressive art of politicking, a failure that made them appear out of touch with the people. Thus, although the vote remained restricted to white male property holders over the age of twenty-one, the Democratic-Republicans brought politics to the people in a new, more personal way. This is what historians mean by **Jeffersonian Democracy**.

Jefferson's Domestic Policies
Reducing the Size of Government

Although Jefferson and his supporters changed America's political culture, they retained much of Hamilton's ambitious

> **Jeffersonian Democracy** Innovation introduced by Jefferson's Democratic-Republicans when they eagerly cultivated popular opinion by campaigning at the grass roots

© iStockphoto.com/Jerry Downs

economic plan. However, Jefferson did seek to make the small federal government even smaller. He proposed two major cutbacks. First, the repeal of many of the taxes Hamilton had imposed allowed Jefferson to reduce the number of federal employees (especially the hated tax assessors). Under Jefferson's plan, tariffs from trading partners, not internal taxes, would fund government operations. Second, Jefferson cut back the military, maintaining just a small army on the western frontier and a small navy that could protect only America's coast. He would pay a substantial price for these two changes, but there was no way for him to know this during his first term. The Federalists, having lost both houses of Congress, could do nothing to prevent these actions, despite the fact that many New England Federalists were concerned that their shipping industry would be jeopardized by the weakened naval fleet. Perhaps taking pity on their powerless status, Jefferson refused to use the Alien and Sedition Acts against the Federalists, as he was legally entitled to.

The Courts

Federalists still had power in the courts, though. This situation birthed two of the most important developments in U.S. judicial history: (1) judicial review, which gave the courts the right to declare an act of Congress unconstitutional and therefore make it void; and (2) the idea that partisanship was not a crime.

Judicial Review

The first of these developments emerged in 1800, when the outgoing president, John Adams, made a number of last-minute "midnight appointments" of Federalist judges. Adams hoped to ensure that the Federalist Party could retain a strong position in the judiciary. But Jefferson and his Democratic-Republicans swiftly repealed the appointments. William Marbury, one of the frustrated judges, sued James Madison (Jefferson's secretary of state) for denying his appointment. This reached the Supreme Court as *Marbury v. Madison* (1803).

Chief Justice John Marshall, a Federalist, headed the Supreme Court from 1801 to 1835. Marshall, suspecting that Jefferson would ignore

his decision whatever it might be, issued a decision, in 1803, declaring that Marbury deserved his appointment, but that the Court could not force the president to grant it. He said that the original Judiciary Act of 1789, which supposedly gave the Court the right to enforce appointments, exceeded the powers granted to the Court in the Constitution. Thus, the original Judiciary Act of 1789 was unconstitutional.

In this roundabout way, Marshall declared that the courts had the right to judge the constitutionality of federal laws, a right called the **doctrine of judicial review**. Based on that ingenious decision, the Supreme Court refused to engage in the partisan bickering of the time, while at the same time carving out its position as the ultimate interpreter of constitutional questions.

The Legality of Partisanship

The second important judicial precedent was established when Jefferson sought to impeach the most politically biased Federalist judges. To Jefferson's chagrin, in 1805, the Senate refused to convict Federalist judge Samuel Chase on purely political grounds. This set the precedent that partisanship was not a crime and that, once appointed, judges could be as partisan as they wished in their decisions without facing rebuke or retribution.

Expanding the Agrarian Republic

Given the republican belief that farming provided the moral basis for good citizenship, Jefferson felt it essential that the United States continue to open new territory to settlement. Without access to new land, Jefferson reasoned, crowding would pressure people into working for others as urban wage laborers. In contrast, territorial expansion allowed every American the chance to be a self-sufficient farmer.

The first step Jefferson took to create this vision was to purchase the city of New Orleans from France. New Orleans was a vital port city at the mouth of the Mississippi River, and the Mississippi was the country's main north-south inland waterway, providing a means of transportation from the Gulf of Mexico to present-day St. Paul, Minnesota. The United States could never guarantee control of the Mississippi unless it controlled New Orleans as well.

In 1803, Jefferson sent emissaries to France to negotiate the purchase of New Orleans. Much to Jefferson's surprise, the French emperor, Napoleon Bonaparte, wanted to sell not only New Orleans, but all of Louisiana, then a huge tract of land that stretched from the Mississippi River to the

>> **Panorama of New Orleans in 1803.**

UNDER MY WINGS EVERY THING PROSPERS

Rocky Mountains. The French treasury was nearly empty, and another war between France and Britain loomed imminently. In addition, after the Haitian Revolution, France had learned how costly it was to maintain colonial possessions. Napoleon asked only $15 million for the 830,000 square miles of Louisiana.

The Constitution did not give the president power to buy new territory, but Jefferson pushed ahead with the **Louisiana Purchase**. Although he claimed to believe that federal power was dangerous and that the Constitution had to be followed strictly, Jefferson was willing to bend his own rules to expand America's western boundary all the way to the Rockies (Map 9.1). The purchase nearly doubled the geographic size of the nation.

Lewis and Clark

Jefferson took responsibility not only for acquiring new territory, but also for exploring it. In 1803, before the Louisiana Purchase

> The Lewis and Clark expedition inspired generations of Americans to move westward.

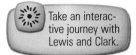
Take an interactive journey with Lewis and Clark.

was completed, Jefferson sent his private secretary Meriwether Lewis with William Clark as co-commander on an exploratory mission to the Pacific. In 1804, Lewis and Clark, along with forty-eight other men, left St. Louis and journeyed northwest toward the Rockies. With the help of Sacajawea, a Shoshone Indian woman who served as their guide, Lewis and Clark traveled to the Pacific. In 1806, the expedition returned to St. Louis with an immense amount of information about the American West. Their journey inspired generations of Americans to move westward and lay claim to the nation's interior.

Land Policies

Jefferson also made access to western lands easier through a revised land policy. The Land Act of 1800, signed by President Adams, had set up land-selling offices in the West, made the parcels smaller (and more affordable), and allowed for payment over time (rather than in a single large lump sum). In 1804, the Democratic-Republicans again reduced the minimum amount that could be purchased, making Western land even more affordable. In a sense, the federal government had become the real

>> **William Clark's diary of the Lewis and Clark expedition.**

> **Louisiana Purchase** Tract of 830,000 square miles that stretched from the Mississippi River to the Rocky Mountains; Jefferson bought it from Napoleon for $15 million in 1803

estate agent for the nation's interior. And, as always, increased westward expansion meant increased contact, and battles, with Native Americans.

Tecumseh and the Prophet

In the early 1800s, two Shawnee brothers, **Tecumseh and the Prophet**, proposed to unite tribes from the Old Northwest (in Ohio and Michigan) and the South (Georgia) to resist the perpetual encroachment of American settlers. The brothers toured across the land preaching a revival of old ways in a **revitalization movement** reminiscent of Neolin's (Chapter 4). The brothers opposed the acceptance of European and American habits, including whiskey and guns.

They set up pan-Indian towns across Indiana. One of the towns was called "Prophetstown" by the surrounding American settlers, and the other was called "Tippecanoe."

Tecumseh and the Prophet grew popular with young Indians, and their increasing power drew international attention. First, the few British who remained in the American West encouraged the growth of the revitalization movement, hoping it would prove too formidable for the American frontiersmen and curb further expansion. But the American settlers had a strong presence in Indiana. In 1811, Indiana Governor William Henry Harrison attacked Tippecanoe, setting the town ablaze. When the War of 1812 broke out, Harrison, then a U.S. Army general, continued his destruction of Indian towns as he led a troop of American soldiers on an attack of British Canada. Tecumseh died in battle, thus ending (for a time) any further attempts at Indian unity.

Map 9.1
The Louisiana Purchase

> The Louisiana Purchase nearly doubled the geographic size of the nation.

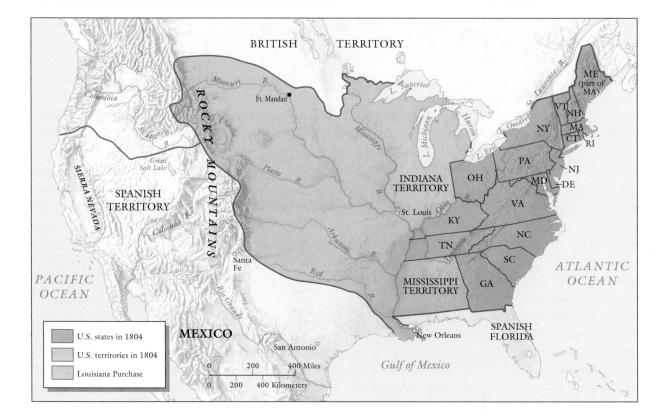

- U.S. states in 1804
- U.S. territories in 1804
- Louisiana Purchase

Reelection

Taking advantage of the new culture of politics, of the expansion of the nation, and of good economic times of the early 1800s, Jefferson coasted to an easy reelection in 1804. The Federalists had once again been beaten badly, and some Federalists were so dismayed at their reversal of fortune that they persuaded Aaron Burr to run for governor of New York and then, if victorious, to separate New York and New England from the rest of the nation. This, in 1804, was the country's first serious plot of secession. Alexander Hamilton—ever the nationalist—learned of the plot and politicked against Burr in New York, leading to Burr's defeat. In his fury, Burr challenged Hamilton to a duel. In that duel, Burr assassinated Hamilton, who, disapproving of duels, had fired his gun into the air. Burr subsequently lost all political respectability because most Americans believed that politics was meant to occupy the realm of discussion and law, not violence and vigilantism. Cast

out from political society, Burr moved west, plotting further secession attempts, until he was tried for treason in the nation's first "Trial of the Century." He was found not guilty by Chief Justice John Marshall, but his widespread unpopularity prompted him to decamp to Europe.

Although Burr is an extreme case, his actions illustrate the bitter divisions between the Federalists and the Democratic-Republicans. His very extremity and singularity, however, also demonstrate that, despite partisanship, the new nation was a nation of laws.

Jefferson's Foreign Affairs

Jefferson's Problematic Diplomacy

While the new nation was weathering the few internal storms that arose (and enjoying good economic times), international events seized attention during Jefferson's two terms. Shortly after the Louisiana Purchase, the long-expected war between France and Great Britain erupted. At first, the United States benefited. With Britain and France fighting each other, America (as a neutral power) took control of the shipping trade between the Americas and Europe. Many American traders grew wealthy. Soon, however, the United States found itself caught in the middle.

England controlled the seas, and France controlled the continent of Europe. With no land to fight on, each nation attempted to starve the other into submission. They restricted other nations from trading with their enemies, raided ships, and prevented them from entering European ports. American shipping was particularly punished. By 1807, about eight

>> **Burr assassinated Hamilton, who, disapproving of duels, had fired his gun into the air.**

hundred American ships had been raided by French and British fleets. Meanwhile, the British began impressing American sailors into the Royal Navy, much as they had in the early 1790s. Estimates of the number of Americans eventually impressed range from four thousand to ten thousand. After one highly publicized attack on the *U.S.S. Chesapeake*, Americans were so angered that some called for war, but it was not to be, for the simple reason that Jefferson had dismantled the U.S. military and was sure to lose any such battle.

The Right of Neutrality

Eager to save face, Jefferson reiterated the rights of a neutral party and initiated a program of "peaceable coercion," which he hoped would get both England and France to stop tormenting America's shipping industry. His plan turned out to be his administration's biggest mistake. The plan centered on the **Embargo Act of 1807**, which stopped American exports from going to Europe and prohibited American ships from trading in foreign ports. Jefferson reasoned that depriving France and Britain of American commerce would force them to recognize America's neutral rights. In essence, he was saying that, if England and France would not respect American rights, Jefferson would punish them by shutting down a large portion of the American economy.

Results

The Embargo Act was a disaster. Europe was not deprived of very much, and British ships took over the Atlantic sea trade. The act imperiled the American economy, especially in the Federalist stronghold of New England, where shipping was a major part of the local economy. Angered by the embargo, American traders began smuggling goods out of the country, an act that the Democratic-Republicans denounced.

Despite the policy's shortcomings, Jefferson refused to admit his mistake. All of these frustrations bubbled into the presidential election of 1808.

> The Embargo Act was a disaster. Europe was not deprived of very much, and British ships took over the Atlantic sea trade.

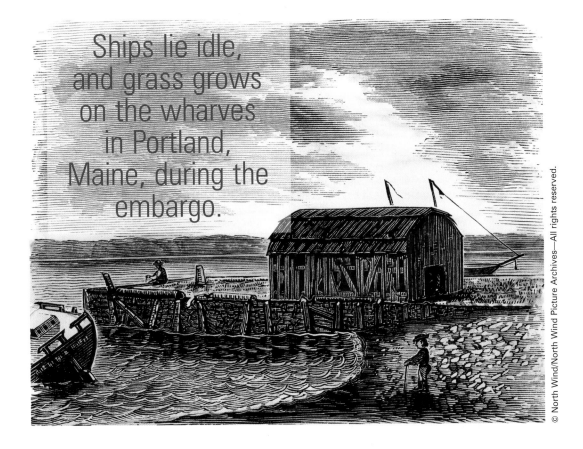

Ships lie idle, and grass grows on the wharves in Portland, Maine, during the embargo.

LO² James Madison and the War of 1812

The Election of 1808 and Declaration of War

The Federalists hoped to capitalize on the unpopularity of the Embargo Act to reclaim the presidency in 1808, but, despite solid support in New England, they did not have the national strength to defeat the Democratic-Republicans. Like Washington, Jefferson had chosen not to run for a third term. Instead, he assured that the nomination would go to his friend and fellow Virginian, James Madison. Madison handily defeated the Federalist candidate, Charles Pinckney, but Pinckney did better than projected, worrying the Democratic-Republicans, who became aware of the widespread anger stirred up by Jefferson's Embargo Act.

The Repeal of the Embargo Act

To prevent the Federalists from gaining ground on the issue of the Embargo Act, Congress repealed it in 1809, shortly before Madison became president. In its place, Congress passed the **Non-Intercourse Act**, which allowed American ships to trade with all nations except Britain and France, and authorized the president to resume trade with those countries once they began respecting America's neutral trading rights.

France Makes Amends

In a brilliant tactical move, France's emperor, Napoleon, announced that he would respect America's neutrality rights, whereupon Madison resumed trade with France and vehemently prohibited trade with Britain. With British trade banned from both continental Europe and the United States, the British economy suffered a depression. On June 16, 1812, the British vowed to respect American neutrality.

Declaration of War

But it was too little, too late. Indeed, war had already been declared. Madison was incensed by Britain's consistent refusal to recognize American neutrality. Moreover, he had been influenced by westerners who wanted war with Britain because they felt the British were to blame for increased Indian violence in the Midwest. These westerners, led in Congress by Kentuckian Henry Clay, were called "war hawks." Their influence meant that the war would be fought against both the British in the Atlantic and hostile Indians to the west.

Under these pressures, James Madison went to Congress on June 1, 1812 (two weeks before Britain pledged to honor America's neutrality), to ask for a declaration of war. Congress split over the question along party lines, with Democratic-Republicans favoring war and Federalists condemning it. Federalists were convinced that war would only hurt American trade further. In contrast, Democratic-Republicans were convinced that a "second war for American independence" was necessary before Britain would recognize America's rights as a neutral nation. Despite Federalist opposition, the Democratic-Republicans carried the vote, and the United States declared war against Britain on June 14, 1812.

The regional support for the war emerged a few months later, in the presidential election of 1812. Madison and the Federalist candidate DeWitt Clinton split the votes of all the eastern states, while the five western states voted solidly for Madison, catapulting him to a second term.

> **Non-Intercourse Act** Legislation passed in 1809 which allowed American ships to trade with all nations except Britain and France, and authorized the president to resume trade with those countries once they began respecting America's neutral trading rights

The War of 1812

Early Defeats

With Britain still embroiled in conflict with France, many Americans expected to win the War of 1812 handily (Map 9.2). In reality, winning the war proved more difficult. Jefferson's reduction of the American military had left the United States poorly prepared. Nevertheless, American forces initiated an assault on British-controlled Canada in 1812, hoping to conquer it quickly and make it one of the United States.

The invasion of British Canada was a complete fiasco. Instead of striking directly at the St. Lawrence River—the lifeline that linked Canada's principal cities to the Atlantic Ocean—the Americans split into three forces, each too small to crush the opposition. They were further handicapped by Britain's willingness to sign treaties with Native Americans if they would fight against the Americans.

Surprising Victories and Indian Decimation

The following year, the picture brightened for the United States. American forces held their own against the British and won a crucial naval battle at

Map 9.2
The War of 1812

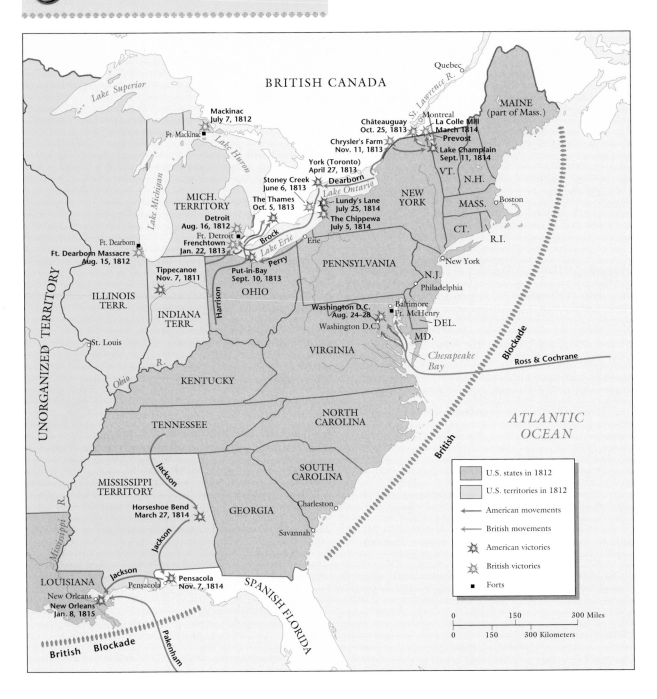

View an interactive version of this map.

Put-in-Bay on Lake Erie. American naval control of the waters in the region made defense of the area north of Lake Erie impossible for the British. The British defeat spelled disaster for a group of Indian tribes that had united with the British in order to fight for tribal rights, as the victorious Americans now felt entitled to plunder their villages.

In the South in 1813, a frontier army under Andrew Jackson defeated the Creek Indians (who viewed the War of 1812 as an opportunity to take

Take an online course on the Battle of Horse Shoe Bend.

advantage of a distracted American army and finally secure land in Georgia). At the Battle of Horse Shoe Bend, in today's Alabama, in March 1814, Jackson's troops forced the Creeks to accept a treaty that ceded their best lands to the Americans.

Culmination

Just as the Americans had seemed to turn the tide of battle, their position teetered when the British forced the abdication of Napoleon, briefly ending European hostilities and freeing the British to focus on their war with the United States. British leaders planned a three-pronged strategy: attacking Lake Champlain, Washington, D.C., and New Orleans.

At Lake Champlain, in September 1814, the British ground force of 15,000 men faced stiffer-than-expected resistance from American advance units, while U.S. naval forces under Captain Thomas Macdonough defied all expectations and destroyed the British fleet as they waited for ground support. The British assault on Washington, D.C., was more successful. The U.S. militia was overwhelmed and essentially vanished during the fight, leaving only a small force of American soldiers and sailors to serve as the region's defense. President Madison and his wife Dolley were among those compelled to flee the city. The British burned the White House, the Capitol, and other government buildings, but the ultimate objective of the invasion—to capture the port city of Baltimore—eluded them. During the failed invasion of Baltimore, Francis Scott Key wrote the poem "The

> Later set to the tune of an English drinking song, "The Star-Spangled Banner" became the national anthem.

Read the lyrics to "The Star Spangled Banner."

Star-Spangled Banner." Later set to the tune of an English drinking song, this became the national anthem.

The most startling upset took place at New Orleans in January 1815, where the British bungled their invasion plans and were mowed down by American troops serving under Andrew Jackson. The Americans suffered only twenty-one casualties in the Battle of New Orleans, but the British incurred more than two thousand. Jackson became an instant national hero and a symbol of America's determination to be permanently independent of Great Britain.

The Hartford Convention

As Jackson and his men defended New Orleans, Federalists in New England held a meeting at Hartford, Connecticut, to discuss their frustrations with the Democratic-Republicans. At the meeting, the **Hartford Convention**, Federalist leaders expressed their frustrations with the proceedings of the War of 1812, which they had protested from its inception. They were fed up with the government's economic policies, which had hurt the mercantile interests of New England. They proposed a series of constitutional amendments limiting the government's ability to restrict American commerce and repealing the three-fifths clause in order to limit the power of the South in Congress. Some representatives broached the idea of seceding if these measures failed.

Jackson's victory, followed by an announcement that the United States and Britain had negotiated terms for peace, made a mockery of the Hartford Convention. The Federalist Party was immediately tainted with treason, and nearly all support for the party vanished. The nation's first two-party system era was over, as only the Democratic-Republicans remained viable. The period of nonpartisan politics that followed became known as the **"Era of Good Feelings."** This lasted a few years and, although the seeds of factionalism would blossom again in 1819 and 1820, historians generally consider the Era of Good Feelings to have lasted until the presidential election of 1824.

Hartford Convention Meeting of New England Federalists in 1814 where they proposed constitutional amendments limiting the government's ability to restrict American commerce and repealing the three-fifths clause to limit the power of the South in Congress

"Era of Good Feelings" Period of nonpartisan politics following the implosion of the Federalist Party, roughly 1815–1824

View a satirical cartoon poking fun at the Hartford Convention.

The Treaty of Ghent

In 1814, the Treaty of Ghent formally ended the War of 1812, but it did not settle any of the significant issues, principally naval impressments and America's right to neutrality. It did, however, end hostilities, which was a relief to both sides. With the war over, the United States was able to turn its attention away from Europe and back to affairs at home.

The Significance of the War of 1812

The War of 1812 was significant for at least four reasons : (1) it shaped American politics, affirming the importance of a strong national government; (2) it vacated the West; (3) it shaped America's role in world affairs; and (4) it unified the nation and boosted American patriotism.

Political changes. Politically, the War of 1812 demonstrated the weakness of the Republican-Democrats' insistence on a small federal government. It prompted four changes from James Madison: (1) he recognized that having a stronger standing army and navy would have served the country better than the scanty forces that had eked out a victory against Great Britain; (2) he recognized the need for a new national bank to centralize banking, which he chartered as the Second United States Bank in 1816; (3) he agreed to new protective tariffs designed to support the growth of American industries; and (4) he realized the need for a system of national improvements, such as roads and canals to facilitate transportation between the newly settled West and the East Coast. Each of these lessons (some of them very Hamiltonian and Federalist) would play an integral role in the future development of the United States.

Vacating the West. In the West, the War of 1812 produced decisive defeats against the most powerful Native American tribes in the Southwest (in today's Tennessee and Arkansas) and the Northwest (in the Ohio River Valley). The conclusion of the war also meant that Britain would no longer impede settlement in the American interior, leaving the United States free to expand in the West—at the continued cost of Native Americans, who were running out of room further to the west.

America's role in the world. The War of 1812 also showed the European powers that the United States was a relatively strong, modern nation. Twice in three decades the United States had defeated Britain. America had earned greater respect and entered a prolonged period of relative isolation, safe from invasions and incursions from abroad.

American patriotism and American culture. Pride in their victory in the War of 1812 generated a strong urge to define America as fundamentally different from England. Hatred of the British prompted some to propose that the United States make German its official language. This movement obviously did not succeed, and during the course of the 1800s, Noah Webster developed a more practical solution. He noticed that a new American idiom had arisen over the 150-year colonial period; in 1828 he codified this new idiom in his Webster's *American Dictionary of the English Language.* Webster's dictionary included such uniquely American words as *skunk* and *squash*, and replaced British spellings, such as *colour*, with American versions, such as *color*.

At the same time, a group of poets called the "Hartford Wits" became the first well-known creative authors on American soil. The most prominent of the Hartford Wits was Francis Scott Key. Other "Wits" composed such enduring songs as "Hail Columbia." At the same time, the first American magazine of note—the *North American Review*—began publica-

>> Trumbull's "The Signing of the Declaration of Independence" (1819)

tion in 1815. The very title of the magazine denoted Americans' attempt to separate culturally from Europe.

In the graphic arts, talented painters in early America crafted pictures with patriotic themes, expressing their gratitude for liberty. The best remembered are the portraits of the founding fathers, many of them painted by Gilbert Stuart (1755–1828) and John Trumbull (1756–1843). Trumbull was also known for his patriotic images, the most popular of which is *The Signing of the Declaration of Independence* (1819), which today appears on the back of the two dollar bill.

The most notable artistic expression of early American nationalism developed in architecture, as American architects, identifying with the ancient republican Romans, revived classical architecture styles and motifs. Both Thomas Jefferson, who designed the University of Virginia and his home, Monticello, and Charles Bulfinch, who designed the Massachusetts

State House in Boston, excelled in this flourishing realm. Pierre l'Enfant, the French architect commissioned to design the capitol buildings in Washington, D.C., also participated in this revival, which explains the plethora of classical architecture to be found today in Washington, D.C.

View more pictures of the classical revival in America.

And in the end . . .

With the rise of the Democratic-Republicans in the early 1800s, the American nation had survived its first significant transfer of power. The Democratic-Republicans had also introduced a new, livelier style of politics into the political culture, one that focused on courting voters and asserting a specific kind of patriotism.

But Jefferson's attempts to create an idealized agrarian republic proved disastrous. By curbing the size of the military and limiting federal income to only tariffs, Jefferson exposed the nation to a variety of geopolitical upheavals taking place in Europe. Only heroic fighting and some good luck during the War of 1812 kept the young nation politically solvent.

Shortly thereafter, the nation would turn another corner and embark on a period of economic growth that ran counter to the image idealized by Jefferson and his followers. In place of an agrarian republic governed by large landholders who disdained city life, the nation developed into a trading center, bustling with markets and commerce. America was still largely a nation of farmers, but these farmers became more intent on bringing their product to market than on merely remaining self-sufficient. Although the Democratic-Republicans established much of the political and diplomatic security for the new nation, their vision for the nation would not carry the day. It is to the Market Revolution and its manifestations that we now turn.

>> Thomas Jefferson's home, Monticello

What else was happening . . .

1808	End of legal slave importation in the United States.
1810	Peter Durand invents the tin can.
1811	Steamboat service begins on the Mississippi River.
1814	First plastic surgery is performed in England.

The *Market* Revolution

Learning Outcomes

After reading this chapter, you should be able to do the following:

LO **1**   Describe the economic system known as the American System.

LO **2**   List the three specific parts of the Market Revolution in early-nineteenth-century America, and evaluate how America and Americans developed during this era.

LO **3**   Describe the growth of America's middle class during the first half of the 1800s, and discuss some of the stronger movements toward reform during the era.

"The American System of economics was a fantastic success."

In the years following the War of 1812, America became relatively isolated from Europe. It focused inward. There was a strong feeling that the United States needed to strengthen its economy in order to protect itself against further incursion from outside powers. This view took tangible form as politicians and citizens designed what they called an "American System" of economics, which focused on keeping American goods within the United States.

What do you think?

The period between 1812 and the 1860s was the social and economic equivalent of the political revolution of the 1770s.

Strongly Disagree   *Strongly Agree*

1   2   3   4   5   6   7

The American System of economics was a fantastic success, and it facilitated so many economic and social changes between 1812 and the 1860s that historians refer to this period as the social and economic equivalent of the political revolution of the 1770s. Historians describe all these transitions under the umbrella term **Market Revolution**. Aided by numerous transportation, communication, and technological innovations, the Market Revolution refers to the time when an increasing number of farmers willingly turned away from the ideal of being self-sufficient, in order to focus on a single crop that could be sold at market. This encouraged specialization and the growth of a dynamic string of market hubs within the United States. The United States had always been a part of the colonial world market, and between 1810 and 1860 the markets moved closer to home. Instead of American commerce focusing on transactions between the Atlantic seaboard and Europe, it shifted, focusing now on transactions between the East Coast and the lands extending to and beyond the Mississippi River.

The rise of localized, commercial agriculture changed the way Americans lived their lives. It moved them closer to the world of the marketplace and allowed many to leave the world of agriculture altogether. At the dawn of the 1800s, more than 80 percent of the American labor force worked in agriculture. By 1850, that figure had declined to 55 percent. By the 1880s, less than half of America's work force was engaged in farming. Local markets needed local salesmen, lawyers, factories, marketers, economists, and bookkeepers. The changes associated with this transition affected nearly every American, and America in 1860 looked dramatically different than it did in 1810.

This chapter examines the Market Revolution, its causes and effects, and the variety of responses to it.

LO¹ Economic Nationalism

The second generation of American politicians (James Monroe was the last American revolutionary to be president, serving from 1817 to 1825) did not have the distrust of centralized authority

> **Market Revolution**
> Umbrella term for the many economic and social changes that took place between 1812 and the 1860s

that characterized the revolutionary era. Several men of this younger generation developed a nationalist program for economic growth similar to the one proposed by Alexander Hamilton during the Federalist era. Updated to fit the demands of the 1810s and 1820s, they called this economic plan the **American System**.

The American System

The American System came from a surprising source: young Democratic-Republican politicians from the West, the South, and the Middle Atlantic states who had superficially embraced Jefferson's vision of a small federal government but in fact eagerly sought the patronage that a large federal government could dole out. Henry Clay from Kentucky and John C. Calhoun from South Carolina led this group. Together, they advanced a vision that the federal government should encourage economic enterprise in three ways: (1) by creating roads and canals, collectively called **internal improvements**; (2) by developing secure economic institutions, such as banks; and (3) by providing for the security of America's economic interests through high tariffs. After seeing the weaknesses of Jefferson's vision of a disparate

collection of states, the leaders of the American System wanted to strengthen the nation and secure the advancement of the West through the creation of tremendous public works projects.

A New National Bank

One of the key components of the American System was the creation of a national bank. When Congress, before the War of 1812, refused to recharter the First National Bank in 1811, the states chartered their own banks, offering a bewildering variety of credit and currencies. This created hundreds of different currencies. More than four hundred banks were operating in 1818, each offering its own form of currency and credit. Speculation ran rampant, as investors attempted to pick which currency would appreciate the quickest. Fortunes were won and lost very quickly, and investors had little idea which currencies would be the most durable.

To end the mayhem and strengthen the national government, proponents of the American System designed the **Second Bank of the United States**. In a bill drafted in committee by Calhoun, the Second National Bank was established with support from western and southern congressmen. New Englanders, who had adequate and secure banks in the North, opposed the creation of the bank. With Democratic-Republicans mostly supporting a national bank and former New England Federalists opposing it, times had changed since

>> The states chartered their own banks, offering a bewildering variety of currencies and credit.

the Federalist era; now each party was advocating what it had opposed just two decades prior. The new bank was chartered in 1816.

A Protective Tariff

Calhoun and Clay also supervised the passage of the Tariff of 1816, which taxed all incoming goods at the stiff rate of 25 percent. They designed the tariff to limit consumption of foreign goods in the United States and to encourage the development of American commerce and industries. This meant that the goods in the American System were to be American.

Court Cases

During these years, the Supreme Court issued a number of decisions that advocated economic growth at the expense of the states or of previous contracts. One of the most consequential cases was *Dartmouth College* v. *Woodward* (1819), which forbade state legislatures from altering college charters in order to gain control over them, because a corporation (the university) had drafted the charter. This decision prioritized the rights of a corporation over those of the state, thus clearing the path for increased economic development.

A Protected Hemisphere

The War of 1812 and the economics of nationalism also allowed the United States to assert its dominance throughout the Western Hemisphere. In 1818, it established a northern boundary at the 49th parallel between the United States and British Canada, and in 1819 it won from Spain both Florida and lands extending nearly to today's Oregon, all in exchange for parts of Texas. Now the United States extended from the southern tip of Florida to the current-day northern boundary with Canada, and from the Atlantic almost to the Pacific (although it still did not claim today's American Southwest).

The new dominance was expressed most clearly in the

© James Monroe (1758–1831) (colour litho), Morse, Samuel F. B. (1791–1872)/ Private Collection, Peter Newark American Pictures/The Bridgeman Art Library

Monroe Doctrine of 1823. This doctrine declared that any European nation attempting to colonize Latin America would be treated as a party hostile to the United States. President James Monroe announced that the Western Hemisphere was the domain of the United States and was to remain separate from the affairs of Europe. At the same time, Monroe agreed to refrain from any interference with existing European colonies or with the internal affairs or wars of the European powers. Although the Monroe Doctrine was little noted at the time, it later became a foundation for American foreign policy, used to justify American expansion into and involvement with the countries of Latin America.

> **Monroe Doctrine**
> Declaration of 1823 proclaiming that any European nation attempting to colonize Latin America would be treated as a party hostile to the United States; President James Monroe announced that the Western Hemisphere was the domain of the United States and was to remain separate from the affairs of Europe

Opponents of the American System

Not everyone favored the American System. Some southerners saw it as merely an attempt to wrangle taxes from wealthy cotton planters and give it to northern and western business interests. Others liked the American System well enough when the money was spent in their home state but opposed it when resources were spent elsewhere. War-hero-turned-politician Andrew Jackson at first enjoyed the fruits of the plan but eventually came to see it as a vehicle for corruption. Despite these mounting complaints, which would increase throughout the first half of the 1800s, the American System was the prevailing economic plan for the nation until the 1830s and 1840s.

>> James Monroe. Although the Monroe Doctrine was little noted at the time, it later became a foundation for American foreign policy.

LO² The Market Revolution

Combining tariffs, internal improvements, and a national bank, the American System of economics facilitated the Market Revolution. Farmers, more than ever before, could focus on producing what they produced best, bring their goods to local American markets, and purchase the items they could not grow or make themselves. The result was a change in people's notions about their role in the economy, leaving behind the idea that they had to be self-sustaining farmers and advancing the idea that they were participants in the national and international marketplace. This made them more accepting of commercial and capitalist goals, for they were becoming not only producers, but also *consumers*. For the most part, the Market Revolution had to do with commercialized agriculture and not with industrialization (although the beginnings of the Industrial Revolution can be identified in this period).

The Market Revolution was made up of three parts, in roughly this order: (1) a transportation and communications revolution, (2) a transition to commercialized farming, and (3) industrialization. Each transition provoked significant social changes.

The Transportation and Communications Revolution

The Market Revolution could not have happened without a revolution in the way people and goods moved around and the way people communicated with one another. Since the start of European settlement in North America, long-distance travel had meant using rivers or the sea. Water offered the quickest and most reliable means of moving goods from their place of origin to a market where they could be sold. However, America's rivers run primarily from north to south, making travel from east to west difficult. For instance, there was not a single navigable river connecting the northeastern cities of New York, Philadelphia, or Boston to the farmlands of the Ohio River Valley.

Recognizing the importance of speedy transportation, in the years after 1800 some states began internal improvements. They financed, for the most part through tax dollars, the construction of toll roads, canals, and other modes of transportation. This increased funding sparked four eras of transportation innovation: the turnpike era, the canal era, the steamboat era, and the railroad era (Map 10.1).

The Turnpike Era

The first improvements were roads and turnpikes (private roads with tolls), and the 1810s were the turnpike era. Between 1800 and 1825, hundreds of miles of toll roads crisscrossed the nation. The Cumberland Road was the best known, extending from Maryland to West Virginia. But these early roads were mostly unpaved, and huge ruts and tree stumps made them dangerous. The roads were too unpredictable for Americans to use reliably in order to transport large amounts of commercial goods.

The Canal Era

To solve this problem, human ingenuity provided the country with something that nature had not—a series of east-to-west canals—and the 1820s were the canal era. New York led the way in 1817, when the New York legislature paid for the construction of the **Erie Canal**, an artificial river connecting Buffalo—on the shore of Lake Erie—to Albany. Because Albany was linked to New York City by the

>> These early roads were mostly unpaved, and huge ruts and tree stumps made them dangerous.

Map 10.1
Rivers, Roads, and Canals, 1825–1860

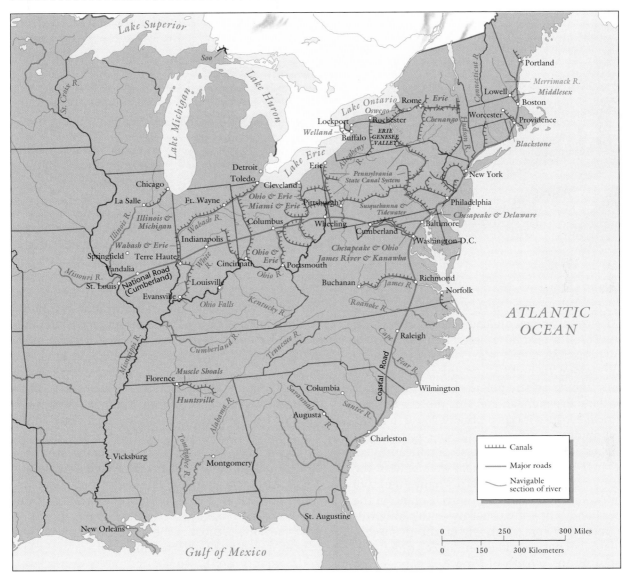

Hudson River, the Erie Canal provided a continuous water route from the shores of the Atlantic to the Great Lakes. This was an immensely complex project. At the time, the longest canal in the world was 28 miles long. The Erie was 364 miles long and 40 feet wide. New Yorkers completed construction in eight years. When it was done, mules on paths along the shore could tow with a rope a barge filled with more than a ton of goods. The barge moved as fast as the mules. The Erie Canal opening was a landmark event for four reasons.

- The project was a tremendous economic success. The cost of moving one ton of goods from Buffalo to New York City dropped from nineteen cents per mile to a little more than one cent. The canal cut the time it took to move goods between Buffalo and New York City from twenty

>> The Erie Canal provided a continuous water route from the shores of the Atlantic to the Great Lakes.

days to six. The State of New York charged tolls on the canal, which yielded a huge profit.

- These profits pushed other states to invest in transportation. Many states chartered private corporations to build those internal improvements, which greatly politicized the role of corporations in American life. This process became political because it was profitable to run a canal, so winning a charter to build one was comparable to winning the lottery. Significantly, all but three of the largest canals were built in the North, signifying a northern commitment to the Market Revolution. Southern leaders, on the other hand, who were usually wealthy landowners, remained content to rely on the rivers that transported cotton and other staple crops.

- It spurred the growth of New York City. As the major trading link between the interior of the United States and the Atlantic Ocean, New York City became the nation's major economic center.

- The creation of a cheap way to move goods to market made it more enticing to farmers in the interior to produce only the few items that would be the most profitable.

The Steamboat Era

Despite the general reluctance of the South to invest in transportation improvements, there were innova-tions in the South and the West as well. There, steamboats, developed in the early 1800s, proved to be effective transport on the regions' broad rivers. By the 1830s, they carried much of the commerce in those regions and succeeded in reducing cargo rates across the country. Their fabulous success made many southerners consider funding other internal improvements unnecessary.

The Railroad Era

The most transformative new form of transportation was the railroad, which became the cornerstone of the American transportation revolution of the 1840s and 1850s. The development of railroads further extended the transportation improvements begun during the canal and steamboat eras, but railroads had three crucial advantages over water travel: (1) unlike canals, rail lines did not depend on natural waterways as their end points; (2) railroads did not freeze; and (3) trains traveled significantly faster than mules.

For these reasons, railroads completed the full transition to a market-based economy. In the 1830s, American builders laid over three thousand miles of track. By the 1860s, more than thirty thousand miles of track ran through the country. As with the canals, most of the nation's railroads were concentrated in the North, laid by merchants and state governments eager to develop a diversified economy. The South, meanwhile, maintained its plantation-based culture and its dependence on natural waterways to move its key staple crops.

Read more about roads, canals, steamboats, and railroads.

From 1810 to 1850, the speed with which goods and people could be moved across vast stretches of land increased considerably. In the 1810s, a journey via horseback from the Atlantic coast to the Great Lakes would have taken several weeks. In the 1850s, one could take either the Erie Canal or a railroad and be there in a matter of days.

>> Trains traveled significantly faster than mules.

>> "What Hath God Wrought?" –Samuel F. B. Morse

The Communications Revolution

At the same time, Americans were inventing and incorporating new methods of communication. The key development was Samuel F. B. Morse's successful transmission via the first telegraph, which used electric wires to send a message instantaneously from one place to another. The telegraph facilitated nationwide commerce and lowered the cost of communication. It also symbolized the energy of the era, when, for the first time in human history, communication was set free from the realm of physical transit. Americans at the time were unaware of the kinds of communications that would emerge in future years, but they were aware that they were living at a transformative time in human history. Morse emphasized this notion when he chose the first words to be transmitted: "What Hath God Wrought?"

Commercialized Farming

The transportation and communications revolutions caused a transition in how farmers (that is, most Americans) farmed their land. No longer did each family have to produce almost everything it consumed. This transition was not entirely new to farmers in the South and in areas of the Middle

Colonies, where colonial-era farmers had already oriented their production around staple crops. But the rest of the nation had concentrated on self-sufficiency and diversified farming, and this market transition led to dramatic changes in the South, the West, and New England.

Changes in the South

Before 1793, southern agriculture consisted of the staple crops of tobacco and rice, but farmers had added a few more varieties of crops during the 1700s. After 1793, when Eli Whitney promoted a new invention called the cotton gin, everything changed. The cotton gin allowed for the profitable cultivation of cotton even in land with poor soil by allowing the harvesting of "short staple" (or hard-to-reach) cotton. This meant that cotton was easy and profitable to produce throughout the South (not just in areas rich in nutrients), and cotton production rapidly took over southern agriculture and the southern economy. By 1825, the American South was the world's largest producer of cotton. Between 1816 and 1840 cotton constituted more than half the value of all American exports, nearly all of it grown in the South.

This created obvious opportunities for white southerners. If you could get a little land and a few slaves, you could earn huge profits. The ease with which wealth could be generated spurred a large westward migration throughout the South, as small farmers searched for land to grow cotton. The development of the cotton gin reinforced the farmers' dependence on slaves, because it made their labor even more valuable (slaves could be used profitably on even poor land). At the same time, slavery moved west with the cotton farmers. These farmers revived the domestic slave trade. Any ideas

Land Act of 1820
Legislation which promoted settlement west of the Appalachians by setting affordable prices for manageable plots of land

that emancipation might be plausible in the South during these years vanished after the introduction of the cotton gin.

This cotton boom had two other key outcomes. First, cotton impeded any significant internal improvements in the South because wealthy southerners considered waterways sufficient to transport cotton. This hurt small farmers, who could not afford land along waterways, and it stalled the development of any major railroad lines in the southern states. Second, the roaring success of cotton, in combination with the Market Revolution elsewhere in the nation, hindered southerners from developing a diversified economy. They could rely on other parts of the nation for the goods they needed.

> Read more about cotton production in the South.

Changes in the West

The Market Revolution also meant that farmers in the Midwest (Ohio, Indiana, and Illinois)

© iStockphoto.com/Oktay Ortakcioglu

could take maximum advantage of the land's rich soil and plentiful rain. Reflecting the Market Revolution's transition to commercialized agriculture, a wheat belt stretched from western New York to Wisconsin, a corn belt reached from Ohio to Illinois, a tobacco belt extended from Kentucky to Missouri, and a cotton belt spread from Georgia to Mississippi. Each area continued to grow a diverse range of crops, but each increasingly specialized in what it grew best.

The commercial development of these regions prompted a huge shift of the American population (Map 10.2). With the **Land Act of 1820**, the federal government helped promote settlement of land west of the Appalachians by setting affordable prices for manageable plots of land. They would succeed, prompting one of the largest internal migrations in American history. In 1789, two-thirds of all Americans (about 3 million people) lived within fifty miles of the Atlantic Ocean, while only 5 percent lived west of the Appalachians. By 1840, one-third of the population (more than 5 million people) lived in new states west of the Appalachians. Several new areas applied for statehood, almost all of them as a result of westward migration: Indiana (1816), Mississippi (1817), Illinois (1818), Alabama (1819), Maine (1820), Missouri (1821), Arkansas (1836), Michigan (1837), Florida (1845), Texas (1845), Iowa (1846), and Wisconsin (1848). During these years, between 5 and 10 percent of all Americans moved each year.

The West and Slavery

Westward migration exposed another significant problem: what to do about slavery. In 1819, Missouri sought entry into the union as a slave state. Its request provoked a debate in Congress that Congress wished desperately to avoid. Even the aging Thomas Jefferson wrote that the issue of slavery frightened him like a "fire bell in the night."

The issue of whether slavery would be allowed in Missouri was pivotal for two reasons: (1) Missouri lay along the same latitude as several free states, and its entry into the Union as a slave state would have moved slavery northward; and (2) the admission of Missouri as a slave state would have upset the congressional balance of eleven slave states and eleven free states. Northerners, mindful of the ideals of the revolution and intent on avoiding a large black population in the North, sought to keep slavery in the South. Southerners sought to expand the development of cotton, which, they felt, required the labor of slaves.

When Representative James Tallmadge, Jr., proposed the **Tallmadge Amendment**, which would have enforced gradual emancipation in Missouri, a vicious debate broke out on the floor of Congress. Henry Clay brokered a compromise: Missouri could enter as a slave state if Maine could enter as a free state. In addition, Clay drew a line at the latitude of **36°30'**. Territories north of the line would remain free, south of it could maintain slavery. This was the **Missouri Compromise**, passed in 1820, which would dictate the spread of slavery in the West for the next thirty years.

> **The aging Thomas Jefferson wrote that the issue of slavery frightened him like a "fire bell in the night."**

The New England Transition

New England farmers had long developed diversified farms that could fulfill many of their family's needs, while local markets provided the items that could not be grown or manufactured easily.

The Market Revolution (combined with soil exhaustion) slowly eroded this lifestyle. Rocky, cold New England had never been a great place to farm, and access to cheap western products furthered the decline in farming during the 1820s.

Without a central profitable crop to turn to, New Englanders reorganized their economy. Giving up on corn and wheat, New Englanders began to grow garden vegetables, fruit, dairy products, meat, eggs, and other perishable goods that could sustain growing urban markets. They took advantage of the new methods of transportation to get their goods to market. In 1820, about one-third of all New England produce was

Tallmadge Amendment
Proposal that would have enforced gradual emancipation in Missouri

36°30'
Line of latitude specified by Henry Clay in the Missouri Compromise; territories north of the line would remain free, south of it could maintain slavery

Missouri Compromise
Arrangement brokered by Henry Clay that set 36°30' as the divider between free and slave territories, and allowed Missouri to enter the nation as a slave state if Maine were allowed to enter as free

Map 10.2
Population Density, 1790–1820

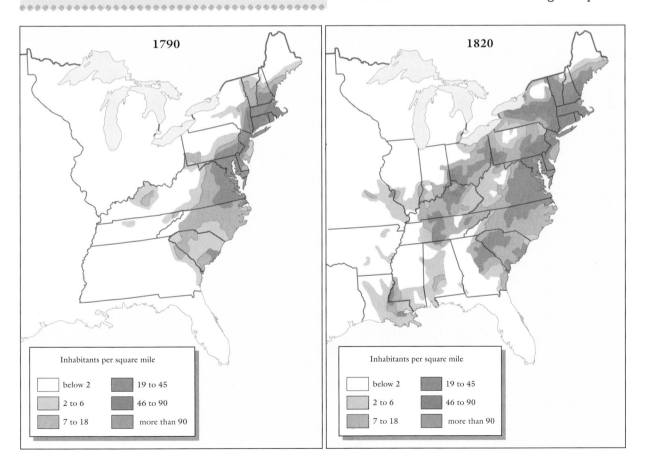

1790

1820

Inhabitants per square mile

below 2
2 to 6
7 to 18
19 to 45
46 to 90
more than 90

sent to market. By 1850, that percentage had jumped to about half.

The result was dazzling success—for those who owned land. Those who did not own land confronted rising land prices. Many headed west, where land was cheaper. Others worked as wage laborers on farms, hoping one day to earn enough money to buy land of their own.

Women's output was similarly affected. Many women stopped weaving clothes, because store-bought cloth was cheaper. They churned butter and made cheese instead, participating in the new market economy by selling these dairy products at market.

Industrialization

The transportation revolution and the conversion to commercial agriculture required machines. Railroads needed machinery to fabricate engines, cars, and tracks. Cotton crops required factories to turn the raw product into cloth. Specialized farming in the West demanded large reapers and tough plows. Thus, the third aspect of the Market Revolution was the rise of industrialization and the creation of factories. It is important to remember that this was not yet the full-scale industrialization associated with today's large factories. But it was the beginning of that process.

The Mechanization of Agriculture

Cyrus McCormick's development of the reaper in 1831 was the most significant industrial development in agriculture. A twenty-five-year-old Virginia farmer, McCormick created a machine that harvested grain much faster than manual labor could. This was a boon for the western states, because they had miles of flat farmland that was perfect for the reaper. In 1837, McCormick moved his factory from Virginia to Chicago, the principal city of the booming Midwest, and sold his reapers to farmers there. In the same way, John Deere's steel plow (1837) made it easier to plow tough fields, and the cotton gin (1793) sped up the process of separating short-staple cottonseed from its fiber.

The Mechanization of Machine Tools

McCormick and Whitney noted the precise specifications of the many moving parts that made up their machines. They then reproduced those parts in large quantities, thus introducing the system of interchangeable parts. Eli Whitney was chiefly credited for this development (more than he deserved) and won government contracts to develop muskets that used interchangeable parts. With interchangeable parts, producers could make products more quickly and cheaply instead of handcrafting each item one by one. Watches, clocks, and locks—all luxury items in 1800—became inexpensive household goods by 1840 because of interchangeable parts.

Factories

Factories were the most efficient way to produce the large quantities of goods that were needed to accommodate the Market Revolution, but they did not prosper as quickly as one might imagine. Before 1800, most production was done in a decentralized system of family- or artisan-based manufacturing. Large manufacturers would pay one family to perform one task, then pass the item on to the next family or artisan to perform the next task. This was called the **"putting out" system**.

The rise of the factory in the 1820s altered this system by bringing nearly all aspects of production under one roof. Samuel Slater was the first to develop the workings of a factory on American soil, designing in 1789 a factory that spun cotton into thread. Within its first ten years of operation, Slater's textile mill hired more than one hundred people, mostly women and young children. The amount of thread produced by Slater's mill prompted a rise in the volume of thread-based goods (mainly clothes, but also towels and curtains) and a drop in their price.

© iStockphoto.com/Sergey Kulikov

>> Watches, clocks, and locks—all luxury items in 1800— became inexpensive household goods by 1840 because of interchangeable parts.

Entrepreneurs opened other factories, and these new factories continued to improve production. Slater could not weave thread into cloth at his mill, for example (he still had to "put out" his thread to home workers for this task). In 1813, Boston merchants developed a power loom to weave cloth. Headed by Francis Lowell, the new factory brought all the processes of clothmaking under one roof. This quickened the pace and cheapened the price of production. Between 1820 and 1860 textile mills sprouted all over the northern and Middle Atlantic states, harnessing the power of swift-moving rivers. Americans began purchasing their clothing rather than making it, which boosted the rise of retail clothing stores. Other manufacturing industries, such as shoemaking and clockmaking, followed.

Social Changes Associated with the Market Revolution

The Market Revolution had many social ramifications. The most significant were the growth of cities, the impact on the environment, the changing face of the labor force, an increase in religious divisions, the beginnings of a working class and a middle class, and increased protest movements.

The Growth of Cities

The expansion of markets and the growth of factories led to a slow process of urbanization. In 1830, only 5 percent of Americans lived in towns of 8,000 people or more. By 1850, that number had more than tripled, to 16 percent. With the development of the Erie Canal, New York City solidified its position as the largest city in the nation, with a population of more than 300,000 in 1840. Philadelphia, Boston, and Baltimore experienced robust growth as well. Of the ten largest cities in 1860, only one, New Orleans, was in the South.

Environmental Costs of the Market Revolution

There were significant environmental costs of the Market Revolution. Steamboats and early railroads burned wood as a source of power, which caused rapid deforestation in the Northeast. Similarly, as the transportation revolution enabled more people to move west, new settlers cleared land and chopped wood, destroying animal habitats and western landscapes. Sawmills and textile mills, relying on waterways for their power, interrupted the paths of spawning fish. These costs would only increase as industrialization expanded through the rest of the century.

Women and Immigrants in the Labor Force

Great Irish Famine
Years of miserable poverty and hunger in Ireland that peaked during 1845–1851

There was also a dramatic change in the composition of the labor force. Setting a pattern followed by other factory owners, Lowell hired single women from New England farms to work in his clothmaking factory. He needed cheap labor, and young women would work for lower wages than men. To present a wholesome image to the farm families who might send their daughters to work there, Lowell built boarding houses for his "mill girls," where they were taught Christian ethics and monitored by chaperones. Factory life was harsh for these workers, however, and most sought to return home to start families after a short tenure in a Lowell mill. Most stayed just five years. They worked without insurance, wage guarantees, or legal protections of any kind, and when times were hard, these factory workers were the first to suffer.

For the most part, working in a factory was arduous, and wages were low. People often worked fifteen-hour days, six days a week, and usually an entire family had to work in order to get by. Men, women, and young children spent long hours in the hot, noisy factories.

But mill owners were not obligated to listen to complaints; they could always find eager replacements. After 1840, the number of immi-

Read a first-hand description of the Lowell mills from one young female worker.

grants arriving in the United States suddenly soared, causing the nation's population to increase a whopping 36 percent in the 1840s. Roughly two-thirds of these new arrivals were Irish, fleeing years of miserable poverty and hunger that peaked during the **Great Irish Famine** of 1845–1851. The majority of Irish immigrants settled in northeastern cities and worked at industrial jobs, replacing New England women and children. By the 1860s, half of the employees in most American factories were immigrants, most of them Irish. The Irish became a distinct underclass in the nineteenth-century United States.

Challenges to the Protestant Consensus

The Irish immigrants brought Roman Catholicism. Catholicism had been present in the United States since the first European settlements, but Catholics had always been a small minority compared to the Protestant majority. With the wave of Irish immigrants, Catholics formed the first sizeable religious

>> "The early millgirls were of different ages. Some were not over ten years old; a few were in middle life, but the majority were between the ages of sixteen and twenty-five." –Harriet Hanson Robinson, Lowell mill girl for fourteen years, starting at age ten

© The London Art Archive/Alamy

minority in American history. Many Americans feared this development, believing that rising levels of Catholic immigration threatened the character of America, which they considered a "Protestant nation." Catholics, most nineteenth-century Americans believed, were too bound to the teachings of the pope to behave like free and independent republicans. They were also prone to the excesses of drinking and licentiousness, or so claimed Protestant nativists.

To counteract the growing Catholic presence, some Protestants began seeking an official proclamation of Protestantism as the religion of the nation. Such efforts did not succeed, but they stirred controversy. For instance, the efforts of Protestant educators to introduce Protestant religious study into the curriculum of the nation's public schools prompted the development of the first Catholic parochial schools.

A New Working Class

In their new jobs, Irish workers earned little pay. Indeed, what made Irish laborers so attractive to factory owners was their willingness to work for low wages. Moreover, as urban land prices skyrocketed, the Irish were forced to accept the worst housing available. Irish families crowded together in basement apartments or in attics, and Irish slums became hotbeds for diseases like cholera and tuberculosis. To the eyes of native-born Americans, these conditions served as unhappy notice that the squalor of Britain's industrial towns had been transplanted to America. In fact, the Irish slums were simply a part of the new working class that worked in the factories, earned day wages, and were increasingly removed from the fruits of their labor. Over the course of the

1800s, these laborers would begin to feel aligned with one another, creating a sense of belonging to a particular class.

Protest Movements

Several movements arose to protest the living and working conditions experienced by the working class. Protest movements of the early nineteenth century were usually one of two kinds: (1) an organization of middle-class reformers seeking to safeguard the morality of workers or (2) laborers fighting for economic and work-related protections, such as a shorter work day. The two movements often opposed each other, sometimes because the middle-class reformers were anti-immigrant, while the labor movement was made up of Irish and non-Irish immigrants. Furthermore, the federal and state governments firmly supported economic development; ceding to the demands of laborers did not seem to offer immediate gains for the economy.

Despite these hurdles, the laborers enjoyed some successes. Neighborhood groups began to meet up in citywide trade assemblies that delved into politics and rallied to elect politicians sympathetic to their cause. They then attempted to unify the citywide assemblies into nationwide unions. One such union, the **Workingmen's Party** was formed in 1828, spreading through fifteen states. It was surpassed in 1834 by the **National Trades Union**, which is usually regarded as the nation's first large-scale union. And, although the power of the trade unions varied depending on the economy, in 1840, President Martin Van Buren instituted the ten-hour day for federal employees, yielding to one of the long-standing demands of the laboring classes.

LO³ Reformers

But the most influential reform movement of the early nineteenth century emerged from the middle class. Spurred by a religious revival known as the Second Great Awakening, a large group of middle-class social reformers attempted to control the changes brought about by the Market Revolution. The men and especially the women who led the reform movement promoted a vision of a more caring nation, one more considerate of human life. In doing so, these reformers broached some of the most consequential issues the nation would face during the next two hundred years, including racism, the rights of workers, and the rights of women.

The Creation of the Middle Class

As more and more unskilled laborers transitioned to factory work, a need arose for paper-pushing bureaucrats who could manage others, balance the books, and sell goods. This was new. In 1800, a shoemaker would have made shoes himself, selling them at his own shop. By 1860, however, many "shoemakers" did not actually make shoes at all. Rather, they supervised a group of semiskilled or unskilled laborers, each of whom completed a part of the shoemaking process. Similarly, large factories needed bookkeepers, accountants, salesmen, and clerks.

This management class formed the backbone of an emerging middle class. Before 1800, Americans had hardly ever used the term *middle class*. By 1850, the term was part of the popular vocabulary. The middle class began to develop a culture distinct from that of the elite property owners or that of the workers. In the middle class of the mid-1800s, men were presumed to be the sole income earners, usually working outside the home. Their wives, meanwhile, transitioned from income providers to guardians of the home and family, a concept that came to be called the "cult of female domesticity." Middle-class women developed their own social and cultural outlets. Manufacturers were quick to recognize this trend, providing products exclusively geared to women, in a feminization of consumerism. Publishers introduced a "lady's" literature, a feminization of culture. But a woman's first priority was making the family home a sanctuary for her laboring husband, a "haven in a heartless world."

The Religious Foundations of Reform

The Second Great Awakening

For most people, and especially for women, new evangelical churches lay at the center of middle-class culture. More than any other group in American society, the middle class—the shopkeepers, clerks, and managers—was most active in the evangelical sects that developed in the 1830s and formed the center of what historians call the Second Great Awakening. The Second Great Awakening was a Protestant religious revival that began in the West but shortly moved to the Northeast and the South. It lasted from the 1790s to the 1840s, and reached its high tide between the 1820s and 1840s.

>> **A woman's first priority was making the family home a sanctuary for her laboring husband, a "haven in a heartless world."**

burned-over district
Area in upstate New York which had many converts who had been inspired by the fiery orators speaking the Word of God during the Second Great Awakening

Transcendentalists
Group of thinkers and writers in the Northeast who believed that ultimate truths were beyond human grasp

lyceum circuit
Schedule of lectures in which clergymen, reformers, Transcendentalists, socialists, feminists, and other speakers would speak to large crowds in small towns

The Theology

The central theological idea behind the Second Great Awakening was that an individual's soul could be saved through human agency (meaning hard work) and his or her acceptance of responsibility for a sinful nature. This meant that divine revelation was not the only path to salvation. This stood in contrast to Jonathan Edwards's and George Whitefield's theology of relying on divine benevolence for salvation, which was paramount during the First Great Awakening. The ideas behind the Second Great Awakening were that humans could achieve a level of perfectibility—both individual and social—by doing good works and by promoting what they understood to be God's intent. Action was the key. Humans had the power to choose good or evil and, by choosing good, they could eventually alleviate sin or, put another way, become perfect. The name for the idea that humans can accept or reject divine grace is Arminianism.

How it Spread

The Second Great Awakening spread through a series of three- or four-day revivals orchestrated by itinerant preachers. The most prominent was Charles G. Finney, a New York lawyer who gave up the law in 1821 in order to convert souls. Finney was a spellbinding orator whose sermons were particularly effective in the towns that had experienced the most changes during the Market Revolution. One area in upstate New York had so many converts it was called the **burned-over district**, having been penetrated by fiery orators speaking the Word of God. Shopkeepers and others who were adapting to the new economic realities of the Market Revolution relied heavily on faith to justify their new mode of living. In the South, women and African Americans were particularly moved by the Christian message of salvation and hope. American Catholics and Jews responded to the newfound fervor as well, usually by upgrading the importance of the sermon in their worship ceremonies. Alas, this awakening of the mainstream did not extend to that mainstream accepting the beliefs of Catholics and Jews. The Methodists and the Baptists capitalized on the religious fervor to the greatest extent. By the

Learn more about the burned-over district.

1820s, both denominations had surpassed all others to become the two largest churches in America.

Why a Revival?

Some historians have argued that middle-class interest in religion stemmed from a desire for economic security. As the American economy became more competitive, those who aspired to succeed embraced religion for a sense of hope and confidence in the future. In addition, evangelical religion promoted the values—frugality, sobriety, diligence, and zeal—that Americans needed in order to achieve their economic goals. More prosaically, church membership also bestowed social respectability, and those who joined were more likely to impress their superiors at work, which might lead to promotions. Both religion and the cult of female domesticity were central aspects of the emerging American middle class.

The Transcendentalists

The theology of perfectibility appeared in secular form in writings by the **Transcendentalists**, a group of thinkers and writers in the Northeast who believed that ultimate truths were beyond human grasp. They believed that these truths "transcended" our capacity for understanding. As such, they turned inward—to themselves and to their society—asking what could be done to improve the human condition. The best-known Transcendentalists were Ralph Waldo Emerson and Henry David Thoreau, two genuine celebrities of the time. Seeking to live by their ideals, Thoreau's attempt to return to nature was narrated in his book *Walden*. Telling the tale of his two-year journey living in the wilderness, the book demonstrated Thoreau's desire for self-sufficiency, living outside of society. He also protested slavery and war. His friend Emerson, meanwhile, critiqued economic competition and social conformity.

Read portions of Thoreau's *Walden*.

The purity of their ideals struck a chord with their generation and with the generation that followed, whose luminaries included Nathaniel Hawthorne and Herman Melville. These writers debated in their fiction the perfectibility of humankind. Perhaps ironically, all of these thinkers were speakers on the **lyceum circuit**, a touring lecture circuit that was made possible only by the transportation breakthroughs of the Market Revolution.

Utopianism

Utopianism provided another response to the quest for perfectibility. After their inception in Europe,

>> "Every morning was a cheerful invitation to make my life of equal simplicity, and I may say innocence, with Nature herself."
–Henry David Thoreau, *Walden*

© iStockphoto.com/Christian Harberts

several "perfectionist" communities popped up in the 1840s and 1850s, mostly in the Northeast, but also in the Midwest. One was in Oneida, New York, where John Humphrey Noyes led a group of fifty-one followers to develop what he viewed as a perfect community. The Oneida community had open sexual mores, communal child rearing, a unique division of labor, and a therapeutic milieu where people freely offered constructive criticism of one another under the watchful eye of Noyes. The Shakers, who developed from a group of Quakers, also believed in perfectionism and communal property. Their communities developed a tradition of rejecting commercial endeavors, one result being their creation of beautiful handcrafted furniture. There were many more of these groups. More than one hundred utopian communities were established between the 1820s and the 1850s.

See a narrated slide show about the Oneida Community.

The Latter-day Saints

Creating a utopia was not for everyone. Some preferred to anticipate the Second Coming of Christ, when perfection would reign for the chosen. The most significant group was the Mormons, founded by Joseph Smith, a Protestant convert who witnessed one of Charles Finney's revivals. After his conversion in the burned-over district, Smith claimed to have been visited by the angel Moroni, who showed him several golden tablets that revealed the foundations for a new religion based on the lost tribe of Israel. According to Smith, these tablets contained *The Book of Mormon* (he said he returned the tablets to the angel after he had transcribed them, so no one has seen them). Smith asserted that the tablets possessed an ancient revelation of God that predicted the "end-times," making the Mormons "saints" called out by God to usher in the new millennium; this is why Mormons called themselves the Latter-day Saints.

Smith's vision appealed to a growing number of people who were dissatisfied with the new social order unfolding during the Market Revolution. Chastised as heretics, Joseph Smith led his congregation to Ohio, then Missouri, then Illinois, in an attempt to avoid persecution. By 1844, Smith was tried for treason and, facing persecution once again, the Mormons headed west in 1846, ultimately settling in the territory of Utah. (For more on the Mormons, see Chapter 13.)

Read more about Mormonism.

>> Even routine chores, such as shelling peas, were communal activities at Oneida.

The Reform Impulse

The Benevolent Empire

While movements striving for perfectibility continued to blossom throughout the first half of the 1800s, most Americans preferred more subtle attempts at reform. Instead of drastically altering the entire society, most Americans sought to change one element at a time. This led to a series of single-issue reforms. Many of the reformers felt that, all together, their various efforts would create a "Benevolent Empire" on American soil. Led by individuals like Arthur and Lewis Tappan, evangelical brothers who advocated numerous reforms, the reformers of the 1820s, 1830s, and 1840s sought social change with a messianic fervor. In their advocacy, they sometimes questioned the morality of impoverished immigrants and non-Protestants, but they claimed to do so only in an effort to improve American society.

Female Reform Societies

The reforming impulse was particularly meaningful for nineteenth-century women. Politics were thought of as men's arena, but social reform was considered within women's sphere, and thus activist women played a large role in the movement for social reform. This was most dramatically illustrated by the **American Female Moral Reform Society**, which by 1840 had more than five hundred local chapters throughout the country and had successfully lobbied for legislation governing prostitution.

Temperance

By far the largest reforming effort went into moderating the consumption of alcohol in America. In 1800, Americans per capita drank five gallons of alcohol every year (today we drink about two gallons per capita). Booze was especially integral to the new culture of politics, but it permeated the rest of American culture too. At the same time, the Irish immigrants who streamed into the country in the 1840s brought with them a tradition of alcohol consumption and of gathering in saloons.

Female reformers attacked the habit, claiming that men who drank often beat their wives and children. They maintained that drinking also affected their work habits, sometimes forcing families into financial hardship. In 1826, temperance workers founded the **American Temperance Society**, and by the middle of the 1830s, five thousand local and state temperance organizations had appeared. In 1851, Maine prohibited the sale of alcohol. By 1855, these temperance and prohibition laws spread throughout New England and the Midwest. The temperance movement also played a prominent moral role in the presidential elections of the 1840s and 1850s, as temperance workers vigorously promoted candidates who shared their ideals.

View an online exhibition of the American Temperance Society.

Education

Between 1800 and 1860, free public education expanded across parts of the United States. Overcoming the mainstream perception that free schools were only for poor people, reformers such as Horace Mann and Henry Barnard fought to establish the public elementary school as a fixture in antebellum America. By the 1820s, public secondary schools increased in number, although they were generally reserved for those interested in a profession. Schools expanded in every region, although the South was the slowest to adopt the institution. A few state-supported colleges also opened in these years. Women gained access to public education as well, highlighted by the founding of a series of coeducational colleges. Most schools took for granted America's Protestant majority and subsequently instituted courses in Protestant moral theology and Bible readings from the King James, or Protestant, Bible.

Read more about Horace Mann.

Prison Reform

Prisons also attracted significant attention from middle-class reformers. Before 1800, punishment was usually doled out financially (in fines) or physically (in lashes). But during these reform years, reformers designed a criminal justice system whereby criminals were incarcerated for a fixed period of time. Solitary confinement—another old-time punishment—was limited to extreme cases. Inmates were allowed (mostly forced) to work together in the daytime, a practice thought to bring about personal reform. The reformer Dorothea Dix was crucial in focusing public interest on the criminal justice system and in removing large numbers of the mentally ill from prisons.

Abolition

Of deeper importance was the small but growing movement for abolition. The moral perfectibility preached during the Second Great Awakening openly exposed the greatest sin of the nation: slavery. And, as the cotton gin enabled cotton production to expand westward, slavery became firmly established in the expanding South during the first quarter of the 1800s.

Free African Americans had long advocated abolition, and in the 1820s they accelerated their protests. Richard Allen, head of the African Methodist Episcopal Church, and David Walker, a vocal pamphleteer, advocated immediate emancipation. Walker's essay *Appeal to the Coloured Citizens of the World* (1829) serves as the strongest statement from an African American during the era; it provoked many small slave riots across the South.

While African Americans advocated immediate emancipation, most white Americans favored gradual emancipation, or gradualism. In the North, slavery had been phased out after the Revolution, and the problem seemed less pressing to northern white reformers. Some white Americans demonstrated racism in other ways, however, most significantly in founding the **American Colonization Society**. The Society advocated sending all black Americans to Africa, and they even established the colony of Liberia on the West African coast for this purpose in the 1820s.

Read a selection from Walker's *Appeal*.

View a Library of Congress exhibit about the American Colonization Society.

Garrison and the Liberator

Public opinion began to shift in 1831, when William Lloyd Garrison, a white journalist advocating immediate emancipation, began publishing the anti-slavery newspaper *The Liberator*. *The Liberator* served for thirty years as the central voice of the abolition movement. It drew together a group of anti-slavery advocates, many of whom were evangelical preachers affiliated with the Lane Theological Seminary in Cincinnati (men like Lyman Beecher and Theodore Weld). The ideas of the Second Great Awakening prodded these leaders to advocate immediate emancipation, although many other northern white churches were

Read Garrison's remarks from the Anti-Slavery Convention.

slower to adopt the cause of emancipation, prompting Garrison to attack them for their complicity. Garrison was clearly the most steadfast in his pursuit of abolition: at one point, he publicly burned a copy of the U.S. Constitution, suggesting that it too was complicit in allowing slavery (which, of course, it was). This action, and others like it, alienated Garrison from many white abolitionists who favored gradualism. In 1833, Garrison founded the **American Anti-Slavery Society**, an organization that served as a point of contact for escaped slaves like Frederick Douglass and Harriet Tubman.

Resistance

Abolitionists faced fierce, stubborn resistance in both the South and the North. In northern states like New York and Illinois, merchants and laborers challenged abolitionists, mainly because they were afraid that poor black people would be willing to work for low wages, thus depressing the economy. In the South, southerners sometimes violently prevented abolitionists from distributing anti-slavery tracts. Georgia offered a $5,000 reward to anyone who delivered Garrison to state authorities.

Congressional "Gag Rule"

Abolitionists continued to fight, though, sending thousands of petitions to Congress. In an effort to prevent Congress from discussing slavery (and therefore threatening the free state/slave state balance), the House of Representatives adopted, in 1836, what opponents called the **"gag rule."** This was a legal provision that automatically tabled any discussion of abolition. Under this law, slavery was not open for discussion in Congress. Former President John Quincy Adams, now a representative from Massachusetts, repeatedly protested the rule, but persistent opposition frustrated his efforts for eight years, when Congress finally rescinded the rule.

By the 1850s, the movement for abolition was growing, and so was its opposition. As the debate

---

American Colonization Society
Group that advocated sending all black Americans to Africa; the Society established the colony of Liberia on the West African coast for this purpose in the 1820s

American Anti-Slavery Society
Organization founded by journalist William Lloyd Garrison in 1833 that served as a point of contact for escaped slaves like Frederick Douglass and Harriet Tubman

"gag rule"
Legal provision of 1836 that automatically tabled any discussion of abolition in Congress; under this law, slavery was not open for discussion

Women's Rights Convention
gathering of women activists in Seneca Falls, New York in 1848; their goal was securing the vote for women

> "A discussion of the rights of animals would be regarded with far more complacency by many of what are called the wise and the good of our land, than would be a discussion of the rights of woman."
> *—Frederick Douglass, editorial after the Seneca Falls Convention*

became increasingly polarized, more and more people had to weigh the costs associated with slavery.

The Women's Movement

Women, both black and white, were some of the most ardent abolitionists. The sisters Angelina and Sarah Grimké, Lydia Maria Child, Maria Chapman, and Lucretia Mott were all active in the crusade. For many of these women, advocating the rights of African Americans highlighted the absence of basic civil rights for women. In one notable instance, the Grimké sisters were criticized for their abolitionist activism by a pastor who suggested that the sisters should obey their male role models. This quite pointedly turned their attention to the condition of women. In response, in 1838, Sarah Grimké published *Letters on the Equality of the Sexes and the Condition of Men* and Angelina Grimké published her *Letters to Catherine E. Beecher*, both landmark tracts in the struggle for women's equality. Together, these works brought together a group of like-minded reformers interested in the place of women in American society. They found eager constituents in the women who had found their voices during the Second Great Awakening and in the new occupations generated during the Market Revolution.

In 1848, several women, including the leading abolitionists mentioned above and Elizabeth Cady Stanton, organized the **Women's Rights Convention** at Seneca Falls, New York. The convention adopted a Declaration of Sentiments, which was modeled after the Declaration of Independence and articulated the injustices that women faced in American society. As a political tactic, the women's movement put securing the vote for women atop their list of demands. But they faced two challenges: (1) from men reluctant to admit women into the raucous world of nineteenth-century politics, and (2) by the rising issue of racial equality, which would culminate in the Civil War and make all other attempts at social reform seem less pressing. The movements for justice by African Americans and women have always been linked (for example, Frederick Douglass spoke at the 1848 Seneca Falls Convention), but the thorny issue of whether to concentrate on establishing African American rights or women's rights perpetually divided the various women's movements, at least until the latter half of the twentieth century.

Read more about Seneca Falls.

And in the end ...

Between 1812 and the 1860s, the nation changed dramatically. With the American System of economics as a model, the United States became increasingly market oriented. Production was implemented on a larger scale and became more and more mechanized. The transportation and communications revolutions altered the way in which people thought of the vast expanse that was their nation. And urbanization and the creation of a sizeable working class served as reminders that certain advances come with ancillary costs, with both positive and negative effects.

The significant changes associated with the Market Revolution provoked various reactions, from the perfection seekers of the Second Great Awakening to calls for social reform from the working class, American Catholics, African Americans, and women. A new form of politics also arose during these years, years that are usually associated with one dynamic character. It is to Andrew Jackson whom we now turn.

What else was happening ...

1815	John Roulstone writes the first three verses of "Mary Had a Little Lamb" after his classmate Mary Sawyer comes to school followed by her pet lamb.
1823	The game of rugby is invented.
1838	Massachusetts prohibits sale of liquor. One man gets around the law by painting stripes on a pig and advertising that it could be viewed for 6 cents and a free glass of whiskey.
1847	Hanson Gregory, a New England mariner, invents the donut.

Politics *of the* Market Revolution

Learning Outcomes

After reading this chapter, you should be able to do the following:

1 Describe the changes that took place in American politics during the first decades of the 1800s, and explain reasons for these changes.

2 Enumerate the political developments of the Jacksonian era, including President Jackson's responses to the "spoils system," the nullification crisis, the battle over the National Bank, Indian removal, and the Panic of 1837.

3 Explain the development of America's second two-party political system, the parties being the Democrats and the Whigs.

> **❝***Despite what his appearance on today's $20 bill might suggest, Andrew Jackson ruined the national currency, which did not revive again until the Civil War.***❞**

The first half of the 1800s saw political developments just as momentous as the social and economic changes brought on by the Market Revolution. While the American economy was booming and busting and booming again between 1814 and 1850, American politics were becoming more and more democratic. The politics of deference—in which people were expected to defer to the wisdom of the more educated elite—were dying out. A new period was beginning. Historians have called it "the era of the common man," in which politics expanded beyond its elite origins and the vote was extended to more and more of the population.

What do you think?

New techniques of mass mobilization, such as campaign leaflets, public speeches, and other kinds of political propaganda, became essential to running a successful campaign in the 1820s and 1830s.

Strongly Disagree						Strongly Agree
1	2	3	4	5	6	7

To be sure, the America of the early 1800s considered the "common man" to be white and, quite literally, a man. However, while racial minorities and women were still excluded from the franchise, many states ceased requiring property ownership as mandatory for full citizenship. This meant that a much higher percentage of Americans could vote in 1840 than in 1790. Large political parties arose to woo the new voters. The result was a vibrant, sometimes raucous political life for men which featured the rise of two new parties to replace the Federalists and the Democratic-Republicans from the Founding Era. These new parties—the Democrats and the Whigs—mostly argued about the best way to manage the economy during the Market Revolution. Because Andrew Jackson symbolized this new style of politics, the period is often called the Age of Jackson.

LO¹ Politics in the Age of Jackson

A New Kind of Politics

Four factors contributed to the rise of a new kind of politics in the 1820s and 1830s: (1) economic booms and busts caused Americans to feel that the government should be more responsive to their needs; (2) the expansion of the franchise, or vote, allowed greater numbers of American men to participate in politics; and (3) the contentious presidential election of 1824 led the entire nation to become increasingly political, which drove (4) the rise of mass parties and the second two-party system.

The Panic of 1819

As we saw in the last chapter, during the first half of the nineteenth century, the United States became a more market-driven society, with increasingly rapid communications and transportation. At the same time, Americans were on the move, settling western lands and building railroads to connect the new settlements with eastern cities. The South was booming as well, becoming Europe's principal supplier of cotton. With these developments, many Americans felt they were destined to reap continued economic success.

Such optimism did not last. In 1819, global demand for American agricultural production (particularly cotton) plummeted, in part because of Europe's recovery after the end of the Napoleonic Wars in 1815. At the same time, the Second Bank of the United States tightened credit, due to fears about overinvestment in factories and land. With fewer people buying American goods and with credit tightened, the United States entered its first major economic depression. Land values tumbled across the nation, and the demand for goods and foodstuffs slackened. Every bank south and west of Pennsylvania failed except two. Thousands of people declared bankruptcy or were sentenced to debtors' prison.

The Panic of 1819 deeply affected the average American. Farmers in the West were particularly hard pressed. Having bought their farms on credit, many could not make their payments. This led banks to foreclose the loans. In desperation, people turned to their state governments, demanding financial assistance during these tough times. In Kentucky and other states, voters agitated in vain for the government to declare a moratorium on the collection of debts. In general, Americans began to feel that the government should protect its constituents from economic disaster.

Expansion of the Franchise

This push to make government more responsive to the common people coincided with the opening up of the political process. In the first years after the Revolution, most states limited the vote to white men who owned a certain amount of property. Such requirements were designed to place political power in the hands of men who were considered to have a "real stake" in society.

These limits did not last long. During the first part of the 1800s, almost every state removed property restrictions on citizenship. By 1824, most states had liberalized their laws so that every free white man was allowed to vote. After 1824, only Rhode

>> During the Panic of 1819, every bank south and west of Pennsylvania failed except two.

© English School/The Bridgeman Art Library/Getty Images

Island, Virginia, North Carolina, and Louisiana maintained property restrictions.

As they expanded the franchise to all white men, legislators of the early 1800s also developed restrictions that prevented African Americans from voting. For example, the New York Constitution of 1777 did not mention race at all, but in 1821, the revised New York Constitution restricted the vote to all white men and to wealthy African Americans. Women and poor black men were specifically excluded. The world of politics was becoming more democratic, and more people were allowed to participate, but it still maintained significant limits to participation.

The Election of 1824

Nowhere was this new politics better reflected than in the election of 1824 (Map 11.1). Since the Federalist

Map 11.1
The Election of 1824

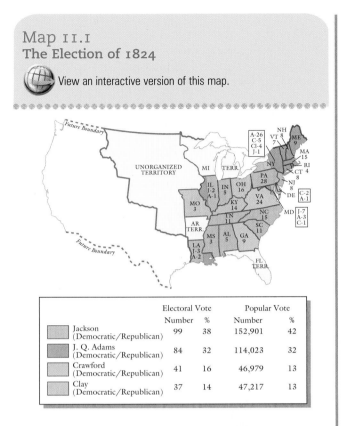

View an interactive version of this map.

	Electoral Vote		Popular Vote	
	Number	%	Number	%
Jackson (Democratic/Republican)	99	38	152,901	42
J. Q. Adams (Democratic/Republican)	84	32	114,023	32
Crawford (Democratic/Republican)	41	16	46,979	13
Clay (Democratic/Republican)	37	14	47,217	13

Party fell apart in the late 1810s (after contemplating secession at the Hartford Convention), all national politicians of the 1820s considered themselves Democratic-Republicans. Five Democratic-Republicans were nominated to the presidency in 1824, for example, and each had strong regional support. Yet no single candidate was able to muster a majority.

Per the Constitution, the election was handed over to the House of Representatives, which was, by law, instructed to consider only the top three candidates. They were Andrew Jackson, John Quincy Adams, and William H. Crawford. The candidate who had come in fourth place (and was thus no longer on the ballot) was Henry Clay. Clay instructed his backers to support Adams—an action that infuriated Jackson, who had won the most popular and electoral votes. With Clay's support, then, John Quincy Adams, the son of former president John Adams, was elected president of the United States on the next vote of the House.

When Adams shortly thereafter appointed Clay his secretary of state (a frequent stepping-stone to the presidency), Andrew Jackson and his followers protested that there had been a "**corrupt bargain**" between the two men. Jackson and his supporters vowed revenge, and revenge they would get.

The split between Clay and Adams on the one hand and Jackson on the other was the key step in the development of the **second two-party system**. By 1824, the followers of Jackson called themselves the Jacksonians, and a few years later the followers of Clay and Adams chose to be called the National Republicans. They later changed their name to the Whigs, in honor of Britain's Whigs, who had protested the authoritarian actions of the king of England (thus insinuating that Jackson yearned to be a dictatorial king). But the more immediate effect of the "corrupt bargain" was to stimulate partisanship and get more people interested in politics. In the election of 1824, national voter turnout was just 24 percent. By 1840, turnout was nearly 80 percent. National parties had developed in the intervening years to capitalize on and profit from the newfound interest in politics.

A New Culture of Politics

These national parties fed a new culture of politics in the 1820s and 1830s. Between the increased number of eligible voters and the expansion of political parties, popular interest in politics soared. Because most "common men" now had the right to vote, political candidates had no choice but to mingle with the masses and earn their respect and attention. As a result, politics for the first time became mass entertainment. Partisan newspapers flourished. Campaigns were conducted to appeal to popular tastes and featured public rallies, picnics, and elaborate parades with marching bands. Alcohol flowed freely at these events. What better way for a candidate to prove to be a man of the people than to raise a glass of whiskey to their health? In this jovial atmosphere, no one charmed the people better than Andrew Jackson.

> **What better way for a candidate to prove to be a man of the people than to raise a glass of whiskey to their health? In this jovial atmosphere, no one charmed the people better than Andrew Jackson.**

Use historical evidence to evaluate how corrupt the "corrupt bargain" truly was.

Hear music for an Andrew Jackson campaign song, and be sure to read the lyrics!

Andrew Jackson and the Politics of the "Common Man"

The Election of 1828

Resentful of the "corrupt bargain," in 1828 Jackson and his newly emerging Democratic Party set out to mobilize voters and achieve the presidential victory he felt he deserved. They had a busy four years between 1824 and 1828, barnstorming all twenty-two states. Jackson's opponent in 1828 was the incumbent president, John Quincy Adams, an old-style, patrician politician in the mold of his father. He made no effort to reach out to the people, relying instead on his record as president. He did propose financing roads and other internal improvements, funding explorations of the western interior, and leveraging American manufacturing in order to win votes, but he did so from the White House, not the campaign trail.

Jackson took a different route. Instead of focusing on specific issues, he used a campaign strategy all too familiar to American voters today: mudslinging. While Jackson defamed the personal character of his political adversaries, his fellow Democratic leaders organized rallies and barbecues to attract and mobilize voters. The Democrats amplified Jackson's biography as a war hero, and his biography changed slightly depending on where he campaigned. He was most successful with three groups: (1) southerners, who appreciated the fact that some of the Indians he had killed were Florida's Seminoles, who were hated by southerners because the tribe had invited slaves to escape to freedom in Seminole lands; (2) westerners, who viewed him as a hearty frontiersman. His supporters avoided revealing the fact that his frontier lifestyle depended largely on the hundred slaves he owned; and (3) the working classes of the North,

who had come to resent what they called the "elitism" of the Federalists and their political offspring. Jackson won the election of 1828 (Map 11.2) by a wide margin—all the more impressive because the total number of voters had tripled in just four years.

A New Politics

The election of 1828 marked a major turning point in American political history. A new style of politics had emerged, characterized by pandering to the masses. Style over substance became the rule. Moreover, new techniques of mass mobilization, such as campaign leaflets, public speeches, and other kinds of political propaganda, became essential to running a successful campaign. The election of 1828 signaled the beginning of the kind of political culture that persists in America today.

White Male Democracy

Jackson's ascendance to the presidency is often described as the dawning of the age of the common man, or the revolt of westerners and southerners

>> John Quincy Adams made no effort to reach out to the people, relying instead on his record as president.

Map 11.2
The Election of 1828

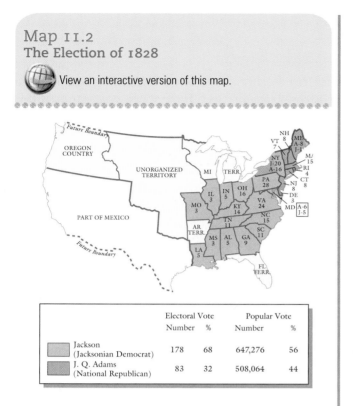

View an interactive version of this map.

	Electoral Vote		Popular Vote	
	Number	%	Number	%
Jackson (Jacksonian Democrat)	178	68	647,276	56
J. Q. Adams (National Republican)	83	32	508,064	44

against a northeastern elite. Both interpretations are somewhat misleading. Jackson was a successful lawyer and a wealthy slaveholder and, in political acumen at least, he was far from common. And, in the 1828 triumph, he won large northern states such as New York.

Nevertheless, it was Jackson's appeal to the American masses that got him elected in 1828. More than anyone else, Jackson symbolized the power of the people in the new political system. He was the first president from the West (Tennessee) rather than from the aristocracy of New England or Virginia. He was supported by a coalition of western frontiersmen, southern planters, and the northern working class who supported manhood suffrage (extending the vote to all white men regardless of property ownership) and opposed anyone they considered an aristocrat, even if those aristocrats were interested in extending rights to other, less privileged minorities.

Read Andrew Jackson's First Annual Message and see what might have appealed to the "common man."

Anti-Black

One group that did not support Jackson, largely because they did not have the legal right to do so but also because of the racism of Jackson's supporters, was African Americans. Slavery remained legal in the South, and although Jackson did not design any

policies specifically against free blacks, the Democrats were hostile to any suggestion of improving the condition of free blacks living in the North. These northern free blacks were denied basic civil rights. Only in Massachusetts, for example, could a black person sit on a jury. Worse still, Ohio, Indiana, and Illinois passed laws that prohibited free blacks from settling within their borders. By custom, segregation was the rule in the North. Blacks had to sit in separate sections on railroads, steamboats, and stagecoaches. They were barred from entering many hotels and restaurants. Thus, although the North had abolished slavery during the first quarter of the 1800s, society-wide racism made blacks an underclass, separate from the "common men" who Jackson came to represent.

patronage
Exchange of a government job in return for political campaign work

LO² Jackson as President

He may have symbolized the "common man," but Andrew Jackson's presidency was anything but common. Four issues dominated his presidency—patronage, the nullification crisis, the Bank War, and Indian removal—and the way he handled them had long-lasting ramifications, some of which we live with today.

Patronage

When Jackson and his followers came to power, they sought to exact revenge on Adams, Clay, and their supporters. Following the advice of the masterful New York politician Martin Van Buren, Jackson took control of the federal government through a system of political **patronage**. Patronage is defined as the direct exchange of a government job in return for political campaign work. This means that, rather than seek out the best-qualified person for a job, a politician simply awards the job based on the campaign support one has given him. This system was routinely called the "spoils system," as in "to the victor go the spoils." Upon his victory in 1828, Jackson fired many federal workers and replaced them with committed Jacksonians. Jackson surrounded himself with like-minded men.

The one non-Jacksonian who could not be fired was Vice President John C. Calhoun, a former senator from South Carolina and a strong advocate of states' rights. The battles between Jackson and Calhoun were legendary, especially during what came to be known as the nullification crisis.

The Nullification Crisis

By far, the most serious crisis Jackson confronted—in fact, the most serious crisis in the nation between the Revolution and the Civil War—developed around the concept of states' rights and whether or not a state could "nullify" a federal law. Nullification emerged as a major issue during Jackson's first term.

The Context of Nullification

By the time Jackson was elected president in 1828, the Panic of 1819 was just an ugly memory, but Americans were still anxious about economic matters. The economy was changing so rapidly during the Market Revolution that many Americans felt they could hardly keep up. This was especially true in South Carolina, where the cotton market had been hit hard by the depression and by soil depletion. South Carolinians focused the blame for their economic problems on the high tariff placed on their goods.

Tariffs

Congress had begun increasing America's tariffs in 1816 in order to protect American industries, especially the newly mechanized textile industry taking root in New England, which used southern cotton as its raw material. The western states also benefited from the tax on imported goods because taxes on European wheat, hemp, and other agricultural products made them more expensive; with the tariff, Americans would buy American goods. The South, however, felt left out. American tariffs did not affect southern staple crops because Europeans did not grow competing crops. As southerners saw it, they were forced to pay higher prices for goods in order to subsidize the economic development of the North and West.

When Congress raised these tariffs in 1824, South Carolina and other southern states vigorously objected. Despite these complaints, Congress narrowly approved the tariff. Then, in a move that backfired, in 1828, Jackson, running for president against Adams, advocated a ridiculously high tariff, assuming it would not pass. Jackson's promotion of the tariff would have gained him the support of the West and the North (which might otherwise have supported Adams), while the South would be content that no tariff had been passed.

To Jackson's shock, the Tariff of 1828, which came to be known as the "Tariff of Abominations," passed in Congress. Adams, the outgoing president, did not veto the measure, leaving Jackson with a tariff that made many of his supporters unhappy. The South was furious and, in response, the South Carolina legislature issued a document called the *South Carolina Exposition and Protest*. The anonymous author of this document was John C. Calhoun, Jackson's incoming vice president.

What Was Nullification?

The *South Carolina Exposition and Protest* gave voice to a new political idea: **nullification**. Calhoun's concept of nullification was designed to answer a serious problem of political theory: how to protect the rights of a minority in a government based on the rule of the majority. (This is something we have seen before, in Jefferson's Virginia and Kentucky Resolutions of 1798.) Calhoun's theory of nullification asserted that the United States was made up of independent and sovereign states. In joining the Union, Calhoun argued, states did not agree to give up their autonomy. Therefore, every state reserved the right to reject any federal law it deemed unconstitutional.

In 1828, South Carolina did nothing more than articulate the idea of nullification, but in 1832, after Congress failed to revise the Tariff of Abominations, South Carolina actually put nullification into practice. The state legislature authorized the election of delegates to a popular convention, and, in November 1832, that convention passed an ordinance declaring the tariffs of 1828 and 1832 null and void in South Carolina, effective February 1, 1833.

 Read South Carolina's Ordinance of Nullification.

Jackson's Response

As an ardent nationalist, President Jackson was not about to let South Carolina challenge the authority of the federal government. In his Proclamation on Nullification, delivered in December 1832, Jackson emphasized that the states of the Union were not independent and that, therefore, no state had the right to reject a federal law; only the Supreme Court had the authority to do that. Moreover, Jackson declared that the Union was perpetual. By this logic, Calhoun's assertion that a state could withdraw from the Union was treason.

 Read Jackson's Proclamation of Nullification (especially the last four paragraphs).

To demonstrate how seriously they took the threat, Jacksonians in Congress passed the Force Bill in March 1833, which confirmed the president's authority to use the army and navy to put down insurrection. But Jackson was wise enough to use the carrot as well as the stick. While threatening South Carolina with the possibility of force, Jackson also urged Congress to lower the tariff. By doing so, Jackson isolated South Carolina. No other state would defend South Carolina when the federal government was trying to be accommodating. As a result, Calhoun himself backed away from nullification and supported a compromise tariff bill. It went into effect on the same day as the Force Bill, March 1, 1833. South Carolina promptly repealed its nullification of the tariff, but, in a final display of spiteful defiance, it nullified the Force Bill. Jackson sagely ignored this and allowed the nullification crisis to die out. For the moment, Jackson's brand of nationalism had triumphed over the forces of nullification and secession.

The Bank War

As strong as Jackson's sense of nationalism was, it did not prevent him from attacking and eventually destroying one major national institution: the Second Bank of the United States. The crisis surrounding the charter of the Second Bank of the United States was the third issue that polarized the politics of the 1830s.

The Bank

The Second Bank of the United States, located in Philadelphia, had been created by Congress in 1816 and granted a twenty-year charter. During its first years, the Bank extended credit easily, helping grow the economy in the aftermath of the War of 1812. Americans were on the move, buying and cultivating new lands in the West, and credit from the Bank underwrote much of this economic activity. In 1819, however, the Bank reversed course and began calling in its loans, contributing to the Panic of 1819. People late on their payments now had to pay up. Many Americans went to debtors' prisons; others suffered bankruptcy. Although the Bank was not the sole cause of the panic, many citizens considered the Bank a monstrous institution.

In 1823, Nicholas Biddle, a Philadelphia businessman, assumed leadership of the Bank. Biddle believed that the Bank could serve as a stabilizing influence over the American economy by preventing the national credit supply from expanding too far or contracting too quickly. It is important to remember that America's monetary system in the nineteenth century was dramatically different than today's. Until 1863, there was no standardized national currency. Several forms of money existed, and payments were made in: (1) specie (gold or silver);

>> **The Second Bank of the United States in Philadelphia.**

(2) barter (goods exchanged for other goods without the use of money); and (3) state bank notes (paper money issued by state-chartered banks). The problem with the paper money was that its value fluctuated depending on the status and solvency of the bank. When too many notes were in circulation, their value declined. Biddle promised to use the Bank to control fluctuations in the value of paper money by limiting the amount in circulation.

Jackson's Opposition

Jackson personally distrusted the Bank. After losing his money in a bank in the 1790s, he viewed paper money as dangerous. In his eyes, only specie provided stability. Outright conflict between Jackson and Biddle erupted in 1832, when Biddle applied for a renewal of the Bank's charter four years before the charter was set to expire. Jackson presumed that Biddle was trying to make the Bank an issue in the presidential election of 1832. Already reeling from the nullification crisis, Jackson had no patience for Biddle's request and vowed to destroy the Bank altogether. Despite Jackson's objections, Congress renewed the Bank's charter in the summer of 1832. Undeterred, Jackson vetoed the charter. He justified his veto with a powerful message, arguing that the Bank was a nest of special privileges for the wealthy who were out to hurt America's humble poor. He also argued that the Constitution did not allow for the creation of a national bank or for the use of paper money. His veto was popular with the working classes, westerners, and southerners.

Crushing the Bank

Once Jackson was reelected at the end of 1832, the bank still had four years of its charter left. Jackson brashly resolved to crush the Bank before its charter expired. He ordered that all $10 million of federal deposits be withdrawn and redeposited in state banks. The Senate censured Jackson for defying its wishes, but it could not prevent the Bank from going under. When the Bank's charter expired in 1836, the institution closed its doors for good.

Wildcat Banking

The result was not what Jackson had planned. Jackson deposited all of the government's money in several state banks, many of which were owned by his friends. (This was another example of Jackson's controversial use of political patronage.) The absence of a central bank allowed for the rise of many state and local banks that had less than adequate credit and little government regulation.

Hundreds of paper currencies appeared, many of which were valueless. Counterfeiting was popular. Ironically, the only people who were knowledgeable about currencies were the commercial elite, reinforcing the notion that paper money only helped the wealthy. With no regulation, Jackson's rhetoric about the insecurity of paper money made sense, and some states, such as California in 1849, outlawed paper money entirely. But on the whole, the financial instability handicapped economic growth. Despite what his appearance on today's $20 bill might suggest, Andrew Jackson ruined the national currency, which did not revive again until the Civil War.

Westward Expansion and Indian Removal

While all this was happening, Americans continued their perpetual move west. Soil exhaustion in the Southeast, a shortage of land in New England, and the alluring broad expanses of the Midwest drew Americans to the Great Plains. Southerners usually moved west to find land where they could grow cotton. Cotton growers moved through Alabama, Mississippi, and Arkansas, populating Texas (with freemen and slaves) in the 1840s. Similarly, northerners moved in order to cultivate the fields of the Midwest, pushing as far as Iowa by the 1840s.

All this growth boosted the development of several cities, which served as trading and transportation hubs for the growing West. Louisville, Cincinnati, Detroit, Chicago, and St. Louis grew into the largest cities in the region. Connected to the East Coast by a chain of steamboats, canals, or trains, these cities boomed as centers of America's westward expansion. Rapidly they, too, became industrial centers, with mills and factories lining their riverways.

Indian Resistance

And, as before, the tribes of Native America were the chief obstacles to westward migration and settlement. Although the U.S. government pursued numerous treaties with the various tribes during the first part of the 1800s, such agreements proved untenable because the federal government would not keep its word. In addition, westward pioneers did not heed the restrictions placed on them; they often strayed into Indian territory. In some instances, Indians were invited to trade with the Americans at specified trading posts, but the result often plunged the Indians into debt, forcing them to sell their lands in order to find economic relief. The Choctaw, Creek, and Chickasaw tribes all succumbed in this way. And, as Americans moved west, they introduced disease. Smallpox wiped out the Pawnees, Omahas, Otoes, Missouris, and Kansas in the Midwest during the 1830s and 1840s. Where debt and disease did not crush Indian resistance, war did: for example, the small tribes in the Midwest were decimated in the Blackhawk War of 1832. This ended any significant Indian presence in today's Midwest.

Indian Removal Act of 1830

In the South, the tribes were larger and better organized. Constant battles raged, and complete Indian removal became established U.S. policy. After some harsh political debate, Congress passed the **Indian Removal Act of 1830**, which allowed the federal government to trade land west of the Mississippi River for land east of the river. Citing the act, Jackson forced several tribes, including the Creek and the Lower Creek, to move west throughout the 1830s. This, however, would not happen so easily.

The Cherokee Nation versus Georgia

The Cherokees had accommodated to the American way of life more than any other Indian tribe. They had adopted a American-style bicameral government, translated a Christian Bible into the Cherokee language, and adopted American rules regarding property and slaveholding. By 1833, the Cherokees owned 1,500 black slaves.

But when gold was discovered in western Georgia, white Georgians wanted the Cherokees removed so they could mine the gold. The white Georgians attempted to dissolve the Cherokee constitution and take away their property rights. To resist, the Cherokees sued the Georgians in federal court. And they won. In *Worcester* v. *Georgia* (1832), which followed a similar case from the year before, *Cherokee* v. *Georgia*, the Supreme Court ruled that the Cherokee nation was a sovereign nation and that the state of Georgia could not enter it without Cherokee permission. According to the court, if the U.S. government wanted to move the Cherokeess, it would have to do so in a treaty, not through the Removal Act.

Amazingly, Jackson simply ignored the decision. One newspaper reported the president as saying, "[Chief Justice] John Marshall has made his decision: now let him enforce it." With the prospect of violence looming, a tiny faction of Cherokee (500 out of 17,000) attempted to end hostilities by signing a treaty with Jackson. The treaty traded Cherokee land for land west of the Mississippi, and when Congress ratified the treaty (by a single vote, over the strenuous objections of Henry Clay and Daniel Webster), the Cherokees lost title to their land. (The tribe later murdered the Cherokee treaty makers, who were viewed by the majority as traitors.) After one American general resigned in protest, in 1838 General Winfield Scott invaded the Cherokee nation and forced the Cherokees to walk a thousand miles, from Georgia to Oklahoma, enduring hardship and death on what was called the **Trail of Tears**. About 4,000 Cherokees died along the way, and, when they arrived in Oklahoma, they faced conflict with the tribes that had already settled there.

Was Jackson Anti-Indian?

Jackson had a complicated relationship with Native Americans. His Indian Removal Bill of 1830 forced all Native Americans to move west of the Mississippi, clearing their lands for white settlement. But he defended these actions under the guise of paternalism—the idea that Jackson was

> **Indian Removal Act of 1830**
> Legislation that allowed the federal government to trade land west of the Mississippi River for land east of the river

> **Trail of Tears**
> Forced removal of the Cherokee nation from Georgia to Oklahoma in 1838; the Cherokees were forced to walk more than a thousand miles

> **"I have recommended them to quit their possessions on this side the Mississippi, and go to a country in the west where there is every probability that they will always be free from the mercenary influence of White men, and undisturbed by the local authority of the states: Under such circumstances the General Government can exercise a parental control over their interests and possibly perpetuate their race."**
> *—Andrew Jackson, in a letter to Captain James Gadsden, 1829*

View an interactive account of Indian removal.

The Trail of Tears

© The Trail of Tears (oil on canvas), Lindneux, Robert Ottokar (1871–1970)/ Woolaroc Museum, Oklahoma, USA, Peter Newark Western Americana/The Bridgeman Art Library

moving Indians for their own good, saving them from the ravages and greed of the white man. He put this idea into practice when he adopted a Creek Indian as a son after the Creek War.

The Seminole Revolt

Jackson's paternalism had limited appeal for those who were being patronized, and Jackson's Indian removal plan and his attitude toward African Americans combined to provoke what may have been the largest slave revolt in American history. Seminole Indians in northern Florida had long provided a refuge for escaped slaves. Beginning in 1835, Seminoles had been fighting a perpetual war with American settlers over land in Florida. In 1836, the Seminoles and their free black population (called Black Seminoles) attacked at least twelve white-owned sugar plantations. Enslaved plantation workers joined the fray, striking back at their slave masters.

In the mayhem that followed, many slaves freed themselves and burned all the sugar plantations in the region. The residents of St. Augustine watched the smoke drift from the south, as the plantations burned to the ground. Sugar was never again a viable product in northern Florida. The war between the Seminoles and the settlers lasted until 1842 without a clear victor.

Learn more about the Seminole Revolt.

The Panic of 1837

The Specie Circular

Once Indian removal became the official policy of the federal government in 1830, speculators began purchasing land in the West. And many of them used paper money from the wildcat banks that had emerged in the aftermath of Jackson's Bank War.

This proved a bad combination because the cash was not stable, and it often lost much of its value. In an attempt to protect the settlers and to affirm his distrust of paper money, Jackson, in 1836, passed the **Specie Circular**, which was an executive order requiring that the government cease accepting paper money as credible currency, accepting only gold or silver (specie) for all items, including public land. The result of the federal government's saying it did not trust the value of paper money was to devalue paper money even further, abandoning settlers to worse economic trouble and sending much of America's specie west.

The Panic of 1837

The Specie Circular could not have happened at a worse time. The rollicking economy of the Market Revolution experienced a boom in the early 1830s, mostly due to rampant speculation in the West along new transportation routes. The Specie Circular caused an immediate drop in demand for western lands and drained most of the specie from New York banks.

Unable to match its paper money with specie reserves, several hundred banks in New York City closed their doors in April. In May 1837, every bank in New York refused to accept paper money for specie. Paper money lost nearly all of its value, and nearly a quarter of all banks in the United States closed. After the Bank War, there was no central

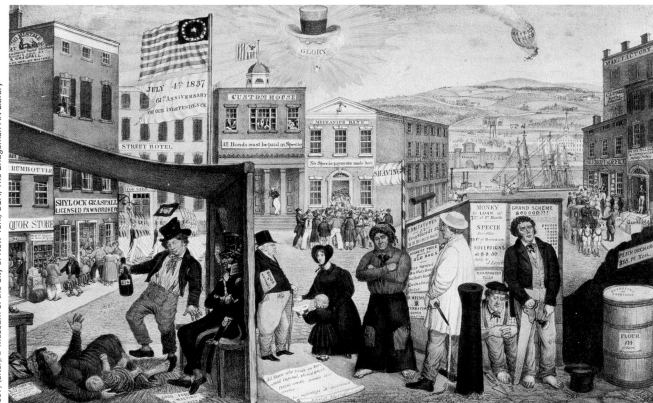

>> In 1837, the United States plummeted into an economic depression that, ever since, has been rivaled only by the Great Depression of the 1930s.

bank to control the economic contraction, and the United States plummeted into an economic depression that, ever since, has been rivaled only by the Great Depression of the 1930s.

LO³ The Development of the Second Two-Party System

Jackson's contentious presidency stirred up a vibrant, flourishing opposition, and during the 1830s the second two-party system in American history took hold, pitting Jackson's Democrats against Adams's and Clay's Whigs. More than anything else, it was opposition to Jackson's Bank veto that spurred the rise of the Whigs. In choosing their name, the Whigs (who had been calling themselves the National Republicans) were alluding to the American Revolution, when the Whig Party of England opposed the king; their name expressed their feeling that Jackson was acting like an authoritarian, king-like ruler.

Jackson's Democrats

For their part, Jackson's Democrats were extremely nationalistic and believed it was best to keep the federal government small. They fashioned themselves as the heirs of Jefferson, who considered government as nothing more than a necessary evil. To Jackson's Democrats, the government was not supposed to control the way that people conducted themselves privately. This made them less aggressive in pushing America's economic development, viewing American society as being divided between two hostile camps: "the people" (farmers, planters, workers), who worked hard to make an honest living, and "the aristocracy" (merchants, bankers, financial agents), who manipulated markets for their own private enrichment. This of course did not preclude Jackson's Democrats from supporting America's westward expansion. Jackson's Indian Removal Bill secured much new territory for white settlement, and subsequent Democratic presidents would eventually push the boundaries of the United States all the way to the Pacific.

The Whigs

The Whigs, on the other hand, favored a more active federal government. They supported using federal funds to finance internal improvements like turnpikes and railroads. They believed that government power could be used to promote the moral health of the nation through temperance laws or antislavery legislation. And the Whigs were more comfortable with market capitalism. As they saw it, economic development made people richer, increased popular demand for foodstuffs and other agricultural products, and created jobs. The Whigs denied that there was any conflict between the common people and big business. According to their view, banks were not evil; they were essential for controlling the flow of money. Many Whigs also opposed the expansion of slavery into new territory, but they did form alliances with southern states' rights groups. Prominent Whigs included Henry Clay, Daniel Webster, and William Henry Harrison.

Constituencies

Although it is tempting to categorize the Democrats as the party of the poor and the Whigs as the party of the rich, this was not the case. Most Americans were farmers of the "middling sort" who were neither miserably impoverished nor impressively wealthy. It was true that most businessmen joined the Whig Party, but the Whigs had several other key constituencies: farmers who wanted better methods to transport their produce to market; workers who believed they would benefit from economic growth; and planters who wanted the United States to have a stable bank system that would float loans. The Whigs also appealed to people concerned about the increasing numbers of Irish Catholics entering the country. In short, the Whigs did well in cities and rural areas that embraced market competition. Appealing to these various constituencies, and playing the new politics developed by the Jacksonians, the Whigs developed a solid party by the late 1830s, symbolized by William Henry Harrison's presidential victory over Martin Van Buren in 1840 (Map 11.3).

The Democrats, in contrast, attracted farmers and workers who felt alienated by America's increasingly commercialized economy, as well as small businessmen who hoped the Democratic Party would stand watch against monopolies and give "little guys" a chance to succeed. They also found a ready constituency in the Irish immigrants who immigrated in large numbers during the 1840s.

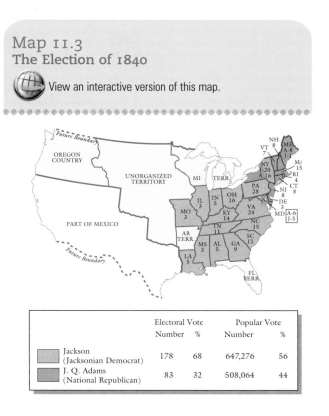

Map 11.3
The Election of 1840

View an interactive version of this map.

	Electoral Vote		Popular Vote	
	Number	%	Number	%
Jackson (Jacksonian Democrat)	178	68	647,276	56
J. Q. Adams (National Republican)	83	32	508,064	44

Political Stability

By the election of 1840, Americans had succeeded in building a stable two-party system. Each party held together a coalition of northerners and southerners, and the party system helped relieve sectional tensions over slavery. (Basically, neither party wanted to talk about slavery and its westward expansion for fear of dividing their party.) As long as the two-party system existed, hostilities between the North and South faded into the background. Such tensions never disappeared entirely, however, and territorial expansion in the 1840s set in motion a breakdown of America's second two-party system, leading to renewed sectional conflict and, ultimately, civil war.

And in the end ...

As the Market Revolution changed the economy and the ways of living associated with it, politicians sought to manage the changes and profit from them politically. They expanded patronage and developed a new political culture that was defined by race and gender. In one respect, the politicians were struggling to keep an increasingly disparate nation together through a series of political endeavors. At the same time, however, reformers were provoking questions that only increased sectional divisions, the most prominent of which was the slavery issue.

In the end, the economic tugs of the Market Revolution would be too strong to preserve this unity and, between the 1830s and the 1850s, America to a large degree fractured into a regionalized nation. This is the subject of the next chapter.

What else was happening . . .

1822–1834	English mathematician Charles Babbage proposes constructing machines to perform mathematical calculations: the Difference and Analytical Engines, forerunners of the modern computer. He runs out of money before completing either.
1824	Michael Faraday invents the first toy balloon.
July 4, 1826	Both John Adams and Thomas Jefferson—longtime friends, rivals, and, in the end, correspondents—die, on the fiftieth anniversary of the Declaration of Independence.
1837	The first kindergarten, called "small child occupation institute," opens in Germany.

Regionalized America, 1830–1860

Learning Outcomes

After reading this chapter, you should be able to do the following:

LO **1**   Describe social life in the commercial North as it developed between 1830 and 1860.

LO **2**   Describe social life as it developed in the South between 1830 and 1860 as a result of dependence on cotton.

> ## "*Regionalized identities persisted despite the best efforts of politicians to bridge sectional gaps.*"

Between 1830 and 1860, American life became increasingly regionalized. Different ways of living emerged in the North, the South, and the West. Work relations were different, communities developed in different ways, and people often thought of themselves in regional terms. "I'm a northerner," they might say, "and I don't work for slave wages." Another might say, "In the West, we operate by a different law."

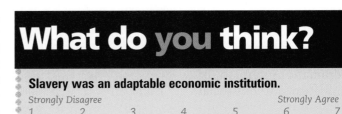

What do you think?

Slavery was an adaptable economic institution.

Strongly Disagree						Strongly Agree
1	2	3	4	5	6	7

Slavery and western expansion were the vital issues that perpetuated regionalized identities, although the transportation revolution bound the West with either the North or the South. These regionalized identities persisted despite the best efforts of politicians to bridge sectional gaps.

This chapter describes social life in the North and the South as they developed during the Market Revolution. The next chapter describes life in the West, which had an identity all its own.

LO¹ Social Life in the Commercial North

Three forces dramatically altered life in the northern United States in the three decades before the Civil War: the Market Revolution, massive immigration, and urbanization.

The Market Revolution

Although some protested the Market Revolution, most northerners accommodated and even promoted the transitions associated with it. The beginnings of an industrial urban sector, the opening of the farmlands of the West, and the interconnectedness of the different groups living in the North affected the social life of every northerner. For the most part, northerners acclimated themselves to these changes. Railroads crisscrossed the North. Commerce blossomed. The Market Revolution ignited the processes that made the North look like a modern society.

Immigration

The massive wave of immigrants to the U.S. between 1830 and 1860 was the second dramatic change. By 1860, about one-third of the total population of the United States was foreign-born. Most of the immigrants came from Europe, and nearly two-thirds came from just two countries: Ireland and Germany. These immigrants settled mostly in the North, creating distinctly immigrant neighborhoods in the cities. As these immigrant groups established themselves, they prompted new definitions of what it meant to be an American. These were not descendants of the American Revolution.

Urbanization

The third dramatic change to affect the northern states was urbanization. In 1860, the cities still housed a minority of the American population, but within their borders the dramatic interplay of America's obvious social divisions played out. Differences between black and white, rich and poor, and native-born and foreign-born all became flashpoints in early nineteenth-century urban American life. Each of these developments contributed to a unique and tumultuous social life in the antebellum North. And the cities would continue to grow.

Life in the Northern Countryside

These events had widespread ramifications for all groups, but life in the North varied depending on whether one lived in the cities or in the countryside.

Communal Values

For the most part, communal values still prevailed in the northern countryside. Farm families gathered regularly to raise barns, participate in politics, and attend church. Social networks were strong. Sewing bees and apple bees brought communities together. Most farming families in the "Old Northwest" of Illinois, western Pennsylvania, and Indiana (areas west of the Appalachians but east of the Mississippi River) found a balance between their roles as consumers and as producers. Some, like the Shakers and the utopians, rejected these impulses, but most northerners adapted to them.

© iStockphoto.com/Dennis Guyitt

Decreased Isolation

Nevertheless, change did come to the northern countryside. For one, the countryside was less isolated than it had been. Americans in the "Old Northwest" easily accommodated the economic changes associated with the Market Revolution. Markets sprang up at railroad depots, and mail and news traveled rapidly from one part of the country to the next.

Meanwhile, the transportation revolution communicated new ideas to once-isolated areas. The itinerant ministers of the Second Great Awakening, for example, moved across the country on the canals and, later, the railroads. The countryside also enjoyed an active lyceum circuit, where clergymen, reformers, Transcendentalists, socialists, feminists, and other provocative speakers would speak. The North opened some public schools and enjoyed a burgeoning newspaper industry. The press was heavily partisan, because it was usually financed by political parties. This meant that in almost every town there were at least two papers: one Democrat, one Whig. The entire North, including the countryside, achieved almost universal literacy in those years. Immigrants from Germany and Scandinavia moved into the Old Northwest to continue the farming life they had left behind in Europe. These newcomers slightly altered midwestern accents, politics, and social life, while

> Immigrants from Germany and Scandinavia moved into the Old Northwest to continue the farming life they had left behind in Europe.

upholding steadfast rural ideals. Descendants of these immigrant groups still have a significant presence in these areas today.

City Life

City life in the North was changing much more rapidly than life in the country. The cities were growing at a tremendous rate. Between 1830 and 1860, the number of towns with 10,000 or more people quintupled, totaling ninety-three in 1860. There were seven towns in the North with more than 100,000 people. In 1830, there had been just one city that large, New York City, which had just over 200,000 inhabitants. By 1860, more than 814,000 people lived in New York, making it by far the nation's largest city.

Immigrants

Immigrants contributed to much of the urban growth. In all, more than 5 million immigrants came to America between 1830 and 1860. The peak period of immigration came in the late 1840s and 1850s, when nearly 1 million Irish came to the United States to escape the potato famine. Many Germans came at this time, especially in 1848, after a failed revolution in Germany forced many political dissidents to flee. Unlike the Irish, these German immigrants, called **the 48ers**, were educated and often financially well off.

The immigrants arrived in such numbers that they changed the nature of the cities. For example, more than half of all the inhabitants of New York City were foreign-born in 1855. More than a third of Bostonians were. Within the cities, immigrants usually created enclaves of ethnic neighborhoods, starting their own churches, leisure societies, sporting clubs, and charitable organizations.

While most of these new immigrants stayed in the cities, some moved west. In 1855, for example, more than 60 percent of St. Louis was foreign-born. And many of the 48ers moved to the rural western provinces, where they could farm and where they could vote after just one or two years of residency. These new immigrants largely avoided the South because of its dependence on slave labor, which limited access to jobs.

Racial and Ethnic Identities

With the arrival of these millions of immigrants, many Americans began to consider what it was that made someone an American. One response was to define an American as someone with an English background who was born in the United States. The most ardent supporters of these views formulated a racial and ethnic identity that differentiated the various immigrant groups and proclaimed the superiority of their own group, usually labeled "native Americans." They chastised the Irish, equating them with black slaves in the South. And they were offended by the German tradition of gathering at beer gardens on Sundays, which these "native Americans" considered a day of worship. The native American movement, sometimes called **Nativism**, moved into politics and into the social and economic life of America as well. Nativists placed restrictions on what fields of business the new immigrants could enter, where they could live, and where they could find work. The influential temperance movement also contained within it a large amount of

the 48ers
Germans who came to the United States in 1848, after a failed revolution in Germany forced many political dissidents to flee

Nativism
Political identity that defined an American as someone with an English background who was born in the United States; supporters formulated a racial and ethnic identity that proclaimed the superiority of their group, usually labeled "Native Americans"

>> **The immigrants arrived in such numbers that they changed the nature of the cities.**

Read a song written by a recent Irish immigrant about his struggle to find a job.

anti-Irish and anti-German nativism. This was the era when the term *yankee* came to have meaningful social significance, differentiating between those whose family lineage predated the Revolution and those who arrived later.

Related to this racial and ethnic stereotyping was a brutal form of anti-Catholicism. The Irish were usually willing to work for lower wages than anyone else, which provoked anti-Irish sentiment from workers who felt threatened by this cheap labor force. Because the Irish were identifiable by their Catholicism, mobs, angry at how the nation was changing, sometimes attacked Catholic churches, convents, and priests. In Boston, where large numbers of Irish had settled, anti-Catholic riots broke out regularly. Public education became more visibly influenced by Protestantism in the 1840s and 1850s, prompting many American Catholics to establish alternative parochial schools.

Read a newspaper account of an anti-Catholic riot in Philadelphia.

But identity formation went both ways. Upon their initial arrival, Irish and German immigrants routinely referred to themselves by the town or county from which they came. But after just a short time in America these immigrants began to consciously think of themselves as "Irish" or "German" or "Swedish." A common language was one feature that bound certain groups together. Religion also helped newcomers feel part of a cohesive group, especially for the Irish. Restricted to certain neighborhoods, immigrant groups developed communities that embraced cultural forms harking back to the homeland. Milwaukee and St. Louis maintain extensive brewing industries today, a legacy of the German immigrants who settled in these cities during the middle of the nineteenth century. Several of these communities also still have *Turnvereine,* or turnvereins, gymnasiums founded in the spirit of the German liberation movement that erupted in 1848.

Class Consciousness

In addition to the formation of racial and ethnic identities, the combination of ethnic enclaves, middle-class professions, and the incredible wealth earned by canal builders and others led to highly visible social divisions. While most of the working class lived in tenements, wealthy Americans were constructing large mansions. By the 1850s, affluent neighborhoods had access to indoor plumbing and gas lighting. The wealthy moved through

Milwaukee and St. Louis maintain extensive brewing industries today, a legacy of the German immigrants.

© iStockphoto.com/Aleksandru Chiriac

Take a virtual tour of a New York tenement.

Read about Beechwood, built in 1851 in Newport, Rhode Island, for a New York City merchant.

the cities via horse-drawn cars, and they built neighborhoods away from industrial hubs. And the rich were getting richer: in 1845, almost 80 percent of New York City's individual wealth was owned by just 4 percent of the population. Poorer people had none of these luxuries and were often forced to live in the least desirable neighborhoods, near stockyards or slaughterhouses.

One result of these increasing economic distinctions was the creation of identities associated with being a member of a specific class. Although never distinct from ethnic, racial, and religious divisions, there was a growing commonality in how poor people talked, voted, and fought. Much of the lower-class consciousness developed not in the workplace, but in places of leisure, where workers felt most free. It was in these locations that organizers had success developing the political parties of the working class.

Women and the Middle Class

The cities became crucibles of the middle class, made up mostly of managers, desk workers, and educators. This group of educated middlemen and their families cultivated a middle-class identity between wealth and poverty. Their children slept one to a bed, they owned several pieces of large furniture, and their sons often went to college. Women were central to the formation of the middle class, and indeed, one hallmark of a middle-class family (in contrast to working-class

>> Teaching became the main profession open to middle-class women.

families) was that its women rarely worked outside the home. As work moved out of the home and into factories and commercial centers, the home became idealized as a haven in a heartless world, and middle-class women were expected to cultivate and maintain this idealized perception. In serving as the moral centerpieces of middle-class society, women became the backbone of reform efforts designed to improve the moral character of the nation. Consequently, teaching became the main profession open to middle-class women. Catharine and Mary Beecher headed up efforts to ensure that middle-class women were prepared to teach middle-class children the proper disciplines.

Leisure

Also during this period, several forms of leisure became commodities to be purchased rather than merely games to play. Although urban Americans still gathered at taverns and competed in physical contests, enterprising merchants developed networks of theaters and professional sports. Boxing, horse racing, track and field, and, in the 1850s, baseball, all evolved into professional sports during this era, attracting large crowds and meriting their own pages in the newspapers. In contrast to male-dominated professional sports, theaters provided social spaces for both men and women. Towns routinely constructed theaters early in their development, featuring plays by Shakespeare and other luminaries. Minstrel shows, featuring white men smeared with burnt cork (to make them look black), were also popular, and ran concurrently with Shakespeare's plays. Throughout the 1800s, audience participation was expected at plays, and the interaction between performer and audience made plays a democratic form of entertainment rather than a polished form reserved for the educated elite.

In the private spaces of their homes (and with increased access to indoor gas lighting), Americans also began to read more. The number of newspapers skyrocketed during these years (funded mostly by political parties), and American novelists flourished. Herman Melville, Nathaniel Hawthorne, and Fanny Fern were some of the most popular authors. The best-selling book of the period was Harriet Beecher Stowe's antislavery novel, *Uncle Tom's Cabin; or, Life Among the Lowly* (1852). Stowe and Fanny Fern were part of the growth of a "ladies' literature" in which middle-class women used their leisure time to cultivate what historians have since called a "sentimental

Uncle Tom's Cabin
Antislavery novel published by Harriet Beecher Stowe in 1852; best-selling book of that period

African Methodist Episcopal (AME) Church
National religious organization founded by African Americans in the 1790s

Read reviews and other items about *Uncle Tom's Cabin.*

Read Chapter 1 of *Uncle Tom's Cabin.*

culture." Stowe's *Uncle Tom's Cabin* emerged from the sentimental culture and had far-reaching political ramifications, enlightening people across the country to the conditions of southern slavery. Many of the other works of ladies' literature were less politically engaged, more often propagating middle-class morality tales than espousing abolitionist ideology.

Free People of Color

The cities of the North also housed free people of color, albeit in small numbers. In all, there were about 500,000 free people of color in the United States in 1860, about half of whom lived in northern cities. The remainder lived in border states, especially in and around Baltimore, Maryland. These enclaves were important not so much for provoking nativist opposition (as the Irish did), but because they created lasting institutions that perpetually supported movements for freedom. One institution was the organization of African American freemasons named after its founder, Prince Hall.

The most influential institution for free people of color was the black church. During the Second Great Awakening, a majority of African Americans became Christians. Barred from worshiping in several houses of the Christian religion, black Americans founded the **African Methodist Episcopal (AME) Church** in

the 1790s. By 1816, there were enough branches to merit a national organization, and by 1824 the AME Church had several thousand congregants. More than just places of worship, the churches functioned as schools and community centers. Because white people were unwilling to block church development for fear they would be accused of preventing Christian worship, the churches developed a separate sphere of freedom for black Americans.

In the wake of the development of the black church, several African American voluntary groups appeared, promoting abolition, temperance, and other reform causes. Black social fraternities prospered as well. If free blacks could not successfully conquer white racism, they could create institutions that developed a class of black leaders and an ideology of independence. Leaders such as James Forten and Reverend Henry Highland Garnet became political advocates for the abolition of slavery during these years. And the educated members of this society began referring to themselves as "Colored Americans" rather than "Africans" in order to assert their membership in the American nation. Throughout the 1840s and 1850s, these black Americans swayed between optimism and pessimism about the place of black people in America, and with the Civil War, their struggle would become central to the nation's political agenda and its very survival.

Conclusion

In general, most Americans in the North accommodated the Market Revolution. The wealthy got

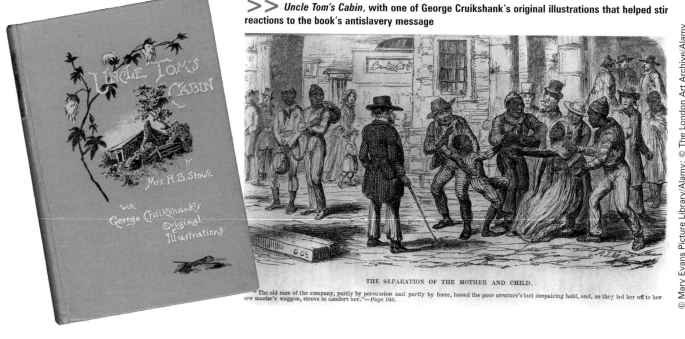

>> *Uncle Tom's Cabin,* with one of George Cruikshank's original illustrations that helped stir reactions to the book's antislavery message

THE SEPARATION OF THE MOTHER AND CHILD.

" The old men of the company, partly by persuasion and partly by force, loosed the poor creature's last despairing hold, and, as they led her off to her new master's waggon, strove to comfort her."—Page 103.

© Mary Evans Picture Library/Alamy; © The London Art Archive/Alamy

wealthier, and the middle class created a unique and comfortable life for itself. Immigrants poured in and, although the working class faced brutal working hours, painstaking labor, and few benefits beyond a paycheck, all they had to do was look south to see that they were much better off than the laborers there, a great majority of whom were enslaved and had no hope of freedom.

LO^2 Social Life in the Cotton South

Between 1830 and 1860, southerners experienced dramatically different developments than northerners. In every way, cotton became king. It constituted nearly half of the exports of the entire nation, and southerners knew that they could get rich if they could succeed as cotton farmers. But growing cotton required slaves and land, so southerners brought slaves and slavery with them into the southwestern territories of the United States. This ended any

>> The vision of the antebellum South presented in *Gone With the Wind* (1939) correctly identifies only a tiny percentage of southerners living during the era.

potential talk of gradual emancipation during this period. Furthermore, southerners had little need for big cities, and, without jobs to offer, they did not attract immigrants in the same numbers as the North. This was the period when southerners solidified their plantation economy and developed a vehement defense of it—one based on the superiority of the white race.

When we think of the antebellum South, we are prone to think of images culled from the novel and film *Gone With the Wind*, which portrayed the leisurely lifestyle of a landed and cultured white elite being served by willing and subservient black slaves. But three facts are vital in understanding how the actual prewar South contrasted with this image. First, of the 8 million southern white people, only 338,000 owned slaves, meaning that a huge majority of southern white people had no direct connection to slavery. Most were isolated yeoman farmers seeking self-sufficiency. Second, of those 338,000 slave owners, most owned very few slaves. More than 60 percent of slaveowners owned only 5 or fewer slaves, and only 3 percent owned 20 or more slaves. Finally, a vast majority of southern white people had no connection to a plantation, but the majority of slaves did. Indeed, the few massive plantations housed as many as half of all the slaves. As such, plantations were vital in the development of a unique slave culture. But the wealthy plantation life of *Gone With the Wind* was lived by only a very small minority of white southerners.

Southern White Society

The North was notable for distinctions between the countryside and the city, but there were no similar complexities in southern society, because there were so few cities. White southern society was stratified between yeoman farmers and wealthy planters. A group of landless white people ranked below the farmers (but above slaves), mostly working as laborers on farms or as frontiersmen settling the Southwest. But most white southerners were either wealthy planters or yeoman farmers.

The Planters

The planters viewed themselves as paternalistic aristocrats managing preindustrial fiefdoms. They were deeply involved in national and international markets, but they usually preferred to keep the marketplace at a distance. The development of the telegraph in 1845 allowed them to monitor cotton prices in England. They spent their summers abroad

>> Content with the society they had created, southern planters resisted change unless it could earn them greater profits.

and sent their children to be educated in Europe and at the Ivy League colleges. The planters entered politics, considering themselves the natural leaders of society. Financially and politically powerful, the planter class fought all attempts to make their society more democratic. The planter class resisted funding public education through taxation and defeated similar attempts to create internal improvements that would have invited more commerce and industry to the South. Content with the society they had created, southern planters resisted change unless it could earn them greater profits.

Yeoman Farmers

Only a tiny minority of white southerners were planters; the majority were yeoman farmers. Yeoman farmers were largely self-sufficient, living with their families on remote farms or in small towns, and missing out on much of the Market Revolution. They were usually forced onto less desirable plots of land and, most of the time, these farmers used most of their land to plant cotton and the rest to grow crops needed by the household. They used the money earned from cotton to purchase items that could not be grown in southern soil, such as coffee. Most yeoman farmers remained largely isolated from markets. A few yeoman farmers acquired large plots, bought slaves, and became wealthy, but this was rare. Social mobility was limited in the antebellum South, and when it did occur, it mostly pushed people downward. Thus, nearly one-quarter of white southerners were landless at some point

during their lives, forcing them to search for work on someone else's farms or push west in search of work. With few public schools, most yeoman farmers were uneducated. (At least 20 percent of white adult southerners could not read.) Consumed by the work of their farms, they remained isolated in their folk culture, which was centered on family, church, and region.

The White Defense of Slavery

No matter what their station in society, nearly all white southerners were advocates of slavery. For the planters, this was an easy decision: slavery, while expensive to maintain, was profitable, and profits and social norms overcame any moral difficulties. For yeoman farmers and landless white people, the existence of slavery ensured that there was always a class of people below them socially, that there was always one rung farther down the ladder. The presence of slaves kept alive their hopes that maybe one day they too might own slaves and become wealthy.

Nat Turner

In the 1830s and 1840s, white southerners developed a more militant defense of slavery. In doing so, they were responding to one of the most violent slave revolts in American history. In 1831, Nat Turner, a Christian preacher, led a group of slaves through the Virginia countryside, brutally murdering sixty white people of both sexes and all ages during a two-day stretch. Turner's plan was to raise an army of freed slaves and lead an insurrection against the southern white planters. The white response was overwhelming and harsh. White militiamen attacked the group associated with Turner, but also

>> Although photographed in 1940, this homestead looks much the same as a yeoman farmer's home would have appeared in the South before the Civil War.

Read more about *The Confessions of Nat Turner*.

Read Harriet Ann Jacobs's account of life in the South after Nat Turner's Rebellion.

indiscriminately killed slaves not involved in the insurrection. Perhaps more than two hundred slaves were killed in retaliation. Turner was eventually captured and hanged, but not before being interviewed by southern physician Thomas R. Gray, who published the interview as *The Confessions of Nat Turner*. The book sold well from its first publication, and it is one of the most haunting tales of American slavery.

Black Codes

Besides the violent damage done to black bodies, Nat Turner's insurrection also caused white southerners to pass further laws restricting black freedoms. Their reaction was nearly hysterical in its ferocity. Many states prohibited slave literacy. Others required all slave meetings to be supervised by whites. Slave behavior was monitored. In 1832, the Virginia legislature developed a plan that would simultaneously emancipate its slaves gradually and then deport them all to Africa. The plan did not pass, and no other open discussion of emancipation ever occurred in the South until the Civil War.

A Sterner Defense

Beyond punitive and legal ramifications, the reaction to Nat Turner stimulated a change in the way slavery was understood. In this period, southern writers developed a defense of slavery that suggested that slavery was good for both races, because black people were not equipped to take care of themselves and needed white, pater-

nalistic masters to protect them. White slaveholders began to cite biblical references to slavery, suggesting that the institution was somehow sanctioned by God. Thomas R. Dew, George Fitzhugh, and J. D. B. DuBow all advocated the benefits of slavery in widely read publications. Through them, the South's understanding of slavery transitioned from being a "necessary evil" (as it was conceived during the revolutionary period) to being a "positive good."

Slave Society

Certainly no slave would agree with the notion that slavery was a positive good. Life for slaves was arduous, a relentless grind of forced labor in uncertain social conditions, shadowed by the constant threat of abuse. Most slaves were field hands growing sugar, rice, tobacco, and especially cotton. Some were house servants who cooked and cleaned for their masters and helped take care of their children. Some were skilled artisans, such as blacksmiths, carpenters, or ironworkers. A few worked as longshoremen or shipbuilders in port cities such as New Orleans, Louisiana, and Charleston, South Carolina. Yet all were regarded as property, to be bought, sold, or bartered at the whim of their owners. The law did not protect slave families. Husbands and wives, as well as parents and children, could be separated from each other permanently, without notice. Although there were official limits on the treatment of slaves (the murder or unjustifiable

> 66 The calm, deliberate composure with which he spoke of his late deeds and intentions, the expression of his fiend-like face when excited by enthusiasm; still bearing the stains of the blood of helpless innocence about him; clothed with rags and covered with chains, yet daring to raise his manacled hands to heaven; with a spirit soaring above the attributes of man, I looked on him and my blood curdled in my veins. 99
>
> —*Thomas R. Gray*, **The Confessions of Nat Turner**

gang system
Work arrangement under which slaves were organized into groups of twenty to twenty-five workers, supervised by an overseer

slavedriver
Supervisor or overseer of slave labor, usually employed on a cotton plantation

task system
Work arrangement under which slaves were assigned a specific set of tasks to accomplish each day; often employed on rice plantations and in domestic service situations

mutilation of slaves was illegal in most states, and state laws set minimum standards for the amount of food, clothing, and shelter that must be provided for slaves), such laws were unenforceable because slaves were prohibited from taking their masters to court.

Despite severely restricting the rights of slaves, many slave masters believed it was in their best interest to treat slaves decently—as long as the slaves remained obedient. Masters were generally profit-minded men who understood that healthy laborers were more productive than those who were sick or abused.

Owners also recognized that healthy slaves were more likely to produce healthy offspring. Slave reproduction mattered to plantation owners because the United States had outlawed participation in the international slave trade in 1808. While Caribbean slaveholders frequently worked slaves to death only to replace them with new imports, this was impossible in the United States. Nevertheless, the fact that slaveholders had an interest in keeping their slaves alive did not mean that slaves were treated humanely in the antebellum South.

Work

The work conditions endured by slaves were as varied as the tasks they performed, but plantation labor was usually organized in one of two ways. The first was the **gang system**. Under this system, masters organized slaves into groups of twenty to twenty-five workers, supervised by a white overseer or a black **slavedriver**. This method of organizing labor was most commonly used on cotton plantations. During the major seasons of cotton cultivation, slaves labored in the fields for up to sixteen hours a day. Although most masters, in keeping with their Christian beliefs, gave their slaves Sundays off and required only a half-day of work on Saturday, working under the gang system was backbreaking.

The second major labor system was the **task system**. As the name suggests, this system assigned each slave a specific set of tasks to accomplish each day. Once slaves had accomplished these tasks, their time was largely their own. The task system was common on rice plantations, because rice did not

>> An idealized view of the master's role reads:

Slaves: God bless you massa! you feed and clothe us. When we are sick you nurse us. and when too old to work, you provide for us!

Master: These poor creatures are a sacred legacy From my ancestors and while a dollar is left me, nothing shall be spared to increase their comfort and happiness.

require the constant care and toil that cotton did. Slaves working as domestic servants also commonly labored under the task system. Although the task system often gave slaves more freedom, slaveholders frequently set unrealistic expectations for slaves and then punished them for failing to finish their work.

Some slaves did not work in either of these two systems. Instead, they had special arrangements that allowed them an unusual amount of freedom. This was especially common among slaves living in the cities. Although urbanization did not unfold as quickly as it had in the North, slave states had a small number of cities, including Baltimore, Richmond, Charleston, Mobile, and New Orleans. Each city housed large slave populations and, even though urban slaves remained the property of their masters, owners could not exercise complete authority over their slaves in the city. For instance, a skilled slave carpenter needed the freedom to move about the city to reach job sites. Craftsmen, such as blacksmiths or jewelers, often worked independently, sharing a portion of their earnings with their master. As these slaves' experiences attest, slavery was an adaptable economic institution.

Quarters

Despite the wide variety of possible slaving conditions, most slaves were owned by planters who lived on large plantations. In these conditions, most slaves lived in slave quarters, defined as a group of cabins set away from the master's home. The cabins were usually organized around families, who tended personal gardens and raised their own animals. On the largest plantations, slave quarters were significant-sized communities with ample freedom away from the watchful eye of the master.

Community

In slave quarters, slaves created a culture far removed from that dictated by white southerners. From the beginning, Africans came to America with their own cultures, and the experience of slavery did not completely obliterate those cultures. The influence of African cultures was especially strong in the music, dancing, and verbal expressions that slaves used in their everyday lives and religious ceremonies.

Family lay at the center of slave culture. Although masters retained the right to separate spouses, siblings, parents, and children from each other, slaves remained determined to preserve a sense of family. Slave marriages were not legally recognized, but slaves entered marital unions with great joy and celebration. Some marriages were made by obtaining the master's verbal consent.

When possible, slaves maintained traditional nuclear families with a father, a mother, and children living together. Within this family unit, men and women followed traditional gender roles, although they worked side by side, doing the same work in the fields. At home, women did the indoor work, such as cooking, cleaning, sewing, and raising children, while men did chores outside the home, like hauling water and gathering wood. Although premarital sex was common in slave quarters, at some point every slave was expected to choose a mate and settle down. Maintaining a two-parent family was not within their control, however. Whenever it was convenient or profitable, many masters sold off married slaves, leaving mates behind. One estimate suggests that, in the four decades preceding the Civil

>> An unusual sight—five generations of a slave family, together, on Smith's Plantation, Beaufort, South Carolina, 1862

Library of Congress, Prints & Photographs Division, LC-B8171-152-A

❝I heard them [slaves] get up with a powerful force of spirit, clapping they hands and walking around the place. They'd shout, 'I got the glory. I got the old time religion in my heart.'❞
—Mose Hursey, former slave from Red River County, Texas

Underground Railroad
Network of men and women, both white and black, who were opposed to slavery, sheltered runaway slaves, and expedited their journey to freedom

War, around 600,000 slave husbands and wives were separated from each other in this way.

Religion served as another pillar of slave culture. Most slaves arrived in America holding some form of West African religious belief. They usually believed in a Supreme God or Creator, as well as in the existence of a number of lesser gods. During the colonial period most slaves continued to practice their native religions, and slave owners did little to introduce their slaves to Christianity, fearing that if slaves became Christians they would have to be freed.

During the Second Great Awakening, however, most slaves became Christians. And despite the controlling efforts of the masters, slaves formed their own ideas about Christianity, melding their native practices with Christian beliefs. Many slaves also maintained belief in benevolent spirits and in the practice of conjuring or foreseeing the future. Theirs was a jubilant faith, promising deliverance. Religious services in the slave quarters included dancing, singing, and clapping. Spirituals were the most significant form of African American music developed during this period. For obvious reasons, the biblical lessons

Learn more about slave religion.

Research slave religion further.

the slaves emphasized were not those that commanded obedience and docility, but those that inspired hope for the future. The God they worshipped was one who would redeem the downtrodden and lift them up to heaven on Judgment Day. The master might be rich and powerful in this life, but many slaves took solace in the conviction that they would attain glory in the next one.

Resistance and Revolt

Although several slave revolts are well remembered today, it is important to note that there were not more of them. Still, the low number of slave revolts in American history should not be interpreted as a lack of resistance on the part of American slaves. Most slaves who wanted to buck the system simply found less overt ways of insulting or irritating their masters, especially considering that punishments for revolt were so severe. Slaves broke tools and machinery in order to slow production. Some feigned illness and injury to avoid work. Still others stole goods from their master to sell or trade for other goods. Even in their everyday demeanor, slaves occasionally outsmarted their owners. They

could pretend to be ignorant and happy, as whites believed them to be, and use white stereotypes of them as a way to escape work. For example, intelligent slaves often faked confusion to avoid being assigned certain tasks or to explain why work was not completed. They were resisting their condition in a subtle, undetectable manner.

Those who wanted to resist white authority in more dramatic fashion, but did not want to take the chance of organizing widespread revolts, had another option. They ran away. However, few slaves found permanent freedom in this way, especially if they were trying to flee states in the Deep South, defined as Alabama, Georgia, Louisiana, Mississippi, and South Carolina. Southerners organized slave patrols to watch for runaways and used hunting dogs to track escaped slaves. Slaveowners also used newspapers to alert whites across the South to be on the lookout for certain runaways. Because so few southern blacks were free (only about 8 percent), slaves on the run were easily sighted.

Despite the odds, many slaves did flee, and a few found permanent freedom. Some runaways found help from the **Underground Railroad**, defined as a network of men and women (white and black) who opposed slavery, who sheltered runaway slaves, and expedited their journey to freedom. One slave who successfully escaped bondage and settled in the North was Frederick Douglass. After his escape, Douglass became one of the foremost figures in the abolition movement. He wrote

Read an excerpt from *Narrative of the Life of Frederick Douglass.*

Read other slave narratives.

Take an interactive journey on the Underground Railroad.

© iStockphoto.com/Rick Rhay

>> Runaways were told that they could recognize a "safe house," a stop on the Underground Railroad, by a lantern hung on its hitching post.

about his experiences in his autobiography, *Narrative of the Life of Frederick Douglass* (1845), which traces his personal journey from slavery to freedom.

And in the end …

By the 1830s, the North and the South had begun to develop divergent societies. The Market Revolution and slavery served as obvious battle lines. For instance, although most northerners did not favor abolition, they generally agreed that slavery contradicted the way of life that the Market Revolution was bringing about, one that underscored the presence and importance of labor that was free to choose its manner and place of employment. The North was also becoming increasingly urbanized and industrialized, with a large population of landless (often immigrant) workers.

Southerners, meanwhile, had begun to articulate the concept that slavery was not shameful, but essential to the protection and improvement of the black race. The region remained a predominantly agrarian society that depended on slave labor for the cultivation of its most profitable crop, cotton. Many in the South viewed the growth of cities and commerce in the North as a move away from the values on which the country had been founded and toward materialism and greed. Northerners, in turn, tended to view the South as a region stuck in the past, venerating the kind of class system and aristocracy against which the revolutionary patriots had rebelled decades earlier.

In addition, the two regions had widely differing attitudes toward the role of the federal government. The North depended on the high tariffs of the American System to protect its growing manufacturing concerns, and the government used the income from the tariffs to finance the roads, canals, and other internal improvements that northerners needed to bring goods to market. Southerners opposed high tariffs. They did not need tariffs to protect their cotton production, so tariffs accomplished nothing for southerners beyond raising the cost of the imported goods they wanted to purchase.

Until the 1830s, most northerners had been content to tolerate slavery outside their own state borders but, as the nation expanded geographically, Americans were forced to confront the issue repeatedly. Should slavery be allowed to move west? Over the next few decades, the question of whether or not slavery would be allowed in new western territories reappeared continually, and conflict over this question would lead to sectional tensions, political conflicts, and eventually, a civil war. What made the issue so pervasive was the revived move to the West, which had a culture and society all its own. The revived move westward is the subject of the next chapter.

What else was happening . . .

1849	The first safety pin is patented.
1850	Beer is first sold in glass bottles. Before that, patrons had their beer poured into a bucket or cup that they brought with them.
1857	The words and music to "Jingle Bells" are registered, under the title "One Horse Open Sleigh"—which didn't stick.
1857	Elisha Graves Otis demonstrates his passenger safety elevator at the Crystal Palace Exposition in New York by cutting the elevator's cables as it ascends a 300-foot tower.

13

The Revived Move West

Learning Outcomes

After reading this chapter, you should be able to do the following:

LO **1** Describe the conquest and development of the West between 1820 and 1850 by white Americans.

LO **2** Explain how the expansionist spirit in the West led to political conflict at home as well as conflict with Mexico, even as it gave the United States its modern boundaries.

> **"The 'opening' of the frontier kept alive the democratic promise that poor but free men could make it on their own."**

Beginning in the 1820s, white Americans began settling west of the Mississippi River for the first time. They did so for a variety of reasons, the three foremost being to flee religious persecution, to pursue greater social freedom, and, most often, to seek riches.

Between the 1820s and 1860, Americans' westward migration across the Mississippi occurred in two general phases. The first phase, which lasted from the 1820s to 1844, saw Americans move west without their government's consent or decree; they moved mostly for personal reasons. The second phase of westward migration began in 1844, after the election of President James K. Polk, an active evangelist of American expansion. On his watch, the American nation doubled in size. This second, deeply nationalistic phase was promoted under the banner of manifest destiny, the idea that America was destined by God to conquer North America and spread American civilization far and wide.

The perpetual westward movement of Americans had at least four significant consequences: (1) further decimation of Native America; (2) continued expansion of the Market Revolution; (3) the "opening" of the frontier, which kept alive the democratic promise that poor but free men could make it on their own instead of subjugating themselves to capitalist chieftains; and (4) perhaps most important, the explosion of the slavery issue onto the American political stage. After decades of cobbled-together political compromises, the question of whether slavery would be allowed in the new territories of the West led to a political breakdown that ignited the Civil War. But, first, to the great westward expansion between the 1820s and 1860.

What do you think?

By taking responsibility for the actions of white settlers, government officials committed themselves to defending, and defining the course of, westward expansion.

Strongly Disagree						Strongly Agree
1	2	3	4	5	6	7

LO¹ Western Conquest and Development, 1820–1844

Americans developed four unique territories in the West between 1820 and 1844: Texas, Oregon, Utah, and California. Each territory was developed for a different reason, and each bore the imprint of its initial conquest long after the territory was settled.

Texas

Before the late 1840s, the most popular destination of westward migrants was Texas. It was a Spanish colony until 1821, when it became part of the newly independent nation

© John Gast/The Bridgeman Art Library/Getty Images

of Mexico. Americans seeking land for growing cotton had been hesitant to settle in Texas while it was a Spanish colony. But the new nation of Mexico seemed much less powerful than Spain, and Americans in the 1820s seized their chance to settle in Texas. During that decade, about twenty thousand Americans streamed into the province, rapidly outnumbering the five thousand Mexicans who were living there. A few Anglo-Americans assimilated to Mexican culture, but most chose not to. The new settlers continued to speak English, created separate schools, and conducted most of their trade with the United States. American cotton planters brought slaves along with them, ignoring Mexico's 1829 abolition of slavery.

By 1830, the Mexican government became worried that it was losing control of Texas. Objecting to the persistence of slavery there, it sought to curtail U.S. immigration to the region. It raised taxes there, built new military posts, and prohibited further American settlement. But it was too late. The floodgates had opened, and Americans, both free and enslaved, continued to pour into the province. Predictably, the new regulations frustrated the American immigrants, who eventually demanded autonomy from Mexican rule. When Mexico resisted, bitter conflict was destined to erupt.

Mexican-American Hostilities

Between 1829 and 1834, Mexico suffered a series of internal political coups, leading up to General Antonio López de Santa Anna's seizing power in Mexico City. He abolished the Mexican constitution and declared himself absolute dictator. He intended to rein in Texas's autonomy. Led by Stephen F. Austin and William B. Travis, and with Sam Houston as commander-in-chief of the new Texas army, Texans rebelled, declaring their independence and creating an interim government. Santa Anna refused to tolerate this insurrection, and in 1836, he led 5,000 troops to San Antonio, attacking the Americans at an abandoned mission called the Alamo. Some 187 Texans, including western pioneer legends Davy Crockett and James Bowie, were killed during the battle. But before they lost the Alamo, the Texans had killed between 1,200 and 1,600 Mexican troops. Their stand became a source of inspiration for the Texas military, which continued to "remember the Alamo" at later battles.

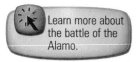
Learn more about the battle of the Alamo.

A Victory for Texas . . . and for Slavery

Two months later, Texans scored the decisive victory over Santa Anna when Sam Houston surprised the

>> "I recognized Col. Crockett lying dead and mutilated. . .and even remember seeing his peculiar cap lying by his side. Col. Bowie was sick in bed and not expected to live, but as the victorious Mexicans entered his room, he killed two of them with his pistols. . . ."
–Susanna Dickinson Hanning, a survivor of the Alamo battle

The Alamo

© iStockphoto.com/Stephen Finn

Mexican forces at San Jacinto, near today's city of Houston. Santa Anna himself was captured (while napping in his slippers), and the Texans forced him to sign treaties guaranteeing Texan independence. Soon after this victory, Texas drew up a new constitution, which guaranteed its white citizens the right to own slaves. It also prohibited free black people from immigrating to the new nation of Texas. Texans formally petitioned the United States for immediate annexation. Many northern members of Congress feared that admitting Texas as a slave state would disrupt the Compromise of 1820, which had crafted a delicate balance between slave and free states. American leaders therefore rebuffed the appeals for annexation and left the new Texas Republic to make its own way as an independent nation. Despite this temporary rebuff (Texas would become an official part of the Union in 1845), settlers continued to flood into Texas, most often to develop cotton farms.

Oregon and the Oregon Trail

Early Battles

The next region to be colonized by American settlers was Oregon. The U.S. government had asserted its sovereignty over Oregon ever since maritime merchant Robert Gray's expedition to the region in 1792, which helped inspire Jefferson to send Lewis and Clark on their expedition. But there were also prior British, Spanish, and Russian claims on the territory. In the early 1800s, as the Oregon fur-trade competition increased, American diplomats took steps to ensure that their merchants would not be excluded from trading in the region. Before 1830, only a few American citizens (usually Protestant missionaries) ventured into distant Oregon, because most of it was controlled by Native American tribes and British fur trading companies.

As the area's beaver population dwindled, the British slowly withdrew. Their departure left the territory open to settlement, and in the 1830s and 1840s American settlers began to move into Oregon's Willamette River valley. Between 1842 and 1845, the number of Americans in Oregon increased tenfold, from about five hundred to about five thousand.

>> ... a new route through the Rockies, called the Oregon Trail.

New Settlements and Indian Violence

Predictably, as the new settlements spread throughout the valley, tensions between Indians and settlers increased. Indians felt crowded, and many were dying from diseases imported by American settlers. In 1847, discontent erupted into violence when a group of Cayuse Indians killed fourteen settlers, including a white doctor who had been treating infectious diseases in white people but refused to treat Indians. The violent attack prompted outrage in Washington, D.C., and a provoked Congress sought to establish more direct control over Oregon by organizing it as a formal American territory.

Oregon Fever

Although violence persisted between Indians and American settlers, increased government control prompted a surge of new arrivals. After the opening in the early 1840s of a new route through the Rockies, called the Oregon Trail, more and more Americans moved to the territory (see Map 13.1, page 209).

Utah and the Mormons

Most American settlers in Texas and Oregon moved for economic reasons, but another group—the Mormons—went west seeking a haven from religious persecution. The Mormons found refuge in the area around the Great Salt Lake, in what would become the state of Utah.

Joseph Smith and the Origins of Mormonism

In 1830, Joseph Smith organized a new religion called the Church of Jesus Christ of Latter-day Saints, known colloquially as the Mormons. Like other new religious communities founded during the Second Great Awakening, Mormonism emphasized a direct and ecstatic connection with God. It attracted people who wanted to renounce the sinfulness and social disorder that they saw all around them. Mormonism grew quickly and gained converts by the thousands. But many Christians viewed Mormons with suspicion because of their community's isolated ways and curious practices, such as polygamy. Joseph Smith, for instance, was reputed to have had thirty-four wives between the ages of fourteen and sixty. Each time tension grew with neighboring "gentiles," the Mormons moved their headquarters, first from New York to Ohio, then to several locations in Missouri. In 1838, they settled in Commerce, Illinois, which they renamed "Nauvoo" (as it is known today).

For five years, the Mormon community grew and prospered in Nauvoo. But in 1844 trouble erupted after a local newspaper, fearful of Smith's growing power, published an exposé of the polygamy practiced by Smith and other Mormon men. As the mayor of Nauvoo and the head of its court and its militia, Smith demanded that the newspaper be suppressed. During the controversy, non-Mormons grew increasingly hostile toward the religion and appealed to state authorities to help drive the Mormons out. Soon after, Joseph Smith and his brother Hyrum were arrested for treason, and on June 27, 1844, a lynch mob entered the jail where the men were being held and shot them both dead. In 1845, in what was referred to as "the Mormon War in Illinois," Mormon opponents torched more than two hundred Mormon-owned buildings in Nauvoo. Rumors surfaced that the federal government was planning a raid, and the Nauvoo city charter was revoked. The Mormons, now led by Smith's successor Brigham Young, negotiated a truce so that they could leave Illinois peacefully.

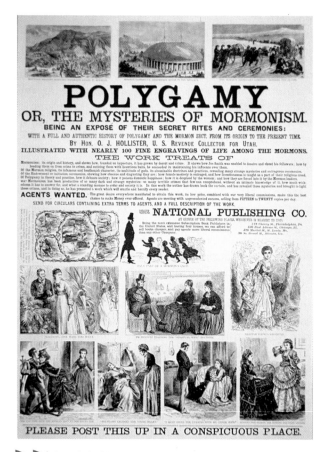

>> Joseph Smith was reputed to have had thirty-four wives between the ages of fourteen and sixty, prompting responses such as this anti-Mormon poster advertising a book critical of *Polygamy or, the Mysteries of Mormonism.*

Brigham Young

From published journals celebrating the western frontier, Young learned of an inland sea—the Great Salt Lake—that lay north of New Mexico. Although surrounded by inhospitable deserts and mountains, the land immediately next to the lake seemed ideal for settlement. To Young, the area also appeared sufficiently remote to guarantee that the Mormons would not encounter persecution. In addition, Utah was still technically under Mexican control and therefore outside U.S. jurisdiction. This meant that the Mormons could function independently and follow their own laws and customs. They set out to find their promised land on what came to be known as the Mormon Trek (see Map 13.1).

To Utah

A dynamic leader, Young had little difficulty persuading his followers that the Great Salt Lake area would be their home. In 1847 and 1848, thousands of Mormons settled in the Salt Lake basin. There they developed an irrigation system, which expanded their acreage of arable land, and laid the foundation for today's Salt Lake City.

But the Mormon dream of settling beyond the reach of the U.S. government did not last long. The United States won control of Utah in February 1848 as part of the settlement of the Mexican War, thus continuing the contentious relationship between Mormons and the federal government for the next fifty years. From 1856 to 1858, relations soured over the issue of who controlled the Utah territory, leading to a brief "Utah War." One notable episode of this conflict was the Mountain Meadows massacre. In the massacre, more than one hundred California-bound migrants from Arkansas were slaughtered by a collection of Mormon militiamen and Paiute Indians, both of whom feared the continued presence of American settlers in their territory.

California: Ranches and Gold

Still farther west, American citizens were beginning to settle the Mexican state of Alta California. In the early 1840s, new Republican leaders awarded huge land grants in California to a handful of its American citizens and retired Mexican soldiers. Word of California's bountiful, fertile lands spread quickly. With the opening of the Oregon Trail and its offshoot, the California Trail (Map 13.1), more and more Americans made their way to the distant Mexican state. By early 1846, about eight hundred

Map 13.1
Overland Trails, 1846

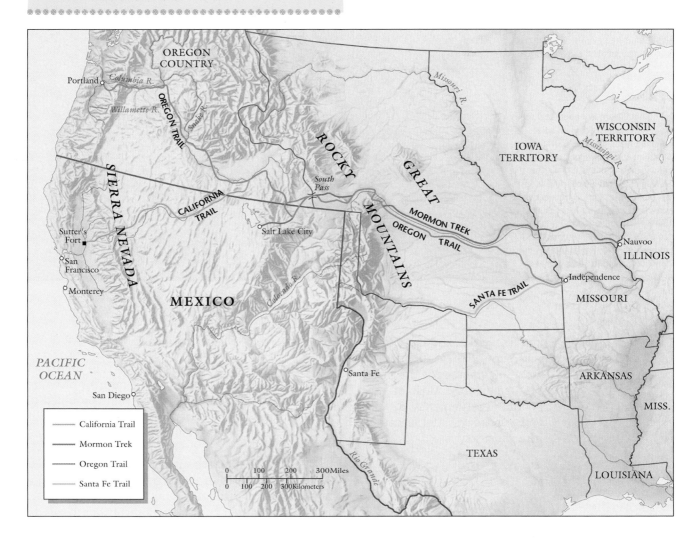

Americans and about eight to twelve thousand *californios* lived there.

This all changed in January 1848, when gold was discovered along California's American River. Emigration to California exploded. In 1849, an estimated eighty thousand fortune hunters reached California, half of them Americans, the rest immigrants from across the globe. Most of the miners were young, unmarried men who had no intention of settling in California; they wanted to get rich and return home. But whether or not mines "proved out" and produced the riches expected of them, many of these "forty-niners" ended up staying in California. They set up temporary businesses, such as saloons, stores, and brothels, which soon surrounded the hastily erected shacks of mining camps. Once

© iStockphoto.com/Phil Morley

Fort Laramie Treaty
Agreement of 1851 between Plains Indian tribes and the U.S. government; the government agreed to make cash restitution for disruptions to the buffalo grounds, while tribal leaders agreed not to attack the large number of settlers moving through the area

>> "There is a good deal of sin & wickedness going on here, Stealing, lying, Swearing, Drinking, Gambling & murdering. . . . Almost every public House is a place for Gambling. . . . Men make & lose thousands in a night, & frequently small boys will go up & bet $5 or 10—& if they lose all, go the next day & dig more. We are trying to get laws here to regulate things but it will be very difficult to get them executed." –S. Shufelt, gold miner

Read a letter from a gold miner in Placerville, California.

View a map of California Gold Country.

miners had exhausted the gold supply, they abandoned the area, looking for the next profitable mine. Most of the booming settlements of the gold-rush days later decayed into ghost towns.

Tribal Conflicts

Reasons for Conflict

No matter where Americans went, they moved onto lands that were already claimed by other parties. While Mexicans in Texas and British settlers in Oregon suffered from the American expansion, no group was more dislocated than Indians. Most dramatically, the hunters of the Western Plains—the Arapahoe, Blackfoot, Cheyenne, Kiowa, and Sioux—depended on the migratory hunting of buffalo for food. White settlers moving through buffalo ranges disrupted the natural hunting process, threatening the livelihood of these tribes. The interference eventually prompted the Plains Indians (as these tribes are collectively called) to attack white pioneers on the emigrant trails, sparking many bloody battles. As for white settlers during the colonial era in New England and Virginia, conflict with the tribes of Native America was part of daily life for the westward bound.

Government Response

The U.S. government's response to this increased Indian conflict was typical: as the number of white settlers increased, the U.S. government continued to cajole or force Native Americans into giving up their land. In the 1851 **Fort Laramie Treaty** with Plains Indian tribes, the U.S. government agreed to make cash restitution for disruptions to the buffalo grounds, while tribal leaders in turn agreed not to attack the large number of settlers moving through the area. But in 1854 yet another transportation corridor for white pioneers was carved out of land that was once set aside as Indian territory. Following the development of this new route, Indian tribes were relocated once again. As they were being shuffled from one area to another, the creation of a defined system of reservations for Native Americans was not far off.

Read the Fort Laramie Treaty.

Mountain Men

In addition to new territories, from the 1820s to the 1840s a new breed of Americans emerged. These so-called mountain men roamed the Rocky Mountains and the various trails carved out by settlers traveling across the harsh landscape. Mountain men were frequently employed as trappers, working for one of the fur companies that bought and sold beaver pelts. But their main occupation was exploration. Men like

> *"... a very companionable man. In person he was over six feet tall, spare, straight as an arrow, agile, rawboned and of powerful frame, eyes gray, hair brown and abundant even in old age, expression mild and manners agreeable. He was hospitable and generous, and was always trusted and respected.*
>
> *–Biographer Grenville Dodge, on mountain man James "Old Gabe" Bridger*

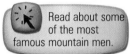 Read about some of the most famous mountain men.

Jim Bridger, James Beckwourth, and Christopher "Kit" Carson are some of the best-known mountain men. Their names are largely remembered in either the names of mountain passes and Rocky Mountain locales or in the folklore of the West that blossomed during these years, coloring the image of the West as a dangerous and exciting place.

Conclusion

Western settlement complicated matters reaching far beyond the lives of the settlers themselves. The haphazard manner in which westward movement took place forced politicians in the East to bring some form of governing order to the West. And independent-minded settlers, accustomed to managing their own affairs, did not welcome the imposition of eastern ide-

>> **James "Old Gabe" Bridger, from a photograph**

als. Friction was inevitable. Moreover, by taking responsibility for the actions of white settlers—particularly the rebels in Texas and the pioneers traversing Native American territories—government officials committed themselves to defending, and defining the course of, westward expansion. This led to westward expansion's second phase.

LO^2 The Expansionist Spirit Rebounds

During the 1840s, America's official interest in acquiring western territory surged for three principal reasons: (1) the government had targeted land that it wanted and was willing to fight for; (2) political leaders discovered that proposals to annex new lands were popular with American voters, despite the festering question of whether to allow slavery there; and (3) the U.S. government sought a rapid expansion of its power, which meant owning as much land as foreign powers, if not more. These arguments motivated the American government to aggressively resume the game of territorial expansion. Journalists and others who favored national expansion embraced an ideology justifying the sometimes brutal methods used to expand American civilization: manifest destiny.

Texas and the Rise of James K. Polk

Texas and Slavery

Because of Texas's substantial number of American settlers, annexing it was at the top of the U.S. government's agenda. But the task proved arduous. The Texas Republic, upon winning its independence from Mexico in 1836, had already applied to become a U.S. state. But the Texas constitution guaranteed the perpetuation of slavery, so if Texas entered the Union, it would be as a slave state. President Andrew Jackson knew that this would disturb the balance in the Senate between free and slave states established by the Compromise of 1820. Moreover, U.S. annexation

Liberty Party
Political party created by northern antislavery activists who left the Whig Party; they were outraged at Henry Clay's reversing his position against annexation of Texas

of Texas would surely start a war with Mexico, which had never recognized Texan independence and therefore still claimed Texas as a part of Mexican territory.

Jackson also refused to annex the Texas Republic because the 1836 presidential election was pending, and he badly wanted Vice President Martin Van Buren to succeed him. Annexing Texas might infuriate northern voters (because of the slavery issue), and Jackson was not willing to risk Van Buren's loss. Van Buren, who did win the election and served as president from 1837 to 1841, avoided discussions of Texas altogether during his campaign. In response to this official silence, Texans suspended all efforts to gain admittance to the Union and focused on developing their own political and economic institutions.

During the decade following Van Buren's election, the dilemma of whether to annex Texas loomed in the shadows of American politics. Foreign policy issues in the 1840s forced it back into the limelight. Britain considered establishing relations with the independent Texas to gain a stronger hold in North America. This prospect alarmed many Americans, and in 1843 Secretary of State John C. Calhoun signed a treaty with Texas that would admit it to the Union. President John Tyler (who became president in April 1841) then sent the treaty to the Senate for ratification. Would Texas finally become a state? Northerners in Congress reasoned that the excuse of foreign diplomacy was just a thinly veiled power play by southern slave owners. Swayed by this argument, the Senate defeated the proposed treaty. Texas would await statehood a little longer.

Texas and the Whigs

Besides the threats from Britain, a second reason Tyler advocated the annexation of Texas was because he was seeking reelection in the 1844 presidential race. He knew the issue would attract voters. He had little support from his party—although he was officially a Whig, he opposed much of the Whig platform and had vetoed several measures passed by Whigs in Congress. Ultimately, despite his interest in annexing Texas, Tyler failed to attract much public support in his bid for reelection, and he dropped out of the race before the November vote.

Texas and the Democrats

With Tyler out of the race, the Democrats were now in an ideal position to "steal" Texas annexation as

their national campaign issue. They made overall territorial acquisition a key issue in their strategy to spread American civilization far and wide. They blustered on and on about how America's territorial growth would make it a first-class nation. Their platform called for the "re-annexation" of Texas and the "re-occupation" of Oregon up to a northern boundary of 54° 40', an outrageous land grab that included nearly all of today's British Columbia, extending to the southern border of today's Alaska.

The Democrats' plan, though greedy, was perceptive. By offering to acquire both Texas and Oregon, they intended to give something to the North and to the South, thus unifying the nation and securing a Democratic victory. The party's presidential nominee was James K. Polk, a former Tennessee governor and congressman (whose nickname was "Young Hickory," aligning him with Andrew Jackson, "Old Hickory"), and he became the loudest spokesperson for the benefits to be gained from American expansion.

Texas and the Liberty Party

Henry Clay replaced Tyler as the new Whig candidate. Clay initially opposed annexing Texas. But midway through the campaign, he decided that the issue was too popular to resist; he needed the votes. Outraged at his reversal—and his political gaffe of not offering to acquire Oregon as well—a group of northern antislavery activists left the Whig Party. They created the **Liberty Party**, which opposed admitting any new slave territory to the United States. The Liberty Party nominated James G. Birney, who attracted voters who would otherwise have supported Clay. This division strengthened the Democratic Party and allowed Polk to win the election fairly easily. But the introduction of the Liberty Party revealed hairline fractures in the second two-party system—fractures that would steadily grow into an outright break.

Read a dramatic antislavery letter by a member of the new Liberty Party.

Tyler and Texas

Tyler, who had a few months left in his term before being succeeded by Polk, interpreted Polk's victory as a sign that the public did indeed support efforts to admit Texas. Thus, during his last months in office, in an effort to ensure himself a positive legacy, Tyler again pushed Congress to annex Texas through a congressional resolution. (A resolution is similar to a treaty but requires only a simple majority to pass instead of the two-thirds majority needed for a treaty.) This time, the Senate, swayed by the public enthusiasm it had witnessed during the election, narrowly voted in favor of the

 Read more about Texas statehood.

resolution. On March 1, 1845, the United States formally offered Texas statehood, which Texas accepted in December.

In response to admission of Texas as an American state, Mexico broke off diplomatic relations with the United States, setting the stage for conflict between the two nations.

Oregon and American Dominance in the West

Polk as President

Despite Tyler's role in granting Texas statehood, it was Polk who would become the nation's staunchest supporter of acquiring new territory. He was an avid believer that Americans were destined to control the West, and he had the personality, vigor, and power to be a strong cheerleader. However, when it came to the West, Polk was less concerned about

slavery and more concerned about a surge in British influence in North America. Thus his first action as president was to snuff out any plans Britain had for reentering Oregon and California. Polk also had to live up to his campaign promise of bringing in a northern state to balance the recent addition of Texas.

54° 40′

During Polk's presidential campaign, he pledged to fight for exclusive title to the Oregon Territory and to settle for nothing less than the entirety of American claims, which extended all the way up to a northern line of 54° 40'—close to what is now the southernmost point of Alaska's border with British Columbia (see Map 13.2). Britain, however, would certainly not concede that the United States owned a territory that Britain had long explored and claimed. After his inauguration in early 1845, Polk softened his position and returned to the demand made by every president since James Monroe: the United States would be willing to settle for a border along the 49th parallel—Oregon's northern border today. Britain rejected the offer; it wanted to control the Columbia River, two hundred miles south of the 49th parallel. Angered at British stubbornness and inspired by the partisan cry of **"Fifty-four Forty or Fight!"** Polk returned to his more aggressive position. In early December 1845, he asked Congress to extend U.S. military protection to the Oregon Trail. He hoped that feigning military intervention would persuade the British to concede the vast Oregon Territory.

49′

His tenacious talk was merely a bluff. Polk had long believed that the land north of the 49th parallel, where few American settlers had reached, was not that important. What he really wanted was Puget Sound and access to the ports of California for trading. Britain's government, meanwhile, decided that its interest in the region, originally based on the once-robust fur trade which was now rapidly declining, was not worth a war. In late December 1845, Britain and

> **"Fifty-four Forty or Fight!"**
> Rallying cry referring to the Americans' intended latitude for the contested border between the United States and Canada; Britain was willing to settle for the 49th parallel

Map 13.2
The Oregon Boundary Dispute

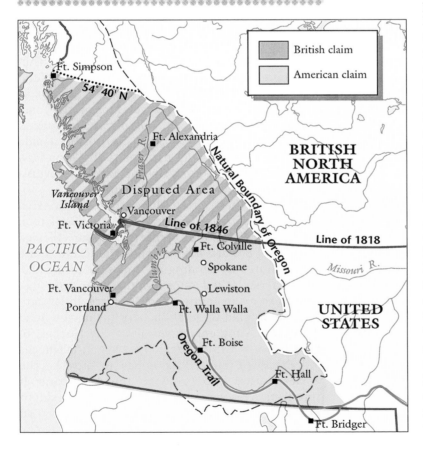

British claim

American claim

Ft. Simpson

54° 40′ N

Ft. Alexandria

Fraser R.

BRITISH NORTH AMERICA

Natural Boundary of Oregon

Disputed Area

Vancouver Island

Vancouver

Ft. Victoria

Line of 1846

Line of 1818

PACIFIC OCEAN

Ft. Colville

Spokane

Missouri R.

Columbia R.

Ft. Vancouver

Lewiston

Portland

Ft. Walla Walla

UNITED STATES

Oregon Trail

Ft. Boise

Ft. Hall

Ft. Bridger

the United States reopened negotiations over the issue, intending to prevent what would have been the third war in seventy-five years between the two nations. The British proposed a treaty accepting the 49th parallel as a border, although it sought to retain the right to navigate the Columbia River. The Senate approved the resulting **Buchanan-Pakenham Treaty** in July 1846, and America now had uncontested access to the Pacific.

Manifest Destiny

Amid the frenzy stirred by the Oregon and Texas statehood issues, a new expression of the spirit of an American empire was born. The term **manifest destiny**—meaning that the United States was *fated* to possess North America from the Atlantic to the Pacific—was coined by New York journalist John O'Sullivan. In July 1845, O'Sullivan wrote an editorial in his *United States Magazine and Democratic Review* urging Whigs and Democrats to join together in support of "the right of our manifest destiny to overspread and to possess the whole of the continent, which Providence has given us." Manifest destiny was popularized in political debates over Oregon, where it was used as an argument for why Britain should not block U.S. expansion. Soon the rhetoric made its way into American popular culture.

Though the term *manifest destiny* was newly coined, it reflected a much older American belief that divine providence was directing the nation. Many Americans felt that their country—by virtue of its strong Christian faith, its commitment to "civilization" and democracy, and the supposed "emptiness" of the West—would dominate North America as a great Empire for Liberty, thriving under God's benevolent guiding hand. The phrase was explicitly chauvinistic, implying the need to "subdue" and "fertilize" the "virgin land" of the West. It was also explicitly racist, referring to the God-given rights of the white man to conquer the "red man's lands." Manifest destiny interpreted the conquest of the West as a story of triumph in the cause of freedom rather than a saga of conflict, death, and destruction. The concept grew in popularity throughout the 1840s, justifying much westward expansion.

The Mexican War

Read John O'Sullivan's "Annexation" essay.

When Texas won its independence from Mexico in 1836, Mexican dictator General Antonio López de Santa Anna vowed that any move by the United States to annex Texas would be met with military force. When Texas did become the twenty-eighth state in 1845, President Polk privately relished Mexico's threat. Polk hoped that by provoking Mexico to make good on its promise of war, the United States could crush the Mexicans and gain control of even more Mexican territory, particularly the far western prizes of California and New Mexico. During the next two years, Polk tried peaceful negotiations with Mexico for these territories (he offered to buy them many times) but all the while he was prepared to order a military strike if negotiations broke down.

Polk Seeks a Fight

Polk's preparations for attack, however, seemed to be in vain. The Mexican officials, though they would not accept the annexation of Texas as legal, did not want to wage war over the matter. Instead, they chose to haggle over the precise boundary of Texas's southern border. Texas state officials insisted that the proper boundary between Texas and Mexico was the Rio Grande River. The Mexicans, however, considered the Nueces River (130 miles north of the Rio Grande) to be the border. Polk decided that the United States had a responsibility to defend Texas's land claims, and the first action he took as president was to station U.S. warships off the coast of Texas. In October 1845, Polk dispatched nearly four thousand U.S. troops to the northern side of the Nueces River. By demonstrating American strength, Polk hoped to bully the Mexican government into ceding the disputed lands.

Despite these intimidation efforts, Mexico refused to respond. So, in November 1845, Polk took another approach, attempting to pressure Mexico into selling both New Mexico and California to the United States by sending an emissary to Mexico. Polk's tactics failed once again. Frustrated, Polk decided to make another show of force. In January 1846, he ordered General Zachary Taylor, the head of the U.S. Army encamped along the Nueces, to move into the disputed region between the Nueces and the Rio Grande. Polk hoped to provoke the Mexican army into firing on the Americans. If American lives were endangered, the president reasoned, it would be easy to declare war on Mexico.

Read President Polk's "Message on War with Mexico."

He finally got his fight. On April 25, 1846, Mexican forces crossed the Rio Grande and attacked Taylor's men, killing eleven soldiers. Polk immediately declared that Mexico had "shed American blood upon the American soil." According to the president, Americans had no choice but to avenge the lives of their slain countrymen.

Patriotic Fervor

On May 13, 1846, as patriotic fervor swept the country, Congress passed a declaration of war by an overwhelming majority. Volunteers responded en masse to fill the ranks of the army. The war was not universally popular, especially not among northerners who considered it a strategy to expand slavery into new western territory. Leading intellectuals, such as Henry David Thoreau, Frederick Douglass, and William Lloyd Garrison, opposed the war, rightly viewing it as an unjust aggression against Mexico and an opportunity for slave owners to annex new land for their plantations. These views were overpowered by the louder voices advocating America's "manifest destiny."

Read Whig Senator Thomas Corwin's speech opposing the Mexican War.

Read Democratic Senator Donald S. Dickinson's speech justifying the U.S. acquisition of territory.

California and New Mexico

Now that the battle with Mexico had begun, Polk also planned to seize Mexico's other northern states, California and New Mexico (Map 13.3). In June 1846, a small group of American rebels, flying a flag decorated with a bear and a red star, seized the California town of Sonoma (north of San

Francisco) and declared the state an independent republic. John C. Frémont led an armed expeditionary group in what came to be called the "Bear Flag Revolt." By the end of July 1846, Frémont's men were inducted into the U.S. Army as the "California Battalion." By August, the U.S. had taken control of California's key ports, and Frémont became a national hero.

Further south, a group of American troops marched through what is today New Mexico. In August, this force seized Santa Fé, the capital of the Mexican region, without firing a shot. By January 1847, the troops had finished their mission and had moved to the California coast. They arrived just in time to put down a Mexican revolt against American rule that had been raging in Los Angeles since the previous September. Relatively easily, and within about six months, Americans had taken control of the large territories of California and New Mexico. Now all that was left was formalizing the land grab.

Invading Mexico

After the United States seized both territories, Polk was prepared to offer Santa Anna a deal. Overthrown in an 1844 coup, Santa Anna was now living in Cuba, plotting his return to Mexico. Polk offered him the chance to do so, in exchange for a promise to end the war and to cede California, New Mexico, and Texas to the United States. Santa Anna

> *If American lives were endangered, the president reasoned, it would be easy to declare war on Mexico.*

>> Inspired by patriotic fervor, seventeen-year-old Bostonian Sam Chamberlain joined the 1st Regiment of Dragoons and saw service in northern Mexico under the command of General Zachary Taylor. His illustrated account of the Mexican War, entitled "Recollections of a Rogue," has all the color of a young American's first experiences in a foreign conflict—not all of them military, as this watercolor of a Mexican dance hall demonstrates.

The San Jacinto Museum of History, Houston.

El Fandango.

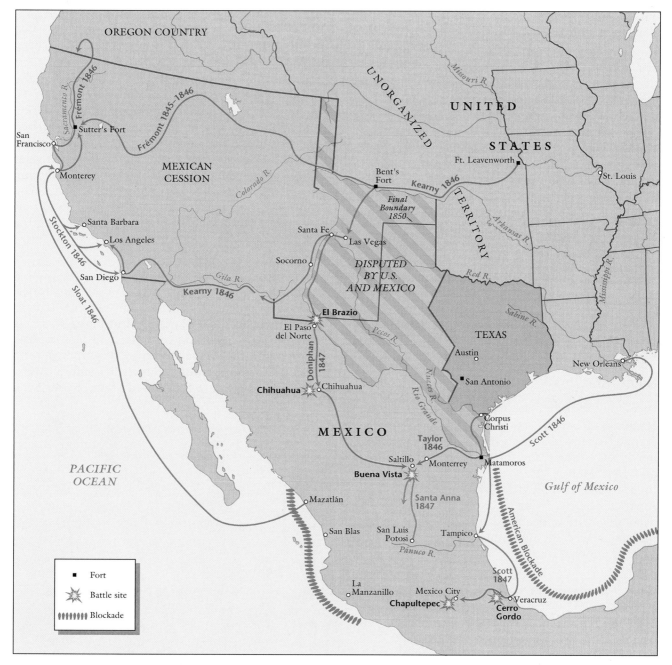

Map 13.3
Principal Campaigns of the Mexican War, 1846–1847

View an interactive version of this map.

OREGON COUNTRY

UNITED STATES

UNORGANIZED TERRITORY

Missouri R.

Sacramento R.

Frémont 1846

Frémont 1845–1846

■ Sutter's Fort

San Francisco

○ Monterey

MEXICAN CESSION

Colorado R.

Bent's Fort ■

Kearny 1846

Ft. Leavenworth ■

○ St. Louis

Stockton 1846

○ Santa Barbara

○ Los Angeles

Final Boundary 1850

Santa Fe ○

○ Las Vegas

Socorno ○

DISPUTED BY U.S. AND MEXICO

Arkansas R.

Red R.

Sloat 1846

San Diego ○

Kearny 1846

Gila R.

El Brazio

El Paso del Norte ○

Doniphan 1847

○ Chihuahua

Chihuahua

TEXAS

Austin ○

■ San Antonio

Pecos R.

Rio Grande

Nueces R.

Sabine R.

Mississippi R.

New Orleans ○

PACIFIC OCEAN

MEXICO

Taylor 1846

Saltillo ○

○ Monterrey

Corpus Christi ○

Scott 1846

Matamoros ■

Buena Vista

Santa Anna 1847

Gulf of Mexico

○ Mazatlán

○ San Blas

San Luis Potosi ○

Tampico ○

Pánuco R.

American Blockade

Scott 1847

La Manzanillo ○

Mexico City ○

Chapultepec

Veracruz ○

Cerro Gordo

■ Fort

✳ Battle site

〰 Blockade

agreed. Once he arrived in Mexico, however, Santa Anna reneged on this promise and rallied Mexican forces against the Americans.

To counter this revolt, Polk ordered his generals, Zachary Taylor and Winfield Scott, to invade Mexico from the sea. With this daring move, he hoped to take control of Mexico City, thus undercutting Santa Anna and his men, who had moved north to attack Americans along the border. In March 1847, after capturing the Mexican port of Veracruz, fourteen thousand American troops marched inland toward Mexico City, and, after numerous battles and several bouts with yellow fever, on September 13 the American troops entered the Mexican capital. Within three days, Santa Anna, flanked on both the north and the south, surrendered to the American forces.

Treaty of Guadalupe Hidalgo

In February 1848, an American envoy named Nicholas Trist negotiated the **Treaty of Guadalupe Hidalgo**, which officially ended the Mexican War. The treaty gave the United States control of Utah, Nevada, California, western Colorado, and parts of Arizona and New Mexico, and it set the Mexican-American border at the Rio Grande River. This was everything the U.S. government wanted, all in exchange for $15 million.

Learn more about the Mexican War.

And in the end . . .

The Mexican cession, comprising nearly 500,000 square miles of territory, turned the rhetoric of manifest destiny into reality. With Texas's annexation and the acquisition of Oregon, New Mexico, and California, the United States had become an empire spanning the width of the continent—all within four short years.

But the struggle involved in taking all this land provoked the issue that no American politician wanted to engage: slavery. The issue of whether or not slavery should exist in the western territories would lead to the political crisis of the 1850s, which would ultimately bring about the American Civil War. It is to this impending crisis that we now turn.

> **Treaty of Guadalupe Hidalgo**
> Agreement ending the Mexican War in 1848, which gave the United States control of Utah, Nevada, California, western Colorado, and parts of Arizona and New Mexico, and established the Rio Grande as the border, in exchange for $15 million

What else was happening . . .

1822	A yellow fever epidemic leaves New York City with 16,000 corpses and no readily available space to bury them.
1835	The Liberty Bell becomes cracked.
1840	The saxophone is invented.
1845	The New York Baseball Club plays the Knickerbockers in the first recorded baseball game, at Elysian Fields in Hoboken, New Jersey.

The *Impending* Crisis

Learning Outcomes

After reading this chapter, you should be able to do the following:

LO **1**   Describe the arguments that took place over whether slavery should be allowed to expand into the new territories, and explain how the Compromise of 1850 was supposed to settle the issue.

LO **2**   Explain how the Kansas-Nebraska Act affected the territories of Kansas and Nebraska, and describe the events that made "Bleeding Kansas" an accurate description for the region.

LO **3**   Discuss the events that propelled the United States into a civil war in 1861.

LO **4**   Explain why and how the southern states seceded from the Union, discuss President Lincoln's reaction, and describe the earliest physical conflict between the two sides.

> ## "In the end, the election to the presidency of an antislavery northerner provoked southerners to withdraw from the Union altogether."

In the 1850s, the controversy over the spread of slavery to the West froze America's territorial expansion. The gains of the 1840s were impressive: the United States had acquired California, Texas, Oregon, Washington, New Mexico, and more. But in the 1850s, except for a small stretch of land on the southern edge of today's Arizona, the United States made no further territorial gains.

Nevertheless, the territorial expansion of the previous fifty years had made it nearly impossible for the two political parties to retain support from all the nation's various regions. In general, although northerners were not often hard-core abolitionists, they protested the spread of slavery in the West, favoring the expansion of free labor, in which men could chose the kind of labor they would perform. Most southern whites, meanwhile, fiercely supported the institution of slavery, seeing it as integral to the American economy and the cotton culture they had developed since the 1793 invention of the cotton gin. As for the political parties, neither Democrats nor Whigs could afford to alienate the South by appearing overtly against slavery or the North by seeming too supportive of the institution. The risk was that each party would become strictly regional or that they would implode in trying to find a balance.

This political conundrum provoked the development of splinter parties, and without the hedging and compromising of the two mainstream parties, the center of American politics could not hold. In the end, the election to the presidency of an antislavery northerner provoked southerners to withdraw from the Union altogether. Considering that people in democratic societies ideally intend to settle their differences without killing one another, how had things gone so wrong?

LO¹ Arguments over Slavery in the New Territories

The Mexican War had, from 1846 to 1848, temporarily united the North and the South in a common enthusiasm for military conquest. But tensions between the two regions always lay just beneath the surface. During and after the war, American politicians became consumed with the issue of whether extensive territories won from Mexico should permit or prohibit slavery.

© James Thomas Linnell/The Bridgeman Art Library/Getty Images

The Democratic Response

Southern Democrats

Andrew Jackson's Democratic Party had always claimed to defend the rights of the "common man." Yet southern Democrats, by demanding that the new territories allow slavery, hardly seemed to be advocating policies that helped every common man. Indeed, many northerners of both parties believed that if slavery were allowed in Texas and other parts of the West, wealthy plantation owners would buy up all the new land, leaving little for less-affluent farmers. And southern Democrats were at a loss to reconcile their image as protectors of the common man with the implications of their position.

Racist, but Antislavery, Northern Democrats

More importantly, new plantations meant that the western territories would be populated with black people. Despite the fact that many northern Democrats were opposed to slavery, they shared the racist beliefs of the day and had no desire to live amid a large African American population. The belief in white supremacy led northern and southern Democrats to radically different conclusions. Many northern Democrats turned against slavery in order to avoid living and competing with black people in the western territories, whereas southern Democrats retained their proslavery stance in order to defend the plantation economy, which theoretically promised even the common man great wealth. This splintered the Democratic Party into southern and northern branches.

The Wilmot Proviso and the "Free Soil" Movement

The Wilmot Proviso and Popular Sovereignty

The splintering intensified in 1846 when one of the alienated northern Democrats, Pennsylvania congressman David Wilmot, proposed that slavery be prohibited from any new territories that the United States might acquire from Mexico. Wilmot was no abolitionist. He wanted slavery kept out of

the West so the land would be available to average white farmers (who could not afford slaves) rather than to wealthy slave owners who would establish massive plantations. The **Wilmot Proviso** passed in the House of Representatives several times but was repeatedly rejected by the Senate, where southerners had the edge because of the support of several "**dough face**" senators, defined as senators from the North who supported southern slavery.

Meanwhile, each round of voting exacerbated regional tensions. Many northern Whigs, such as Abraham Lincoln, joined northern Democrats in voting for the measure. At the same time, southern Democrats, such as John Calhoun (now a senator from South Carolina), argued that the Constitution guaranteed the option of slavery in federal territories, thus joining southern Whigs in voting against it. Now the Whigs were beginning to divide along regional lines too.

The Presidential Election of 1848

The presidential election of 1848 deepened these tensions. At first, the campaigners tried to ignore slavery altogether. When this proved impossible, Democratic nominee Lewis Cass hoped to sidestep the issue by proposing the idea of **popular sovereignty**, which

The Wilmot Proviso

Provided that, as an express and fundamental condition to the acquisition of any territory from the Republic of Mexico by the United States, by virtue of any treaty which may be negotiated between them, and to the use by the Executive of the moneys herein appropriated, neither slavery nor involuntary servitude shall ever exist in any part of said territory, except for crime, whereof the party shall first be duly convicted.

meant letting the settlers in the territories decide whether they wanted slavery or not. The Whigs, meanwhile, who had nominated Mexican War hero Zachary Taylor (who had never voted before, much less held political office), made no mention of slavery in their platform.

The Free Soil Party

Neither of these positions satisfied all Democrats or all Whigs, and disaffected Democrats launched a political movement under the banner of the **Free Soil Party**. The new party was headed by former Democratic president Martin Van Buren and advanced a platform centered on the Wilmot Proviso. The party was antisouthern, but not staunchly abolitionist. It argued that southern slave owners were blocking the development of northern progress. Southern congressmen, said the Free Soilers, refused to advance national programs for internal improvements, which would facilitate access to the West and extend the progress made by the Market Revolution. Free Soilers wanted western lands to be made available to small, ambitious white farmers, and they wanted to save the land for white people.

In its platform, the party called for "free soil, free speech, free labor, and free men," focusing not on ending slavery where it already existed but on keeping slave-based plantations out of western lands. Significantly, the Free Soil movement brought together all those who opposed slavery in the West. These groups opposed the expansion of slavery for different reasons. The abolitionists sympathized with the slaves; the racists disliked African Americans and did not want to compete with them economically in the new territories. The Free Soil Party also brought together northern Democrats, such as Wilmot, with northern Whigs, who were unhappy about their party's nomination of slaveowner Zachary Taylor.

Taylor and the Whigs cobbled together enough votes to win the election of 1848, but they failed to win a congressional majority, and in the long run, they were greatly weakened by the rise of the Free Soil Party. Democrats, too, had seen a split within their ranks that would grow in coming years. During the 1850s, the Free Soil Party and the slavery issue set the stage for a reconfiguration of American politics. The first instance of this would arise in 1850.

The Compromise of 1850

California as the Problem

California provoked the next round of compromises in Congress. When Zachary Taylor took office in 1849, California, brimming with new settlers driven by the gold rush, applied for statehood. But would it enter as a free or a slave state? Either way, its statehood was destined to upset the balance between free and slave states that had held since the Compromise of 1820.

Taylor tried to address the crisis as soon as he took office. He hoped to simply bypass the slavery issue by granting immediate statehood to California and New Mexico without specifying whether they were free or slave states.

Southern politicians attacked Taylor's plan. They worried that once California was admitted, its citizens would vote to be a free state, thus setting a precedent for prohibiting slavery from all western territories. They also feared that someday slave states would be greatly outnumbered by free ones in Congress—an event that could lead to the permanent decline of southern interests and the permanent abolition of all slavery.

The Compromise of 1850

To allay these fears, Henry Clay, author of the Missouri Compromise of 1820 and now a powerful senator, stepped forward with yet another compromise. In January 1850, Clay proposed a five-part bill, which came to be called the **Compromise of 1850** (Map 14.1, page 224):

1. California would be admitted to the Union as a free state.
2. The remaining land won from Mexico would be divided into two new territories, New Mexico and Utah, and would remain open to slavery until they became states, at which time the state legislatures could vote on the issue.
3. To mollify antislavery northerners, slave auctions (but not slavery itself) would be banned in the nation's capital, Washington, D.C.
4. Texas would receive $10 million in compensation but be prohibited from further influencing New Mexico, where it had hoped to extend slavery.
5. For southerners, the federal government would create and enforce a new and tougher Fugitive Slave Act. By punishing white northerners who helped slaves escape from the South, the measure would ensure that the North and the South would cooperate in protecting the slave system.

Free Soil Party
Political movement started by disaffected anti-South Democrats, headed by former Democratic president Martin Van Buren; they wanted new lands to be made available to small, ambitious white farmers

Compromise of 1850
Five-part bill proposed by Henry Clay, which outlined specific arrangements that accommodated both antislavery northerners and slaveowning southerners

The Controversy

The compromise contained elements to appeal to both sides, but it also set off a storm of political controversy. Opposed by hardliners on both sides of the slave-state issue, the compromise gave rise to the first focused talk of secession in the South. This alarmed President Taylor so much that he decided to oppose the compromise altogether. Months of impassioned arguments for and against the compromise went on in Congress. The debates marked the last time that the great triumvirate of powerful senators, Clay, Calhoun, and Daniel Webster, would discuss the nation's fate with their formidable oratorical skills. Clay and Webster allied in favor of the compromise, and Webster's "Seventh of March" speech rallied northern opinion for the compromise. On the opposite side, Calhoun, dying of tuberculosis, watched his

Read Calhoun's speech.

>> "As much indisposed as I have been, Mr. President and Senators, I have felt it to be my duty to express to you my sentiments upon the great question which has agitated the country and occupied your attentions." –John C. Calhoun, debating the compromise in the Senate as read by his friend James Mason

© The Print Collector/Alamy

friend James Mason deliver Calhoun's last speech in the Senate against the proposed compromise. But the compromise remained in limbo.

Becoming Law

When, in 1850, Zachary Taylor died of food poisoning and was replaced by Millard Fillmore, the compromise's chances of passing improved. Fillmore favored the plan. With Fillmore's support, Clay's political lieutenant in the Senate, Stephen A. Douglas of Illinois, set to work dividing the bill in five parts and finding majorities for each of its separate proposals. By September 1850, the compromise had become law.

The peace that ensued would prove ultimately unstable, however, as many northerners resented the tough Fugitive Slave Act. In fact, during the next decade many northern states passed **Personal Liberty Laws**, which were designed to protect escaped slaves—for instance, by prohibiting the use of a state's jail to restrain runaway slaves. Vermont, Rhode Island, and Connecticut passed Personal Liberty Laws in 1854. Maine, Massachusetts, and Michigan did so in 1855, followed by Kansas and Wisconsin in 1858, Ohio in 1859, and Pennsylvania in 1860.

The debates of 1849 and 1850 only worsened the mutual distrust between North and South. But the Compromise of 1850 bought some time before the ultimate dissolution of the nation's political order.

Western Destiny Deferred

Buying Cuba?

As the debates over the Compromise of 1850 showed, admitting new states to the Union was bound to be contentious. In addition, southerners immediately noticed that there was more territory open for statehood in the North than in the South. Fearful of what this might portend for the future, southern leaders sought to expand America's territorial holdings southward, by expanding into Latin America. Presidents Polk and Pierce, in fact, had both tried to buy the island of Cuba from Spain. When Polk's offer was rebuffed, a group of Americans tried to invade the island in order to bring it into the Union as a slave state. They failed, but the adventurers who attempted to take these lands came to be called **filibusters**, after the Spanish *filibustero*, for "pirate" or "freebooter." The term was subsequently adopted to describe attempts to extend debate over a legislative proposal in order to hijack it or delay its passage.

The Slave Conspiracy

These reckless attempts to create more southern states heightened northerners' suspicions that the Democratic Party was plotting in league with slave owners. Abolitionists and Free Soilers viewed the Cuban plan as an indication that the South, rapidly being outpaced in population growth by the North, was desperate to acquire new slave states to maintain parity in the Senate. Sensing a conspiracy, northerners fought hard to prevent further accessions to slaveholders' power. Both sides were intensifying their opposition to the other.

LO² The Kansas-Nebraska Act and New Political Parties

Slavery in Kansas and Nebraska?

These sentiments erupted in the 1854 debate over the Kansas-Nebraska Act. And, again, it was expansion in the West that brought the issue of slavery to a head within the nation's corridors of power.

By the early 1850s, plans were underway to build the nation's first transcontinental railroad, and Senator Douglas of Illinois wanted Chicago to serve as the new railway's major hub. But Chicago could not serve as the hub if the unorganized northern portion of the Louisiana Purchase remained unorganized and unpopulated; it wouldn't make any sense to put a railroad where there were no people and where the United States had little political presence. To eliminate this problem, Douglas began to push for the creation of several new territories in that northern region, where today sit Kansas and Nebraska.

The problem with Douglas's plan was that, according to the Missouri Compromise of 1820, slavery was prohibited in the northern part of the Louisiana Purchase. Southerners therefore resisted Douglas's efforts, fearing that when those territories eventually became states, they would become free states, tipping the balance of power in the Senate against the South.

The Kansas-Nebraska Act

Douglas, a shrewd statesman, devised a compromise to ensure that southerners would support the development of the new territories. Douglas created two territories, Kansas and Nebraska (Map 14.1), and left the status of slavery in each territory open, to be decided by the popular sovereignty of those who settled there. In the end, this meant that the Missouri Compromise of 1820 did not apply because slavery might have been allowed above 36°30', had the residents of Kansas or Nebraska so chosen. Many northerners were outraged at the prospect, but a coalition of northern Democrats and southerners passed the **Kansas-Nebraska Act** by a narrow margin.

Its passage had two direct results: it contributed to the demise of the Whig Party, and it sparked a race to populate Kansas, because the fate of slavery in Kansas would be decided by voters there. The race would lead to tension, then conflict, and, ultimately, violence.

> **Kansas-Nebraska Act** 1854 act that created two territories, Kansas and Nebraska, and left the status of slavery in each territory open, to be decided by the popular sovereignty of those who settled there

Read the Kansas-Nebraska Act.

Library of Congress, Prints & Photographs Division, LC-DIG-cwpbh-00881

>> "Senator Douglas was very small, not over four and a half feet height, and there was a noticeable disproportion between the long trunk of his body and his short legs. His chest was broad and indicated great strength of lungs. It took but a glance at his face and head to convince one that they belonged to no ordinary man. No beard hid any part of his remarkable, swarthy features. His mouth, nose, and chin were all large and clearly expressive of much boldness and power of will." –Journalist Henry Villard, 1858

The Death of the Second Two-Party System

The Kansas-Nebraska Act fatally weakened America's second two-party system, splitting both parties along regional lines. Northern Whigs found themselves at odds with southern members of the party; southern Whigs abandoned the party altogether to join the Democrats, who were more clearly supporting slavery. Many northern Democrats were increasingly sympathetic to parties like the Free Soilers. At the same time, several new political parties emerged, all of which spoke mostly for regional issues. By 1856, there were no longer any national political parties.

Map 14.1
Kansas-Nebraska and the Slavery Issue

The Know-Nothing Party

One of the new parties to arise in the 1850s was the American Party, which built its base of support on anti-immigrant and anti-Catholic sentiment. The American Party was an outgrowth of a secret society called the Order of the Star-Spangled Banner. As a secret society, its members vowed to answer all inquiries about the Order with the response "I know nothing." Consequently, the American Party came to be known as the **Know-Nothing Party**.

Believing that "Americans should rule America," the Know-Nothings wanted to prevent the masses of new immigrants from gaining political rights. They advocated changing naturalization laws so that immigrants would be required to wait twenty-one years (as opposed to just five) before they could apply for citizenship. Although they resented and feared all immigrants, the Know-Nothings were especially frightened by Irish Catholics. As they saw it, Catholics took their instructions from the pope and did not exercise the independence of mind necessary to function as democratic citizens. The Know-Nothings prided themselves on disdaining

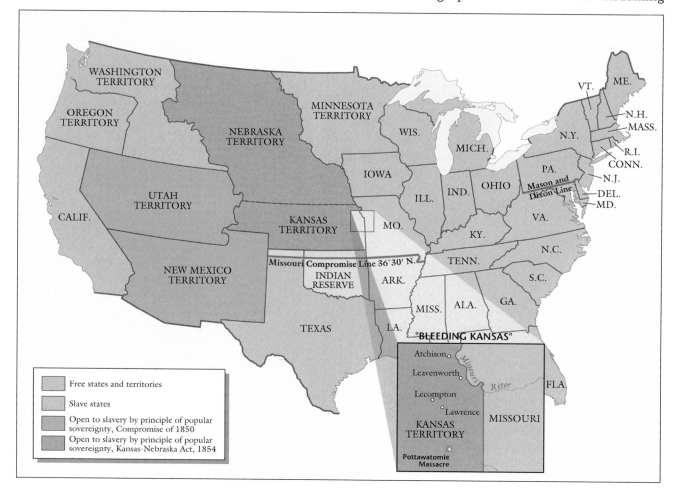

Legend:
- Free states and territories
- Slave states
- Open to slavery by principle of popular sovereignty, Compromise of 1850
- Open to slavery by principle of popular sovereignty, Kansas-Nebraska Act, 1854

>> Popular music was on the rise during the 1850s, so it was inevitable that someone would compose a song for the new political party. Its sheet music cover is loaded with symbols of Americanism, from the eagle and flags to native pumpkins and corn.

Library of Congress, Prints & Photographs Division, LC-US262-19431

the very things that Irish stereotypes supposedly embraced: alcoholism, urban disorder, and poverty. The party appealed to middle-class and working men who saw immigrants as their main competition for industrial jobs.

Very quickly, the Know-Nothings won several elections, suggesting the appeal of nativist ideas in mid-nineteenth-century America. Just a year after they formally established their party, in 1853 the Know-Nothings won important electoral victories in New York, Pennsylvania, Massachusetts, and Ohio, the states that had experienced the most dramatic influx of immigrants. By 1855, the Know-Nothings had more than one million voters enrolled in their various lodges. Although they were never a commanding national party, the rise of the Know-Nothings is significant not only as a testament to the appeal of anti-Catholic nativism in the 1850s, but also because its rise killed off the Whig Party. Southern Whigs had deserted the party in order to join the Democrats, and many northern Whigs flocked to the Know-Nothings.

After its meteoric rise, the popularity of the Know-Nothings plummeted just as rapidly. When the Know-Nothings failed to achieve their goals of changing naturalization laws and restricting the political rights of immigrants, members became disillusioned. By that time there were also other parties to join.

The Republican Party

Most of the disaffected Know-Nothings joined another political party that was forming at the time, the Republicans. Unlike any other party except the Free Soilers, the Republican Party was explicitly antislavery; its main goal was to prevent any further expansion of slavery in the West. Its platform included support for homesteading rights, a protective tariff, and internal improvements—most of the components of the American System. The Republicans succeeded in unifying numerous antislavery groups, including the Free Soilers. They also drew support from northern Whigs and Democrats who were infuriated by the Kansas-Nebraska Act and the idea of popular sovereignty.

Two Parties from Two Regions

The Republicans were a purely sectional party, drawing most of their strength from antislavery sentiment in the North. Because the North had a significantly larger population than the South, the Republicans expected that they could eventually win the presidency without courting southern voters. Therefore, by the late 1850s, after the downfall of the Know-Nothings, a new sectional party system was established, pitting antislavery northern Republicans against proslavery southern Democrats. This decline of national parties would accelerate the political crisis of the 1850s.

"Bleeding Kansas"

Popular Sovereignty

So, what would become of Kansas? Would it enter the Union as a slave state or a free one? Under the doctrine of popular sovereignty, voters in Kansas would decide. The problem was that there weren't many people in Kansas in 1854, so both parties (and their subsequent supporting groups) sent people to Kansas, just in time to vote in the election. Slaveholders in neighboring Missouri were fearful of having a free state just across its border. They were especially eager to see Kansas become a slave state, so they encouraged slaveholding families to migrate to Kansas. At the same time, abolitionists sent northern settlers to Kansas. One effort, led by New Englander Ely Thayer, sent nearly 1,250 colonists to Kansas, where they established Lawrence as a strong antislavery town.

The Stolen Election

With both sides actively working to promote their own interests, Kansas became a bitterly divided territory. When the first territorial legislature was elected in 1855, throngs of men from Missouri, who came to be known as "border ruffians," crossed the border for the day and stuffed the ballot boxes, electing a proslavery government. Only 2,900 registered voters lived in Kansas, but over 6,000 ballots were cast. The advocates of slavery had stolen the election.

Kansas's new proslavery government immediately set out to crush its opposition and make Kansas a slave territory. It expelled antislavery representatives from the legislature and made it a crime to publicly advocate Free Soil principles or help a fugitive slave. Opponents appealed to the White House, but President Franklin Pierce supported southern interests. His opponents called him a "dough face," that derisive name for a northerner who openly supported the South. Forced to fend for themselves, antislavery Kansans formed a rival government in the city of Topeka. For a time, there were two functioning state governments in Kansas.

Read a contemporary account of the "sacking of Lawrence."

Bleeding Kansas

Inevitably, this bitterly contested conflict erupted into violence. In 1856, a mob of proslavery men sacked the Free Soil town of Lawrence. The town was put to the torch, but no one was killed. The violence enraged John Brown, a zealous abolitionist who considered himself God's executioner of justice. To avenge the attack on Lawrence, Brown and his sons entered the town of Pottawatomie Creek, Kansas, rounded up five proslavery advocates, none of whom was a slaveholder, and butchered them. Brown's acts inspired more vigilantism, and atrocities were met with counter-atrocities. As the newspapers reported, Kansas was bleeding.

Kansas's Constitution

In June 1857, the people of Kansas elected another set of delegates to a convention in the town of Lecompton, which was charged with drawing up a state constitution. People opposed to slavery, however, boycotted the election on the grounds that the voting districts had been drawn so as to make it more difficult for them to elect antislavery represen-

>> Throngs of men from Missouri, who came to be known as "border ruffians," crossed the border into Kansas for the day and stuffed ballot boxes. Only 2,900 registered voters lived in Kansas, but more than 6,000 ballots were cast.

tatives. Their boycott assured that most of the men sent to the convention supported slavery, and predictably, they created a state constitution that made slavery legal in Kansas. Their constitution was called the **Lecompton Constitution**.

Read the section on slavery from the Lecompton Constitution.

Free Soilers Strike Back

In a provocative move, the convention refused to allow the citizens of Kansas a chance to challenge or reject the Lecompton Constitution. In the popular referendum that followed, Kansans were allowed to vote only on whether *more* slaves would be allowed into the territory, not on the legality of slavery itself. President James Buchanan, elected to succeed Pierce in 1856, was eager to satisfy the southern branch of the Democratic Party, so he backed the Lecompton Constitution despite what he knew about the antidemocratic convention that had created it. Senator Stephen Douglas, however, refused to support something so questionable, even though doing so angered the southern members of his party. President Buchanan pulled enough political strings to get the Senate to accept the constitution without Douglas's support, but he could not garner enough votes for it to pass in the House of Representatives. When no agreement could be reached on the issue, Congress sent the Lecompton Constitution back to Kansas for another vote by its people. This time, the

Free Soilers participated in the vote and resoundingly rejected the proslavery constitution.

Outcomes

Although the Lecompton Constitution was ultimately defeated, the shenanigans surrounding its creation disgusted northerners, and the controversy convinced many northern Democrats to switch to the Republican Party. With each new political crisis, the sectional divide between northern Republicans and southern Democrats became more and more profound.

"Bleeding Sumner"

Events in the Senate only intensified the animosity. The reports from Kansas had caused emotions to run high among America's congressmen. No one was more vocal in his outrage than Charles Sumner, a Republican from Massachusetts who was perhaps the Senate's most outspoken opponent of slavery. Shortly before the burning of Lawrence (and John Brown's subsequent retaliation), Sumner delivered a speech in Congress entitled **"The Crime Against Kansas,"** which blamed slavery for all the violence. In addition, Sumner made personally insulting remarks about Andrew P. Butler, a proslavery senator from South Carolina, leading many in attendance to believe that Sumner was deliberately provoking an attack.

The Caning of Sumner

Butler was not at the capitol to defend himself, and he was too old and feeble to do so anyway. But his nephew Preston Brooks, a South Carolina representative in the House, stepped in on Butler's behalf. Brooks himself had been a southern moderate before being galvanized by the events in Kansas. On May 22, 1856, just two days after Sumner delivered his vilifying speech, Brooks entered the Senate chamber and proceeded to beat Sumner senseless with his metal-topped cane. With his first blow, Brooks opened a gash in Sumner's head and sent him careening to the floor. Brooks then pounced on his victim and continued to strike him in the head, even after his cane had shattered to pieces. It took more than three years for Sumner to recover from his injuries.

In the opinion of many northerners, "Bleeding Sumner" came to match "Bleeding Kansas" as a symbol of southern barbarity. Certain southerners were proud of the caning, however, for its literal and symbolic value. Many of them mailed new canes to Brooks, with messages like "Hit Him Again." The episode captured in a moment the nation's breakdown of reason on the eve of civil war.

"The Crime Against Kansas" Speech delivered in Congress by Charles Sumner, Republican of Massachusetts, which blamed slavery for the violence between pro- and antislavery activists in Kansas

SOUTHERN CHIVALRY — ARGUMENT versus CLUB'S.

>> With his first blow, Brooks opened a gash in Sumner's head and sent him careening to the floor. Brooks pounced on Sumner and continued to strike him in the head, even after his cane had shattered to pieces.

Slave Power Conspiracy
Specter raised by anti-slavery Republicans who believed that, in order to preserve slavery, southern leaders would be willing to attack and silence anyone who advocated against slavery; allegedly the conspiracy intended to outlaw free speech and make all Americans accept proslavery principles

The Election of 1856

The Republicans

Bleeding Kansas and the caning of Sumner were featured as central images in the 1856 Republican presidential campaign. The Republican candidate, John C. Frémont, founder of the free state of California, ran on a platform that denounced slavery as a "relic of barbarism." Frémont called for Kansas to be admitted to the Union as a free state, as the most recent vote there had suggested. There were several central themes in the Republican agenda, including expanding internal improvements and embracing the Market Revolution. But none were more important than the promotion of personal independence and free labor. Blocking the expansion of slavery in the territories, argued the Republicans, was essential to giving free white men the opportunity to establish homesteads for themselves in the West.

The Slave Power Conspiracy

The Republicans openly condemned the South's planter class. They argued that slaveholders were a minority group wielding a disproportionate amount of power. They believed that, in order to preserve slavery, southern leaders would be willing to attack and silence anyone who advocated against slavery. According to Republican propaganda, the **Slave Power Conspiracy** intended to outlaw free speech and make all Americans accept proslavery principles.

The Election

Northerners comprised the majority of the American population, and the Republicans believed it was time for the northern majority to control the national government. In 1856, Republican rhetoric proved powerful at the ballot box, but not quite powerful enough. Out of the sixteen free states, Frémont won eleven. Millard Fillmore, the American Party candidate, managed to take only Maryland, a slave state. Meanwhile, the Democratic candidate, James Buchanan of Pennsylvania, won thirteen of the fourteen slaveholding states, as well as the five free states that eluded Frémont. It was just enough for Buchanan to get into the White House.

Results

The election made two things clear: American voters were divided into sectional parties, and despite Buchanan's victory, the Republicans were close to having enough support in the North to win a presidential election without winning a single southern state. The South was politically outnumbered and knew it.

LO³ Three Events That Catapulted the Nation into War

In this heated atmosphere, three events pushed sentiments over the top: the Dred Scott controversy, John Brown's raid, and the election of 1860. The events of the 1850s had pushed America to the brink of collapse. These three events would finish the job.

The Dred Scott Controversy

Dred Scott

On March 4, 1857, Buchanan was inaugurated as president, and just two days later, he confronted a controversial Supreme Court decision that threatened to intensify sectional tensions. A Missouri slave named Dred Scott had been taken by his owner to live for a few years in Illinois and the Wisconsin Territory, where slavery was illegal. Eventually, however, Scott and his master returned to Missouri. With the help of antislavery advocates, Scott sued for his freedom on the grounds that his residence in a free state and a free territory had made him a free man.

The case forced the U.S. Supreme Court to rule on whether Scott's residence in Illinois and Wisconsin made him free. By a 7-to-2 decision, the Supreme Court ruled that Dred Scott was still a slave, despite his residence outside of Missouri. As Chief Justice Roger Taney explained, Scott had returned to Missouri before attempting to claim his freedom, and within Missouri he was a slave.

Slavery as Law of the Land

But Chief Justice Taney did more. Taney added remarks to his opinion that were intended to prevent black bondsmen from suing for their freedom ever again. In an incredibly bold statement, Taney asserted that the Missouri Compromise was unconstitutional because Congress had no right to prohibit slavery anywhere in the United States. A slaveholder could take his slaves anywhere he or she wanted within the Union, including free states, without losing title to them. By this logic, any attempt to restrict the westward march of slavery was prohibited by the land's highest court.

Proslavery southerners were pleased by the Dred Scott decision, while Republicans were outraged. Republicans interpreted the Dred Scott decision as proof that the Slave Power Conspiracy was as strong as ever. With the prohibition of slavery declared illegal by the Supreme Court, Republicans wondered if the South would attempt to renationalize slavery, as it had been before the Revolutionary War. Taney had, after all, declared slavery to be the law of the land.

Northerners could not accept this. Their fears made antislavery forces in the North all the more determined to reduce the South's political power in the country, deepening the sense of alienation and crisis between the two regions.

John Brown's Raid

Following the Dred Scott decision, John Brown, the radical abolitionist who had provoked some of the violence in "Bleeding Kansas," intensified the sectional crisis again. In October 1859, with eighteen of his followers, he raided the federal arsenal at Harper's Ferry in northwestern Virginia. Brown envisioned that, after seizing the armory, he would rally the slaves in the surrounding area to join him in revolt against their oppressors.

To Brown's surprise, however, no slaves joined his side after he daringly seized control of the arsenal. Most were afraid Brown would be unsuccessful and did not want to risk their lives for the actions of a crazy man. Within three days, federal troops under the command of Colonel Robert E. Lee captured Brown and six of his cohorts. They were summarily tried for treason. Brown refused to give up the fight; throughout his trial, he spoke passionately against slavery and accepted his conviction and death sentence with the calm resignation of a martyr. On December 2, 1859, the state of Virginia hanged him.

Results

John Brown's raid was a dismal failure which horrified most northerners. Even if they opposed slavery, northern people generally disapproved of Brown's violent tactics. But a few high-profile northerners praised Brown in no uncertain terms. Ralph Waldo Emerson,

> **"** During the affair the negroes about H F were terribly alarmed and clung as closely as they could to master & mistress. One negro hid under a water wheel in the armory canal and didn't come out till Tuesday—and then was afraid Brown might catch him. **"**
>
> *—Charles White, eyewitness account of the 1859 raid on Harper's Ferry*

the prominent philosopher and abolitionist, publicly proclaimed Brown a "saint." Although views like Emerson's were in

Learn more about John Brown's raid.

the minority, southerners fixated on such remarks as evidence that the North was out to destroy slavery and crush the "southern way of life." Brown failed to arouse the revolt he had planned, but he did succeed in inspiring a keen sense of fear and loathing among the southern public. What the Dred Scott decision was to northerners, John Brown's raid was to southerners: an unfathomable, appalling episode that highlighted the gulf between the regions.

John Brown

The Election of 1860

The Democrats

The implosion of national party politics and the sense of isolation felt in the

Lincoln-Douglas Debates Public debates of slavery between Stephen A. Douglas and Abraham Lincoln as they competed for the Illinois Senate seat in 1858

Read the first Lincoln-Douglas debate on the spread of slavery.

Read Lincoln's powerful "House Divided" speech.

North and the South came to a head in the election of 1860. In April of that year, the Democratic Party held its convention in Charleston, South Carolina, and the sectional divide between northern and southern members generated palpable tension. Stephen A. Douglas was a clear favorite for the nomination, but southern Democrats had become disgusted with his leadership after he refused to endorse Kansas's proslavery constitution. Moreover, to nominate Douglas meant accepting the idea of popular sovereignty, which Douglas still supported and which contained within it the chance that antislavery forces would carry the day. Douglas had articulated his advocacy of popular sovereignty in the 1858 **Lincoln-Douglas Debates**, when Douglas and his opponent for the U.S. Senate seat in Illinois, Abraham Lincoln, publicly debated the issue of slavery. After the Dred Scott decision, southern Democrats wanted their party to agree with the Supreme Court that slavery could not be barred from any U.S. territory. Douglas would not accede to such a demand.

❝A house divided against itself cannot stand. I believe this government cannot endure, permanently half slave and half free. I do not expect the Union to be dissolved—I do not expect the house to fall—but I do expect it will cease to be divided.❞

–Abraham Lincoln, June 16, 1858

Thus the Democrats could not agree on a candidate who would satisfy the party's northern and southern members. They decided instead to adjourn

>> **The Lincoln-Douglas debate at Charleston, Illinois, September 18, 1858.**

© Art Resource, NY

the convention and reassemble in Baltimore in July. This second Democratic convention nominated Douglas, but the southern delegates refused the nomination and walked out. That move confirmed the long-standing divide within the party, and the Democratic Party officially split into northern and southern wings. The northern branch stood behind Douglas, and southerners backed the current vice president, John C. Breckinridge of Kentucky, on a platform that called for the creation of a national slave code protecting slavery everywhere in the Union.

The Republicans

Meanwhile, the Republicans nominated Abraham Lincoln, who was an attractive candidate for two reasons. First, Lincoln had become known after the Lincoln-Douglas Debates as a moderate on the slavery question. Although he believed that slavery was an evil institution and he wished to keep it out of the western territories, he did not aspire to end slavery in the southern states where it already existed. Republican leaders felt that this position would appeal to the general public of the North, which hoped to avoid greater conflict if possible. Second, Lincoln was from Illinois, a state the Republicans had failed to carry in 1856. If the Republicans were to win in 1860, they needed to win Illinois.

The Final Sectional Division

In addition to Republicans, northern Democrats, and southern Democrats, a fourth party entered the race with hopes that a showdown between North and South could be averted. The Constitutional Union Party nominated John Bell of Tennessee as their presidential candidate. Its simple platform was to avoid all discussion of slavery in an attempt to raise the Constitution and the Union above all schisms.

Despite the best intentions of the Constitutional Union Party, the election was not really a national contest. In the North, only Lincoln and Douglas held any popular appeal; in the South, the race was between Breckinridge and Bell. When all the votes were in, Lincoln emerged with the most votes, but not a majority of them. But because his base of support was in the populous states of the North, Lincoln won 180 votes in the Electoral College, just enough to secure victory.

Results

Lincoln won the presidency as a sectional candidate. He did not win a single southern state (Map 14.2), and his platform revealed his intention to halt the

Abraham Lincoln circa 1860

westward expansion of slavery. Although Democrats still controlled Congress, the North's ability to dictate the 1860 presidential election outcome confirmed the southern states' worst fear: they had lost control of national politics. The institution of slavery was in peril.

Read Lincoln's Inaugural Address.

LO⁴ Secession and Civil War

In the eyes of many southerners, Lincoln's election spelled the end of the southern way of life. Although Lincoln had actually affirmed the rights of the states in his campaign speeches, the South saw his opposition to the spread of slavery in the West as a serious threat. If all the western territories became free states, southerners assumed they would amend the Constitution and outlaw slavery everywhere. Many southerners believed it would be better to leave the

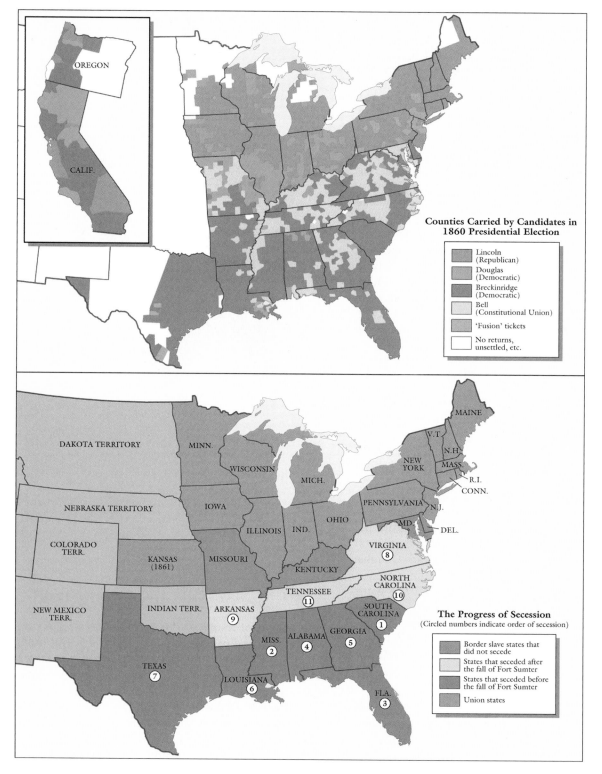

Counties Carried by Candidates in 1860 Presidential Election

- Lincoln (Republican)
- Douglas (Democratic)
- Breckinridge (Democratic)
- Bell (Constitutional Union)
- 'Fusion' tickets
- No returns, unsettled, etc.

The Progress of Secession
(Circled numbers indicate order of secession)

- Border slave states that did not secede
- States that seceded after the fall of Fort Sumter
- States that seceded before the fall of Fort Sumter
- Union states

Union before the horrors of abolition were inflicted upon them.

Americans had considered secession in the past. Ever since the founding of the nation, defenders of "states' rights" had argued that any state should be able to "nullify" laws passed by the federal government and even withdraw from the Union should it so desire. In 1798, Thomas Jefferson claimed the right of nullification in his Kentucky Resolution; disgruntled New England Federalists threatened to leave the Union during the War of 1812; and South Carolina's great statesman John C. Calhoun had in the 1830s defended the South's right to "disunion" in order to protect it from what he called "northern aggression." In these prior cases, however, only the most hotheaded ideologues urged secession. Until 1860, southerners had held back from dividing the country. That changed with Lincoln's election.

The Deep South Secedes

South Carolina and the Confederate States of America

South Carolina took the lead. On December 20, 1860, a state convention repealed South Carolina's ratification of the U.S. Constitution and voted to withdraw from the Union. It did not want to be part of a nation in which it had no control. Over the next six weeks, several other southern states—Mississippi, Florida, Alabama, Georgia, Louisiana, and Texas—followed suit. Together, on February 7, 1861, they established the Confederate States of America: an independent, southern slave republic. The Confederate States of America elected Jefferson Davis of Mississippi as the new nation's first president.

>> **The first flag of the Confederate States of America, called "the Stars and Bars," was flown from March 5, 1861, to May 26, 1863.**

© Shutterstock.com/Patsy Michaud

Lower South versus Upper South

Seceding was not a unanimous choice for these southern states. The planter class was the driving force behind the movement. Those counties that had a large number of slaveholding families tended to vote for secession, while those areas with few slaves typically voted against it. Therefore, the initial wave of secession was confined to the Deep South (Louisiana, Mississippi, Alabama, Georgia, South Carolina, Texas, and Florida), where slave-based agriculture was more fully established. The Upper South (Virginia, North Carolina, Arkansas, Kentucky, and Tennessee), by contrast, had a more diversified economy. Those states chose not to secede in the winter of 1860–1861.

Read South Carolina's declaration of the causes of secession.

Crittenden Compromise Reconciliation proposal advocating that the Missouri Compromise line of 1820 be extended all the way to the Pacific, excluding California, with all land north of the line free, all land south of it open to slavery; also included an "unamendable amendment" to the Constitution, guaranteeing the preservation of slavery in the southern states where it already existed

Conciliatory Efforts

Crittenden Compromise

A last-ditch effort at reconciliation was spearheaded by John Crittenden of Kentucky. Crittenden proposed that the Missouri Compromise line of 1820 be resurrected and extended all the way to the Pacific, excluding California. All land north of the line would be free, all land south of it would be open to slavery. Moreover, he recommended that an "unamendable amendment" be made to the Constitution, guaranteeing the preservation of slavery in the southern states where it already existed.

The **Crittenden Compromise** proved unworkable. Secessionists in the Deep South had no interest in returning to the Union. The Republicans, who had been elected to office on a platform that called for prohibiting the expansion of slavery, did not want to renege on their campaign promises. Thus, the Crittenden Compromise was a nonstarter, and the only question remaining was whether the states of the Deep South would be permitted to withdraw from the Union.

Read the Crittenden Compromise.

Lincoln's Middle Course

After his inauguration on March 4, 1861, Lincoln attempted to chart a middle course. He sought to reassure southerners that he would not interfere with slavery in the states where it already existed. Slave states that did not secede would be allowed to maintain slavery. At the same time, Lincoln, like Andrew Jackson before him, maintained that the Union was perpetual and that no state could withdraw from it. Furthermore, he insisted that federal property in the southern states (forts, arsenals, and customs houses) still belonged to the Union. Lincoln put the ball in the Confederacy's court. It was up to the southern states to either return to the Union or face civil war. He had invited them back and granted them slavery where it already existed, maintaining the status quo. What would the Confederates do?

Fort Sumter

Army rations became the deciding factor. The deadlock was shaken when the federal garrison at Fort Sumter, South Carolina, located just off the coast of Charleston (now a city in the Confederate States of America), ran low on food. Provisions needed to be sent to the U.S. troops there, or they would have to surrender the fort to the Confederacy. By March 1861, only six weeks of supplies remained.

In early April 1861, President Lincoln organized a relief expedition to the fort. Hopeful that war could be avoided, Lincoln assured the governor of South Carolina that the ships sent to supply Fort Sumter would contain only food, not guns or ammunition. Jefferson Davis, however, declared that any attempt to send provisions to Fort Sumter would be considered an aggressive act against the Confederacy. As a preemptive move, Davis ordered General Pierre Beauregard, the Confederate Army commander in Charleston, to demand Fort Sumter's immediate surrender. If the garrison of eighty-five men refused to surrender, Davis ordered Beauregard to open fire. On April 12, 1861, when Beauregard's demands were rejected, Confederate batteries began shelling Fort Sumter. By the evening of April 13, the garrison capitulated.

Explore further information about Fort Sumter.

What else was happening . . .	
1842	Abraham Lincoln accepts a challenge to a duel from James Shields, the Democratic state auditor. (The duel never takes place.)
1845	The rubber band is patented.
1849	The first safety pin is patented.
Feb. 11, 1861	Both Abraham Lincoln and Jefferson Davis leave their homes to be inaugurated president.

>> The bombardment of Fort Sumter

© The London Art Archive/Alamy

And in the end . . .

In the wake of Fort Sumter's surrender, Abraham Lincoln called for 75,000 volunteers to put down the southern rebellion. Northerners eagerly rallied behind Lincoln and resolved to bring the secessionists to their knees. The South was also coming together. In response to Lincoln's attempt to "coerce" the rebel states back into the Union, the Upper South states of Virginia, Tennessee, North Carolina, and Arkansas threw their lot in with the Confederacy. Battle lines were now drawn. What was destined to become the bloodiest war in American history had begun. The political crisis of the 1850s, sparked by the question of whether slavery would be allowed in the west, had erupted into civil war.

The Civil War

Learning Outcomes

After reading this chapter, you should be able to do the following:

LO **1**   Describe the areas of strength and advantage for each side at the beginning of the Civil War.

LO **2**   Explain why both sides in the Civil War believed the war would be brief, and describe the early conflicts that made that outcome unlikely.

LO **3**   Explain how preparing for and prosecuting the Civil War contributed to the transformation of the United States into a fully modern state.

LO **4**   Describe the actions of those who opposed the war in the North and of those who opposed the war in the South.

LO **5**   Discuss the events that occurred during 1863 and up to and including the presidential election of 1864 that demonstrated Lincoln's strong will and his eventual determination that the end of the war should bring a definite end to slavery.

LO **6**   Describe and discuss the events that finally led to the utter defeat of the South and the end of the war.

> ## "The war ended slavery and accelerated America's modernization, shaping the nation we live in today."

In hindsight, we know the Civil War was four years of prolonged and bloody battles. At the outbreak of fighting, however, neither northerners nor southerners took the prospect of fighting one another all that seriously. Both sides expected a short war with few casualties. Southerners believed that northerners were effete cowards lacking the mettle to sustain a prolonged battle. They thought that once the northern armies caught a glimpse of the South's determination, northerners would drop their guns and let the South secede. Northerners, meanwhile, were certain that only southern slaveholders supported secession, and because they were a tiny minority in the South, that their lack of support would become evident. Northerners also considered southerners ill prepared and ill equipped to take on the U.S. Army. The North expected the South's will to fight to diminish rapidly.

As a consequence, northerners and southerners predicted that the war would not change their societies very dramatically. Southerners presumed that their plantation-based, slaveholding civilization would continue to thrive as it had for decades. Northerners imagined that the southern states would realize their error and return to the Union to resume amicable relations. Southerners would keep their slaves, most northerners thought, but slavery would be prevented from spreading westward.

All these predictions proved inaccurate. The fighting between North and South became fierce and vindictive, and casualties were high. In addition, when the North and the South emerged from the war in 1865, both were transformed from what they had been in 1861. The war ended slavery and accelerated America's modernization, shaping the nation we live in today.

What do you think?

Lincoln's proclamation did not end slavery; slaves themselves ended slavery.

Strongly Disagree						Strongly Agree
1	2	3	4	5	6	7

LO¹ Each Side's Strengths

Northern Advantages

Population

In some ways, northern expectations for a quick victory were reasonable, because the Union possessed overwhelming material advantages over the South. In 1861, the total population of the Union was around 22 million, compared to 9 million in the Confederacy. This statistic becomes even more impressive when one considers that 3.5 million of the Confederacy's people were slaves, people clearly unwilling to fight on behalf of the perpetuation of slavery. In terms of military-age white males, the Union outnumbered the Confederacy four to one.

Materials and Industry

The northern states had other advantages as well. The North had an existing navy and produced more firearms than the South. It also produced more of the essential provisions of war, including coal, textiles, corn, and wheat. By all estimates, the North was better able to outfit its men with weapons, clothing, shoes, and food. The North also had a more extensive network of railroad lines for transporting those supplies and a larger pool of money to finance its war effort. The Union possessed about $200 million in bank deposits, while the Confederacy had only $47 million.

> **In terms of military-age white males, the Union outnumbered the Confederacy four to one.**

> **Most men in the South were more comfortable with firearms than soldiers raised in the urban North**

Southern Advantages

Will to Fight

The Confederacy did have certain strengths, however. Three of these advantages were vitally important. First, northerners severely underestimated the southern will to fight. While only slaveholders had taken the lead in the secession movement, by April 1861, most southerners supported the bid for Confederate independence, and they were willing to fight to win it.

A Defensive Battle

The Union also had to wage an offensive war to occupy the South, while the Confederacy had the simpler task of fighting on the defensive. The Confederacy did not have to overwhelm or occupy the North; it merely had to frustrate northern efforts to conquer it.

Military Leaders and Morale

At the beginning of the war, the South also had more well-trained military leaders and a stronger tradition of military service. Many of the West Point–trained officers in the U.S. Army, including Jefferson Davis, Robert E. Lee, Albert Sydney Johnston, Thomas "Stonewall" Jackson, and James Longstreet, sided with the Confederacy. In addition, living in a rural environment, most men in the South were more comfortable with firearms than soldiers raised in the urban North. And, in terms of morale, the Confederacy had the advantage of fighting for its existence.

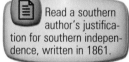

Library of Congress, Prints & Photographs Division, LC-USZ62-96445

>> **Filling cartridges at the U.S. Arsenal at Watertown, Massachusetts, 1861.**

© iStockphoto.com/Melissa Carroll

LO² The Fallacy of an "Easy War": 1861–1862

The Battle of Manassas (Bull Run)

The fallacy of expecting a brief war became apparent at the first major battle of the Civil War, in northern Virginia on July 21, 1861. Union General Irvin McDowell moved 30,000 troops toward the Confederate soldiers clustered at Manassas Junction, just south of Washington, D.C. At the same time, civilians and congressmen from the capital packed picnic lunches and made the twenty-five-mile journey to witness the battle. After all, they anticipated fighting to be light and the battle to end shortly.

To the surprise of both sides, the Battle of Manassas, called the Battle of Bull Run by the Union (the North named battles after nearby creeks or rivers, the South after nearby towns), was hard-fought and bloody. Some 22,000 Confederate soldiers, led by General Pierre Beauregard, battled tenaciously against McDowell's men, and Confederate reinforcements under General Thomas "Stonewall" Jackson turned the tide decisively in the South's favor. When McDowell ordered a retreat, his troops panicked and stampeded from the fray.

A Costly Confederate Victory

Although the Confederates had won the field of battle, they were not prepared to pursue the fleeing federal troops. The victory had been too costly. Each side had suffered nearly 10 percent casualties, with the northern forces having 2,896 killed, wounded, or missing, and the southern forces suffering 1,982 similar casualties. In light of such carnage, northerners and southerners alike were stripped of their assumptions about an easy war. The change in tone was especially marked in the North. After the defeat at Manassas, fearing that victorious southern forces would head straight to Washington, D.C., Congress authorized, and received, the enlistment of 500,000 volunteers. They were now preparing for a major armed conflict, a bigger war than anyone had predicted.

Learn more about the Battle of Manassas.

Read Stonewall Jackson's official report on the Battle of Manassas.

Limited War

Although northerners no longer believed that the war would be won quickly, they clung to the idea that most southerners still loved the Union but had been pressured into fighting by a small clique of powerful slaveholders. They viewed it as a rich man's war and a poor man's fight.

In keeping with this view, the Union army in 1861 and 1862 fought a limited war, which meant that, in attacking the Confederacy, Union troops were careful not to assault southern civilians or damage their property. Their goal was to occupy southern territory and defeat the Confederate army. They were not aiming to subjugate the southern

© iStockphoto.com/ngirish

>> "You come to see the gladiator's show, But from a high place, as befits the wise: You will not see the long windrows of men Strewn like dead pears . . ."
—From Stephen Vincent Benét, "The Congressmen Came Out to See Bull Run"

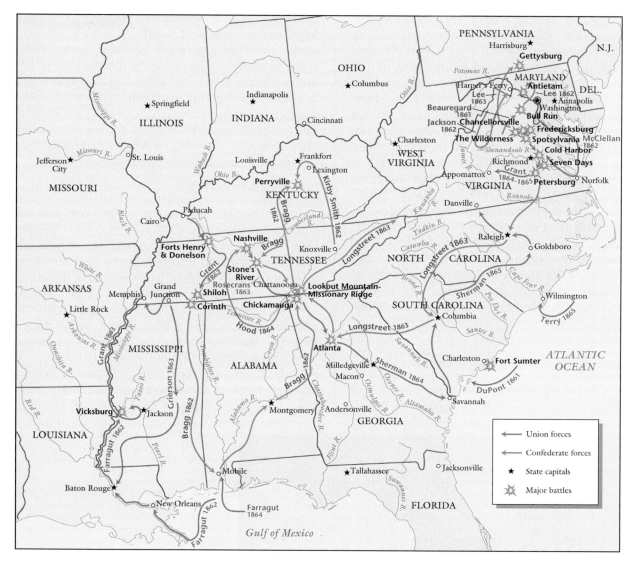

people. They attempted this strategy of "limited war" in three theaters: the water, the West, and the East.

The Water

Naval Blockade

The imposition of a naval blockade of the Confederacy was part of the Union strategy. In April 1861, Lincoln formally declared a blockade of the southern coastline, hoping to prevent European supplies from reaching southern harbors.

Cutting the Confederacy off from sea-borne commerce proved difficult at first because the U.S. Navy only had forty-two ships to patrol 3,550 miles of Confederate coastline. After the first year of the war, however, blockading the South became easier, as the Union took control of several southern coastal locations, including Roanoke Island in North Carolina, the sea islands of South Carolina, and New Orleans. Taking New Orleans was a significant coup; it was the South's largest and richest city, its biggest port, and it opened the Mississippi River valley to invasion from the south.

>> **Crew of the Union ironclad *Monitor* in front of their rotating turret**

If the Union could not yet beat the Confederacy on the battlefield, they could prevent European goods from reaching it and eventually starve southerners into submission.

The blockade effort also stimulated the development of the ironclad battleship. Instead of wood, these ships used iron (later steel) siding, sat low in the water to ram targets more efficiently, and one in particular, the U.S.S. *Monitor*, had a two-gun rotating turret on top. The first battle between ironclads, a four-hour barrage in March 1862 between the U.S.S. *Monitor* and the C.S.S. *Virginia*, ended inconclusively. But the news coverage it garnered signaled to the world a shift in military technology. Notably slow, however, the ironclads were only marginally successful in stopping Confederate blockade runners throughout the war.

The West

Some Union Successes

While the Union navy was taking control of the southern coast, the Union army achieved some success in the western theater of the war, located west of the Allegheny Mountains. Although the Confederacy won many of the battles waged in 1861 (including those at Wilson's Creek, Lexington, and Belmont),

Union general Ulysses S. Grant earned the first decisive victories in the first half of 1862. In February 1862, with the support of Union gunboats, Grant's forces captured Fort Henry on the Tennessee River and then Fort Donelson on the Cumberland River.

> **Battle of Shiloh**
> Bloody conflict near the Tennessee-Mississippi border in April 1862; also called the Battle of Pittsburg Landing; 23,000 casualties

Shiloh

These losses forced Confederate troops to withdraw from Kentucky and Tennessee. A few months later, as Grant's army moved farther south, they encountered fierce resistance from Confederate troops under the command of General Albert Sydney Johnston. Johnston's army took Grant's men by surprise near the Tennessee-Mississippi border in April 1862. The ensuing **Battle of Shiloh** (or the Battle of Pittsburg Landing) was incredibly bloody, resulting in 23,000 combined northern and southern casualties. Grant took the victory on the second day, but at a heavy price. The casualties at Shiloh exceeded American losses in the Revolutionary War, the War of 1812, and the Mexican-American War put together, and they were almost five times as great as the losses suffered at the Battle of Manassas. And, in the end, it would turn out to be only the ninth bloodiest battle of the Civil War. The enormity of the fatalities was felt nationwide. The North was securing the western theater, but it was doing so at a tremendous cost. Not only would this be a massive war, it would be a tragic one as well.

>> **The casualties at Shiloh exceeded American losses in the Revolutionary War, the War of 1812, and the Mexican-American War put together.**

The East

McClellan

The Union army was less successful in the east. Here, General George B. McClellan headed the Union's Army of the Potomac. Despite his outward arrogance, McClellan was an insecure man and an excessively cautious commander. His troops appreciated his reluctance to expose them in bloody battles, but McClellan's self-defeating attitude hurt the Union cause.

Throughout most of 1861, McClellan resisted pressures to pursue the Confederate army in Virginia, insisting that he needed time to discipline and drill his men. In spring 1862, McClellan finally decided to make a move on Richmond, the Confederate capital. After transporting his troops to the mouth of the James River, McClellan slowly made his way up the peninsula between the James and York Rivers. But he had waited too long to attack. This gave the Confederate army a chance to organize and respond. On May 31, 1862, McClellan was within five miles of

General George B. McClellan at repose

Portrait of George Brinton McClellan (1826–85) (litho), Chappel, Alonzo (1828–87) (after)/Private Collection, Ken Welsh/The Bridgeman Art Library.

>> "If General McClellan does not want to use the army, I would like to borrow it for a time." –attributed to Abraham Lincoln, 1862

Richmond when General Joseph Johnston and the Confederacy's Army of Northern Virginia attacked his troops at Fair Oaks (or Seven Pines). Johnston was badly wounded in the battle, but he succeeded in halting McClellan's advance.

Robert E. Lee

Matters only worsened for McClellan after Robert E. Lee replaced Johnston as the head of the Army of Northern Virginia. Lee was as audacious as McClellan was cautious, and with the help of Stonewall Jackson, Lee repulsed the Army of the Potomac during the Seven Days' Battles, which raged from June 25 to July 1, 1862. The Army of the Potomac was pushed north, out of Virginia.

With that defeat, Lincoln ordered the abandonment of McClellan's peninsula campaign, removed McClellan from his post, and put General John Pope in command of the Army of the Potomac. Pope was no more successful than McClellan had been. At the second Battle of Manassas, on August 29, 1862, Lee routed the Union troops and disgraced Pope. Despite McClellan's flaws, Lincoln reinstalled him at the head of the floundering Army of the Potomac. The Union armies were generally successful in the west and on the seas, but they were unable to beat their opponents where it mattered most—in Virginia, the heart of the Confederacy.

Results

Battles in these three theaters were hard fought, suggesting that the war would last longer than anyone had expected. War would require each side to mobilize its resources and, in the end, establish what is thought of today as a modern nation-state.

LO³ Full Mobilization and the Making of a Modern State

In order to amass the manpower and money necessary to wage a serious prolonged war, northerners and southerners were forced to concentrate authority in the hands of their national governments. This process transformed the Union and the Confederacy into truly modern nations with intricate bureaucracies capable of controlling the resources of its states. The irony of this was felt strongly by Confederate president Jefferson Davis. After all, one of the principal reasons for southern secession was defending the rights of states over the rights of the national government. Yet in order to secure the South's independence, Davis found it necessary to concentrate power under a centralized authority. But northerners, too, felt the tightening grip of the federal government.

Raising Armies

The Confederacy

Nowhere was this truer than when it came to raising armies. During the first year of the war, the Confederacy had only a small national army. Most soldiers volunteered for service through state militias controlled by state governors, not through the Confederacy. However, Jefferson Davis understood that engineering a strong war effort required greater coordination. So he convinced the Confederate Congress to implement a national draft in April 1862.

All men between eighteen and thirty-five became eligible for military service in the Confederate army. Exemptions could be purchased, traded in return for supplying a substitute, or simply granted to wealthy landholders who owned twenty or more slaves. This **"20 Negro Law"** was designed to keep the planters producing their valuable cotton yield. The Confederate Conscription Act also contained occupational exemptions, whereby workers at gun and munitions factories would not be forced to leave jobs valuable to the war effort (the list of occupational exemptions immediately became political, such that, by the end of the war, the list of war-related jobs could not be contained on two finely printed pages). By 1863, the Confederate government, not the various state governments, had assumed control of the army.

The Union

The North implemented a national draft in 1863. Like the Confederacy, the Union had initially relied on state armies to enlist soldiers, but the high desertion and low enlistment rates of state officers forced the federal government to establish a national conscription law, making all able-bodied men ages twenty to forty-five eligible for the draft. To ease the burden of conscription, the Union also established volunteer quotas for each of its states. Only when a state failed to provide its allotted number of volunteer soldiers was the draft employed in that state.

Very few men were ever drafted. Most volunteered. Others tried to fail medical exams in order to escape the war altogether. Similarly, under the conscription law, a person could be exempted until the next draft by paying a $300 **commutation fee.** The Union draft law, too, allowed men to be exempt from service by hiring a substitute to take their place. Some men, known as bounty jumpers, would receive a bounty to take another man's place in the Army, then desert, only to do the trick again and again. Thus, in both the Union and the Confederacy, exemptions were made for rich men, who could afford to buy their way out of service, while ordinary workers and farmers could not. The accusation that this was a rich man's war and a poor man's fight applied to both sides of the conflict.

Read about life in the armies of the Civil War.

"20 Negro Law"
Exemption from Confederate military service granted to wealthy landholders who owned twenty or more slaves; designed to keep the planters producing their valuable cotton yield

commutation fee
Sum of money that guaranteed a draft-age man's exemption from enlisting in the Union Army until the next draft

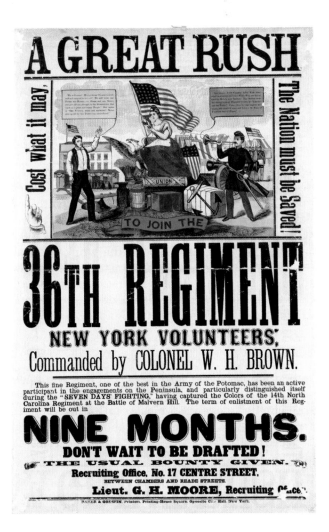

© 'A Great Rush,' recruitment poster for 36th Regiment, published by Baker & Goodwin (colour litho), American School, (19th century)/© Collection of the New York Historical Society, USA, The Bridgeman Art Library

Suspension of Civil Liberties

In the Union

The expansion of federal control also affected wartime civil liberties. In the first year of the war, both Union and Confederate governments suspended civil liberties. Abraham Lincoln took the lead. From the start of fighting in April 1861, some northerners opposed the war and worked to hamper the Union's effort. For instance, on April 19, 1861, Confederate sympathizers in Baltimore destroyed telegraph lines, sabotaged railroads, and attacked Union soldiers who were passing through on their way to Washington, which was threatened after the Battle of Manassas.

To deal with the dissent, Lincoln used his authority as commander-in-chief to suspend the writ of habeas corpus in Maryland, which made it possible for Union soldiers to arrest any northern civilians suspected of disloyalty and imprison them without benefit of trial. Eventually, Lincoln suspended the writ in all other states, hoping to control disloyalty and dissent everywhere in the North. During the course of the conflict, roughly fourteen thousand people were arrested for undefined reasons.

Read Lincoln's proclamation suspending habeas corpus.

In the Confederacy

Jefferson Davis followed Lincoln's lead. As in the North, antiwar sentiment existed in the Confederacy from the outset, especially in poorer areas with few slaves. Several military losses in 1862 incited a level of dissent that provoked Davis to action. Unlike Lincoln, Davis did not suspend the writ of habeas corpus by his own authority. Instead, he sought approval from the Confederate Congress, which gave Davis the power to clamp down on citizens who opposed southern independence.

Taxation

Both sides also exercised new controls over their national economies. Before the war, the federal government had depended mostly on tariff revenues and land sales to finance its operations. In fact, aside from the tariffs, the federal government had levied no taxes on the American people since the War of 1812.

Tariffs, Taxes, and Bonds in the Union

At the outbreak of hostilities in the Civil War, the U.S. Congress began raising tariff rates in order to pay for the war, and by 1865 the average tariff rate was an astronomical 47 percent. Despite these rates, tariffs failed to generate enough revenue to fully finance the military operation.

To compensate, Congress introduced direct taxation measures. Congress enacted a 3 percent income tax during the first year of the war. Then, in 1862, Congress enacted a graduated tax schedule to bring in more revenue from wealthier citizens. Congress also passed a comprehensive tax bill that levied new occupational and licensing taxes, corporate taxes, stamp taxes, insurance company taxes, dividend taxes, sales taxes, food taxes, and so-called sin taxes on alcohol and tobacco. To streamline the collection of these new levies, Congress created the Internal Revenue Service in 1862.

The U.S. government also tried to raise money by selling war bonds, or bonds that a person or corporation could buy that would earn interest over a fixed period of time. The bondholder could then redeem the bond within from five to twenty years for their initial investment plus interest (they were called **five-twenties**). New York banker Jay Cooke took the reins on this prospect and rapidly sold more than $500 million worth of bonds, to both large corporations and individual buyers.

Inflation and Impressment in the Confederacy

At first, the Confederacy resisted creating a national system of taxation. It preferred instead to finance the war by simply printing more and more paper money—a plan that succeeded only in creating runaway inflation. The cost of living at the end of the war was an astounding 92 times what it had been before the war began. Only in 1863, once Confederate currency became nearly worthless, did the Confederate Congress institute a graduated income tax similar to the Union's. Nevertheless, while these types of taxes financed 21 percent of the Union's expenses, they furnished only 1 percent of the Confederacy's.

In addition, the Confederacy enacted a policy of impressment, authorizing armies to seize food, supplies, and even slaves for use in the war effort. Theoretically, citizens would be compensated, but many people complained that the government paid too little and that the payments were made in inflated and increasingly worthless Confederate dollars. The war was a financial disaster for the Confederacy, which never figured out the best method to pay for it.

A Changing Nation

Between the new system of conscription, suspension of the writ of habeas corpus, and new taxes,

>> The Confederacy preferred to finance the war by simply printing more and more paper money—a plan that succeeded only in creating runaway inflation.

© iStockphoto.com/Lee Pettet

the Union and the Confederacy became powerful nation-states with great control over the lives of their citizens. Before 1861, Americans had little contact with their federal government. Most Americans encountered the federal government only when the U.S. postal service delivered their mail. By 1865, however, northerners and southerners lived under large and powerful national governments. After the war, the writ of habeas corpus was restored, but other powers assumed by the federal government were not rolled back. The Civil War established innovative and permanent changes in the scope of government authority in the United States.

LO⁴ Dissent

These changes stirred dissent, and governments in both the North and the South found themselves confronted by those who opposed the war.

Dissent in the North

Peace Democrats

The entire body of Lincoln's policies came to elicit a great deal of opposition on the northern home front. For example, a minority of Democrats refused to support the war. These Democrats came to be called "Peace Democrats" or "Copperheads." They believed that secession was legal, such that the Union had no right to force southern states to remain within

it. Although their numbers were small in 1861, the Peace Democrats soon capitalized on popular dissatisfaction with Lincoln's leadership to become a formidable force in northern society.

Lincoln the Tyrant

The Peace Democrats jumped on Lincoln's suspension of the writ of habeas corpus as proof that the president was a tyrant undeserving of popular support. Although the Constitution did allow the government to suspend the writ in times of national crisis, it had always been assumed that the power rested with Congress. Lincoln, however, acted without prior consent from Congress. This gave rise to the notion that Lincoln, like Jackson before him, was a dangerous tyrant, ready to sacrifice liberties in order to exercise and expand his own power.

The Draft

Even more than suspension of habeas corpus, the draft became an important symbol of Lincoln's dictatorial ways which angered the Peace Democrats. Conscription seemed to contradict America's commitment to individual freedoms. In addition, the 1863 draft law seemed unfair to poor men, who, unlike the wealthy, could not afford to buy their way out of fighting.

The New York Draft Riot

This inequity generated violence as well as political opposition. In July 1863, when the first national draft was about to be held in New York City, Democratic working men, most of them Irish, rampaged through the streets and shut down the draft office. They attacked anyone who was rich or a known pro-war Republican. The rioters also expressed hostility to the idea of fighting to free the slaves, and they acted most violently toward black people, who had recently been used to replace Irish longshoremen during a labor strike. It took four days before order was finally restored, and by then, more than one hundred people had been killed. This was the largest loss of life caused by any civilian riot in American history up to that point.

Take a virtual tour of the draft riots.

Dissent in the South

Economic Woes

The South faced its own dire problems on the home front. The prospect of a long war had put the

> **"**The number composing this first mob has been so differently estimated, that it would be impossible from reports merely, to approximate the truth. A pretty accurate idea, however, can be gained of its immense size, from a statement made by Mr. King, son of President King, of Columbia College. Struck by its magnitude, he had the curiosity to get some estimate of it by timing its progress, and he found that although it filled the broad street from curbstone to curbstone, and was moving rapidly, it took between twenty and twenty-five minutes for it to pass a single point. A ragged, coatless, heterogeneously weaponed army, it heaved tumultuously along toward Third Avenue.**"**
>
> *—Journalist Joel Tyler Headley*, **Pen and Pencil Sketches of the Great Riots [of 1863],** *1877*

Confederate economy in desperate straits by 1863. With the institution of slavery disintegrating (as explained below), the women and men who remained on the southern home front were unable to maintain sufficient production of corn, grain, and other foodstuffs. The shortages caused the price of food to skyrocket. Manufactured goods also became scarce as the Union blockade of the Confederacy cut off the region from European suppliers. Merchants made matters worse by hoarding goods, which also drove prices up.

Riots

In this economy, the average southerner could not afford basic necessities. High prices and food shortages provoked riots throughout the Confederacy in 1863. In April, in the Confederate capital of Richmond, three hundred women and children took to the streets armed with knives and pistols, broke into stores, and stole the items they needed but could not afford.

In the face of months of scarcity and starvation, many women on the Confederate home front started to lose their will to sacrifice for independence. Jefferson Davis and the other leaders of the Confederate States of America were ineffective in sustaining popular morale. This was not due to their personal qualities, but principally because the South's poor transportation networks, never fully developed during the Market Revolution, hindered leaders from making rallying trips across the land. In addition to this inability to communicate with its citizens, the government also did little to alleviate their economic hardships. Focusing solely on the military problem of keeping the Union armies at bay, Davis made no attempt to provide his constituents with government assistance. Davis's wartime policies—the suspension of the writ of habeas corpus, conscription, and impressments—only increased popular dissatisfaction. As in the North by 1863, there was a full-blown peace faction in the South working to undermine Davis's leadership.

By the midpoint of the war, both the Union and the Confederacy had become bitterly divided societies.

Read excerpts from Mary Boykin Chesnut's wartime diary from the South.

>> An engraving entitled "Sowing and Reaping" depicts Southern women persuading their husbands to join in the rebellion (left) and the same women rioting for bread during the hard times of the war (right).

SOWING AND REAPING.

[SOUTHERN WOMEN HOUNDING THEIR MEN ON TO REBELLION.]   SOUTHERN WOMEN FEELING THE EFFECTS OF REBELLION, AND CREATING BREAD RIOTS.

contraband
Smuggled goods

Confiscation Act
Legislation that officially declared that any slaves used for military purposes would be freed if they came into Union hands

LO⁵ The Tide of Battle Turns, 1863–1865

Wars continue despite dissent, of course. During the Civil War, men fought brutal battles, combining ancient methods of fighting (using sabers and knives) with modern warfare (using long-range rifles, cannons, and other instruments that could kill opponents without ever having to see them up close). As the conflict deepened, the war turned from a "limited war" to an all-encompassing one by 1863.

Lincoln struggled to keep up morale in the North, and one way he did this was by performing a delicate political dance on the subject of slavery, leading ultimately to his powerful and eloquent Emancipation Proclamation. Seeking to outlaw slavery was a definitive move toward challenging the very existence of southern society.

Slavery and Emancipation

Although slavery was clearly the root of the Civil War, Lincoln made no immediate move to end slavery. Lincoln understood that in 1861 most northerners did not support broad emancipation. Northern people generally agreed that slavery was an evil institution, but they also balked at the thought of creating a large, free black population in the United States.

Lincoln also feared that immediate emancipation would alienate the four border states that remained within the Union; Missouri, Kentucky, Maryland, and Delaware all retained slavery but still sought to preserve the Union. In order to defeat the Confederacy, Lincoln knew he needed to keep those states relatively happy, something emancipation would undoubtedly jeopardize. Therefore, as part of the Union's limited war strategy, U.S. soldiers were initially instructed to leave southern slave property alone and return any escaped slaves who tried to hide behind Union lines.

Overtures to Emancipation

As the war dragged on, however, Union practice gradually deviated from this policy. The South depended on its slaves to provide food and manual labor for the war effort, so in May 1861, General Benjamin Butler of Massachusetts began the practice of treating runaway slaves as **contraband** (smuggled goods), refusing to return them to their owners. Then, in August 1861, Congress passed its first **Confiscation Act**, which officially declared that any slaves used for military purposes would be freed if they came into Union hands.

Congress also freed the two thousand slaves living in the nation's capital, providing compensation to their owners. At the same time, it banned slavery from all U.S. territories. This officially put an end to the issue of the expansion of slavery that had aroused sectional tensions in the 1840s and 1850s. And in July 1862 Congress passed the Second Confiscation Act, which stated that all slaves owned by rebel masters (not just those being used for military purposes) would be set free if they fell under Union control. With southerners absent from Congress, northern Republicans were making rapid strides toward eliminating slavery in the United States.

Although Lincoln signed the Second Confiscation Act, he generally ignored it. Lincoln wanted the slave states to choose emancipation, not to have it forced upon them. After the Second Confiscation Act became law, Lincoln summoned to the White House representatives from the border states of Missouri, Kentucky, Maryland, and Delaware, and presented

Read the Second Confiscation Act.

them with a plan to free their slaves. Unfortunately, the border states resisted any suggestion that they end the practice of slavery.

Deciding on Emancipation

Eventually, Lincoln decided to initiate an emancipation policy himself, explicitly making slavery the central issue of the war. On July 22, 1862, Lincoln told his cabinet that he planned to issue a presidential proclamation freeing at least some of the slaves. Emancipation carried clear military benefits, he argued. For one thing, it would weaken the Confederacy by depriving southerners of slave labor. In addition, emancipation would earn moral support from the rest of the free world, making it difficult for nations such as Britain and France to ally with the Confederacy.

Taking the advice of his secretary of state, William H. Seward, Lincoln waited for a Union military victory before announcing his proclamation, in order to appear to speak from a position of strength, not desperation. Lincoln got his chance after the Battle of Antietam (Battle of Sharpsburg) on September 17, 1862, when the Union's Army of the Potomac forced Lee's Army of Northern Virginia to retreat from Union territory in Maryland back into the Confederacy.

The Emancipation Proclamation

Five days after the Battle of Antietam, on September 22, 1862, Lincoln made his preliminary Emancipation Proclamation, which declared that all slaves within rebel territory would be freed on January 1, 1863, unless the southern states returned to the Union. To make the proclamation more palatable to white northerners, Lincoln averred that he had given the order out of military necessity. Emancipation would weaken the Confederacy, he argued, and as commander in chief, he was obliged to initiate and enforce such policies. In addition, it would not free a single slave in the slave states that were already part of the Union. When the southern states failed to return to the Union as requested, Lincoln issued the formal Emancipation Proclamation on January 1, 1863. The North no longer fought for the reconstruction of the old Union. It was seeking the creation of a new Union, one without slavery.

Although undeniably bold, the proclamation was far from a comprehensive plan for emancipation. Lincoln exempted Missouri, Kentucky, Maryland, and Delaware (the border states), as well as Tennessee and areas of Virginia and Louisiana already under Union occupation. Only areas actively engaged in rebellion were affected. Moreover, those places where the proclamation was intended to free slaves were precisely those places where the Union lacked the power to enforce its policies.

A Factor in the End of Slavery, but Not *the* Factor

Even before Lincoln issued the Emancipation Proclamation, however, slavery was disintegrating, as the dislocations of war made it impossible for southerners to maintain control over their slaves. As more southern men left their farms to enter the army, slaves took more and more liberties and, in some cases, openly challenged white authority. They shirked work, and attempts to impose discipline only made them more defiant. When word spread that the Union Army was nearby, thousands of slaves would run away and attempt to take refuge behind Union lines.

Lincoln's proclamation thus did not end slavery; slaves themselves ended slavery. But the Proclamation emboldened slaves to increase their resistance, and it offered hope that, if the Union won the war, slavery would be outlawed.

Learn more about the Emancipation Proclamation.

Read the Emancipation Proclamation.

Black Americans in the Union Military

Black Americans had been trying to volunteer for service in the Union Army all along, but, afraid

>> *Harper's Weekly* of March 14, 1863, illustrates a Union officer teaching black recruits how to use the relatively new French Minié rifle.

of the effect on white soldiers' morale, Lincoln rejected them. This changed with the Emancipation Proclamation, which included an announcement that black Americans would be accepted into the U.S. Army and Navy. During the next two years, 180,000 black men, many of them runaway slaves, joined the Union military. They faced difficult conditions, however, serving in segregated units headed by white officers and receiving only half the compensation paid to white soldiers. Despite the prejudicial treatment, the Union's black soldiers signed up readily, and, in June 1864, Lincoln persuaded Congress to grant them equal pay retroactively. By the end of the conflict, 37,000 black servicemen had lost their lives in the battle for the Union.

The Fort Pillow Massacre

Confederate soldiers resented the presence of African American troops in the U.S. Army. In one controversial incident, after a Confederate victory in the Battle of Fort Pillow, Tennessee, on April 12, 1864, Confederate soldiers, led by Major General

Nathan Bedford Forrest (later the first leader of the Ku Klux Klan), massacred most of an African American regiment, who may have been attempting to surrender. The interracial Union troops suffered defeat in the battle, and some witnesses said the Union troops were attempting to surrender when Confederate troops opened fire. Only about 20 percent of the black soldiers were taken as prisoners, while 60 percent of white soldiers were. The rest were casualties of war. The Fort Pillow Massacre became a rallying cry in the North at a pivotal time in the war.

Read the report from the congressional committee investigating Fort Pillow.

Criticism of Lincoln's Proclamation

Although Lincoln's fellow Republicans generally supported the Emancipation Proclamation, many other northerners criticized it. Predictably, northern Democrats lambasted the proclamation as an act of tyranny. As they saw it, the government had no right to deprive anyone of their property. Moreover, the proclamation suggested that Republicans might actually allow black Americans to exist on a level of equality with white people in America. Given the depths of racism in the United States, the proclamation was hard for many northerners to accept, especially northern Democrats.

Union Military Triumphs

In 1863 and 1864, while both Union and Confederacy dealt with rising dissent and the expansion of their governments, the Union military won a number of important victories. The turning point was Gettysburg.

Lee's Hopes

After Antietam in September 1862, Confederate forces under Robert E. Lee had won impressive victories at Fredericksburg, Virginia, in December 1862, and at nearby Chancellorsville in May 1863. With the momentum from these victories, Lee invaded the North with 75,000 troops. By invading the North, Lee (1) sought to allow the southern soil time to recuperate from months of battles; (2) was hoping that, strategically, a major victory in the North would buttress the Union's peace movement and force Lincoln to accept Confederate terms for peace; and (3) thought a major victory in the North would also compel the British to reconsider recognition of the Confederacy, thus giving the Confederacy a valuable partner in the war.

Gettysburg

Despite Lee's intention of waging a northern battle in a major city, circumstances conspired to force a showdown at the small town of Gettysburg, Pennsylvania. Lee's Army of Northern Virginia had invaded Pennsylvania and had come close to taking Harrisburg, the state's capital. The Union's Army of the Potomac, however, now led by General George Gordon Meade, set off to chase Lee, ultimately confronting him in Gettysburg. The battle that ensued was one of the epic battles of the Civil War, and many historians consider it the turning point of the war.

Engagement was vicious and bloody. After two days of trying unsuccessfully to break the Union line, Lee made an ill-fated move on July 3. In an attempt to split the Union forces, he sent about 12,500 men in a charge into the well-entrenched center of the Union line. This attack is known as Pickett's Charge because General George Pickett was one of the three division commanders leading it. It was a disastrous move by Lee. Nearly two-thirds of the attacking Confederates were killed, wounded, or captured during the assault, and the Union took the victory. All told, Lee lost roughly 28,000 soldiers

Read Lincoln's Gettysburg Address.

Read General Carl Schurz's impressions of Gettysburg after the battle.

at Gettysburg (approximately one-third of his army) and never again had the manpower to go on the offensive. The federal losses numbered about 23,000, but the Union's great advantage in manpower made such losses easier to overcome than they were for the South. Indeed, in his Gettysburg Address, Lincoln memorably used the battle to motivate his side to continue the struggle under the belief that what they were doing was right, destined to give the nation a "new birth of freedom."

Victories in the West

Meanwhile, Union General Ulysses S. Grant continued to triumph in the West. On July 4, 1863, after a six-week siege, his troops forced the fortress town of Vicksburg, Mississippi to surrender. Four days later, he captured Port Hudson in Louisiana. With those two victories, the Union controlled the entire Mississippi

> ❝All that I had ever read in battle stories of the booming of heavy guns out-thundering the thunders of heaven and making the earth tremble, and almost stopping one's breath from the concussions of the air—was here made real, in terrific effect.❞
>
> –From "The Reminiscences of Carl Schurz," general at Gettysburg

River, severing the Confederacy into eastern and western halves. The battle at Gettysburg received more public notice at the time, but Grant's victories on the Mississippi were perhaps more strategically important.

In light of Grant's success, Lincoln brought him east in March 1864 and made him commander of all the Union armies. From his new post, Grant prepared for an offensive against Lee in Virginia, while General William Tecumseh Sherman took over for Grant in the West.

Northern Momentum?

While northern momentum was strong, the Union again faced the strategic problem of having to completely subdue and conquer its enemy in order to win. In May and June 1864, Grant relentlessly pursued Lee's army in a bloody campaign from the Rappahannock River to the city of Petersburg, south of Richmond, Virginia. Outside Petersburg, the two armies settled into opposing trenches. The siege there lasted more than nine months. Between May and July 1864, Grant lost sixty thousand men, and news of these heavy casualties demoralized the northern home front. Northerners began to fear that the Union armies could never defeat the Confederacy. Despite northern military momentum, was it possible to win a war when the opposition never had to attack?

The Election of 1864

In this atmosphere of uncertainty, the Union continued its pattern of predictable, regular elections as laid out in the Constitution and held a presidential contest. As the war stretched on, the impatience of the northern people during the summer of 1864 did not bode well for Lincoln. But, more than this, the election became a referendum on slavery and Lincoln's Emancipation Proclamation.

McClellan

In 1864, Lincoln's Democratic opponent was none other than the overly cautious George B. McClellan, the former General of the Army of the Potomac. If elected, McClellan promised to restore slavery in the South and negotiate peace with the Confederacy (perhaps leading to the recognition of Confederate independence). His party's slogan was "The Union as it was, the Constitution as it is, and the Negroes where they are." After three years of war, northerners were despairing of the casualties and fearful of the outcome, and even Lincoln did not believe he would be voted into office for a second term.

Timely Military Victories

The Union military, however, saved the day for Lincoln. On August 5, 1864, the Union captured Mobile Bay in Alabama, and less than one month later, Sherman took control of Atlanta. After months of stagnation, the momentum had swung fully to the Union. These victories heartened northern voters and gave them a renewed sense that the Confederacy could be beaten. On Election Day

> "With malice toward none; with charity for all; with firmness in the right, as God gives us to see the right, let us strive on to finish the work we are in. . . ."
> —*Abraham Lincoln, Second Inaugural Address*

in November, Lincoln received 55 percent of the popular vote, giving him a landslide victory in the Electoral College.

Read Lincoln's remarkable Second Inaugural Address.

LO⁶ The Destruction of the South and the End of the War

The Thirteenth Amendment

Abolishing American Slavery Forever

Lincoln's reelection spelled the end of slavery. The Emancipation Proclamation had been made as a war measure, so Lincoln concluded that, once the war ended, it would no longer be binding. Therefore, upon his electoral victory, Lincoln and his supporters moved quickly to secure the final, formal demise of American slavery. Lincoln used all of the influence he had in Congress to ensure the passage of a constitutional amendment freeing all the slaves in the United States without compensating their owners. On January 31, 1865, Congress passed the Thirteenth Amendment, and by the end of the year, enough Union states had ratified the amendment to make it part of the Constitution, abolishing slavery from the United States forever.

The Destruction of the South

Sherman's March to the Sea

Lincoln's victory in November 1864 marked the beginning of the end for the Confederacy. With the Union now set to defeat the rebels rapidly, Sherman waged his **"March to the Sea,"** mowing a path of destruction sixty miles wide and several hundred miles long, through Georgia. The March to the Sea stretched from Atlanta to the Atlantic. Sherman designed the move to encircle Lee's army, which was still in Virginia and, more importantly, to prove to the southern people that the Confederate government lacked the ability to protect them. The soldiers burned fields, tore up vital infrastructure, such as railroad ties, and killed and consumed all the livestock they encountered. By Christmas, Sherman's soldiers had reached Savannah. As much as the Union soldiers relished this punishment of the rebels, they relished the prospect of moving north and destroying South Carolina, the birthplace of the Civil War. After hitting the coast, Sherman's troops continued their march through South and North Carolina, heading north to join forces with Grant in Virginia, an act that would encircle Lee's Army of Northern Virginia and end the war once and for all.

Sherman's March showed how much the war had changed since 1861. Having started with a strategy of limited war, intending to fight only against soldiers and leaving private property alone, by 1864 the Union was fighting a total war, destroying railroads, bridges, cotton gins, and anything else that the rebels could use to support their war effort.

The Southern Will to Fight?

The Confederacy's ravaged economy, the demoralization of its home front, and the dangers of the Union army all combined to erode the southern people's will to fight. By the spring of 1865, more than half of Confederate soldiers had deserted. Meanwhile, Grant tenaciously attacked the Army of Northern Virginia, knowing that when Lee surrendered, the South would be forced to give up entirely. Lee finally capitulated on April 9, 1865, at Appomattox Courthouse, Virginia. Although there was sporadic fighting in the West until the end of May, with Lee's surrender the war was effectively over.

And in the end . . .

The Civil War left the nation irrevocably different than it had been in 1861. The physical destruction was inconceivable: 360,000 Union men and 260,000 Confederates lost their lives. Farms and cities were destroyed. Railroads and other forms of infrastructure were uprooted. And the American government had been transformed into a powerful, centralized force no longer divided between freedom and slavery.

And in the end, the North won the war for three reasons:

{ The reasons why . . . }

- The North had integrated the breakthroughs of the Market Revolution better than the South had. With a well-developed manufacturing sector, varied agricultural supplies, a diverse labor force, and a transportation system able to move food, troops, and supplies rapidly, the North outmaneuvered, outpaced, and outproduced the South.

- The Union simply had more men than the Confederacy, meaning that it could afford a long and costly war better than the South.

- The political party system surrounding Lincoln provided him with an infrastructure to spread propaganda and garner widespread support. Jefferson Davis never had such an infrastructure and thus failed to create sustained enthusiasm for the war effort.

Despite the reunification of the Union and the Confederacy, however, exactly how northerners and southerners would come to live together again remained unclear. Reconstructing the nation would be a difficult process full of conflict and disappointment, and that is the subject of the next chapter.

What else was happening . . .

1862	The first black troops are used in battle, at Island Mount, Missouri.
1863	Former Union nurse Louisa May Alcott (author of *Little Women*) publishes a collection of wartime letters, "Hospital Sketches."
1864	The *H. L. Hunley,* a Confederate submarine, is the first sub to sink an enemy ship. It sank the U.S.S. *Housatonic* on February 17, only to find itself sinking that same night.
1864	Photograph of Lincoln is taken that appears on today's five-dollar bill.

Reconstruction

1865–1871

Learning Outcomes

After reading this chapter, you should be able to do the following:

LO **1**   Describe the changed world of ex-slaves after the Civil War.

LO **2**   Outline the different phases of Reconstruction, beginning with Lincoln's plan and moving through presidential Reconstruction to Radical Reconstruction.

LO **3**   Explain how Reconstruction evolved at the individual states' level.

LO **4**   Evaluate and understand the relative success of Reconstruction.

Confederate soldiers returned home to a devastated South in 1865. While northern trains and cities hummed with activity, the South's farms and factories, its railroads and bridges—its entire infrastructure—had been destroyed by war. Nearly 23 percent of the South's fighting-age men had died in the war. Thousands more bore the physical scars of battle. The physical rebuilding of the region began quickly and progressed rapidly, but reconstructing southern society was a much more difficult process, especially considering the political questions about how to integrate rebel states back into the nation and the social questions about how to deal with 4 million newly freed slaves.

The North was also vastly changed, albeit in another way. Northern politicians seized the opportunity to pass many of the laws that southerners in Congress had long resisted. During and shortly after the war, Congress passed laws supporting internal improvements, outlawing slavery, and expanding the development of the Market Revolution. Indeed, some historians argue that the Civil War was crucial in turning the Market Revolution into the Industrial Revolution. Regardless of the term you use, the North after the Civil War was beginning to take the shape of what we think of today as a modern industrial society. In addition to material changes, many northerners also became skeptical of hard and fixed ideas, which, as they saw it, led to the unbending ideologies that had led to war. The result was the development of the highly practical philosophy of pragmatism, one of America's most important contributions to the world of philosophy. Furthermore, the need to understand the magnitude of the war's death toll compelled many Americans to abandon or modify their Christianity, leading to the advent of both secularism (the belief that religion should stand apart from public life) and liberal Protestantism.

But, first, to the era of **Reconstruction**, the federal government's attempts to resolve the issues resulting from the end of the Civil War, which lasted from 1865 to 1877.

LO¹ Freedmen, Freedwomen

After the Civil War, blacks found a world of new opportunities. Many freedmen and women sought the education that had been denied them during slavery. Black schools opened up in the South, for parents and for children. Family life stabilized for black families throughout the South, not only because thousands of ex-slaves

What do you think?

The post–Civil War reconstruction of the South had some significant achievements but was ultimately a failure.

Strongly Disagree   Strongly Agree
1   2   3   4   5   6   7

Reconstruction
The federal government's attempts to resolve the issues resulting from the end of the Civil War

traveled to reunite with their families, but also because the transition to freedom meant that men and women had more control over familial roles. Reflecting the priorities of nineteenth-century American society, ex-slaves often moved women from the fields in order for them to occupy a "women's sphere of domesticity." Most black women had to work for economic reasons and began work as domestics rather than as field hands. Meanwhile, freedmen often desperately sought to purchase land and continue the planting life they knew best, sometimes by simply purchasing a piece of the land on which they had labored before the Civil War. African Americans also expressed their religious independence by expanding the huge independent network of black churches that had been established since the Revolution. During the Reconstruction era, the number of black churches multiplied.

Politically, African Americans sought to vote. They marched in demand of it. They paraded to advocate for bills that came forward endorsing it. They lionized black Revolutionary heroes to establish their credentials as vote-casting Americans. And they held mock elections in order to show their capacity and desire to participate in the American political process. Freedom was an intoxicating concept indeed.

> **Freedom was an intoxicating concept indeed.**

The Freedmen's Bureau

While ex-slaves explored a life based on the free-labor vision, members of the defeated Confederacy sought to maintain as much of the old order as possible. They worked to prevent ex-slaves from acquiring economic autonomy or political rights. Although they had lost the war, ex-Confederates feared a complete disruption of the lives they had led before it.

To adjudicate these differences, in 1865, Congress established the **Freedmen's Bureau**, a government agency designed to create a new social order by government mandate. Under the management of northerner O. O. Howard (after whom Howard University is named), Congress designed the Freedman's Bureau to build and manage new schools, provide food and medical care to needy southern black and white people, and ensure equal access to the judicial system for southerners both black and white. They had some success with this Herculean task: the Freedman's Bureau built three thousand schools and expanded medical care throughout much of the South, paying particular attention to the freed slaves and the areas where they had settled.

Its task of redesigning economic relations would prove more challenging. Although Lincoln's Republicans in Congress succeeded in putting into the bureau's charter a provision that plantations be divided into 40-acre plots and sold to former slaves, that plan was

Read the congressional act establishing the Freedmen's Bureau.

{ What it meant to be free. . . }

After the Civil War, African Americans in the South demonstrated their freedom in numerous ways, large and small. Many bought dogs, some purchased firearms, and several held mass meetings without white supervision, all actions that were often denied them under slavery. Many quickly moved after the war, almost always traveling in search of lost relatives who had been sold to other plantations during the era of slavery, when slave families were secondary to profits. Many newly freed persons simply sought to be far away from the plantations on which they had been enslaved. Ex-slaves who traveled around the country demonstrated their freedom to make their own choices.

Library of Congress, Prints & Photographs Division, LC-DIG-cwpb-00468

>> "... the Secretary of War may direct such issues of provisions, clothing, and fuel, as he may deem needful for the immediate and temporary shelter and supply of destitute and suffering refugees and freedmen and their wives and children, under such rules and regulations as he may direct." –Freedman's Bureau Bill, 1865

© New York Public Library/Art Resource, NY

upended by politicians intending to enforce their own plans for reconstructing the South. Because politics were vitally important in determining how Reconstruction would unfold, it is to politics we must turn.

LO² Political Plans for Reconstruction

Lincoln's Plan for Reconstruction and His Assassination

The Ten-Percent Plan

Even before the war was over, President Lincoln had pondered what it would take to bring the South back into the nation. In 1863, he issued his **Ten-Percent Plan**, which offered amnesty to any southerner who proclaimed loyalty to the Union and support of the emancipation of slaves. When 10 percent of a state's voters in the election of 1860 had taken the oath to the United States, they could develop a new state government, which would be required to abolish slavery. Then that state could reenter the Union with full privileges, including the crucial apportionment to the House of Representatives and Senate. Although requiring just 10 percent of a population to declare loyalty seems extremely lenient toward the opposition (besides the fact that it left out any role for the ex-slaves), Lincoln was attempting to drain support from the Confederacy and shorten the war by making appeasement look easy.

Congress Bristles

Republicans in Congress, more interested in punishing the South than Lincoln was, bristled at Lincoln's leniency. In opposition to Lincoln's plan, they passed the **Wade-Davis Bill**, which would have allowed a southern state back into the Union only after 50 percent of the population had taken the loyalty oath. Furthermore, to earn the right to vote or to serve in a constitutional convention, southerners would have to take a second oath, called the **iron-clad oath**, which testified that they had never voluntarily aided or abetted the rebellion. The iron-clad oath was designed to assure that only staunch Unionists in the South could hold political power. Lincoln vetoed the bill, but the battle about Reconstruction continued.

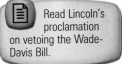

Read Lincoln's proclamation on vetoing the Wade-Davis Bill.

Lincoln's Assassination

As this battle wore on between Congress and the president, the hostilities of the American Civil War finally ended. Although the South had lost the war, a few disgruntled southerners would attempt to get revenge. Three days after Appomattox, John Wilkes Booth, a local actor and Confederate sympathizer, shot and killed Lincoln during a play at Ford's Theater in Washington, D.C. Eleven days

View a Library of Congress picture gallery about Lincoln's assassination.

Library of Congress, Prints & Photographs Division, LC-USZC4-1155

later, a Union soldier shot and killed Booth as he tried to escape from a burning barn. In the coming political showdown, Lincoln's deep empathy and political acumen would be missed, as the battle to reconstruct the nation now took place between defiant congressional Republicans and the insecure man who had stumbled into the presidency—Andrew Johnson.

Andrew Johnson and Presidential Reconstruction

President Johnson

Upon Lincoln's assassination, Andrew Johnson became president. Johnson was a native southerner, born in North Carolina and then residing in Tennessee. Throughout the war, however, Johnson proved a loyal Unionist, and he served as Tennessee's military governor after the state was taken over by the Union army. Despite Johnson's being a Democrat, in 1864, Lincoln selected Johnson as his running mate because Lincoln hoped to quiet dissent by running with a non-northerner and a non-Republican. While it may have helped him win the election, Lincoln's plan would ultimately backfire.

Presidential Reconstruction, 1865–1867

Johnson was a lonely man who had a tough time handling criticism. Since his youth, he had looked up to the South's planter aristocracy and constantly sought their approval. Reflecting these insecurities, within a month of assuming the presidency, Johnson unveiled his plan for Reconstruction: he scrapped the "40-acres-and-a-mule" plan suggested in the charter of the Freedman's Bureau and created a tough loyalty oath that many southerners could take in order to receive a pardon for their participation in the rebellion. However, Johnson added a caveat

>> The insecure man who had stumbled into the presidency—Andrew Johnson.

that Confederate leaders and wealthy planters—who were not allowed to take the standard oath—could appeal directly to Johnson for a pardon. Anyone who received amnesty through either of these measures regained their citizenship rights and retained all of their property, except for their slaves. Under Johnson's plan, a governor appointed by the president would then control each rebel state until the loyalty oath was administered to the citizens. At that point, southerners could create new state constitutions and elect their own governors, state legislatures, and federal representatives. Johnson showed no concern for the future of black people in America.

Southern states made the most of the leeway Johnson afforded them. Even Robert E. Lee applied to be pardoned (although his pardon was never granted during his lifetime). A line of southern planters literally appeared at the White House to ask Johnson's personal forgiveness; doing so allowed the southern elite to return to its former privileged status. In the end, Johnson granted amnesty to more than thirteen thousand Confederates, many of whom had been combative leaders in the Confederacy. Once Johnson had granted these pardons, he ensured that there would be no social revolution in the South.

> **Even Robert E. Lee applied to be pardoned.**

Read Johnson's Proclamation of Amnesty for the Confederate States.

Black Codes

Most of the new southern state governments returned Confederate leaders to political power. These leaders then created **black codes** modeled on the slave codes that existed before the Civil War. Although the codes legalized black marriages and allowed African Americans to hold and sell property, freed slaves were prohibited from serving on juries or testifying against white people in court. Intermarriage between black and white Americans was also strictly forbidden. Some states even had special rules that limited the economic freedoms of its black population. Mississippi, for example, barred African Americans from purchasing or renting farmland. Most states created laws that allowed police officials to round up black vagrants and hire them out as

Read the Mississippi legislature's Black Codes.

laborers to white landowners. In the end, these new laws hardened the separation of black Americans from white Americans, ending the intermingling and interaction that had been more common during slavery. With the rise of post–Civil War black codes, black and white southerners began a long process of physical separation that was not present before the war, and which would last for at least a century.

Radical Reconstruction

The Radical Republicans

Johnson did nothing to prevent the South from reimposing these conditions on the black population. In Johnson's eyes, reconstruction of the Union would be finished as soon as southern states returned to the Union without slavery. Conservative members of Congress agreed. The **Radical Republicans**, however, disagreed.

Indeed, the Republican Party had never been squarely behind Lincoln's plan for Reconstruction. In fact, Radical Republicans, known as the wing of the party most hostile to slavery, had opposed Lincoln's plans fiercely. Radicals in Congress, including Thaddeus Stevens of Pennsylvania, Charles Sumner of Massachusetts (of "Bleeding Kansas" fame), and Benjamin Wade of Ohio, had pushed for emancipation long before Lincoln issued the Emancipation Proclamation, and they considered Lincoln's lenient Reconstruction program outrageous. As they looked toward the end of the war, Radicals hoped to use the Confederacy's defeat as an opportunity to overhaul southern society. At the very least, they hoped to strip the southern planter class of its power and ensure that freed slaves would acquire basic rights.

The Radicals versus Johnson

As we have seen, Johnson, considering himself somewhat of a moderate, took office intending to wrap up the process of Reconstruction quickly. Radicals in Congress, however, continued to devise measures for protecting the interests of the newly freed black population. With no southerners yet in Congress, the Radical Republicans wielded considerable power.

Read a *Harper's Weekly* editorial about the Civil Rights Bill.

Their first move was to expand the role of the Freedmen's Bureau, creating a stronger organization with greater enforcement powers and a bigger budget. Congress also passed the important **Civil Rights Bill**, which was designed to counteract the South's new black codes. The Civil Rights Bill granted all citizens mandatory rights, regardless of racial considerations. Johnson vetoed both the second Freedmen's Bureau bill and the Civil Rights Bill, but Congress overrode the veto on the Civil Rights Bill, making it the first law ever passed over presidential veto. Their willingness to override a presidential veto suggests the importance that Radical Republicans placed on a meaningful reconstruction effort. It was the first of many vetoes the Radical Republicans would override.

The Fourteenth Amendment

Congress's success in circumventing Johnson's veto began a new phase of Reconstruction known as **Radical Reconstruction** in which Congress wielded more power than the president. Congress introduced a constitutional amendment in 1866 that would bar Confederate leaders from ever holding public office in the United States and give Congress the right to reduce the representation of any state that did not give black people the right to vote. It also declared that any person born or naturalized in the United States was, by that very act, an American citizen deserving of "equal protection of the law." This, in essence, granted full citizenship to all black people; states were prohibited from restricting the rights and privileges of any citizen.

To the frustration of Radicals like Thaddeus Stevens and Charles Sumner, the amendment, which became the Fourteenth Amendment to the U.S. Constitution, did not also protect the voting rights of African Americans. Nevertheless, Congress passed the amendment and it went to the states for ratification. Tennessee approved it and, in 1866, was invited by Congress to reenter the Union. Every other state of the former Confederacy rejected the amendment,

> Congress overrode the veto on the Civil Rights Bill, making it the first law ever passed over presidential veto.

Read the Fourteenth Amendment to the U.S. Constitution.

Radical Republicans
Wing of the Republican Party most hostile to slavery

Civil Rights Bill
Bill that granted all citizens mandatory rights, regardless of racial considerations; designed to counteract the South's new black codes

Radical Reconstruction
Phase of Reconstruction during which Radical Republicans wielded more power than the president, allowing for the passage of the Fourteenth and Fifteenth Amendments, and the Military Reconstruction Act

Military Reconstruction Act
Act that divided the former rebel states, with the exception of Tennessee, into five military districts; a military commander took control of the state governments and federal soldiers enforced the law and kept order

suggesting that the Radicals' hopes for restructuring the South would not be realized easily.

Radical Reconstruction, 1867–1877

The midterm elections of 1866, however, gave the Republicans a two-thirds majority in both houses of Congress, and they began to push their program of Reconstruction more vigorously. The election was vicious, as Johnson and his supporters went around the country on what was called the "swing around the circle" to castigate and even threaten the execution of several Radical Republicans. Despite Andrew Johnson's claim that Reconstruction was over, the Radical-led Congress easily passed (again over Johnson's veto) the **Military Reconstruction Act** in March 1867. This act divided the former rebel states, with the exception of Tennessee, into five military districts. In each district, a military commander took control of the state governments, and federal soldiers enforced the law and kept order.

Congress also made requirements for readmission to the Union more stringent. Each state was instructed to register voters and hold elections for a state constitutional convention. In enrolling voters, southern officials were required to include black people and exclude any white people who had held leadership positions in the Confederacy, although this provision proved easy to ignore. Once the conventions were organized, the delegates then needed to create constitutions that protected black voting rights and to agree to ratify the Fourteenth Amendment. Only then would Congress ratify the new state constitutions and accept southern state representatives back into the national Congress. Holding a fair state election and agreeing to the Fourteenth Amendment became the litmus tests for reentry to the nation. Without doing so and thereby becoming full-fledged members of the Union again, the southern states would remain without congressional apportionment and under military control.

Read the Military Reconstruction Act.

The Second Reconstruction Act

At first, these provisions proved to be both too harsh and too lenient. The Military Reconstruction Act so outraged southerners that they refused to enroll the voters needed to put Reconstruction into motion. But southerners also preferred military rule to civilian control by those hostile to the South. In response to these various objections (and to the South's subsequent foot-dragging), Congress passed a second Reconstruction Act, authorizing the Union military commanders to register southern voters and assemble the constitutional conventions (since the southerners were not eager to do this themselves). The southern states continued to stall, so, in the summer of 1867, Congress passed two more acts designed to force southerners to proceed with Reconstruction. President Johnson vetoed all these measures, but his vetoes were all overridden by Radical Republicans in Congress. He was helpless to stop Congress's actions.

Eventually, the southern states had no choice but to follow the Military Reconstruction Act's instructions to establish new state governments. There was nothing worse than being part of a nation and having no say in how that nation was governed. They wanted congressional representation back and, in order to get it, they had to acquiesce to Congress's demands. In June 1868, Congress readmitted representatives and senators from seven states: North Carolina, South Carolina, Georgia, Florida, Alabama, Arkansas, and Louisiana. By 1870, the remaining three southern states— Virginia, Mississippi, and Texas—had also agreed to the required provisions and they too received permission to send congressmen to Washington. As more and more Confederate states came back into the Union, the Fourteenth Amendment became the law of the land in 1868.

> There was nothing worse than being part of a nation and having no say in how that nation was governed.

Read the Second Reconstruction Act.

Frustrations

Although the Radical Republicans in Congress had considerable successes, in many important ways they did not produce the social revolution that they had envisioned: they did not redistribute land to freed slaves; they did not provide black people with guaranteed access to education; they did not forbid racial segregation; and they did not call for absolute racial equality for black and white people. The process of reconciliation meant that both sides had to give at least a little, and President Johnson's leniency at the outset of Reconstruction had caused Radicals the most consternation.

>> "The ponderous two-handed engine of impeachment, designed to be kept in cryptic darkness until some crisis of the nation's life cried out for interposition, was being dragged into open day to crush a formidable political antagonist a few months before the appointed time when the people might get rid of him altogether." –Historian David Dewitt , referring to the Radical Republicans' impeachment of Andrew Johnson

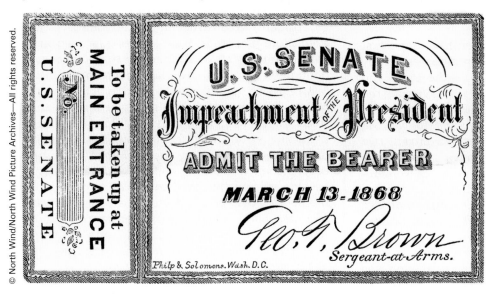

Johnson's Impeachment

The Tenure of Office Act

Still stung by Johnson's initial act of granting pardons to the southern aristocracy, Radicals were equally stymied by his constant string of vetoes. Frustrated by all this, Congress took steps in 1867 to limit the president's authority by passing the Tenure of Office Act, which required the president to obtain the consent of the Senate before removing any appointed government official from office. In essence, the law declared that Johnson could not fire anyone who had earned congressional approval, especially Republicans who had been appointed by Lincoln. Johnson of course vetoed the act, but Congress once again overrode his veto.

The Impeachment

A showdown over the new law occurred in August 1867, when Johnson wanted to remove from office Secretary of War Edwin M. Stanton. Stanton sympathized with the Radicals and had fallen out of favor with Johnson, so Johnson ordered his dismissal. The Senate, however, refused to authorize the firing. Undeterred, Johnson ordered Stanton to resign his position. When Republicans in the House of Representatives learned that Johnson had defied the Senate's Tenure of Office Act, they responded by drafting a resolution to impeach Johnson. This could be the chance they had sought to eliminate a major obstacle to Radical Reconstruction. The House made eleven charges against Johnson, stemming mostly from his refusal to heed the Tenure of Office Act, and a majority of the representatives voted in favor of putting him on trial. This made Andrew Johnson the first president in the nation's history to be impeached.

Radical Republicans in the House of Representatives (especially Thaddeus Stevens) powered the vote for impeachment, but the Constitution dictates that impeachment trials take place in the Senate and are to be judged by the Chief Justice of the U.S. Supreme Court. Moderate Republicans and Democrats in the Senate refused to join the House Radicals in condemning Johnson, and, by one vote, the Senate lacked the two-thirds majority needed to convict the president and remove him from office.

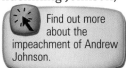

Find out more about the impeachment of Andrew Johnson.

The Fifteenth Amendment

In 1868, the Republicans nominated the war hero Ulysses S. Grant for president, hoping that Grant's tremendous popularity in the North would help them control the White House and propel their Reconstruction plans through the federal government. The Democrats nominated Horatio Seymour, the governor of New York. To the shock of the Republicans, the race between Grant and Seymour was relatively close. Although Grant obtained a majority in the Electoral College, he won the popular vote by only 300,000 ballots. Since an estimated 450,000 black people had voted for Grant, it was clear that a narrow majority of white Americans had cast their ballots for Seymour.

Recognizing the importance of their newest support base—and aware that their time in power might be limited—Republicans in Congress moved quickly to create a constitutional amendment guaranteeing the suffrage rights of black males, and the Fifteenth Amendment was ratified and adopted in 1870. It prohibited any state from denying citizens the right

Read the Fifteenth Amendment to the U.S. Constitution.

to vote on the grounds of race, color, or previous condition of servitude.

Women's Rights

Advocates for the rights of women have often first fought for the rights of racial minorities, especially black people. This was the case in the 1830s and 1840s, and again in the 1860s and 1870s. Viewing the overhauling of the U.S. Constitution as a moment ripe for extending various freedoms to women, Elizabeth Cady Stanton and Olympia Brown, two veterans of the struggle to expand women's rights, pushed for a constitutional guarantee of women's suffrage. Using new journals such as *The Agitator*, activist women also pushed for a reform of marriage laws, changes in inheritance laws, and, as always, the vote.

But they were frustrated at almost every turn. Even Republicans declared that Reconstruction was designed solely for black men. Indeed, the Fourteenth Amendment introduced the word *male* into the Constitution for the first time. Women were torn about whether or not to support the Reconstruction amendments, even if they excluded provisions for women's rights. These bitter differences led to divisions within the women's suffrage movement that would last until the 1890s.

Two other developments revolutionized the lives of American women in this period. First, the typewriter was invented in the 1860s and marketed by Eliphalet Remington and Sons beginning in 1873. The typewriter created a number of office jobs that opened up to women during these years. In the otherwise patriarchal business world of the nineteenth century, the typewriter helped make women earners in an industrializing economy. The second development was an extraordinary proliferation of women's clubs and voluntary associations. These clubs, sometimes purely social, more often to advocate a social cause, created a network of women who were interested in the dynamics of the changing American society. These clubs foreshadowed the dramatic women's involvement in politics in the Progressive Era during the first decades of the twentieth century.

LO³ Grassroots Reconstruction

With all the political jockeying within the federal government, Reconstruction at the state level was even more rancorous. Freed slaves exercised more muscle at the state level, ensuring that Republicans dominated all of the new state governments in the South. Newly freed slaves steadfastly cast their ballots for the party that had given them their freedom. To support this voter bloc, Republican politicians—from the North and the South—sought dramatic Reconstruction efforts. But at every turn they encountered strong opposition. Before long, it became evident that the process of reconstructing the South would be a process of two steps forward, one step back. And the most substantive change that could have happened—land and economic redistribution to the ex-slaves—remained perpetually frustrated.

Black Officeholders

Even with the admission of black voters, the proportion of government positions held by black Americans was still smaller than their proportion in the population. They were rarely elected to high positions, and until 1990 no black person was ever elected or nominated to serve as governor. South Carolina was the only state where a black judge served in the state supreme court and, because the state was 60 percent African American, only in South Carolina did African Americans form a plurality of the legislature. Nevertheless, more than two thousand black citizens gained political office in the Reconstruction South. Some were policemen, some were sheriffs, some were tax assessors. Their roles were important because they ensured that fairness would be enforced and that the rule of law would be upheld.

Analyze an image of the South Carolina legislature.

© Red Rocket Stock/Alamy

>> **In the otherwise patriarchal business world of the nineteenth century, the typewriter helped make women earners in an industrializing economy.**

Carpetbaggers and Scalawags

Yet white men held most of the offices in the new state governments. Some of these new officials were northern-born white men who moved south after the Confederacy's defeat. Southerners called these men **carpetbaggers** because they supposedly journeyed to the South with nothing more than what they could carry in a ratty old carpetbag. The carpetbag was meant to symbolize corruption and lowliness, as supposedly poor and pretentious northerners headed south seeking to capitalize on the region's fall from grace. Not all the so-called carpetbaggers were corrupt, of course. Many of them came to the South with a desire to improve the lot of America's black people.

Southern-born, white Republicans were given the name **scalawag**. Scalawag was originally a term used by cattle drivers to describe livestock that was too filthy for consumption, even by dogs. Although southern Democrats insisted that only the "dirtiest" citizens became scalawags, in reality, many elite men joined the Republican Party, including Confederate generals Pierre Beauregard and James Longstreet. Most of the scalawags, however, had been nonslaveholding poor white farmers who worked and lived in the hill country. Many of these scalawags believed that participating in the Republicans' plan was the fastest way to return their region to peaceful and prosperous conditions.

Southern Republican Successes

Although they faced considerable opposition from the old antebellum elite, southern Republicans managed to construct the South's first public school system, develop a system of antidiscrimination measures, strengthen the rights and privileges of agricultural workers, and begin efforts at internal improvements in the various states. Under the leadership of southern Republicans, for example, every state in the South financed a system of railroads and attempted to lure northern industries to the South. They met with mixed results, but they showed a newfound commitment to greater equality and to bringing the gains of the Market Revolution southward.

© Hulton Archive/Getty Images

>> American comedian Jack Benny in convincing costume as a carpetbagger, in the short 1949 film *Spirit of '49.*

Sharecropping

Despite the new opportunities put forward by southern Republicans, freed slaves had to struggle hard to enjoy their new liberty. There was no serious land reform and the Market and Industrial Revolutions were slow to move southward, so most black southerners had no choice but to accept work as agricultural wage laborers for white landholders, many of whom had been slaveholders before the war.

The Battle of Labor

Many of these white landowners attempted to re-create as much of the slave system as they could, closely overseeing their black workers, forcing them to work in gangs, and even trying to use the whip to maintain discipline. The freedmen, however, refused to be reduced to slavery again. They insisted on working shorter hours, and they often refused to work in gangs. To limit the amount of white surveillance, freedmen often built their own log cabins far away from the houses of their white employers. Unless they were willing to go beyond the rule of law, most white landowners could do nothing to stop them.

Sharecropping

The power struggle between southern whites and the freedmen led former slaveholders to establish and develop the **sharecropping** system. As sharecroppers, black families farmed a plot of land owned by a white person and shared the crop yield with the owner of the property. Typically, the black farmer and the white owner split the yield in half, but the owner often claimed an even larger share if he supplied the seeds or tools

carpetbagger
Northern-born white who moved south after the Confederacy's defeat

scalawag
Southern-born white Republican; many had been nonslaveholding poor farmers

sharecropping
System in which a family farmed a plot of land owned by someone else and shared the crop yield with the owner

Civil Rights Act of 1875 Act that forbade racial discrimination in all public facilities, transportation lines, places of amusement, and juries; it proved largely ineffective

Civil Rights Cases Cases in which, in 1883, the Supreme Court declared all of the provisions of the Civil Rights Act of 1875 unconstitutional, except for the prohibition of discrimination on juries

necessary for cultivating the crop or if he provided housing and food. Black farmers had earned the right to work in a familial setting, as opposed to the gang labor system of the slave era, but white landowners had managed to curtail black freedom by preventing many of them from owning property.

Despite sharecropping's prominent place in southern black history, there were more white sharecroppers in the South than black. It was a sign of the South's poverty after the war. The sharecropping system offered little hope for economic or social advancement. Sharecroppers could rarely earn enough money to buy land, and they were constantly in debt to their landlords. The landlord was always paid first when crops were sold at market, so if crop prices were lower than expected, sharecroppers were left with little or no income. Although sharecropping was not slavery, it was still a harsh and limited form of economic existence, which permeated the South after the Civil War.

LO⁴ The Collapse of Reconstruction

The reconstruction of the South had some significant achievements, including two new constitutional amendments and the passage of the nation's first civil rights law. These positive achievements could have continued to accumulate, but they did not, for two reasons: growing northern disinterest in the plight of America's southern black population and southern resistance to Reconstruction.

In the North

On the whole, the eight years of Grant's presidency (1869–1877) were not marked by great strides for African American civil rights. Instead, Grant's term became infamous for economic chicanery and corruption. The president's personal secretary was caught embezzling federal whiskey revenues in the so-called "Whiskey Ring," while Grant's own family was implicated in a plot to corner the gold market. Charges of corruption even led to a split in the Republican Party, further draining support for Reconstruction efforts. As more upstanding political leaders became preoccupied with efforts to clean up the government and institute civil service reform, securing equal rights for black people in the South ceased to be the most pressing issue. Other things seemed to matter more. And, as Reconstruction moved into the background, northerners' racism—always just under the surface—became more visible.

Despite charges of corruption, Grant was reelected to the presidency in 1872, and during his second term, only one major piece of Reconstruction legislation was passed. Even that had several key limitations. The **Civil Rights Act of 1875** forbade racial discrimination in all public facilities, transportation lines, places of amusement, and juries. Segregation in public schools, however, was not prohibited. Moreover, there was no effort whatsoever to legislate against racial discrimination by individuals or corporations, so discrimination in the workplace remained legal.

In addition to these flaws, the Civil Rights Act proved ineffective anyway. The federal government did not enforce the law vigorously, so the southern states ignored it. And in 1883, in what would come to be called the **Civil Rights Cases**, the Supreme

The sharecropping system offered little hope. . .

Court delivered a final blow to this last act of Reconstruction by declaring all of its provisions unconstitutional, except for the prohibition of discrimination on juries. In 1890, Henry Cabot Lodge, a Republican from Massachusetts, led the House of Representatives in passing a Federal Elections Bill that would have revived protection of voting rights for African Americans, but a Senate filibuster prevented the piece of legislation from becoming law. It would be nearly seven decades before another civil rights bill made its way through Congress.

The failure of the Civil Rights Act of 1875 reflected a larger northern disinterest in Reconstruction. For many northerners, support for black rights had been an outgrowth of their animosity toward the South. In 1865, such feelings burned hotly, and northerners were willing to support federal efforts to guarantee the liberties of former slaves. As the bitterness of war faded, northerners were tired of the antagonism between North and South, so their interest in civil rights faded, too.

Analyze a *Harper's Weekly* cartoon on the Civil Rights Act of 1875.

Instead, northerners became consumed with economic matters, especially after the United States entered a deep recession in 1873. The **Panic of 1873** erupted when numerous factors, including overspeculation, high postwar inflation, and disruptions from Europe, emptied the financial reserves in America's banks. Rather than honor their loans, many banks simply closed their doors, which led to a panic on Wall Street. Although Grant acted quickly to end the immediate panic, many businesses were forced to shut down. The Panic lasted four years and left 3 million Americans unemployed. In the years after 1873, Americans became concerned more with jump-starting the economy than with forging new laws to protect the needs and interests of black citizens.

The Republicans, meanwhile, took the blame for the nation's economic troubles, so, in the congressional elections of 1874, the Republicans lost 77 seats, depriving them of control of the House. The party that had spearheaded civil rights legislation in America was no longer in a position to control federal policy. Instead, the Democrats were back.

Analyze a *Harper's Weekly* cartoon on the Panic of 1873.

In the South

The decline of northern support for Reconstruction emboldened southern Democrats, who worked to reclaim political control of their region. In order to create white solidarity against Republican rule in the South, the Democrats shamelessly asserted white superiority.

Racism proved to be a powerful incentive for the Democratic Party, especially to attract poor southerners worried about their economic fortunes. Keeping black people as an underclass in southern society was important to poor white people's sense of self-worth (and economic well-being), and Democrats promised to protect the racial hierarchy as it had been before the Civil War. Democrats earned the backing of the vast majority of white southerners—mostly by playing the race card.

Intimidation of Black and Republican Voters

To control black votes, white Democrats used economic intimidation. In the nineteenth century, voting was not done by secret ballot, so it was easy to know how every individual cast his ballot. Democratic landowners fired black tenant farmers who voted Republican and publicized their names in local newspapers to prevent other landowners from hiring them. Thus the threat of starvation and poverty kept many black citizens from participating in elections and voting for the Republican Party.

More than economic intimidation, however, southern Democrats used violence in order to seize control of southern politics. A number of paramilitary groups, including the Ku Klux Klan, formed in Tennessee in 1866, used violent tactics to promote Democratic control. They harassed black and white Republicans. They disrupted Republican Party meetings. They physically blocked black southerners from casting ballots in elections. They even assassinated Republican Party leaders and organizers. Their goal was to erode the base of Republican support in the South and to ensure election victories for the Democratic Party, which promised to uphold white superiority. Prior to the presidential election of 1868, two thousand people were killed or injured in Louisiana alone. In Texas, the federal military commander said murders were so common he could not keep track of them.

Grant's Response

Although not known for its civil rights activism, the Grant administration did respond to the upsurge in

> **Panic of 1873**
> Financial crisis provoked when overspeculation, high postwar inflation, and disruptions from Europe emptied the financial reserves in America's banks; many banks simply closed their doors

southern violence by pushing two important measures through Congress—the Force Act of 1870 and the Ku Klux Klan Act of 1871. The new laws declared that interfering with the right to vote was a felony; they also authorized the federal government to use the army and suspend the writ of habeas corpus in order to end Klan violence. Grant proceeded to suspend the writ in nine South Carolina counties and arrest hundreds of suspected Klan members. These efforts crushed the Klan in 1871 (although it would resurge in the 1910s and 1920s).

The Mississippi Plan

Southern Democrats, however, did not always relent when faced with pressure from the federal government. In 1875, Democrats in Mississippi initiated a policy called the **Mississippi Plan**, which called for using as much violence as necessary to put the state back under Democratic control. Democratic

clubs began to function much as the Klan had, terrorizing Republican Party leaders and the black and white citizens who supported them. This time, the Grant administration refused to step in to stop the violence. Most northerners no longer seemed willing to support federal intervention into southern strife.

Read an official report on the success of the Mississippi Plan of 1875.

In 1876, the Mississippi Plan formally succeeded. By keeping tens of thousands of Republicans from casting ballots, the Democrats took charge of the state government. In the vocabulary of the time, Mississippi had been "redeemed" from Republican misrule. In fact, it had been tortured into submission; official reports proclaiming as much were generally ignored.

"Redeemers" Win the Presidential Election of 1876

The presidential election of 1876 put the final nail in Reconstruction's coffin. Through violence and intimidation, the Democrats had already succeeded in winning control of all the southern states except Louisiana, Florida, and South Carolina. They intended to use the Mississippi Plan to "redeem" those three states and win the presidency as well.

The presidential campaign pitted Ohio Republican Rutherford B. Hayes against New York Democrat Samuel Tilden, who had a reputation as a reformer and a fighter against political corruption. The election was a mess. Violence prevented as many as 250,000 southerners from voting for the Republican ticket, and as southern Democrats had hoped, Democratic governors triumphed in Louisiana, Florida, and South Carolina. The Democrats in those states also reported that the majority of voters favored Tilden for the presidency. Republicans were suspicious, however, and did a canvass of their own. They claimed that the Democrats had used violence to fix the results. Louisiana, Florida, and South Carolina, the Republicans argued, should have gone to Hayes. These disputed states carried enough Electoral College votes to swing the entire election one way or the other.

The Compromise of 1877

After receiving two versions of the final tallies, Congress needed help deciding

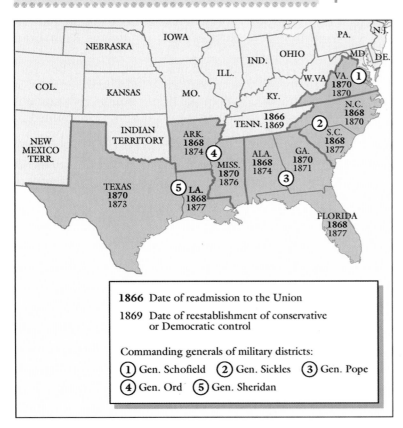

Map 16.1
Reconstruction in the South

1866 Date of readmission to the Union

1869 Date of reestablishment of conservative or Democratic control

Commanding generals of military districts:
① Gen. Schofield ② Gen. Sickles ③ Gen. Pope
④ Gen. Ord ⑤ Gen. Sheridan

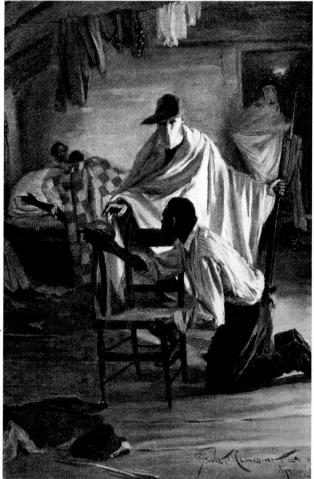

>> Before the election of 1876, two thousand people were killed or injured in Louisiana alone by the Klu Klux Klan.

© North Wind Picture Archives/Alamy

what to do. Congress created a 15-member electoral commission, with 5 members from the Senate, 5 from the House, and 5 from the Supreme Court. The commission was composed of 8 Republicans and 7 Democrats, and, by a purely partisan vote of 8 to 7, the commission gave the disputed states of Louisiana, Florida, and South Carolina to Hayes, the Republican. The Democratic Party leaders were furious but, in order to prevent further violence, Republican leaders proposed a compromise that became known as the **Compromise of 1877** (see Map 16.2).

In the compromise, Republicans promised not to dispute the Democratic gubernatorial victories in the South and to withdraw federal troops from the region. The white redeemers would be in control throughout the entire South. In return,

the Republicans asked the Democrats to accept Hayes's presidential victory and to respect the rights of its black citizens. The Democrats accepted these terms and, with that, Hayes withdrew the federal military from the South. Of course, without a federal military to protect black Americans, Reconstruction was over, and the South was left under the control of Democratic "redeemers" who used violence, intimidation, and the law to create the society they envisioned. Freed blacks lost whatever political and social gains they had achieved during the previous twelve years. This failure ensured that racial oppression would continue. In the words of one historian, Reconstruction was America's unfinished revolution, and a great chance to correct the colossal wrong that was slavery vanished.

> **Compromise of 1877** Compromise in which Republicans promised not to dispute the Democratic gubernatorial victories in the South and to withdraw federal troops from the region, if southern Democrats accepted Hayes's presidential victory and respected the rights of its black citizens

And in the end ...

Why did Reconstruction fail? So boldly stated, the question is perhaps unfair. There were some major accomplishments. Slavery was abolished. Federal laws were established that provided support for further political gains for America's black population. There have been only five black senators ever elected to the U.S. Senate, and two of them were elected during Reconstruction (Hiram Rhodes Revels and Blanche K. Bruce, both from Mississippi). About a fifth of the 101 black Americans ever to serve in the U.S. House of Representatives were elected during Reconstruction.

But there was a dramatic decline of black political participation in the South (where a large majority of black people lived) beginning in 1876 and lasting until after the Second World War. There was an even more dramatic increase in physical segregation between America's black and white populations during and after Reconstruction too. The failures are many. First, President Johnson's unwillingness to participate in a wholesale social revolution meant that land would not be redistributed in the South, signifying that, for the most part, the wealthy would remain wealthy and the poor would remain poor. The development of sharecropping as an institution further paralyzed black advancements, especially after the

> *Reconstruction was America's unfinished revolution, and a great chance to correct the colossal wrong that was slavery.*

Map 16.2
The Disputed Election of 1876

View an interactive version of this map.

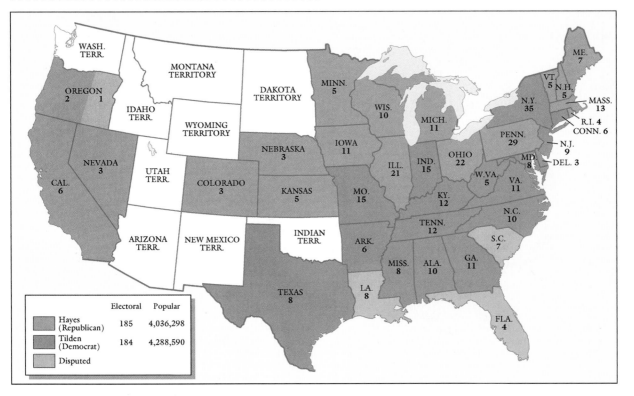

	Electoral	Popular
Hayes (Republican)	185	4,036,298
Tilden (Democrat)	184	4,288,590
Disputed		

emergence of black codes limited black Americans' abilities to protest economic injustices. The violence used by the southern "redeemers" served as an emblem of the wrongs felt by white southerners and, when northerners became more focused on the rollicking economy of the Industrial Revolution, there was no one left to monitor the henhouse. Plainly enough, most white southerners strongly opposed racial change, and after 1876, they were left in power to do as they wished.

What else was happening . . .

1865	William Bullock invents printing press that can feed paper on a continuous roll and print both sides of the paper at once.
1867	Bullock dies of gangrene after getting caught in his own invention.
1870	First New York City subway line opens.
1871	Euphemia Allen, age sixteen, composes simple piano tune "Chopsticks."
1873	Mark Twain patents the scrapbook.

To help you take your reading outside the covers of *HIST*, each new text comes with access to the exciting learning environment of a robust eBook.

Working with Your eBook

You can read HIST wherever and whenever you're online by paging through the eBook on your computer. But you can do more than just read. Your eBook also contains over 300 tested, live links to

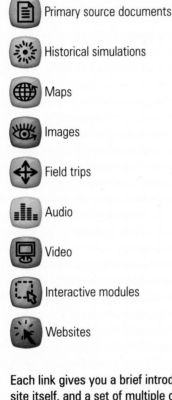

Primary source documents

Historical simulations

Maps

Images

Field trips

Audio

Video

Interactive modules

Websites

Each link gives you a brief introduction to the site, a direct connection to the site itself, and a set of multiple choice and reflection questions that you can answer online, print, and/or email to your instructor.

Your eBook also features easy page navigation, different page views, highlighting, note taking, a search engine, a print function, and a complete user's manual (under Help).

You can save your HIST user name and password for future reference **here**:

User Name: _____   Password: _____

Accessing Your eBook
Go to 4ltrpress.cengage.com/hist/ and select the book you're using.

Enter the Student area of the site, and register using the access code on the card bound into your textbook.

Click on the eBook circle.

an innovative approach to teaching and learning history

Chapter in Review

1

LO¹ Paleo-Indians
The first people to settle North America, roughly 15,000 to 10,000 years ago

Paleo-Indian era
Era beginning about 15,000 years ago and ending about 10,000 years ago, characterized by initial North American settlement

Archaic era
Era beginning about 10,000 years ago and lasting until about 2,500 years ago, characterized by increased agricultural development

sedentary existence
Life in which settlers can remain in one place cultivating agriculture, instead of pursuing herd animals

pre-Columbian era
North American era lasting from 500 BCE–1492 CE, before Columbus landed

clan system
Living arrangement in which a tribe was divided into a number of large family groups

matrilineal
Family arrangement in which children typically follow the clan of their mother; married men move into the clan of their wives; most often seen in agricultural societies

polytheistic
Belief system consisting of belief in many deities

animistic
Belief system consisting of belief that supernatural beings, or souls, inhabit all objects and govern their actions

Iroquois Confederacy
Group of northeastern tribes that joined together to form a political and trading entity and later created an elaborate political system; also known as the Haudenosaunee Confederation

Pueblo people
Southwestern conglomeration of tribes including the Apache, Navajo, Hopi, Taos, and Zunis, who lived in today's New Mexico and Arizona

wampum
Beads made of polished shell, used as currency in trading for goods

roanoke
Bracelet-like bands made of wampum

LO² Islam
Modern religion that flourished throughout the world in the fourteenth and fifteenth centuries; its adherents are called Muslims

Ghana
West African kingdom that prospered from the eighth to the thirteenth centuries; famous for its gold deposits

TIMELINE

20,000–10,000 years ago	People arrive from Asia across Bering Strait, possibly by boat
15,000–10,000 years ago	People of Paleo-Indian era develop different languages, economies, beliefs
10,000–2,500 years ago	Agriculture and sedentary existence become dominant in Archaic era
9,000 years ago	Kennewick man dies; discovery suggests several migrant waves and origins
500 BCE–1492 CE	Pre-Columbian societies develop trade, cities, social hierarchies, science
900–1150	Anasazi build multi-story "apartment houses" in Chaco Canyon
1000	Italian long-distance trade begins, empowering rich mercantilist city-states
1096–1291	European crusaders try to capture Jerusalem; return with spices and luxury goods
1100	Mississippian city of Cahokia has 20,000 inhabitants—the size of London
1225–1274	Life of Thomas Aquinas marks the height of Catholic power in Europe
1235	North African Muslims conquer trade and gold empire Ghana
1300	Timbuktu is Africa's cultural and artistic capital
1300–1500	Modern religion of Islam spreads rapidly through Africa, Middle East, Spain
1337–1453	French and English Hundred Years' War prompts new trade routes, larger kingdoms
1346	Bubonic plague kills one in three Europeans and weakens feudal order
14th–17th century	Urban wealth and expansion engender Renaissance of culture and humanism
1440s	Invention of printing press
1500	Empires of Benin and Kongo rise with Mali's demise; first Catholic conversions
1517–1648	Christian humanism and secular church practices trigger Protestant Reformation

LO¹
Explain current beliefs about how the first peoples settled North America, and discuss the ways in which they became differentiated from one another over time. The long-held belief about the settlement of North America was that Asian peoples following herds of wooly mammoths crossed a land bridge across the Bering Sea during the last Ice Age, about 12,000 years ago. Some scholars now suggest that people from Europe could have arrived much earlier, and perhaps that they came from both Europe and Asia.

During the Archaic era (10,000 to 2,500 years ago), agriculture began to develop, and some peoples settled in one place long enough to see their crops through to the harvest. From about 500 BCE to 1500 CE (the pre-Columbian era), agriculture became more complex and societies became more diverse based in large part on what area a particular people settled.

In the future United States, the variety was everywhere apparent. Northeastern tribes banded together in loose confederations but had many enemies in neighboring areas. Most tribes developed as their physical environment would permit; they fished in the Northwest, built canyon apartments in the Southwest, hunted buffalo on the High Plains, and traded with each other across wide areas.

Mali
Flourishing Islamic kingdom; it enveloped the kingdom of Ghana by the thirteenth century

Timbuktu
Principal city of the kingdom of Mali; cultural capital of Africa in the thirteenth century

Lower Guinea
Southernmost part of Mali; home to the majority of the Africans who came to America

Songhay Empire
Portion of Mali after that kingdom collapsed around 1500; this empire controlled Timbuktu

Benin
African empire on the Malian coast

Kongo
African empire on the Malian coast

LO³ **manor**
Agricultural estate operated by a lord and worked by peasants in exchange for protection and sustenance

feudalism
System of labor in which a lord granted control over a piece of land, and authority over all the land's inhabitants, to an upper-class ally, or vassal

serf
Laborer in the feudal system; protected and controlled by the vassal of the estate

mercantilism
Theory that a nation or state's prosperity was determined by the total volume of its trade

Crusades
Series of campaigns in which Europeans marched to the Middle East in an effort to take control of the Holy Land of Jerusalem, which at the time was controlled by Muslims; battles lasted from 1096 to at least 1291

Black Death
Bubonic plague, which started to spread in 1346 and eventually killed one-third of all Europeans

Hundred Years' War
War waged between France and England in the fourteenth century over who controlled the French throne

Renaissance
Intellectual and artistic reconnection to the age of Greco-Roman antiquity, starting in the fourteenth century, which lionized the individual

Catholicism
Central religious force in Western Europe; sole institution with moral authority and political power over all of medieval Europe

Christian humanism
Belief in the importance of the singular individual, as opposed to the institution of the Church; characterized by optimism, curiosity, and emphasis on naturalism

selling of indulgences
Practice of popes using their authority to limit the time a person's soul spent in purgatory, in exchange for cash

Protestant Reformation
Movement that challenged the Catholic Church to return to its unornamented origins; protesters criticized Church rituals, including the Mass, confession rites, and pilgrimages to holy sites

LO² Describe the African societies that existed at the time the first Africans were brought to the New World as slaves. Most Africans brought to the New World were from West Africa, mainly Lower Guinea. Politically, much of West Africa had known sophisticated kingdoms with powerful rulers. Their wealth was based on large gold resources and their cities, which were important trade centers. Kingdoms such as Ghana and Mali lost out to Songhay,

Benin, and Kongo only shortly before European contact began in the 1500s.

Kinship networks were vital to the maintenance of African societies. Most people here were farmers, and quite a number of these held slaves—often a result of warfare, and not in a hereditary fashion. Though Islam held sway across much of northern Africa, in the West most people clung to native religions which included elaborate ceremonies designed to honor the gods and receive their blessings. Africans who first encountered the Europeans, then, were a mixed group: experienced at farming, skilled in arts, polytheistic, often matrilineal, and experienced in trade. One would not have expected such peoples to lose out so quickly to the Europeans.

LO³ Describe Europe's experiences during the last centuries before Columbus made his first voyage to the New World in 1492. Europe during the Middle Ages was for the most part organized as a feudalistic system. Feudal lords owned large manorial holdings, and most members of the population were tied

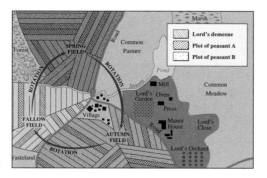

to them as serfs with hardly any freedoms. Feudalism declined only after Europe's terrible losses due to the Black Death in the mid-1300s and the Hundred Years' War which strengthened kings and weakened feudal lords. The Crusades that ended only a half century before the Black Death had made a new class of people very wealthy, and these people began to balk at feudalism as well.

Europe also experienced a Renaissance of intellectual and artistic excellence and a decline in the dominance of the Roman Catholic faith, which led to the world-changing Protestant Reformation. With people beginning to think more for themselves, becoming more wealthy and more adventurous, and gaining more knowledge about other parts of the world, the age of exploration was inevitable. England, especially, became more powerful and secure.

printing press
Invention of the 1440s using metal letter faces to print words on paper

Chapter in Review

2

LO² Line of Demarcation
Line drawn by Pope Alexander IV through a map of the Western Hemisphere. He granted the eastern half to Portugal and the western half to Spain, in what could be considered the first act of modern European colonialism

conquistador
One of the Spanish noblemen who sailed to the New World with small armies to vanquish kingdoms there

encomienda
Tribute, usually payable in gold or slaves, demanded of conquered Indian villages by the conquistadors

viceroy
Representative of the Spanish crown who governed conquered Indian villages

price revolution
Inflationary event, such as the huge influx of silver to Spain in the mid-1500s, that causes the price of goods to surpass the wages paid to laborers and landless agricultural workers

Columbian Exchange
Biological crossover of agricultural products, domesticated animals, and microbial diseases from Europe to the New World and vice versa

plantation
Large farm staffed by an entire family in an agricultural economy

lost colony of Roanoke
Second settlement by English colonists at Roanoke; deserted sometime before 1590

joint stock company
Company that sold stock to numerous investors in order to raise large sums of money

LO³ Jamestown
English settlement of 1607 in present-day Virginia

starving time
Winter of 1609–1610 in Jamestown, when food supplies were so scarce that at least one colonist resorted to cannibalism

Powhatan Confederacy
Group of six Algonquian villages in present-day Virginia, named after its leader

cash crop
Agricultural product grown primarily for sale. Examples include sugar and tobacco harvests.

TIMELINE

ca. 1000	Scandinavian expeditions to North America
1440s	Portuguese begin trade with Africa
1492	First Spanish voyage of discovery: Christopher Columbus
1493	Pope Alexander VI draws Line of Demarcation
1497	Englishman John Cabot lands in Canada
1498	Vasco da Gama reaches India via Cape of Good Hope
1512	First permanent Spanish settlements in New World
1519–1521	Cortés conquers Mexico
1519–1522	Magellan completes first circumnavigation of world
1532	Pizarro overthrows Incas in Peru
1565	Spanish seize St. Augustine from French
1585	First Roanoke settlement
1607	Jamestown founded by Virginia Company of London
1608	Quebec founded as French trading post
1620	Settlement of Plymouth
1629	Massachusetts becomes royal colony
1632	Founding of Maryland
1630s	Pequot War in New England
1644	Rhode Island receives preliminary charter as independent colony

LO¹
Explain the reasons for Europeans' exploring lands outside Europe, and trace the routes they followed. The Portuguese and other Europeans sought to explore lands outside Europe for two principal reasons: to alleviate a trade deficit (and therefore increase wealth) and to spread the gospel of Christianity.

The search for riches and for lands not already in the hands of Christians drew European explorers to several locations around the globe, many of which they encountered quite accidentally. Portuguese sailors traveled down the western coast of Africa searching for the dramatic left turn that would lead them to India and the Middle East. With Portugal's success, Spanish sailors began advocating the search for a western route to the Orient. Previously, around the year 1000 C.E., Scandinavian explorers had sailed to Greenland and possibly as far south as Cape Cod, Massachusetts.

LO²
Describe the founding of European nations' first colonies in the New World. Two decades after Columbus first crossed the Atlantic, the Spanish established permanent settlements in Hispaniola, Cuba, Puerto Rico, Jamaica, and Panama. In the early sixteenth century, Spanish conquistadors led private armies to the New World—Hernán Cortés to Mexico, Francisco Pizarro to Peru, and others to Florida and the American Southwest.

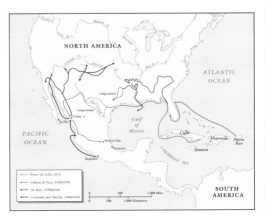

indentured servitude
System of labor whereby Virginia farmers paid the Atlantic passage for English and Irish workers in exchange for four to seven years of their work on farms or plantations

head right
50 acres of land granted by the Virginia Company to any individual who paid his or her own passage across the Atlantic. This put more property in private hands.

"seasoning"
Period of several years during which indentured servants were exposed to the New World's microbes. Many did not survive.

royal colony
English settlement whose governor was chosen by the King

House of Burgesses
Assembly of landholders chosen by other landholders, with which the royal governors were forced to work

proprietary colony
Colony overseen by a proprietor who was allowed to control and distribute the land as he wished

Toleration Act of 1649
Act granting freedom of worship to anyone who accepted the divinity of Jesus Christ. This meant that neither Catholics nor Protestants could be imprisoned for their faith.

LO4 Puritans
Group of believers who wished to reform or purify the Church of England by removing its hierarchy, its emphasis on work as payment to God, its allowance of prayers for communal salvation, and its promotion of missions

Separatists
Group of believers who wished to separate completely from the Church of England because they believed it was irrevocably corrupted

Mayflower
Ship containing Separatists who sailed from Holland and landed in Plymouth, in present-day Massachusetts, in 1620

Mayflower Compact
An agreement that bound each member of the Separatist group in Plymouth to obey majority rule and to promise to defend one another from potential eviction. This agreement set a precedent for democratic rule in Massachusetts.

Antinomianism
Theological philosophy stressing that only God, not ministers, determined who merited grace. Instead of a single orthodox scripture, this belief suggests that humankind's relationship with God was a continual process of divine revelation. Anne Hutchinson led a group of Antinomian dissenters and was banished from Massachusetts for these beliefs.

Pequot War
Bloody battles of the 1630s between New England colonists and the Pequot tribe of Indians

The French established several encampments in present-day Canada that served as French trading posts in the New World. The largest was Quebec.

Sir Walter Raleigh was the first Englishman to found a New World colony—Roanoke in 1585.

LO3 Trace the expansion of England's holdings in the southern colonies. Between 1600 and 1660, more than 150,000 English people left for the New World. Most went to the West Indies, but perhaps slightly less than a third crossed the Atlantic to settle the eastern coast of North America.

Begun by the Virginia Company of London (a joint stock company), Jamestown was founded in 1607. In the early 1610s, the English settlers there successfully cultivated tobacco. Following Virginia's success, in 1632 the king of England granted the region that we now call Maryland to George Calvert.

LO4 Outline the reasons for and timing of England's founding of colonies in New England. Despite the harsh reality of life in the colonies, the promise of wealth and religious freedom fueled England's desire for more colonies.

A group of Separatists departed from England, went to Holland, then, after receiving a land grant from the Virginia Company of London, sailed on the ship *Mayflower* in 1620, destined for Virginia. They were blown off course, landing in present-day Massachusetts, founding a town they called Plymouth. In 1629, Massachusetts was formalized as a royal colony under the name of the Massachusetts Bay Company.

Two groups of Massachusetts dissenters, led by Roger Williams and Anne Hutchinson, settled in Rhode Island. A preliminary charter founding Rhode Island as a colony independent of Massachusetts was granted in 1644. It was followed by another in 1663 that granted political and religious freedoms to the settlers. Puritan dissenters continued to expand outward from Massachusetts, and by the 1630s they had founded towns in what are now Connecticut, Maine, and New Hampshire.

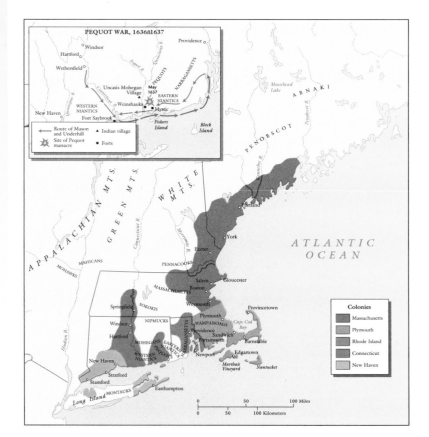

Chapter in Review

3

LO¹ commonwealth
A kingless republican government

Restoration
Period of English history when the Stuarts were restored to the throne (1660–1685)

Navigation Acts
Regulations that dictated where colonial producers could ship their goods, stipulated that colonists must transport their goods in English ships, and listed a group of products that colonists were permitted to sell only to England

enumerated articles
Goods (tobacco, sugar, cotton, indigo) listed in the Navigation Acts that colonists were permitted to sell only to England

proprietary colonies
Colonies owned and ruled by an individual or a private corporation, rather than by the Crown

Quakers
Protestants who believe that God's will was directly transmitted to people through "the inner light" of divine knowledge that a person possesses within his or her being; this belief was in direct opposition to the Bible-centered Protestant mainstream

Pueblo Revolt
An uprising of several villages spanning several hundred miles across the New Mexican landscape in 1680, led by the shaman Popé

LO² Beaver Wars
Bloody intertribal battles over beaver pelts between the Iroquois and the Hurons (1640–1680s)

Metacom's War
First large-scale conflict between colonists and Native Americans, waged in Plymouth, Massachusetts Bay, Rhode Island and Connecticut (1675–1676)

King Philip's War
British colonists' name for Metacom's War, because they referred to Wampanoag leader Metacom as King Philip

Bacon's Rebellion
Revolt among colonists, led by Nathaniel Bacon, triggered by Virginia governor Sir William Berkeley's unwillingness to listen to the demands of the laboring people, who wanted to attack several nearby Indian tribes (1676–1677)

Bacon's Laws
Series of laws that democratized the politics of Virginia, granted the franchise to all freemen, inaugurated elections of the members of the legislature, and granted greater representation in taxation

slave codes
Laws meant to govern the slave system of labor; these laws made it impossible for an African American to live as a free person

TIMELINE

1640–1680s	In Beaver Wars over French fur trade, Iroquois Confederacy defeats Hurons
1649	Oliver Cromwell's execution of King Charles I prompts English civil war
1651	Parliament passes first of colonial trade regulations known as Navigation Acts
1660–1685	Charles II's return to his father's throne signals a new era of royal Restoration
1662–1690s	Colonial assemblies make slavery matrilineal, prohibit miscegenation, separate slaves from servants by race
1664	Charles II invades Dutch colony New Amsterdam, grants it to brother, Duke of York
1674	Penn and Quakers purchase West Jersey
1675–1676	Wampanoags lead pan-Indian fight against Puritan encroachment in Metacom's War
1676–1677	English freemen fight colonial nobility over Indian and land policies in Bacon's Rebellion
1680	Pueblo Revolt expels and kills Spanish Catholic friars
1681	William Penn exchanges father's royal debt claim for colony that offers religious freedom
1689–1697	French-English rivalries reach colonies and Indian allies in King William's War
1693	Rice cultivation expands rapidly in the Carolinas
1698	Rapid growth of southern slave plantations prompts Carolina's split
1701–1713	Europeans fight over French claim to Spanish succession, leaving English victorious in Queen Anne's War
1705	Virginia slave code ties slavery to African origin
1720	African slaves make up two-thirds of South Carolina's population
1726	East and West Jersey unite as New Jersey
1733	James Oglethorpe leads settlers to Georgia to create haven for "worthy poor"
1750	Non-native population in colonial America reaches 1 million

LO¹
Describe the changes in European development of North America during the period from 1660 to 1700, and analyze the four distinct areas that began to emerge. Civil war at home, the Restoration, and a rising debt led the English to alter their treatment of the colonies as well as to develop several more. The new colonies began as proprietary colonies (Carolina, New York, Pennsylvania, the Jerseys, and Georgia). These colonies contained greater diversity than the ones first established, and the distinct environment there encouraged the growth of a slave system. The Spanish tried to preserve their territories in the Southwest, despite two strong uprisings of the Native Americans. By 1700, then, the situation in North America remained fairly fluid and unstable, and the British appeared to have the upper hand over the Spanish.

LO²
Discuss the English colonists' experiences up to 1700 with Native American tribes. Despite some friendly relations between Native Americans and colonists

LO³ King William's War
Battles between the Iroquois, French, and English colonists (1689–1697)

Queen Anne's War
The New World name for the War of the Spanish Succession; twelve years of battle between the Spanish in Florida, the French in the North American interior, the English along the coast, and various Indian tribes

in the early years of settlement, it soon became apparent that the two groups were destined to be enemies more often than not. With increasing settlement, the native tribes were forced from their traditional lands, and several wars (most notably Metacom's War and Bacon's Rebellion) contributed to the problems rather than easing them.

LO³ Discuss the English colonists' experiences up to 1700 with African slaves. When Europeans began to grow more sugar cane in the Caribbean and in South America, they killed off much of the native populations, through either hard work or death from new diseases they brought with them. They then turned to

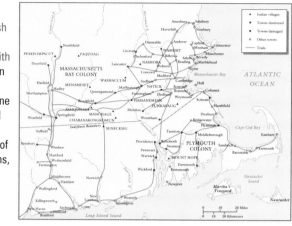

Africa for slaves. The English colonies at first relied on labor from indentured servants, and even some Africans were treated as such at first. Over time, Europeans ceased to indenture themselves, and when Africans were needed in larger numbers, the colonists began to enact slave codes to ensure that they would have the necessary labor supply. It was only then that laws began to forbid mixed marriages and to declare slavery hereditary.

LO⁴ Discuss the European wars that had an impact on North America.
Because both the French and the English had a strong presence in North America (the French for fur trading and the English for settlement), it was to be expected that their conflicts in Europe would bleed over into America. One of these was King William's War, during which the governor of New York instigated warfare between the native groups who supported the two countries. At the end, the Iroquois established closer ties with the French, whom they had first attacked. The second conflict, Queen Anne's War, brought a respite to the conflicts in Europe, at least for a while, and English colonists seized the opportunity to move into the frontier areas and to take control of Hudson Bay.

Chapter in Review

4

LO 1 **diversified farming**
System in which a single home could farm various crops to sustain the household throughout the year

Triangular Trade
Pattern of trade in which fish, grains, spices, sugar, ships, slaves, and gold were traded between the New England colonies, England, southern Europe, the West Indies and Africa

halfway covenants
Processes by which baptized individuals who had never had a personal conversion to Christ were counted as partial members of a Protestant church and were allowed to have their children baptized

jeremiad
A long speech or literaty work emphasizing society's fall from purity and grace to its current depraved state

LO 2 **Enlightenment**
A movement to prioritize the human capacity for reason as the highest form of human attainment

Great Awakening
America's first large-scale religious revival, originated by preachers who stressed that all were equal in Christ

Old Lights
Protestant leaders who condemned emotionalism and favored a more rationalistic theology favored by elements of the Enlightenment

New Lights
Protestant leaders who supported evangelism, the new methods of prayer, and equality before Christ

LO 3 **Atlantic slave trade**
Huge system of trade and migration that brought millions of slaves to the New World and Europe in the 1600s and 1700s

middle passage
Perilous journey across the Atlantic endured by captives from Africa

Stono Rebellion
Slave rebellion in South Carolina in 1739; this was the largest slave uprising of the century

Negro Act
South Carolina state law which consolidated all of the separate slave codes into a single code that forbade slaves from growing their own food, assembling in groups, or learning to read

TIMELINE

1688	Protestants replace James II with William and Mary in Glorious Revolution
1696	The Salem witchcraft trials signal demise of Puritans' religious utopia
1720	Slaves make up 20 percent of Chesapeake population
1734	*New York Weekly Journal* editor J. Peter Zenger is punished for government criticism
1738–1745	In Great Awakening, itinerant preachers such as George Whitefield promote emotional Protestantism
1739	South Carolina whites quell slaves' Stono Rebellion and in turn pass Negro Act
1740	Fearful of slave insurrection, New York City convicts, burns, and hangs 35 suspects
1744–1748	France and Britain continue imperial rivalries in King George's War
1754–1763	The French and Indian War over trade in American interior escalates worldwide
1754	At Albany Congress colonists for the first time discuss common concerns with war
1760	Slaves make up 40 percent of Chesapeake population
1763	Treaty of Paris evicts France from America, draws Proclamation Line, sets borders with Spanish Empire
1763	Brutal pan-Indian Pontiac Rebellion against growing British colonial empire fails

LO 1 Describe the development of the English colonies during the 1700s, including a discussion of each group of colonies: New England, the Middle Colonies, the Chesapeake, and the Southern Colonies. By the beginning of the 1700s, clear differences among the English colonies had become apparent. As the colonies matured, developing local governments of their own, England found them more and more difficult to control.

The New England colonies had long relied on farming for survival, but by the early 1700s fishing and lumber industries led them into trade with other countries. As the population multiplied, a class system emerged and the importance of religion began to recede.

Colonists in the Middle Colonies enjoyed a warmer environment and established individual, mostly self-sufficient farmsteads. The main industries developed around corn and wheat.

Tobacco became the main crop in the Chesapeake. The Chesapeake had few cities, with tobacco farms fairly self-sufficient. A small group of aristocratic families controlled social, political, and religious institutions. Many poor whites eked out a living, and slaves comprised about 40 percent of the population.

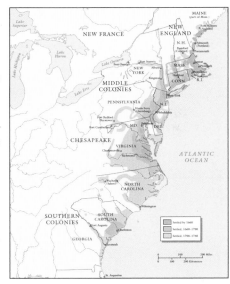

The Southern Colonies had little industry, and the main crops were rice, indigo, and tobacco. The environment was so poor that few English colonists chose to live there. Those who did owned large plantations but lived in cities for comfort.

LO2 Discuss the impact of the Enlightenment and the Great Awakening on colonial society in America. European Enlightenment thinkers contributed greatly to an American Enlightenment based on the concept that mankind had "natural rights" that no government could deny.

A truly American phenomenon was the Great Awakening, a religious revival that personalized religion for people who had once accepted the idea of deferring to church authorities without question. Religion in America took on an individualistic nature.

LO3 Chronicle the development of slavery in the American colonies, and analyze the reasons for changes in attitudes and in the legal system that helped the distinctively American slave system to flourish. Although the Atlantic slave trade took many more Africans to other parts of the Americas, it was in the American colonies, especially the Southern Colonies, that slavery became so entrenched. The journey to the West, known as the "middle passage," lasted up to two months, a time during which many Africans died. Those who survived were sold in slave auctions. Slavery, though legal in all colonies, was most prevalent in the Chesapeake and the Southern Colonies.

Slaves might serve their masters in many ways; in all colonies they were used as domestic servants and field hands. Slave life on the plantations in the Chesapeake and the South made it possible for Africans to retain some aspects of their native culture, but white slave owners soon saw the need to place heavy restrictions on the slaves.

LO4 By 1763, American colonists had become used to making their own decisions and taking care of their own needs. Describe the events in England that contributed to this situation, and explain their effects on the colonists. Religious differences in England, especially among the various monarchs who ruled the country during most of the 1600s, eventually led to the execution of a king, the proclamation of a republic, several years without a monarch, and finally the return of monarchy in 1688 during the Glorious Revolution. During those years, Parliament and the rest of England were caught up in events at home and left the colonists pretty much to their own devices. This period of "salutary neglect" came to an end after 1763.

Several European wars between the French and the English bled over into America. Then a conflict actually began in America, as the English colonists battled the French for control of the Ohio Valley. The Seven Years' War, or French and Indian War, as it was known in America, eventually involved several major countries in Europe and numerous Indian tribes in America. England won the war, but the victory took its toll on British finances. People in the colonies realized that they had begun to develop a degree of unity among themselves that they no longer felt with the Mother Country.

Chapter in Review

LO¹ Privy Council
A group of advisors to the Crown

Sugar Act of 1764
Act which reduced taxes on molasses and sugar, laid taxes on indigo, pimento (allspice), some wines, and coffee, and increased enforcement of tax collection; this Act signaled the end of the era of salutary neglect

Quartering Act of 1765
This act required the colonies to feed and house British troops stationed in their territory

Stamp Act
Passed in 1765, this act mandated the use of stamped (embedded) paper for all official papers, including diplomas, marriage licenses, wills, newspapers, and playing cards

LO² circular letter
Communication among a number of interested parties which was sent from colony to colony in order to keep the disparate colonies together, or united; a primary form of communication for the colonies during the revolutionary period

Stamp Act Congress
Gathering of colonial leaders from nine states in New York City in October 1765 to discuss resistance to the Stamp Act; one of the early instances of collaboration between colonies and of identifying Parliament as the opposition rather than the king

Sons of Liberty
Groups of colonial leaders who organized protests and intimidated stamp officials; their actions caused the resignation of all known stamp officials

Radical Whigs
Political activists and pamphleteers who coined the phrase "no taxation without representation"

external taxes
Duties designed to protect the British empire, part of Parliament's right to regulate trade, as argued by Benjamin Franklin and Daniel Dulany

internal tax
Duties that directly affected the internal affairs of the colonies; according to Benjamin Franklin and Daniel Dulany, this internal legislation threatened private property

virtual representation
Theory endorsed by Parliament that said the House of Commons represented the interests of all the king's subjects, wherever they might reside; this was the pretext for rejecting the colonists' demand for actual representation

deputy representation
The practice of the people's interests being advocated by a deputy; also known as actual representation

TIMELINE

1751 Writs of Assistance allow British search and seizure in private homes
1760 Privy Council issues "Orders of Council" to rein in smugglers and absentee officials
1763 Proclamation Line tries to stop western land sales and settlement, makes Indians royal subjects
1764 Sugar Act cuts taxes and increases enforcements
1765 Quartering Act requires colonists to house and feed British troops
Stamp Act stirs powerful opposition against direct taxation of official paper
1766 Declaratory Act asserts Parliament's right to legislate colonies
Restraining Act suspends New York Assembly for violating Quartering Act
1767 New external duties in Townshend Act stir boycotts, revolutionary ideology
1770 In Boston Massacre, British soldiers shoot into rowdy crowd, killing five
1773 Tea Act cuts duties but establishes monopoly for East India Company
Colonists in Indian disguise board ship to destroy tea cargo in Boston Tea Party
1774 Coercive Acts close Boston harbor and Massachusetts government, tightening
Quartering Acts to protect British officials from colonial courts
Parliament grants Quebec jurisdiction over land west of Proclamation Line
1st Continental Congress signals colonial unified resistance, not submission
1775 In Concord and Lexington, Minutemen engage redcoats in guerrilla tactics
2nd Continental Congress creates Continental Army under Washington
Battle of Bunker Hill triggers colonists' solidarity and British resolve

LO¹
What were Britain's main reasons for attempting to change its management of the American colonies during the mid-1700s? For years Britain had been engaged in wars for empire with the country of France, and such wars gave colonists the opportunity to make more and more of their own decisions. During and after the Seven Years' War, however, England's Privy Council made several decisions that would anger many in the colonies. One dealt with smuggling: Crews who seized smuggling vessels would be rewarded, and smugglers would be punished for trying to avoid taxes.

To the American colonists, this seemed an order aimed directly at them. Adding insult to injury, the end of the war brought the Proclamation of 1763. There was to be no settlement west of the Appalachian Mountains (where settlers had already built up some holdings); no more western lands would be sold by the government; and Indian trade would be under the oversight of the British government. One of the most outrageous changes, in the minds of the colonists, was England's decision to raise revenue in the colonies to pay for the just-ended war. The Sugar Act (1764), the Quartering Act of 1765, and the Stamp Act (1765) angered the colonists. The question remained: What would the colonists do in response?

LO²
Explain how the colonists responded to the new acts, and trace the evolutionary process that brought the colonies closer to true rebellion. The Sugar Act angered colonists illegally trading in rum, but the Stamp Act affected virtually everyone. The Stamp Act Congress was created to deal with this issue, but the colonists continued to unify. They protested the Stamp Act in several ways, with some success. Some appealed directly to Parliament but were ignored. Boycotts against British goods were effective to the point of shutting down the port of New York. Newspaper editorials fanned the flames of discontent and helped spread the protests. Coordinated rioting, led by the Sons of Liberty, was so successful that stamp officials resigned even before the act went into effect.

Phrases such as "external taxes," "internal taxes," "taxation without representation," and "virtual representation" became commonplace in American cities, as people debated the merits of protest. Without support from the king, Parliament repealed the Stamp Act, and the protesters claimed a victory against the crown. People supporting the crown became targets of the mobs, and a growing gap between the two groups signaled rough times ahead. So did the Declaratory Act, wherein Parliament reasserted its right to legislate for the colonies "in all cases whatsoever." Despite these warning signs, the colonists believed they had pulled off a great feat.

Declaratory Act
Passed by Parliament in 1766, this act affirmed its authority to legislate for the colonies "in all cases whatsoever"; largely symbolic, this Act became one of the nonnegotiable claims that Parliament was unwilling to relinquish throughout the struggle

 Restraining Act
In this act, chancellor of the Exchequer Charles Townshend suspended the New York Assembly for failing to comply with the Quartering Act

Townshend Acts
These acts of 1767 instituted duties on glass, lead for paint, tea, paper, and a handful of other items

Boston Massacre
Incendiary riot on March 5, 1770 when British soldiers fired into a crowd and killed five people

***Gaspée* incident**
Conflict that occurred when colonists from Providence boarded and burned the English naval vessel *Gaspée*

committees of correspondence
Organized groups of letter writers

Tea Act
Passed in 1773, this Act was designed to give the East India Company a monopoly on the sale of tea to North America

Boston Tea Party
Protest staged December 16, 1773, when an organized squad of roughly sixty colonists dressed as Mohawk Indians boarded Hutchinson's ship and dumped 342 chests of tea into Boston Harbor

Coercive Acts
Four separate acts, passed in 1774; meant to punish Massachusetts for the Tea Party. The four Acts were: the Boston Port Act, the Massachusetts Government Act, the Administration of Justice Act, and the Quartering Act

Intolerable Acts
Colonists' collective label for the Quebec Act and the Coercive Acts

First Continental Congress
Meeting of twelve colonies at Philadelphia in May 1774 to consider the American response to the Coercive Acts

Continental Association
Group which supervised a boycott of British trade; the association was prefaced with a "Declaration of Rights," which affirmed the natural rights of "life, liberty, and property"

Minutemen
Nickname for American militia soldiers, due to their reputation for being ready on a minute's notice

 Second Continental Congress
Gathering of colonial leaders in May 1775 to determine the colonies' response to the battles of Lexington and Concord; they passed resolutions supporting war, which included a sharp rejection of all authority under the king in America

Olive Branch Petition
Declaration to King George III that the colonists were still loyal to him and imploring the king to seek a peaceful resolution to the conflict

LO3 Trace the path to revolution in America from the Townshend Acts of 1767 to the meeting of the First Continental Congress. In 1767 a new Chancellor of the Exchequer took office in England. Charles Townshend soon showed that the colonists' problems with the English government were far from over. The broad-based Townshend Acts set out to change almost everything about how taxes were raised in the colonies. At first colonists tried the same tactics that had worked with the Stamp Act. The worst confrontation, known as the Boston Massacre, resulted in several deaths among the rioters. Ironically, on that day Parliament was in the midst of repealing most of the Townshend Acts, thus postponing the inevitable day of reckoning. As tensions escalated, colonists urged more people to join them. Committees of correspondence came together to ensure that current news traveled quickly throughout the colonies.

Colonists who began to choose sides knew they were making a monumental decision. Those remaining loyal to the crown were most often wealthy urban residents and those with the most to lose in the Southern Colonies and the Chesapeake.

Two new edicts from Parliament brought matters to a head. The Tea Act passed in 1773 lowered the tax on tea, so as to give the East India Company a monopoly, and the colonists were angered by the manipulation. The result was the Boston Tea Party, which in turn led to the Coercive Acts in 1774. Parliament intended to get the colonies in line: they closed the port of Boston; ordered the colonists to house and feed British troops; removed most of Massachusetts's rights to self-government, etc. Instead of breaking the will of the colonists, however, these maneuvers did the opposite; representatives of twelve colonies met in Philadelphia as the First Continental Congress, where they agreed on another boycott of English goods.

LO4 Explain how the American Revolution began, and describe the first battles of the conflict. Upset with their English government and fearful about what might come next, the protesting colonists began to make military preparations. Britain responded by requesting 20,000 additional troops. In April 1775, General Gage sent his troops to Concord to capture stores of weapons held there by the colonists, but word spread of the troop movements. Colonial volunteers known as "Minutemen" responded, and on their second attempt they drove the Redcoats back to Boston in disarray. To decide what to do next, colonists convened the Second Continental Congress, where they created an army, named George Washington commander, and voted to try to make peace with George III. The Congress stopped just short of declaring war, but the king declared them in rebellion.

After several minor skirmishes, the first major conflict took place at Boston's Bunker Hill (actually Breed's Hill). Though forced from their hilltop position, the colonists inflicted heavy casualties on the British and claimed a victory. Now Parliament declared a state of open rebellion and began a blockade of American ports designed to cripple the colonies into submission.

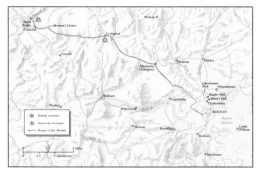

Battle of Bunker Hill
Outbreak of fighting on June 17, 1775, near Boston Harbor; the first all-out battle of the Revolutionary War

American Prohibitory Act
This Act declared the colonies to be "in open rebellion," forbade commerce with the colonies by blockading their ports, and made colonial ships and their cargo subject to seizure as if they were the property "of open enemies"

Chapter in Review

LO 1 Republicanism

The theory that government should be based on the consent of the governed and that the governed had a duty to ensure that their government did not infringe on individual rights

Cato's Letters

Book that spread Republican ideas throughout the colonies; written by English authors John Trenchard and Thomas Gordon

Common Sense

Influential political pamphlet written by Thomas Paine, published in January 1776, containing a simple wording of republican ideals

LO 2 bills of credit

Currency printed by the Continental Congress

Battle of Saratoga

Battle in New York state in 1777 between the Continental Army and General Burgoyne's British army troops; Burgoyne surrendered

LO 3 manumit

To willingly free one's slaves

Virginia Statute of Religious Freedom

Bill drafted by Thomas Jefferson in 1776 articulating distrust of an established state church and the value of religious liberty

TIMELINE

Aug. 1775	King George III denounces colonists as rebels
Nov. 1775	Dunmore promises slaves freedom for fighting alongside British
January 1776	Thomas Paine's pamphlet *Common Sense* calls for independence
March 1776	Continental Army forces British to evacuate Boston, ending 11-month siege
June 7, 1776	Committee for Declaration of Independence forms, with Jefferson as draftsman
June 28, 1776	Continental Congress debates and edits Declaration of Independence
July 2, 1776	Continental Congress unanimously approves Declaration of Independence
Aug.–Dec. 1776	Continental Army escapes British in New York
Dec. 26, 1776	General Washington defeats British with surprise move in Trenton, NJ
Sept. 19, 1777	Patriot victory at Battle of Saratoga leads to Franco-American Alliance
Sept. 26, 1777	Under General Howe, British take the new capital of Philadelphia
1778	Franco-American Alliance against British expands the war to the Atlantic
1779	Under Cornwallis, British land in South Carolina and advance quickly
1780	To weaken British, patriots draw fighting deeper into South Carolina
1781	Cornwallis gives up South Carolina and awaits reinforcements in Virginia
Oct. 19, 1781	American and French forces trap Cornwallis army on Yorktown peninsula
1782	John Jay, Benjamin Franklin, John Adams travel to Paris for peace talks
Sept. 1783	Treaty of Paris grants American independence and rights to the West
1785	Revolution inspires formation of freedom churches such as the Unitarians
1790	All states but South Carolina and Georgia outlaw slave import from abroad

LO 1

Describe the long-term causes and more immediate events that led the colonists into a true revolution against Britain. From the mid-1600s, the British colonists in America had forged a society very different from the one they had left behind in England. Class differences were less important in the colonies, and there was a greater sense of community. Thus, when Britain passed the various acts that so upset the colonists, it wasn't just the wealthy who were upset, and free men and women from all walks of life drew together to oppose what they saw as unfair treatment. In addition, each colony had established a separate government of one kind or another, and it became clear to the colonists that they were completely capable of governing themselves.

As the disagreements with Britain escalated, more colonists began to talk of complete separation—at the same time that the government in Britain became more determined not to give in to colonial demands, but rather to clamp down on the rebellion. As the Continental Army clashed with British redcoats more frequently, King George grew more angry with the colonists. In time, it became clear that the split between the two had become too wide to repair.

LO 2

Discuss the various phases of the American Revolution, and analyze the circumstances that eventually helped the colonists win a conflict that Britain, by rights, should never have lost. At the outset of hostilities between the colonial revolutionaries and Britain, most analyses would have predicted that Britain would prevail, due to the strength of its military and the relative weakness and inexperience of the colonial forces. The Continental Army was operating on a shoestring, as it would throughout the conflict. Washington's troops were notoriously ill equipped, while the British troops were well equipped, well clothed, and well fed.

Accordingly, the first phase of the war brought successes to the British, who hoped to deflect the colonial forces in the north without having to broaden the conflict to include all of the colonies. After some initial British successes, however, Washington pulled off a victory at Trenton, New Jersey, at the end of 1776. Less than a year later, the Continental Army won a crucial victory at Saratoga that brought the French into the war on the American side.

Hoping to enlist Loyalists to their cause, as well as hold onto the South and its rich natural resources, the British moved the war southward, and most of the remaining fighting took place there. Once pushed, however, many Loyalists joined the American cause. In addition, guerrilla tactics began to take a toll on British forces. Back at home, the English people grew restless over taxes to pay for a war far from home that few of them felt strongly about. The truth was that most people in England wouldn't have cared which side won, as long as the war ended. The Americans, on the other hand, only grew more determined.

LO3 Assess the significance of the American Revolution to the following groups: colonists, slaves, native populations, and women. The experience of joining together in the course of liberty contributed greatly to the sense of American nationalism that grew out of the rebellion, and moving forward to establish a government that would protect their liberties and broaden democracy fed the patriotic nationalism that would become one of the most unique outcomes of the war.

For slaves in the North, the war brought tremendous change, and the polarization between North and South over the slavery issue began in earnest. Some northern states outlawed slavery almost immediately, and by 1840 only one thousand Africans in the North remained slaves. Most states, north and south, banned the importation of slaves, but southerners clung to their right to own slaves, even after their recent fight for their own independence.

The situation for the Native American tribes worsened after the war. Both the Americans and the British recruited Indian tribes, and frequently this pitted one group against the other. When the Americans won, they exacted revenge on several of the tribes that had sided with the British. Americans also felt free to venture onto the frontier, and it was soon clear that there would be many conflicts as time went on.

It is safe to say that the American Revolution would not have been won without the direct aid and support of women; though officially they did no fighting, they upheld boycotts, raised war funds, and did everything in their power to help with the war. Afterward, a few states "rewarded" them with suffrage, but in most states, women returned to their traditional domestic roles.

Chapter in Review

7

 LO¹ bill of rights
List of "natural rights" that many Americans felt were threatened by England's prerevolutionary laws. Most of the bills of rights included in early state constitutions guaranteed the freedom of the press, the right of popular consent before being taxed, and protections against general search warrants

separation of powers
The concept of creating several different branches of government and giving each of them different responsibilities so as to prevent any one body from exerting an excess of authority

LO² Articles of Confederation
Document that defined the colonies' collective sovereignty; drafted by the Continental Congress between 1776 and 1777, then ratified by the thirteen states by 1781

LO³ Northwest Ordinance of 1787
This legislation established territorial governments in the Great Lakes region and set a pattern for future western development

specie
Gold or silver, which has intrinsic value, used as payment instead of paper money, which has extrinsic value

Shays's Rebellion
Potential coup of January 26, 1787, when Daniel Shays led 1,200 men to seize control of the federal arsenal in Springfield, Massachusetts to protest the state legislature's inability to address the debt problems of small farmers

LO⁴ Virginia Plan
This proposal, known as the large states plan, sought to scrap the Articles of Confederation and create a Congress with two houses, with representation in Congress being determined by population, favoring the large states

New Jersey Plan
This proposal suggested revising the Articles of Confederation rather than replacing them altogether

Great Compromise
Plan to grant each state equal representation in the upper house (to be called the Senate) and representation that was proportional to population (1 representative for every thirty thousand people) in the lower house (the House of Representatives)

three-fifths clause
Section of the Constitution that allowed southerners to include three-fifths of their slave population for both representation and the apportionment of federal taxes

TIMELINE

1777–1781	States ratify Articles of Confederation
1783	Continental Congress demobilizes Continental Army
1784	Virginia cedes western land claims to federal government
1786	In vain, Massachusetts farmers petition for debt relief
Jan. 26, 1787	In Shays's Rebellion, Massachusetts farmers try to seize federal armory
1787	Northwest Ordinance creates territorial governments, orders western development
May 1787	State delegate meeting in Philadelphia turns into Constitutional Convention
Sept. 1787	Delegates present new Constitution to states for ratification
Dec. 1787	Delaware, Pennsylvania, New Jersey ratify Constitution
June 1788	New Hampshire becomes ninth state to ratify Constitution
Sept. 1789	Congresses sends Bill of Rights to states for ratification
May 1790	Rhode Island is last state to ratify Constitution
Dec. 1791	Bill of Rights goes into effect

LO¹ Describe the first state constitutions written and adopted after the United States declared its independence. Although the early state constitutions differed in details, they provided models for the Articles of Confederation. Each state constitution included a Bill of Rights designed to protect certain rights of the citizens not directly covered in the constitution. Some states allowed only Christians to participate in the political process. Others retained property-owning qualifications. Women were usually excluded from voting, with New Jersey being a major exception. All states endeavored to implement a separation of powers, as the Enlightenment thinkers had espoused, but only within their respective states, not in the eventual federal plan of government.

LO² Analyze the federal government as it existed under the Articles of Confederation. The Articles of Confederation laid out how the federal government would operate; moreover, the relationship between the rights of states and their responsibilities to the federal government was addressed. Drafted by the Continental Congress in 1777, the Articles did not take effect until 1781, because all states had to ratify the document.

This insistence on absolute unity was a major weakness of the Articles of Confederation, as every proposed change or addition required unanimous consent by all states. There was also no provision for raising funds or overseeing internal trade, nor was the federal government authorized to settle the various issues that began to crop up between the United States and the world's other sovereign nations.

LO³ Describe the most significant issues that the United States had to deal with under the Articles of Confederation, and explain how the Articles failed to live up to the needs of the new country. One of the first issues facing the new United States was how the country's new lands should be settled. With independence, America just about doubled in size, extending from the Atlantic coast to the Mississippi River. At the time, some states claimed all of their settled lands north to south, as well as all lands extending westward to the Mississippi. In 1784, Virginia was persuaded to cede its western lands to the federal government, and the other states eventually did the same. As settlers populated these areas, Congress had to develop a plan for setting up territories and eventually making them eligible for statehood.

Another problem illustrating the weak federal government was foreign relations. As part of the peace treaty, England was supposed to vacate American lands, but lack of military might made it impossible for America to force the issue.

A third problem involved finances. The country was in debt due to the prosecution of the war, and bonds sold to finance the war needed to be repaid. The army also needed back pay that was not available. Shays's Rebellion clearly demonstrated the weakness of the Articles of Confederation.

LO⁴ Explain the need for the Constitutional Convention that met in Philadelphia in 1787, and describe the process of writing the Constitution. The men who met in Philadelphia were officially there to amend the Articles of Confederation, but in reality they knew that an entirely new plan of government was needed. The two main plans presented highlighted the problems of trying to unite such a diverse group of states.

George Washington was unanimously selected as president of the convention, a body comprised mostly of the wealthy and educated members of society. They held the common belief that they needed a strong national government, within reason, and they were concerned about too much democracy.

The Virginia Plan represented the concerns of large states, while the New Jersey Plan represented the small. Both called for a two-house legislature. Most other matters required some degree of compromise; one contentious issue was how to count a state's population for purposes of representation in the House. The solution was the awkward "three-fifths clause," which accepted slavery but counted slaves as less than whole, to keep southern states from being overrepresented. Another compromise allowed the slave trade to continue for twenty more years so that the nation's economic system could get established. The new plan gave the federal government the power to regulate the admission of new states.

LO⁵ Describe and explain the major provisions of the Constitution created by the Philadelphia convention, especially concerning the separation of powers and the rights given to individual states. The new constitution placed several matters under the control of Congress: the power to collect taxes and raise revenue; regulate commerce; maintain an army and declare war; and make modifications. Each state retained a great deal of power over its own internal affairs.

A true separation of powers was achieved through the division of duties into three branches of government. Congress was designed to be the most powerful branch, with the ability to make new laws. The executive branch consisted of an elected president and a cabinet of advisors that he appointed. The election process was removed from the direct control of voters, since the framers of the Constitution feared too much democracy. Thus the Electoral College would meet after a general election, and in theory, override a "bad" decision made by the citizens. Presidential powers included making treaties, overseeing the military, and vetoing acts of Congress. The third branch of government was the judicial, comprised of a Supreme Court and various regional courts. The last word on legal interpretation of the Constitution would reside with the Supreme Court.

LO⁶ Explain the procedure established for ratification of the Constitution, describe the actions of its supporters and its opponents, and explain how and when ratification was eventually achieved. The framers agreed that it would become the law of the land when nine states had ratified it. Some states ratified it almost immediately, but except for Pennsylvania, the larger states held off, wanting to ensure that they would retain enough control within their state borders.

Those supporting the Constitution, the Federalists, campaigned for support with a series of newspaper articles, the Federalist Papers. Those opposed called themselves Anti-Federalists. Much opposition evaporated after the Federalists pledged to add a Bill of Rights. New Hampshire's ratification in June 1788 gave the Constitution legal status, and by the end of that year every state except Rhode Island was on board. Soon Rhode Island made acceptance of the Constitution unanimous.

Chapter in Review

8

1788 First federal election

Judiciary Act creates three circuit and thirteen district courts

1790 Naturalization Act limits citizenship for immigrants to free white persons

Indian tribe coalition attacks American settlers north of Ohio River

Indian Trade and Intercourse Act puts trade with natives under federal control

1791 Congress charters first Bank of the United States

Haitian Revolution becomes only successful slave rebellion in hemisphere

1792 Jefferson becomes leader of Democratic-Republican Party

1793 Genêt affair further splits Democrat-Republicans and Federalists

1794 Western settlers resist federal authority in the Whiskey Rebellion

1795 Conciliatory Jay Treaty with England angers Democratic-Republicans

Treaty of Greenville forces tribes west out of Ohio Valley

1796 Pinckney Treaty with Spain opens Mississippi River to American trade

1796 Federalist John Adams becomes second president of the United States

1797 XYZ Affair prompts quasi-war with revolutionary France

1798 Adams tries to control political conflict with Alien and Sedition Acts

In response, Virginia and Kentucky formulate doctrine of nullification

1800 Virginians crush Gabriel's slave conspiracy and tighten slave laws

Jefferson's election demonstrates peaceful political change in republic

LO 1

Naturalization Act of 1790
Legislation which declared that, among immigrants to the U.S., only "free white persons" could become citizens of the United States

patronage
System of granting rewards for assisting with political victories

Hamilton Tariff of 1789
Act which imposed a 5 to 10 percent tariff on certain imports in order to fund the new government

cabinet
Group of the heads of departments within the executive branch; one of George Washington's innovations as president

LO 2

implied powers
Congress's power to do anything "necessary and proper" to carry out its delegated powers, even if those actions are not explicitly named in the Constitution

loose constructionism
Interpretation of the Constitution suggesting that the Constitution should be flexible to accommodate new demands

Democratic-Republicans
Faction that coalesced in opposition to Alexander Hamilton's economic policies and Jay's Treaty; led by Virginians like Thomas Jefferson and James Madison; also known as the Jeffersonians

strict constructionism
Literal interpretation of the Constitution, arguing that the original meaning of those at the Constitutional Convention should not be adapted to fit more recent times

Whiskey Rebellion
Conflict in which Pennsylvania farmers fought a tax on whiskey, eventually rioting and over-running the city of Pittsburgh in 1794, where they were to be tried for tax evasion

Pinckney Treaty of 1796
Agreement with Spain that opened the Mississippi River to American shipping and allowed Americans the "right of deposit" at New Orleans, which meant that American merchants could warehouse goods in the city

impressment
Practice of capturing and forcing sailors from other nations into naval service

Jay's Treaty
Treaty in which the British agreed to evacuate military posts along the frontier in the Northwest Territory and make reparations for the cargo seized in 1793 and 1794 while the United States lifted duties on British imports for ten years

LO 1 Describe the creation of the federal government under the new Constitution.

The new Constitution was unclear about how the three-branch government should function, and those who helped work out the details felt a great burden to do things as effectively as possible.

In 1788 elections for the first Congress were held, and members met in New York City to begin crafting a federal system. The Judiciary Act of 1789 established the federal court system. Making good on the Federalists' promise to obtain ratification of the Constitution, Congress adopted a number of amendments that would become the Bill of Rights. Congress also dealt with matters of finance, citizenship, the establishment of the executive cabinet, and even what to call the person elected to head the government.

George Washington was unanimously selected as the first president. Washington decided that the best order of business was to negotiate treaties and then obtain consent from the Senate, and he strongly supported delivering a state of the nation speech to Congress once a year. He selected men for his cabinet who held opposing political views, a move he hoped would help keep leaders working together for the good of the country.

LO 2 Describe how disagreements over how the United States should be governed led to political divisions, and discuss some of the individuals who took strong stands on each side.

How to finance the government and how to deal with foreign policy were two issues facing the new federal government. The Federalists (supporters of a strong federal government) included Washington and Hamilton, while the group that became Democratic-Republicans (including Jefferson and Madison) wanted a weaker federal system and stronger states' rights.

The first treasury secretary, Alexander Hamilton, laid out a plan to take care of wartime loans owed by the government, establish a national bank, and raise revenue for the operation of the government. Opponents

Treaty of Greenville
Agreement which forced the Indian tribes of the Old Northwest westward across the Mississippi in 1795

Indian Trade and Intercourse Acts
Laws which made it illegal for Americans to trade with Native American tribes without formal consent from the federal government and also made it illegal to sell land to or buy land from Native Americans without similar federal consent

 3 Federalist Party
Faction of American leaders that endorsed Hamilton's economic policies and Jay's Treaty

Gabriel's Conspiracy
Slave rebellion in 1800 in Richmond, Virginia; twenty-six rebels were hanged

 4 XYZ Affair
Foreign policy crisis with France over the trade wars; three agents designated X, Y, and Z attempted to extort money from American envoys as a prerequisite for negotiations

Alien and Sedition Acts
Legislation signed by President John Adams; included the Alien Enemies Act, the Alien Friends Act, and the Sedition Act; opponents called them a violation of the First Amendment's guarantees

Virginia and Kentucky Resolutions
Declarations written by Thomas Jefferson and James Madison and adopted by the legislatures of Virginia and Kentucky, proclaiming the Sedition Act to be an infringement on rights protected by their state constitutions and that states had the right to nullify federal laws within their borders

doctrine of nullification
The theory that each state had the right to nullify federal laws within its borders

 5 lame duck
Politician who is not returning to office and is serving out the rest of his or her term with little influence; a soon-to-be-out-of-office politician or Congress

---

did not want nationalization of state debts, and many believed that a national bank would benefit only the wealthy. In an unlikely compromise maneuver, those opposed to the bank allowed Hamilton's plan to pass in Congress, and the nation's capital was established permanently along the Potomac River, in the new city of Washington, D.C. Tax collection was a problem, the best example being the whiskey producers' refusal to pay the tax on their product. Washington called out federal troops to put down their rebellion, thereby establishing the supremacy of the federal government.

One well-received treaty allowed the United States to use the mouth of the Mississippi at New Orleans; another, Jay's Treaty, failed to get Britain to fulfill promises made in the peace agreement ending the Revolution.

LO 3 Outline the country's development of a two-party political system. By the presidential election year of 1792, the two opposing groups had coalesced into formal political parties known as the Federalists and the Democratic-Republicans. Federalists tended to be wealthy, property owners, or conservative farmers, with their strongholds centered in New England and the Middle Colonies. Democratic-Republicans strongly supported the continuation of slavery and were found more often in the South and on the frontier.

A revolt of slaves in Haiti in 1791 demonstrated the different belief systems: Federalists supported the revolution, while Democratic-Republicans supported the French in their attempts to quell the rebellion. The Haitian slaves ultimately succeeded in setting up an independent black republic, and unrest among slaves seeped into America's southern states. The result was a short-lived rebellion known as Gabriel's Conspiracy. This, along with a second failed rebellion, led to the passage of slave laws.

LO 4 Discuss the issues of John Adams's presidency, and explain how he and the country dealt with them. After two terms as president, Washington retired from public life, departing with a warning against "entangling alliances" with foreign governments and urging Americans to abandon the two-party system before it became too entrenched. The two presidential candidates were Federalist John Adams and Democratic-Republican Thomas Jefferson. Because of a glitch in the electoral process, Adams became president and Jefferson vice president.

Problems with France plagued the new president. The French were upset with the Americans for preferring to deal with the British rather than with the French. When the French began raiding American ships and Adams sent a representative to negotiate with France, the French demanded payment to set up meetings. When Americans heard of this, they were incensed at the lack of respect. Both countries began raiding each other's ships, and war appeared imminent.

Fearing that partisan battles would make the United States vulnerable during a potential wartime, Adams's promotion of Alien and Sedition Acts backfired, with Democratic-Republicans wrongly accusing the president of targeting their party. Virginia and Kentucky passed resolutions claiming the right of states to ignore within their borders laws that overrode their respective constitutions. Though nothing came of the resolutions then, they anticipated the doctrine of nullification that would cause many problems later.

LO 5 Explain the convoluted political process that made Thomas Jefferson president in 1800, including the constitutional change designed to mend the problem. The election of 1800 proved that the country could hold together even when a different political party took over. Jefferson and Adams both ran again, and the campaign was bitter. When Adams's party divided over his peace treaty with France, the unity of Jefferson's party led to a Democratic-Republican victory.

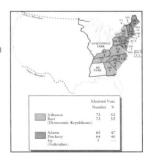

That victory took place in the House of Representatives because Jefferson and his vice presidential candidate received the same number of electoral votes. After the 1796 problem, this situation showed that a better system of electing leaders was needed. The result was the Twelfth Amendment, which stated that electors would elect a president and then elect a vice president, rather than giving the top two offices to the top two vote getters.

Chapter in Review

LO¹ Jeffersonian Democracy
Innovation introduced by Jefferson's Democratic-Republicans when they eagerly cultivated popular opinion by campaigning at the grass roots

Marbury v. Madison (1803)
Court decision declaring that Judge Marbury deserved his appointment, but that the Court could not force the president to grant it, because a federal law was unconstitutional; first U.S. Supreme Court decision to declare a law unconstitutional

doctrine of judicial review
Right of the courts to judge the constitutionality of federal laws; this established the Supreme Court as the ultimate interpreter of constitutional questions

Louisiana Purchase
Tract of 830,000 square miles that stretched from the Mississippi River to the Rocky Mountains; Jefferson bought it from Napoleon for $15 million in 1803

Tecumseh and the Prophet
Shawnee Indian brothers who proposed to unite tribes from the Old Northwest (in Ohio and Michigan) and the South (Georgia) to resist the perpetual encroachment of American settlers in the early 1800s

revitalization movement
Revival of old ways of tribal life and pan-Indianism preached by Tecumseh and the Prophet

Embargo Act of 1807
Legislation which stopped American exports from going to Europe and prohibited American ships from trading in foreign ports

LO² Non-Intercourse Act
Legislation passed in 1809 which allowed American ships to trade with all nations except Britain and France, and authorized the president to resume trade with those countries once they began respecting America's neutral trading rights

Hartford Convention
Meeting of New England Federalists in 1814 where they proposed constitutional amendments limiting the government's ability to restrict American commerce and repealing the three-fifths clause to limit the power of the South in Congress

"Era of Good Feelings"
Period of nonpartisan politics following the implosion of the Federalist Party, roughly 1815–1824

TIMELINE

1800	Land Act creates federal offices for sale of western land to settlers
1801–1835	Chief Justice John Marshall builds Supreme Court's constitutional authority
1803	John Marshall introduces judicial review in *Marbury* v. *Madison*
	Napoleon Bonaparte sells Louisiana territory
1804	Aaron Burr kills Alexander Hamilton; his secessionist plans lead to trial for treason
1804–1806	Lewis and Clark expedition sparks Americans' fascination with West
1807	Embargo Act stops American exports and foreign trade, and imperils economy
1811	William H. Harrison attacks Tecumseh's tribal alliance at Tippecanoe
1812	War with Britain over American neutrality, alleged collusion with Indians
	Invasion of British Canada a fiasco
1813	Andrew Jackson defeats Creek Indians in battle over land in Georgia
March 1814	Creeks lose their land to U.S. after Battle of Horse Shoe Bend
August 1814	British burn White House in assault on Washington, D.C.
October 1814	Defense of New Orleans against British forces makes Jackson national hero
December 1814	New England Federalists invoke states' rights at Hartford Convention
1814	Treaty of Ghent ends hostilities without resolving causes of war
1815–1824	Decline of Federalist party ushers in nonpartisan "Era of Good Feelings"

LO¹ Define Jeffersonian Democracy, and explain how Jefferson's presidency both defined and contradicted that political philosophy.

Jeffersonian Democracy is a term used by historians to describe the political style and belief system of the Democratic-Republicans. In its earliest stages, this kind of politics sought to get "the people" more involved in the election process, and its appeal contributed to the election of Thomas Jefferson in 1800. Over time, however, the term has been broadened to describe the political philosophy of giving less control to the federal government and more control to the individual states and "the people." For Jefferson, as a strong proponent of a strict interpretation of the Constitution, it was wrong for any of the three branches of government to go beyond what was explicitly included in the Constitution and its amendments.

That being the case, the Democratic-Republicans clearly demonstrated Jeffersonian Democracy in action during the 1800 election: partisan newspapers, personal appeals for votes, a demonstrated concern for the needs and hopes of the common people. Jefferson's ideal republic, after all, was a nation of industrious and successful farmers.

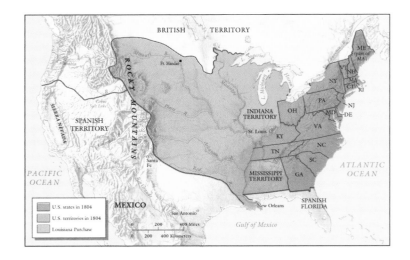

Jefferson's beliefs were also evident in his desire to open new lands on the frontier for settlement, and he sought to purchase the port city of New Orleans from the French. France's leader, Napoleon Bonaparte, needed money, and he offered to sell the entire Louisiana Territory to the United States. Despite his beliefs, the realist won out over the idealist, and the Louisiana Purchase almost doubled the size of the country.

LO^2 Discuss the reasons for and the results of the War of 1812. James Madison, a staunch Democratic-Republican, was elected president in 1808, but the Federalists made a better showing than expected. Fearing their growing popularity, Congress repealed the Embargo Act even before Madison took office, replacing that hated act with the Non-Intercourse Act, which stated that America would trade with every European country except Britain and France. Napoleon agreed first, leading the president to reestablish trade with France and reassert the embargo on Britain. "War hawks" in Congress pushed for war against Britain. Democratic-Republicans believed America would have to fight another war with Britain to get that country, once and for all, to truly recognize the sovereignty of the United States.

That is how this series of events came to pass; Madison asked for a declaration of war against Britain; while Congress debated, Britain recognized American neutrality; still, Congress voted for a declaration of war; and Madison won reelection in the fall of 1812 with the strong support of the western states and their war hawks. Two weeks before Andrew Jackson and his forces soundly defeated the British in New Orleans, the American and British governments reached a peace agreement, making the battle, in reality, unnecessary.

The main issues between the two countries remained, for the most part, unsettled. The War of 1812 led to significant changes within America, however. The Democratic-Republicans realized that the country did need a stronger central government, a stronger military, a national bank, and improvements to America's transportation network. Americans also became more nationalistic and patriotic, and a true American culture, distinctly non-British, began to emerge.

Chapter in Review

10

1789	Samuel Slater builds first American spinning factory
1793	Cotton gin makes fiber a profitable cash crop and revives plantation slavery
1800	Land Act creates federal offices for sale of western land to settlers
1807	First steamboats introduced to American rivers
1811	Congress fails to recharter First Bank of the United States
1813	Lowell system combines all processes in textile production in one factory
1816	Democratic-Republicans push for Second Bank of the United States Congress discourages foreign imports with high tariff
1817	State of New York begins construction of canal from Albany to Buffalo
1819	Supreme Court protects contract clause in *Dartmouth College* v. *Woodward*
	Spain yields Florida and claims to Pacific Northwest in Adams-Onís Treaty
1820	Federal Land Act promotes western migration and farm settlements Compromise admits Missouri as slave, Maine as free, states; sets slavery's northern boundary at 36°30′
1821	American Colonization Society promotes slaves' return to Africa and found Liberia
1820s–1840s	Second Great Awakening promises salvation through good work
1823	Monroe Doctrine claims Western Hemisphere as American domain
1825	364-mile-long Erie Canal connects eastern seaboard with Great Lakes
1826	American Temperance Society becomes century's largest reform movement
1828	Workingmen's Party formed; eventually spreads to sixteen states
1831	Cyrus McCormick's mechanical reaper transforms commercial agriculture Lloyd Garrison becomes leading voice of abolitionists
1834	National Trades Union formed
1838	Grimké sisters publish landmark tract in struggle for women's equality
1844	Samuel P. Morse "wires" first message "What Hath God Wrought?"
1845–1851	Irish potato famine further pushes European immigration to U.S.
1846	Mormons migrate west to escape persecution
1848	Women's Rights Convention at Seneca Falls adopt Declaration of Sentiments
1854	Thoreau's *Walden* typifies transcendentalist response to Market Revolution

LO¹ Market Revolution
Umbrella term for the many economic and social changes that took place between 1812 and the 1860s

American System
Economic plan based on the idea that the federal government should encourage economic enterprise

internal improvements
Building of roads and canals by the federal and state governments

Second Bank of the United States
National bank established in 1816, to curb rampant currency speculation

Monroe Doctrine
Declaration of 1823 proclaiming that any European nation attempting to colonize Latin America would be treated as a party hostile to the United States; President James Monroe announced that the Western Hemisphere was the domain of the United States and was to remain separate from the affairs of Europe

LO² Erie Canal
Artificial river connecting the New York state cities of Buffalo and Albany; provided a continuous water route from the shores of the Atlantic to the Great Lakes; measured 364 miles long and 40 feet wide

Land Act of 1820
Legislation which promoted settlement west of the Appalachians by setting affordable prices for manageable plots of land

Tallmadge Amendment
Proposal that would have enforced gradual emancipation in Missouri

36°30′
Line of latitude specified by Henry Clay in the Missouri Compromise; territories north of the line would remain free, south of it could maintain slavery

Missouri Compromise
Arrangement brokered by Henry Clay that set 36°30′ as the divider between free and slave territories, and allowed Missouri to enter the nation as a slave state if Maine were allowed to enter as free

"putting out" system
Division of labor in which large manufacturers would pay one family to perform one task, then pass the item on to the next family or artisan to perform the next task

Great Irish Famine
Years of miserable poverty and hunger in Ireland that peaked during 1845–1851

LO¹
Describe the economic system known as the American System. As younger men entered Congress, fears of a more powerful central government eased. Younger members embraced a program of internal improvements that would promote economic growth. The American System, as it was called, focused on building roads and canals with federal monies, establishing a sound system of banks, and maintaining high tariffs on imported goods so that America's fledgling industries would be protected from too much competition. A key element of this system was a national bank with a centralized currency, and the Second Bank of the United States was chartered in 1816.

The federal government promoted economic growth in several ways. A tariff of 25 percent was placed on all goods imported into the country, so that domestic goods would find a strong domestic market. A number of court cases during these years also promoted business growth on a national level, often giving states little consideration in making their decisions. America was moving toward more federal control and less independence at the state level; cotton planters in the South protested that the only people helped were those in the North and the West, and that the South lost out all around.

LO²
List the three specific parts of the Market Revolution in early-nineteenth-century America, and evaluate how America and Americans developed during this era. America's Market Revolution consisted of three separate "revolutions": transportation and communications; commercialized farming; and industrialization.

Workingmen's Party
Union of laborers, made up from citywide assemblies, formed in 1828; eventually spread through fifteen states

National Trades Union
First large-scale labor union in the U.S.; formed 1834

LO 3 burned-over district
Area in upstate New York which had many converts who had been inspired by the fiery orators speaking the Word of God during the Second Great Awakening

Transcendentalists
Group of thinkers and writers in the Northeast who believed that ultimate truths were beyond human grasp

lyceum circuit
Schedule of lectures in which clergymen, reformers, Transcendentalists, socialists, feminists, and other speakers would speak to large crowds in small towns

American Female Moral Reform Society
Women's activist group that had more than five hundred local chapters throughout the country by 1840, and had successfully lobbied for legislation governing prostitution

American Temperance Society
Group founded by temperance workers in 1826; they promoted laws prohibiting the sale of alcohol

American Colonization Society
Group that advocated sending all black Americans to Africa; the Society established the colony of Liberia on the West African coast for this purpose in the 1820s

American Anti-Slavery Society
Organization founded by journalist William Lloyd Garrison in 1833 that served as a point of contact for escaped slaves like Frederick Douglass and Harriet Tubman

"gag rule"
Legal provision of 1836 that automatically tabled any discussion of abolition in Congress; under this law, slavery was not open for discussion

Women's Rights Convention
Gathering of women activists in Seneca Falls, New York in 1848; their goal was securing the vote for women

To move people and goods in all directions, the country needed roads, canals, steamboats, and railroads. The first roads were usually financed mostly through taxes; canals were built to connect cities to lakes and rivers in the East; steamboats plied the rivers of the South; and railroads made it possible for the entire country to be connected faster than ever before. Communications also improved, with the telegraph most responsible. The combination of all of these improvements revolutionized the ways in which businesses could operate.

Better equipment allowed farmers to specialize in certain crops, selling their surplus and buying what they needed. The cotton gin allowed cultivation of cotton on large plantations in the lower South, and steamboats could ship the cotton to worldwide markets. Since huge profits were possible, most southern farmers clung to cotton as their main crop, contributing to a growing dependence on slave labor. Goods began to be produced in factories employing more workers who all labored in one place, factories began to employ entire families, and the cities continued to grow. A continual stream of immigrants provided the needed workers, as did rural residents who migrated into the cities. A new urban working class quickly emerged.

LO 3 Describe the growth of America's middle class during the first half of the 1800s, and discuss some of the stronger movements toward reform during the era. Factory work required mostly unskilled laborers, but it also required more people to handle the record-keeping, bookkeeping, planning, and employment records. These people were better educated and commanded greater pay for their specific skills. "Management" became a defined group, separate from "labor," even though they all worked for the same company, often in the same building. Higher wages for a larger group of people led to a tremendous increase in the "middle class." One of the outward signs of success for a middle-class male was for him to be able to provide for his family without his wife or children working outside the home.

Two distinct developments contributed to America's reform movement. One was the Second Great Awakening, a religious period of revival that led many middle-class individuals to see the need for helping those less fortunate than themselves. It should also be pointed out that attending church regularly, actively participating, and "being seen" was a good way to gain social respectability—and perhaps a raise or a better position at work as well. This was also the period of the Transcendentalists, those who believed in humans' ability to create a perfect society, when a number of Utopian societies flourished and then died out. Reform movements of the era included temperance, increased public education, new colleges, prison reform, and abolition. The first stirrings of feminism were also felt; because women were so involved in the various reform efforts, it was only natural that they began to perceive themselves as being left out of a major part of American life: politics.

Chapter in Review

LO¹ **"corrupt bargain"**
Alleged deal between John Quincy Adams and Henry Clay to manipulate the voting in the House of Representatives to install Adams as president and Clay as his secretary of state in 1824

second two-party system
Evolution of political organizations in 1824 into the Jacksonians and the Whigs

LO² **patronage**
Exchange of a government job in return for political campaign work

nullification
Assertion that the United States was made up of independent and sovereign states; states did not agree to give up their autonomy; and every state reserves the right to reject any federal law it deemed unconstitutional

Indian Removal Act of 1830
Legislation that allowed the federal government to trade land west of the Mississippi River for land east of the river

Trail of Tears
Forced removal of the Cherokee nation from Georgia to Oklahoma in 1838; the Cherokees were forced to walk more than a thousand miles

Specie Circular
Executive order of 1836 requiring that the government cease accepting paper money as credible currency, accepting only gold or silver (specie) for all items, including public land

TIMELINE

1819	Europe's postwar recovery hits U.S. agriculture, leading to financial panic
1824	Most states have expanded franchise to all free white men
	Jackson's complaint of Adams's "corrupt bargain" starts second party system
1828	Jacksonian Democrats win presidency with mass appeal
1830	Jackson's Indian Removal Act forces Indians to move west of Mississippi
1832	Supreme Court confirms Cherokee sovereignty in *Worcester* v. *Georgia*
	Tariffs cause nullification crisis between South Carolina and Washington
1836	Jackson refuses to renew charter of Second National Bank
	Jackson's Specie Circular forbids government from accepting paper currency
1837	Severe bank panic spreads from New York across the country
1838	4,000 Cherokees die on the Trail of Tears from Georgia to Oklahoma
1838–1842	Seminole Indians rebel against sugar planters in Florida

LO¹ Describe the changes that took place in American politics during the first decades of the 1800s, and explain reasons for these changes. Boom and bust cycles, more men gaining the right to vote, elections that reeked of corruption—all of these led to greater participation in American politics by the time of the 1828 election. The Panic of 1819 affected almost all Americans, not just the wealthy. Despite optimism fueled by the Market Revolution, Americans realized that global markets could affect the domestic economy. Land prices fell, banks across the country failed even after foreclosing on farm loans, bankruptcies escalated, and the nation experienced its first real economic depression. One political result was a demand by ordinary people for more government intervention during such economic crises.

Another reason for political change was that the franchise was being extended to all white males through the removal of property restrictions. The democratization of politics fed anew the factionalism that would eventually give rise to the country's second two-party system, with the election of 1824 causing many to view the current system as too corrupt to continue unopposed. All five presidential candidates were Democratic-Republicans, and no one received a majority of the votes. When the House of Representatives decided the outcome, Henry Clay threw his support to John Quincy Adams, and Andrew Jackson, who had won the most popular votes and the most electoral votes, was furious. After Adams named Henry Clay his secretary of state, Jackson's supporters protested the "corrupt bargain" and vowed to win the next election for Jackson.

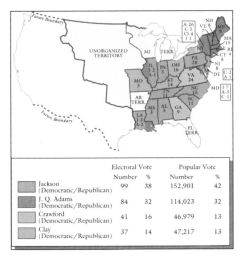

	Electoral Vote		Popular Vote	
	Number	%	Number	%
Jackson (Democratic/Republican)	99	38	152,901	42
J. Q. Adams (Democratic/Republican)	84	32	114,023	32
Crawford (Democratic/Republican)	41	16	46,979	13
Clay (Democratic/Republican)	37	14	47,217	13

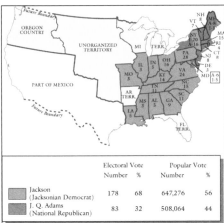

	Electoral Vote		Popular Vote	
	Number	%	Number	%
Jackson (Jacksonian Democrat)	178	68	647,276	56
J. Q. Adams (National Republican)	83	32	508,064	44

LO² Enumerate the political developments of the Jacksonian era, including President Jackson's responses to the "spoils system," the nullification crisis, the battle over the National Bank, Indian removal, and the Panic of 1837. Andrew Jackson ran for president as a new Democrat in 1828 and handily defeated the incumbent, John Quincy Adams, primarily by winning in the South and the West. His presidency is usually described as the era of the "common man," and he set out to reward his supporters with government jobs, a practice known as the "spoils system."

His most serious problem was the issue of protective tariffs. Southerners objected to high tariffs and asserted the right of an individual state to nullify a federal law within its borders that it viewed as unconstitutional. South Carolina threatened to secede if nullification was not accepted, and Jackson responded by obtaining from Congress the power to send federal forces to South Carolina if it tried secession. However, the two sides compromised on the tariff and ended the crisis—temporarily.

Jackson distrusted the Second Bank of the United States, and when Congress renewed the Bank's charter four years early, just before the 1832 election, Jackson vetoed the

measure, arguing that the Bank was unconstitutional. He viewed his landslide reelection as a mandate to break the Bank and ordered that federal funds be removed from the National Bank and placed in various state banks. In 1836, Jackson ordered that all payments to the federal government be made in gold and silver, or specie. This order, the Specie Circular, contributed to the Panic of 1837 and a major depression.

Jackson's attitude on Indian removal was in line with that of most white Americans at the time. Westward expansion brought whites and Indians into greater conflict, and the position of the federal government came to be that the Indians should be "removed" from any contact with white Americans. The Indian Removal Act of 1830, with Jackson's support, gave the government the right to move Indians from east of the Mississippi to lands west of the river. Jackson's paternalistic statements indicate that he believed Americans were doing the Indians a favor, when in truth he was doing expansionists a favor.

LO³ Explain the development of America's second two-party political system, the parties being the Democrats and the Whigs. The old Democratic-Republican Party could not contain Andrew Jackson and his supporters, who felt that they had long been marginalized by the old guard of the party. The new Democrats, as they called themselves, were highly nationalistic and yet supported a smaller government; those who continued to push for

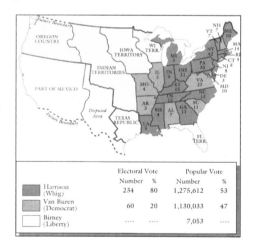

	Electoral Vote		Popular Vote	
	Number	%	Number	%
Harrison (Whig)	234	80	1,275,612	53
Van Buren (Democrat)	60	20	1,130,033	47
Birney (Liberty)	----	----	7,053	----

more federal assistance for financial improvements took the name Whigs. They reasoned that in England, the Whigs were those who had opposed the king during the American Revolution, and since they opposed Jackson's acting like a king, Whig was an appropriate name for them.

So, once again, two strong parties took center stage. This time, however, the primary difference was that the core of Whig support came from those who detested Jackson and were ready to do anything to shut him down. Also, the Whigs pushed for strong government support of economic development through internal improvements and a stronger banking system. Democrats appealed to small farmers, disaffected workers, small businessmen who were feared the growth of big business, and newly arrived Irish immigrants who felt alienated by the successful and somewhat elitist Whig Party.

Chapter in Review

LO¹

the 48ers
Germans who came to the United States in 1848, after a failed revolution in Germany forced many political dissidents to flee

Nativism
Political identity that defined an American as someone with an English background who was born in the United States; supporters formulated a racial and ethnic identity that proclaimed the superiority of their group, usually labeled "Native Americans."

Uncle Tom's Cabin
Antislavery novel published by Harriet Beecher Stowe in 1852; best-selling book of that period

African Methodist Episcopal (AME) Church
National religious organization founded by African Americans in the 1790s

LO²

gang system
Work arrangement under which slaves were organized into groups of twenty to twenty-five workers, supervised by an overseer

slavedriver
Supervisor or overseer of slave labor, usually employed on a cotton plantation

task system
Work arrangement under which slaves were assigned a specific set of tasks to accomplish each day; often employed on rice plantations and in domestic service situations

Underground Railroad
Network of men and women, both white and black, who were opposed to slavery, sheltered runaway slaves, and expedited their journey to freedom

TIMELINE

1816 African Methodist Episcopal Church becomes national organization
1831 Nat Turner's deadly revolt breeds repression and new defense of slavery
1838 Frederick Douglass escapes slavery with help of Underground Railroad
1852 Harriet Beecher Stowe's *Uncle Tom's Cabin* popularizes abolitionism

LO¹ Describe social life in the commercial North as it developed between 1830 and 1860. Social life in the North developed very differently according to where one lived in the North. Despite rapid industrialization, many people still lived in rural areas. They maintained close family ties and communal values, but most embraced consumerism to some degree, because they also produced goods for sale. Improvements in transportation and communication ended their isolation, and traveling lecturers brought new ideas their way, while newspapers provided both local and national news.

Cities grew tremendously during this period in the Northeast and New England, due to both internal migration and the arrival of many more immigrants. Immigrant communities arose in every major city. Irish Catholics became targets of discrimination more than other groups during this period, because they arrived ready to work for whatever wages they could get, and workers already here feared for their jobs. Not all immigrants stayed in the cities; some moved westward and found a greater acceptance on the frontier.

The way the cities grew led to a greater class consciousness, and the newly rich left downtown areas and moved farther out to build their mansions. Most working-class people lived in dirty, disease-ridden tenements and faced uncertain, often brief, futures. Some middle-class women managed to enter the work force, at least until they married. Various leisure activities appealed to wealthy urban residents. Boxing, horse racing, theaters, and a new, uniquely American literary movement engaged those with leisure time to spare, and boxing was especially popular in inner-city immigrant communities.

LO² Describe social life as it developed in the South between 1830 and 1860 as a result of dependence on cotton. The South contained at least three distinct social groups: (1) wealthy planters, businessmen, and politicians; (2) yeoman farmers who hoped to become wealthy at raising cotton, but who almost never did; and (3) a large slave population.

Planters were the self-proclaimed aristocrats of the South who vacationed abroad, sent their children to schools in England, and entered politics because it was their duty to see that their society continued to run smoothly. Though very small in number, they wielded an inordinate amount of power within their society. Their vast plantations were located on waterways so that they could ship their cotton to the North and to Europe easily, and the plantations provided virtually everything they needed; what they did not produce, they could send for. Thus towns and cities were few and far between in the South.

Yeoman farmers sometimes managed to acquire small plots of land—usually not the best, by any means. They often hoped to gain enough wealth to move into the social world of the planters, but this seldom happened, despite what old movies depict.

Most blacks in the South were slaves, with a large majority living and working on large plantations. Many whites owned no slaves, and many owned only a few. Almost all whites in the South, however, supported the slave system. Planters saw slave labor as the only possible way for them to make a decent profit on their cotton. Some slave owners had nothing to do with plantation agriculture, instead purchasing slaves to hire them out as blacksmiths, carpenters, longshoremen, and such. Most blacks, however, had no special skills to speak of and thus were relegated to the arduous work of the plantation. African American slaves sought to hold onto as much of their culture as possible. Religion provided one bond, and after the Second Great Awakening, most accepted Christianity, though with overtones of African beliefs. Strong resistance and rebellions seldom occurred, because whites had put in place so many legal restrictions that they could basically treat their slaves as property. When blacks did openly rebel, the uprisings were quickly put down, and those involved were usually executed in vicious ways that allowed whites to make examples of them. In time, even some southerners began to espouse the cause of abolition that was being promoted in the North, but their numbers remained so small as to be insignificant.

THE REVIVED MOVE WEST

Chapter in Review

13

LO 1 Fort Laramie Treaty
Agreement of 1851 between Plains Indian tribes and the U.S. government; the government agreed to make cash restitution for disruptions to the buffalo grounds, while tribal leaders agreed not to attack the large number of settlers moving through the area

LO 2 Liberty Party
Political party created by northern antislavery activists who left the Whig Party; they were outraged at Henry Clay's reversing his position against annexation of Texas

"Fifty-four Forty or Fight!"
Rallying cry referring to the Americans' intended latitude for the contested border between the United States and Canada; Britain was willing to settle for the 49th parallel

Buchanan-Pakenham Treaty
1846 agreement between the United States and Britain, agreeing on the 49th parallel as the border between the United States and Canada, giving the United States uncontested access to the Pacific

manifest destiny
Idea that America was destined by God to possess North America from the Atlantic to the Pacific; phrase coined by journalist John O'Sullivan in 1845

Treaty of Guadalupe Hidalgo
Agreement ending the Mexican War in 1848, which gave the United States control of Utah, Nevada, California, western Colorado, and parts of Arizona and New Mexico, and established the Rio Grande as the border, in exchange for $15 million

TIMELINE

1821	Mexico's independence draws American settlers to northern province of Texas
1830	Joseph Smith forms Church of Jesus Christ of Latter-day Saints
1834	Texas settlers rebel against Mexican ruler Santa Anna
1836	187 Texan rebels perish in Alamo after killing over 1,200 Mexican troops
1844	James K. Polk wins presidency with promise of annexing Oregon and Texas
1845	Admission of Texas sets stage for war with Mexico "Mormon Wars" follow 1844 murder of Joseph Smith in Nauvoo, Illinois
July 1845	John O'Sullivan coins term *manifest destiny*
April 1846	Polk provokes war with Mexico and seizes northern provinces
June 1846	Rebels under John C. Frémont declare California independent republic Buchanan-Pakenham Treaty establishes Canadian-U.S. border in Northwest
1847	Clashes between Oregonians and Indians show need for territorial government
September 1847	U.S. forces march into Mexico City; Santa Anna surrenders
January 1848	Gold discovery in California triggers global gold rush
February 1848	Treaty of Guadalupe Hidalgo cedes 500,000 sq. miles to U.S. for $15 million
1848	America gains control of the Utah territory one year after Mormons settle there
1851	Fort Laramie treaty with Plains Indians secures settler migration westward

LO 1 Describe the conquest and development of the West between 1820 and 1850 by white Americans.
Settlement of the true American West, the area from Texas to California, presented many challenges and demonstrated the unique spirit of those who were first willing to move into the area. All new territories caused problems of one sort or another, even as their lands beckoned to adventurers, speculators, and not a few ne'er-do-wells.

First controlled by the Spanish, and then by Mexico after 1821, Texas was a sprawling territory. Yet most Americans who moved there settled in the eastern part of the country where rainfall was plentiful. Under its new leader, Santa Anna, Mexico tried to stop the influx of immigrants, fearing that eventually the newcomers would attempt to separate from Mexico. That did happen in 1836, with a series of battles from the Alamo to San Jacinto. By defeating Santa Anna, Texas gained independence and established itself as a republic, a status it would maintain until it gained statehood in 1845.

Oregon and Utah also began to interest Americans during this period. So many people began to migrate to Oregon and surrounding areas that their most favorable route became known as the Oregon Trail. Here, too, local Indians tried to fight off the intruders, but here, too, they were defeated. Mormons, led by Joseph Smith, practiced polygamy and kept to themselves, which led to escalating conflicts with their neighbors. They moved westward, settling in Illinois in 1838. It was there that their founder and several other members were killed, and the Mormons moved farther West. Led by Brigham Young, they turned toward Utah's Great Salt Lake, hoping to avoid government control. That did not last long, for America gained control of the Utah territory at the end of the war with Mexico in 1848. The Mormons chose to stay.

The last territory settled during this period was California. Migrants were converging on the territory even before the discovery of gold in early 1848; after the discovery, the "gold rush" brought many people to the area hoping to strike it rich. Most did not, but most stayed on, with the population concentrating not in the old mining camps but in a handful of cities that began to grow and become prosperous as families were started.

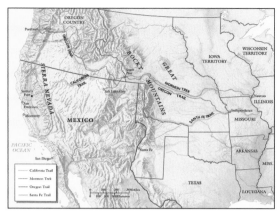

Settlement was somewhat hindered by the presence of Native Americans in the region, especially the Plains Indians, but soon the government had them all settled on a few reservations scattered throughout the Southwest. Mountain men roamed the Rocky Mountains during this period trapping for furs, and they began to chart the areas in which they lived and worked, giving the rest of America a better idea of what the lands there were really like.

LO2 Explain how the expansionist spirit in the West led to political conflict at home as well as conflict with Mexico, even as it gave the United States its modern boundaries. John L. O'Sullivan coined a new term in mid-1845 when he wrote an editorial urging both political parties to join together to carry out America's "manifest destiny"—taking ownership of all lands from the Atlantic Ocean to the Pacific. The process was

already well underway, and within a few years it would be complete. Ending years of argument within the federal government, Texas became part of the United States in March 1845. The most hotly debated issue was whether Americans wanted to expand slavery into new lands, and the Texas constitution guaranteed that slavery would continue. The debate affected presidential elections as well as the terms of three presidents, and James K. Polk assumed office just after Texas joined the Union. Polk and other expansionists set out to goad Mexico into a war so the United States could pick up some more Mexican territory, and they finally succeeded in May 1846. The Treaty of Guadalupe Hidalgo, signed in early 1848, ended the war and left the United States in possession of America's Southwest. The treaty established the border between the two countries at the Rio Grande River as well. In return, Mexico received $15 million as compensation for its losses. Polk also finally settled the long-standing issue of the country's northern border, negotiating a settlement with the British that gave all of the Oregon Territory up to the 49th parallel to the United States.

LO 1 Wilmot Proviso
Legislation proposed in 1846 in the House of Representatives to prohibit slavery from any new territories that the United States might acquire from Mexico

dough face
Derisive name for a northerner who openly supported the South

popular sovereignty
Proposal for letting the settlers in the territories decide whether or not they wanted slavery

Free Soil Party
Political movement started by disaffected anti-South Democrats, headed by former Democratic president Martin Van Buren; they wanted new lands to be made available to small, ambitious white farmers

Compromise of 1850
Five-part bill proposed by Henry Clay, which outlined specific arrangements that accommodated both antislavery northerners and slaveowning southerners

Personal Liberty Laws
A variety of laws designed to protect escaped slaves, such as by prohibiting the use of a state's jail for runaway slaves; these laws passed in many northern states in the 1850s

filibusters
Adventurers who attempted to invade the island of Cuba in order to bring it into the Union as a slave state

LO 2 Kansas-Nebraska Act
1854 act that created two territories, Kansas and Nebraska, and left the status of slavery in each territory open, to be decided by the popular sovereignty of those who settled there

Know-Nothing Party
American Party, a new political party of the 1850s that built its base of support on anti-immigrant and anti-Catholic sentiment

Lecompton Constitution
1857 state constitution that made slavery legal in Kansas; subsequently defeated in 1858

"The Crime Against Kansas"
Speech delivered in Congress by Charles Sumner, Republican of Massachusetts, which blamed slavery for the violence between pro- and antislavery activists in Kansas

Slave Power Conspiracy
Specter raised by antislavery Republicans who believed that, in order to preserve slavery, southern leaders would be willing to attack and silence anyone who advocated against slavery; allegedly the conspiracy intended

TIMELINE

1846	Wilmot Proviso's ban on slavery from new territories alarms southerners
1848	Whigs divide in presidential election; Free Soil Party emerges
1850	Compromise admits a free California, leaves slavery in territories to popular sovereignty, bans slave trade in D.C., expands Fugitive Slave Act
1854	Kansas Nebraska Act leaves slavery to popular sovereignty in territories
1854-1856	As Free Soilers and slaveholders race to settle Kansas, violence ensues
1856	Republican party draws Free Soilers, Whigs, Know-Nothings with antislavery stance
	Multiparty presidential election of James Buchanan highlights sectional rift
1857	Supreme Court's Dred Scott decision prohibits Congress from restricting slavery
	Kansas's proslavery Lecompton Constitution splits Congress
November 1860	Republican Lincoln wins presidential election as sectional candidate
December 1860	South Carolina secedes in reaction to Lincoln's election; Deep South follows
	Crittenden Compromise fails
April 1861	South Carolina attacks federal Fort Sumter near Charleston

LO 1 Describe the arguments that took place over whether slavery should be allowed to expand into the new territories, and explain how the Compromise of 1850 was supposed to settle the issue. Disagreements over the expansion of slavery led to realignment of parties after America's victory over Mexico. Southern Democrats wanted slavery to be allowed in new territories, to protect the southern economy; northern Democrats opposed slavery in the territories because whites did not want to live among African Americans.

The 1848 presidential election illustrated the unrest, with the Democrats proposing the idea of "popular sovereignty," which would allow the voters of a territory, to decide about slavery. The Whigs and, Zachary Taylor, did not discuss the issue. Democrats unhappy with their platform splintered to form the Free Soil Party, proposing that slavery remain where it existed but go no farther. The Free Soil Party made a good showing in the election, but Whig Zachary Taylor won.

Because of the gold rush, the California territory was ready to petition for statehood by the time Taylor took office, but southern Democrats feared California and other southwestern territories might enter the Union as free states, giving nonslave states an advantage in Congress. Over spring and summer 1849, debate raged in Congress. With the groups deadlocked, Henry Clay proposed a compromise: California would enter as a free state; other lands won from Mexico could decide for themselves; slave auctions could no longer be held in the Nation's capital; Texas would get $10 million to stop trying to push New Mexico into accepting slavery; and Congress would enact a new, tougher Fugitive Slave Law Taylor died during the debate, and his successor, Millard Fillmore allowed Congress to decide. The move toward allowing people to decide for themselves worried northern abolitionists, who began to talk of a "slave conspiracy" in the South.

LO 2 Explain how the Kansas-Nebraska Act affected the territories of Kansas and Nebraska, and describe the events that made "Bleeding Kansas" an accurate description for the region. During the 1850s, Congress was making plans to build a transcontinental railroad. Many people wanted it to go through Chicago and westward, but for that to happen, the rest of the Louisiana Purchase needed to be settled. The Missouri Compromise (1820) had provided that slavery would be prohibited in the northern part of the Louisiana Territory, and southerners feared that several slave-free states could be sculpted out of those lands. When they opposed the railroad plan, Senator Stephen Douglas

to outlaw free speech and make all Americans accept proslavery principles

LO3 Lincoln-Douglas Debates
Public debates of slavery between Stephen A. Douglas and Abraham Lincoln as they competed for the Illinois Senate seat in 1858

LO4 Crittenden Compromise
Reconciliation proposal advocating that the Missouri Compromise line of 1820 be extended all the way to the Pacific, excluding California, with all land north of the line free, all land south of it open to slavery; also included an "unamendable amendment" to the Constitution, guaranteeing the preservation of slavery in the southern states where it already existed

offered a compromise that would undo the Missouri Compromise and allow the people to decide in those territories if the South dropped opposition to the railroad. The bill passed.

People raced to populate Kansas, not as true settlers but as outsiders who wanted to be there when the vote on slavery took place. Supporters of slavery crossed the border from Missouri in large numbers, but so did abolitionists from New England. The territory was divided on the issue, and violence became the norm in Kansas. Abolitionist John Brown set out to avenge the sack of Lawrence, and he and his sons killed five proslavery men. "Bleeding Kansas" became an apt name for the territory.

LO3 Discuss the events that propelled the United States into a civil war in 1861. Early in James Buchanan's presidency, the Supreme Court handed down the controversial Dred Scott decision, in which a Missouri slave had sued for his freedom because he had been taken by his master to free territories, and had therefore become free. The Court ruled that he was still a slave, but in the written decision, Chief Justice Taney declared that slaves were not citizens and could not sue in court. Further, slaves were property and could be taken anywhere by their masters without gaining freedom. Taney also declared the Missouri Compromise unconstitutional. Republicans were shocked that the highest court in the land had just validated slavery in any and all territories and states.

John Brown emerged again and carried out a raid at Harper's Ferry, Virginia, to collect weapons that he hoped would start a slave uprising. Brown was tried for treason, convicted, and hanged within a matter of weeks.

By the time of the presidential election in 1860, southern states were discussing secession as a possibility should a Republican win the presidency. The Democrats pretty much ensured that would happen, however, by running two different candidates and splitting their votes. Before Abraham Lincoln was inaugurated, seven southern states had left the Union.

LO4 Explain why and how the southern states seceded from the Union, discuss President Lincoln's reaction, and describe the earliest physical conflict between the two sides. By the time Lincoln took office, seven southern states had repealed the Constitution and come together in the Confederate States of America. States in the Upper South held off on making a decision. Shortly after his inauguration, Lincoln tried to resupply the federal Fort Sumter, in the harbor of Charleston, South Carolina. The fort was surrounded by Confederate forces, and as the federal supply convoy approached, the southern troops opened fire and demanded that the fort surrender. The first shots had been fired; the southern states were in full rebellion; and Lincoln would have no choice but to go to war.

LO **2** **Battle of Shiloh**
Bloody conflict near the Tennessee-Mississippi border in April 1862; also called the Battle of Pittsburg Landing; 23,000 casualties

LO **3** **"20 Negro Law"**
Exemption from Confederate military service granted to wealthy landholders who owned twenty or more slaves; designed to keep the planters producing their valuable cotton yield

commutation fee
Sum of money that guaranteed a draft-age man's exemption from enlisting in the Union Army until the next draft

five-twenties
War bonds, or bonds that would earn interest over a fixed period of time; the bondholder could redeem the bond in anywhere from five to twenty years for their initial investment plus interest

LO **5** **contraband**
Smuggled goods

Confiscation Act
Legislation that officially declared that any slaves used for military purposes would be freed if they came into Union hands

LO **6** **"March to the Sea"**
Path of destruction led by General William Tecumseh Sherman in late 1864; the March was sixty miles wide and several hundred miles long, from Atlanta to the Atlantic; Sherman's army pillaged all it encountered

TIMELINE

April, 1861	Lincoln orders blockade of southern coastline
July 21, 1861	Battle of Bull Run in Virginia shatters hopes for an easy war
August 1861	First Confiscation Act frees captured slaves employed in military service
March 1862	First battle of ironclads signals changes in military technology
April 1862	Union wins Battle of Shiloh and exceeds all American casualties in history
	Confederate Congress implements draft
1862	Congress creates Internal Revenue Service
June–July 1862	Excessive caution at Richmond costs Army of the Potomac dearly
July 1862	Second Confiscation Act frees all slaves owned by rebel masters
August 29, 1862	Lee defeats Union at Second Battle of Bull Run
Sept. 17, 1862	Union Army forces Confederacy back after Battle of Antietam
Sept. 22, 1862	Lincoln's Emancipation Proclamation declares freedom for rebels' slaves
July 1863	Mostly Irish Democratic working men riot in New York over national draft
July 3,1863	Lee's army suffers devastating defeat at Gettysburg
July 4, 1863	Union General Grant forces surrender of Vicksburg, Mississippi
April 12, 1864	Confederates kill surrendering black regiment in Fort Pillow Massacre
June 1864	Lincoln persuades Congress to grant black servicemen equal pay
November 5, 1864	Military victories restore faith in Lincoln, who soundly defeats opponent for presidency
January 31, 1865	Congress passes Thirteenth Amendment abolishing slavery
April 9, 1865	General Lee surrenders at Appomattox Courthouse

LO **1** Describe the areas of strength and advantage for each side at the beginning of the Civil War. The North held a clear advantage over the South in population, with more than twice as many people. The North had four times as many fighting-age men as the South, and it already had a functioning navy. Industrialization allowed the North to produce its own firearms and things needed to outfit an army. It also had better railroad coverage and a larger bankroll—and the value of its currency was already established.

The South had advantages too. One was the southern will to fight. Morale was strong in the South as the war began, and most of its officers had trained, and even taught, at West Point. One should also recognize the importance of a southern upbringing: Most southern boys rode, hunted, and could provide their own food.

LO **2** Explain why both sides in the Civil War believed the war would be brief, and describe the early conflicts that made that outcome unlikely. The North knew its advantages and did not see how the South could withstand its forces for long. The South knew that it just had to maintain a good defensive position and fight off northern aggression. What neither side was prepared for was the toll in casualties for both sides and the fact that both sides were unprepared for warfare.

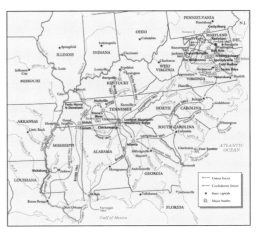

The North blockaded the southern coast with naval vessels, believing it could starve the South into submission. General Grant's troops seized key forts on major southern waterways, but the Battle of Shiloh shocked both sides with its 23,000 combined casualties that really didn't change the situation that much. Union General McClellan trained his troops very well but found it difficult to commit them to a major battle. When Robert E. Lee assumed command of the Army of Northern Virginia, northern successes in the East rarely occurred. It began to appear that both sides would be unable to take down the other side quickly or easily.

LO3 Explain how preparing for and prosecuting the Civil War contributed to the transformation of the United States into a fully modern state. Both sides in the Civil War found it necessary to give more power to a centralized government, something very strange for the Confederacy, which was ostensibly fighting for states' rights. It soon became apparent that a volunteer army would not be sufficient, because volunteers, like most others, had thought the war would be brief; when it wasn't, they often deserted and returned home. The Union was the first to institute a draft, but eventually the Confederacy did also. Both sides had to raise taxes to help finance the war. The president suspended some civil liberties in order to cut down on disloyalty from northerners opposed to the war.

LO4 Describe the actions of those who opposed the war in the North and of those who opposed the war in the South. Some northern Democrats believed secession was legal and opposed the war on those grounds. Known as either Peace Democrats or Copperheads, they gained in strength as more people became unhappy over the war. The suspension of the writ of habeas corpus upset them, but the draft sent them into action. The result was the New York draft riot in July 1863. Peace Democrats did not want to fight for the rich, and they did not want to fight to free the slaves, because in the North they competed with blacks for jobs.

The South experienced riots as well, for different reasons. Men went off to fight, women were left to deal with the shortages at home, and prices continued to rise. Richmond experienced the largest riot, as women and children armed themselves and broke into stores to take what they needed. Nevertheless, the Confederate government remained focused on trying to take care of the military and left those on the home front to fend for themselves. By mid-1863 morale and support for the war were down considerably in both North and South.

LO5 Discuss the events that occurred during 1863 and up to and including the presidential election of 1864 that demonstrated Lincoln's strong will and his eventual determination that the end of the war should bring a definite end to slavery. During the first year of the war, northern troops began to deal with runaway slaves by declaring them "contraband." Still, most northerners did not favor full emancipation. Lincoln knew the issue had to be decided, and shortly after the Battle of Antietam, he issued the Emancipation Proclamation. Contrary to what many believe, this document freed only the slaves in the southern states that were in rebellion against the U.S. government.

In July 1863, it appeared the end of the war might be near. Robert E. Lee was defeated at the Battle of Gettysburg. General Grant gained control of Vicksburg and the Mississippi River. But the next year brought many bloody battles and a few southern victories. Lincoln's chances to win reelection looked slim in the summer of 1864. Even with his former favorite, General McClellan, running against him in the election and supporting the maintenance of slavery, Lincoln stuck to his belief that slavery must end. General Sherman's victorious march through the South late that summer raised Lincoln's numbers, and he handily won reelection.

LO6 Describe and discuss the events that finally led to the utter defeat of the South and the end of the war. General Sherman carried out a "scorched earth" policy in what became known as his "March to the Sea." The war had become a war of attrition. In spring 1865, only about half of the troops remained at their posts. Lee handed over his sword to Grant on April 9, 1865.

Chapter in Review

16

1863	Abraham Lincoln proposes the lenient Ten Percent Plan
1864	Lincoln pocket-vetoes the stricter Wade-Davis Bill for Reconstruction
1865	John Wilkes Booth assassinates Abraham Lincoln
1865–1867	Johnson's Presidential Reconstruction demands loyalty oath from Confederates
	Congress establishes Freedmen's Bureau
	Congress passes Civil Rights Bill
1866	The Ku Klux Klan forms in Tennessee
1867	Congress enacts Military and Second Reconstruction Act
1867–1877	During Radical Reconstruction Congress enforces its rules for readmission
1868	North Carolina, South Carolina, Georgia, Florida, Alabama, Arkansas, Louisiana return to Union
	14th Amendment grants full citizenship to all persons born in U.S.
1870	15th Amendment bans state disfranchisement based on race, but not gender.
	Virginia, Mississippi, Texas return to Union
1871	With Force Act of 1870, Ku Klux Klan Act permits federal government to respond to Klan violence
1873	Marketing of Remington typewriter opens clerical positions for women
	Financial panic causes severe recession and mass unemployment
1875	Civil Rights Act forbids racial discrimination in public places
	Mississippi Plan calls for use of violence to restore Democratic control
1877	To overcome election stalemate, Republicans grant Democrats Home Rule in return for presidency
1883	In Civil Rights Cases, U.S. Supreme Court declares Civil Rights Act unconstitutional

LO¹ Reconstruction
The federal government's attempts to resolve the issues resulting from the end of the Civil War

Freedmen's Bureau
Government agency designed to create a new social order by government mandate; this bureau provided freedmen with education, food, medical care, and access to the justice system

LO² Ten-Percent Plan
Plan issued by Lincoln in 1863 which offered amnesty to any southerner who proclaimed loyalty to the Union and support of the emancipation of slaves; once 10 percent of a state's voters in the election of 1860 signed the oath, it could create a new state government and reenter the Union

Wade-Davis Bill
Bill that would have allowed a southern state back into the Union only after 50 percent of the population had taken the loyalty oath

iron-clad oath
Oath to be taken by southerners to testify that they had never voluntarily aided or abetted the rebellion

black codes
Post–Civil War laws specifically written to govern the behavior of African Americans; modeled on the slave codes that existed before the Civil War

Radical Republicans
Wing of the Republican Party most hostile to slavery

Civil Rights Bill
Bill that granted all citizens mandatory rights, regardless of racial considerations; designed to counteract the South's new black codes

Radical Reconstruction
Phase of Reconstruction during which Radical Republicans wielded more power than the president, allowing for the passage of the Fourteenth and Fifteenth Amendments, and the Military Reconstruction Act

Military Reconstruction Act
Act that divided the former rebel states, with the exception of Tennessee, into five military districts; a military commander took control of the state governments and federal soldiers enforced the law and kept order

LO³ carpetbagger

Northern-born white who moved south after the Confederacy's defeat

LO¹ Describe the changed world of ex-slaves after the Civil War. During the brief twelve years of Reconstruction (1865–1877), ex-slaves experienced at least a degree of freedom, but white southerners used black codes and the so-called "Jim Crow" laws to hold African Americans in the South in a state of servitude akin to slavery. The Freedmen's Bureau provided a fair amount of assistance to black people, and also poor white people, in the South. The planned redistribution of land never took place, but thousands of schools opened, and medical care improved across the South before the Bureau died out.

LO² Outline the different phases of Reconstruction, beginning with Lincoln's plan and moving through presidential Reconstruction to Radical Reconstruction. Trying to persuade southerners to end the war, President Lincoln proposed a plan to allow southern states to return to the Union as soon as 10 percent of the state's voters in the election of 1860 signed an oath of loyalty to the Union. In response, Congress passed the Wade-Davis bill, requiring 50 percent of the population to take the oath. The president's pocket-veto, and then his assassination, effectively killed the bill. Radical Republicans in Congress detested Lincoln's successor, Andrew Johnson, who pardoned virtually everyone who took the oath—even military leaders and the wealthy—after a direct appeal to him. Congress was incensed when southern states returned the same people to office and enacted restrictive black codes.

Radical Republicans expanded the Freedmen's Bureau, passed a Civil Rights Bill, and passed the Fourteenth Amendment. Overriding Johnson's veto, they then passed a Military Reconstruction Act that laid out strict guidelines for the southern states. These included organizing state conventions, writing new constitutions, protecting black voting rights, and passing the Fourteenth Amendment. But after only twelve years, northerners abandoned Reconstruction. Radical Republicans failed to carry out a social revolution; there was no redistribution of land, no guarantee of education for freed slaves, no guarantee of racial

scalawag
Southern-born white Republican; many had been nonslaveholding poor farmers

sharecropping
System in which a family farmed a plot of land owned by someone else and shared the crop yield with the owner

4 Civil Rights Act of 1875
Act that forbade racial discrimination in all public facilities, transportation lines, places of amusement, and juries; it proved largely ineffective

Civil Rights Cases
Cases in which, in 1883, the Supreme Court declared all of the provisions of the Civil Rights Act of 1875 unconstitutional, except for the prohibition of discrimination on juries

Panic of 1873
Financial crisis provoked when overspeculation, high postwar inflation, and disruptions from Europe emptied the financial reserves in America's banks; many banks simply closed their doors

Mississippi Plan
1875 Democratic plan that called for using as much violence as necessary to put Mississippi back under Democratic control

Compromise of 1877
Compromise in which Republicans promised not to dispute the Democratic gubernatorial victories in the South and to withdraw federal troops from the region, if southern Democrats accepted Hayes's presidential victory and respected the rights of its black citizens

equality. Instead, segregation remained legal, and southern whites pushed their agenda to the limits.

LO3 Explain how Reconstruction evolved at the individual states' level. Turbulence ruled politics in the South during Reconstruction. Politically, black people were elected to some state and local positions; overall, about two thousand southern African Americans gained political office during that time, but wealthy white men still dominated state governments. Some northerners came south hoping to help African Americans, and some southerners joined the Republican Party in order to hasten southern recovery, but any gains they achieved were short-lived.

One of the most oppressive systems to develop in the South during Reconstruction was the agricultural system known as sharecropping, developed by white landowners to ensure they had sufficient field hands. Sharecropping kept both black and poor white southerners (the majority of the population) locked in a kind of debt peonage until after World War II.

LO4 Evaluate and understand the relative success of Reconstruction. During Reconstruction, protections were added to the Constitution itself, but most existed on paper only. Clinging to the Democratic Party, white voters reasserted control of elections. Harassment, intimidation, and even murder became the means to maintain control of their society, helped along by the newly founded Ku Klux Klan. During Reconstruction, civil rights legislation was enacted, but little real change in the South occurred. Industrialization ruled the North, and cotton ruled the South. Northerners tired of trying to change southerners, especially after the Panic of 1873 set in. Many also feared an exodus of ex-slaves into the North, and long-held racist tendencies began to emerge. After the Compromise of 1877, federal troops left the South and Reconstruction ended.

Reconstruction was, for the most part then, a failure. For decades African Americans in the South existed as neither slave nor free. In a matter of years, northerners began to turn their backs as southerners created a "solid South" to rally around. Southern whites still sought to "control" African Americans, but the seeds had been sown. After World War II, African Americans would begin the modern Civil Rights Movement, demanding that those Reconstruction era laws be enforced.